U.S.
Immigration
& Citizenship
YOUR COMPLETE GUIDE

For further information, contact the publisher at

Emmis Books
1700 Madison Road
Cincinnati, Ohio 45206

www.emmisbooks.com

books

ISBN1-57860-169-X

Library of Congress Cataloging-in-Publication Data

Wernick, Allan.
  U.S. immigration & citizenship : complete guide / Allan Wernick.-- 4th ed.
    p. cm.
  Previous ed.: Roseville, Calif. : Prima Pub., c2002.
  ISBN 1-57860-169-X
 1. Emigration and immigration law--United States--Popular works. 2. Citizenship--United States--Popular works. 3. Visas--United States--Popular works. I. Title: U.S. immigration and citizenship. II. Title: US immigration & citizenship. III. Title: United States immigration & citizenship. IV. Title.

KF4819.6.W54 2004
342.7308'2--dc22

                                                2004056298

CONTENTS

Section I:

Getting a Green Card 1

Section II:

Naturalization and Citizenship 87

Section III:

Nonimmigrant Visas 138

Section IV:

Asylees and Refugees 199

Section V:

Employer Sanctions 215

Appendices

Allan Wernick is a professor at Baruch College, City University New York (CUNY), and Chair of CUNY's Citizenship and Immigration Project.

Professor Wernick's weekly column, "Immigration and Citizenship" is syndicated by King Features Syndicate, and his column "Immigration Advice" appears every Thursday in the *New York Daily News*. Professor Wernick has taught as a visiting professor in Chicana/o Studies at the University of California, Los Angeles, UCLA, and was a professor at Hostos Community College, CUNY, where he taught immigration law to students pursuing degrees in Paralegal Studies and Public Administration.

Prof. Wernick practices law as of counsel to the firm of Glenn Bank in New York City. He has served on the national Board of Directors of the American Immigration Lawyers Association (AILA), as Chair of the Immigration Committee of the Association of the Bar of the City of New York, and as President of the New York Chapter of AILA. Professor Wernick has appeared on numerous national and local television and radio programs, including CNN's Crossfire and The Phil Donahue Show.

Spanish Language matters:

Among the placements of The King Features Syndicate column is the *Florida Sun-Sentinel* and its weekly Spanish language edition, *El Sentinel*. *El Sentinel* is one of the most read Spanish language newspapers in Central Florida. The column appears as well in Spanish language papers in Kansas and Missouri.

Professor Wernick speaks Spanish and has been interviewed on Spanish TV and Radio. Wernick was profiled in *The Hispanic Outlook in Higher Education*, November 4, 2002.

This fourth edition of *U.S. Immigration & Citizenship: Your Complete Guide* includes major revisions to previously published material. Of particular significance is information on the Child Status Protection Act, CSPA, the law allowing certain children of U.S. citizens, permanent residents, and asylees to keep their benefits as children after turning 21. Also important are the new rules for international students. All chapters have been reviewed and corrected to reflect the latest information available. Based on suggestions from readers, I have rewritten certain parts to make them more easily understandable.

U.S. immigration law is incredibly complex and elastic. Moreover, new laws, regulations, court decisions, and agency interpretations change daily. That's why I regularly update my Immigration Answers Web site: www.allanwernick.com/. Through my Web site, I keep you informed of the latest developments in immigration law and policy.

Throughout *U.S. Immigration & Citizenship*, I point out how important it is that you seek expert assistance if you have any doubts about your rights under U.S. immigration law. Heed that advice. Once you submit an application to the USCIS or a U.S. consulate, it becomes part of your permanent record. This book will point you in the right direction, but you may need expert assistance to reach your goal.

ACKNOWLEDGMENTS

Some outstanding legal experts have helped me with all four editions of *U.S. Immigration & Citizenship: Your Complete Guide.* When writing for the public, as I do in my weekly column for the *New York Daily News* and in my syndicated column for King Features Syndicate, I've got to get it right the first time. I've been able to do this successfully, thanks to those who have reviewed my drafts and helped me understand and present the law. Of course, all final decisions regarding the content of the book are my own.

A few people deserve special mention. Phyllis Jewell, a business immigration law expert in San Francisco, was extremely generous in her contribution to Chapter 14, "H-1B and TN Status for Temporary Professional Workers." In my opinion, that chapter alone is worth the price of this book. Ms. Jewell carefully reviewed the chapter and made important suggestions, greatly improving its accuracy and usefulness. I thank her particularly for allowing me to reprint her fact sheet for employers on the completed LCA regulations. She made important suggestions in other chapters as well, particularly Chapter 6, "Applying for an Immigrant Visa."

Robert Gibbs, an attorney in Seattle, a longtime fighter for the rights of immigrant workers, and a leading expert on immigration law—particularly as it impacts immigrant labor—made many helpful suggestions.

Yvette Nelson and Victoria Orellava, paralegals in Los Angeles, helped with research. Laura Phillips, an excellent writer and a senior passport officer at the Los Angeles Passport Office, helped me understand the Child Citizenship Act and reviewed Chapter 10, "How Children Become U.S. Citizens." For many years, Laura has helped me understand derivative citizenship laws.

Gnoleba Seri, director of the Immigrants' Center at City College, reviewed Chapter 4, "Lottery Green Cards."

Many other lawyers answered questions or reviewed portions of the book. Special mention must go to Glenn Bank, with whom I practice law in New York. Glenn is a tireless and knowledgeable practitioner with high standards. Howard Jordan, a colleague at the City University of New York, used his extensive knowledge of Internet research to help with Appendix O, "Immigration Law and Policy Web Sites."

I must also thank the many attorneys I have consulted over the course of preparing these four editions of this book: James D. Acoba in California; Noreen Quirk in Connecticut; Lynn Neugebauer, Lindsay Curcio, Robert Belluscio, and Carolyn S. Goldfarb in New York; Palma Yanni and Leslie Dellon in Washington, D.C.; Jeffrey E. Gonzalez-Perez in Arlington, Virginia; and Jeanette Alvarado in Phoenix, Arizona.

Others who have been helpful over the years are Mariam Cheikh-Ali, an expert on student visas and former assistant director of international student affairs at the Pratt Institute in Brooklyn, New York; and Mary Todesca, formerly a legal assistant at the law offices of Noreen Quirk, Tracey Dean, and Helena Hungria, who helped with word processing on the first edition.

I'd like to thank Federal Publications, publisher of Interpreter Releases, an indispensable tool for immigration practitioners, for permission to use the citizenship charts in section II, "Naturalization and Citizenship."

My agent, Peter Rubie, himself an excellent writer and editor, provided needed moral support and professional guidance.

Maria Violetta Szulc conceived the stories that introduce the book and each section. A recent immigrant, Maria also has helped make the book understandable to nonlawyers—not an easy task.

Jerold Kress, who teaches video production at the Bresee Community Center in Los Angeles, gave me much-needed moral and logistical support. Thanks to Rory Solomon who designed my web site: www.allanwernick.com.

Finally, I'd like to thank the many people at Emmis Books who contributed to the production of the book, especially Don Prues, Jack Heffron and Richard Hunt.

Getting In and Staying In: A Popular Guide to U.S. Immigration Law

Tom was worried and upset—his wife, Mary, had just moved out. She had sponsored him for a green card, and his interview with the United States Citizenship and Immigration Services, USCIS, was just two weeks away. Tom was sure that Mary's leaving had ended his chances of staying in the United States. Mary still loved Tom, and she hoped that he could get his immigration papers. But she felt their marriage wouldn't last, and she refused to live with him another day.

If Tom had read this book, he'd know that unless his wife withdraws his visa petition, he can still get his immigrant visa. He'd also know what documents to bring to his USCIS interview to help him win his case. Tom's story is typical of the thousands sent to me by readers of my weekly immigration law column published in the *New York Daily News* and my syndicated column for King Features Syndicate. Tom's story teaches you something about U.S. immigration law that you may not have known: Your husband or wife can help you get a green card even if you are separated. Here are some other things you may not have known:

- Some permanent residents can become U.S. citizens without being able to speak, read, or write in the English language.
- If you are married to a U.S. citizen, you can become a naturalized citizen after three years from the time you first became a lawful immigrant.
- If you have a college degree and an employer wants to sponsor you, you can get a temporary work status for up to six years—in certain circumstances, even longer. You can get this status even if you are less qualified than a U.S. worker who wants the job.
- If you are a U.S. citizen, you can bring your fiancé or fiancée to the United States by filing a K-1 Fiancé Petition.
- If you are a naturalized U.S. citizen, your children may have automatically become U.S. citizens when you did.

- Minor legal infractions such as traffic tickets and disorderly conduct usually won't keep you from becoming a naturalized citizen.
- Most applicants for asylum end up in removal proceedings (formerly called deportation proceedings).
- Sometimes you don't have to give up your native citizenship to become a U.S. citizen.
- An employer can sponsor you even if you are in the United States without papers.
- USCIS rules allow foreign students to work.
- Both men and women can petition to bring their out-of-wedlock children to the United States.

WHO NEEDS THIS BOOK?

You need this book if:

- You are in the United States and want to stay.
- You are abroad and want to know how to come legally to the United States.
- You are lost in the complexity of U.S. immigration law or want to get legal status.
- You want to become a U.S. citizen.
- You are an employer, teacher, politician, or journalist who needs to know how our immigration system works.

U.S. Immigration & Citizenship: Your Complete Guide makes immigration law understandable. After answering hundreds of readers' questions, training hundreds of immigration law paralegals, and counseling immigrants for more than twenty five years, I know what you need to know. If you want to make sense out of the U.S. immigration system, you need this book.

Getting Help With Your Immigration Problem

You have a lot at stake when you apply for legal immigration status or U.S. citizenship. Try to get some expert advice for your immigration problem before you submit papers to the USCIS. If you can't afford a lawyer, don't despair. Most people get visas without hiring an attorney. Others get advice from not-for-profit organizations (also known as VOLAGS, which is short for voluntary agencies) that provide low-cost or free services to immigrants. In Appendix M, you'll find a nationwide list of VOLAGS.

If I Read This Book, Do I Still Need a Lawyer?

If you can afford a lawyer to help you with your immigration problem, hire one. The USCIS is sometimes a difficult agency to deal with. Having an experienced immigration lawyer on your side may make a difference. Even if your case is easy, having a lawyer can help you relax as you go through the immigration process.

If you decide to hire a lawyer, find one experienced in immigration and naturalization law. The best way to find a lawyer you'll be happy with is to follow the recommendation of a friend who is satisfied with his or her lawyer. Another good way of finding a lawyer is by calling the local bar association and asking for a referral.

Getting Help From a Not-for-Profit (Voluntary) Agency

Many not-for-profit agencies (or VOLAGS) provide excellent immigration counseling services. Most agencies charge a nominal fee, but some provide free services (again, see Appendix M for information on these agencies). Some immigration counselors and paralegals employed by not-for-profit agencies are accredited by the Board of Immigration Appeals (BIA) to practice immigration law. You can find a list of agencies recognized to represent you in immigration court at www.usdoj.gov/eoir/probono/ freelglchtNY.htm. If you have an immigration problem and you can't afford an attorney, try to get help from a not-for-profit agency.

Representing Yourself

Most people represent themselves when they apply for legal immigration status. If you can't get help, at least make sure that you read the USCIS form instructions carefully. To help you research immigration law, I have provided a list of resources in Appendix A. I have also provided a list of Internet resources in Appendix O.

The USCIS will send you forms for no charge if you call 800-870-3676. You can also get the forms at the USCIS Web site: http://uscis.gov/. Send completed forms and documents to the USCIS by certified mail with return receipt requested, and keep copies for your records.

Who's Who Under U.S. Immigration Law

Let's start our study of what immigration law can do for you by looking at how the law classifies people. I've included some stories to help you understand how the U.S. immigration system works. You'll find similar stories throughout the book.

U.S. immigration law divides all of us into two groups: U.S. citizens and aliens. The term "alien" includes permanent residents (green card holders), asylees, refugees, nonimmigrants, parolees, and undocumented immigrants.

U.S. Citizens

Whether natural born or naturalized, all U.S. citizens have the same rights except one: Only a natural born U.S. citizen can become president or vice president of the United States. Naturalized citizens may work in federal jobs, vote, and hold public office.

The government can't deport (remove) you for something you do after you become a U.S. citizen. However, the government can denaturalize a U.S. citizen who committed a fraud on the way to becoming a citizen. Then the government can deport the denaturalized former citizen.

You can also lose your U.S. citizenship by committing an act of expatriation.

An example of an act of expatriation is joining a foreign government. You can renounce your U.S. citizenship. Renunciation takes place when you voluntarily, knowingly, and willfully give up your U.S. citizenship.

If you are a U.S. citizen, you may petition to bring to the United States as permanent residents your husband or wife; your children of any age, both married and single; and your parents. For more information on how to become a U.S. citizen, see section II.

Permanent Residents (Green Card Holders)

Permanent residents are sometimes called green card holders, lawful permanent residents, and lawful immigrants. Permanent residents can travel freely into and out of the United States. However, if you are out of the United States for more than six continuous months, the government may question whether you have given up your residence. (See the section "Maintaining Your Permanent Residence," in Chapter 1.)

Unlike U.S. citizens (including naturalized citizens), permanent residents can't vote in national, congressional, or state elections. In a few places, permanent residents and undocumented immigrants can vote in community and school board elections.

Permanent residents qualify to work in most jobs. However, many federal and some state and local government jobs, such as police officer and firefighter, are reserved for U.S. citizens. Permanent residents may also be excluded from working for private employers, if the work is to be done under a U.S. government contract.

If you are a permanent resident, you can bring to the United States as permanent residents your husband or wife and unmarried sons and daughters. To learn how you can become a permanent resident, see Section I.

The USCIS gives a permanent resident a permanent resident card, formerly called an alien registration card. This card is also known as a green card. The permanent resident card is a plastic-covered card that shows that its legitimate holder is a permanent resident of the United States. The cards issued today are not green but salmon or rose colored. (The first permanent resident card issued was green and the name stuck.)

Nonimmigrants

Nonimmigrants are aliens who come to the United States temporarily for a limited purpose (see section III). Pierre's and Ying's stories provide examples of how a person goes from being a nonimmigrant to a permanent resident and then a U.S. citizen.

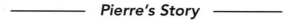
Pierre's Story

Pierre came to visit the United States from France. Pierre had been in the United States for only a month when he met Melanie, a U.S. citizen. They fell madly in love and decided to marry. Melanie petitioned for Pierre to get an immigrant visa.

Within a few weeks after they filed his papers, the USCIS gave Pierre work authorization and he began working. A few months later, a USCIS officer interviewed him for his immigrant visa.

Three years after Pierre became a permanent resident, he was naturalized as a U.S. citizen. He qualified after only three years, instead of the normal five years, because he was still married to and living with his U.S. citizen wife.

Ying's Story

Ying came to the United States from China to study business. She entered the United States using an F-1 student visa. She successfully completed her master's program, so the USCIS gave her one year of practical training work authorization. She immediately got a job with one of the largest financial institutions, Big Money, Inc., in Chicago. After six months on the job, the company offered Ying a permanent position.

To keep her in legal working status while her permanent visa papers were processed, Big Money Inc. sponsored Ying for a temporary professional worker status called H-1B. Two months later, the USCIS approved a change of Ying's status from F-1 student to H-1B worker, valid for three years.

While Ying was in H-1B status, Big Money Inc. sponsored her for a permanent visa in the position of deputy director of their Asian Investment Department. Ying became a permanent resident and five years after that became a U.S. citizen. Once she became a citizen, she petitioned to bring her mother and father to the United States.

Asylees and Refugees

Asylees have a well-founded fear of being persecuted in their home country because of their race, religion, nationality, political opinions, or membership in a particular social group. They apply to the USCIS for asylum either after they enter the United States or while trying to enter the United States.

Refugees are also people afraid of persecution if they return home, but who got refugee status before they came to the United States. For more on refugees and asylees, see Section IV.

Lisa's story provides an example of a successful asylum applicant.

Lisa was running away from a country in turmoil. Her brother had been killed for his opposition to the government, and Lisa was sure that she was next on the government's list. She took what she could in a suitcase and, using a phony passport, came to the United States. She left behind her husband and infant daughter. She was lucky to have gotten away.

Within a week after her arrival, she contacted an immigrants' rights organization, which advised her to apply for political asylum.

The USCIS granted Lisa asylum. She then could bring her husband and child to the United States, regardless of whether or not they had independent claims for asylum. One year after the USCIS granted Lisa asylum, she and her family applied for permanent residence. They qualified for permanent residence because Lisa had been an asylee for one year.

Undocumented Immigrants

We use the term "undocumented immigrants" for aliens living in the United States who haven't yet established the legal right to be here. This includes people who entered the United States by evading inspection at the border as well as people who entered with fraudulent documents. It also includes people such as tourists who entered with a valid nonimmigrant visa but who have overstayed the time allowed them by the USCIS.

Parolees

Parolees are aliens who the USCIS lets into the United States, though at the time they apply to enter they don't qualify as either nonimmigrants or permanent residents. Parolee status is often used to let people into the United States for humanitarian reasons or in emergencies.

If you are in the United States with an application pending for permanent residence, you can sometimes get advanced parole. That's advance permission from the USCIS to be paroled back into the United States after travel abroad. (For more on advance parole, see Chapter 6.) In rare situations, you can get parolee status if you have an urgent need to come to the United States. Most often this humanitarian parole is granted to people needing emergency medical care or to keep families united. To apply for humanitarian parole, write to the USCIS Parole Branch at U.S. Immigration & Naturalization Service, Office of International Affairs, Attn: Parole Branch, 425 I Street, NW, Washington, DC 20536.

The USCIS most often grants parolee status where it has some question as to an alien's admissibility as an immigrant, nonimmigrant, or asylee. An example is the thousands of Cubans who landed in Key West, Florida, in the early 1980s.

Regarding Immigration Law Post-September 11, 2001

The events of September 11, 2001 resulted in important new laws and policies impacting immigration to the United States. While the basic rules for getting immigrant and nonimmigrant status remain in effect, readers need to be aware of the new benefits and burdens. The most important of these are outlined in the following section. Readers should regularly check my Web site, www.allanwernick.com, for updates.

USCIS (UNITED STATES CITIZENSHIP AND IMMIGRATION SERVICES) REPLACES INS

In the wake of September 11, 2001, Congress abolished the INS. Former INS enforcement and service functions were divided among various agencies within the newly-formed Department of Homeland Security. The service functions, such as granting naturalization and deciding relative and employment petitions, are handled by the bureau of United States Citizenship and Immigration Services, called USCIS or CIS. For a short time, the government tried to use the name Bureau of Citizenship and Immigration Services or BCIS, but now the agency is strictly called the bureau of United States Citizenship and Immigration Services (USCIS).

Enforcement functions, including detection and removal and border enforcement are the responsibility of the Directorate of Border and Transportation Security (BTS). The BTS includes the Bureau of Customs and Border Protection (CBP), responsible for the Border Patrol and inspections of individuals entering the United States, and the Bureau of Immigration and Customs Enforcement (ICE), which handles the detention and removal of immigrants.

Immigration Judges and the Board of Immigration Appeals remain part of the DHS's Department of Justice (DOJ).

ANTI-TERRORISM

The main goal of the U.S.A. Patriot Act, according to its proponents, is to make it easier for the U.S. government to fight terrorism. Many of the law's provisions are controversial. Some commentators fear that the new laws infringe on civil liberties; others argue that the new laws will do little to stop terrorism.

New Grounds of Inadmissibility

The U.S.A. Patriot Act added several new grounds of inadmissibility to those discussed in Chapter 5. Representatives of foreign terrorist organizations or representatives of any group that publicly endorses terrorist acts are considered inadmissible (and thus ineligible for permanent residence and entry to the United States). The spouses and children of those inadmissible on any of the terrorism-related grounds are also barred.

What's a terrorist organization? Any group designated as such by the U.S. Secretary of State upon publication of the name of the group in the Federal Register, the publication that notifies the public of all new federal rules and regulations. You can find the list of designated organizations at the Department of State Web site: http://www.state.gov/.

New Grounds of Removal

The U.S.A. Patriot Act also makes activism in support of certain organizations a deportable (the legal term is removable) offense. Under the law, you can be deported for fund-raising, soliciting for membership, or providing material support for designated groups. That includes support for humanitarian projects, even if the activities don't advance terrorist activity.

Moreover, even if an alleged terrorist organization is not on the Department of State's designated list, you can be deported for soliciting funds or providing other material support for a terrorist organization unless you can prove that you "did not know, and should not reasonably have known, that the solicitation would further the organization's terrorist activity."

Detention of Suspected Terrorists

The U.S.A. Patriot Act gives the U.S. Attorney General or the Deputy Attorney General (with no power of delegation) authorization to certify a foreign citizen as a "terrorist." If a person is certified as a terrorist, he or she may be detained without the right to bail or bond until a final decision on deportability is reached. The government has up to seven days to detain a suspected terrorist before bringing immigration or criminal charges.

NEW INVESTIGATION
AND RECORD-KEEPING PROCEDURES

A major goal for the USCIS after the events of September 11, 2001 is to keep track of foreign students and other nonimmigrants residing in the United States. In the past, keeping track of such people has been difficult. Now, however, the USCIS is doing its best to monitor such individuals and their whereabouts.

Tracking Foreign Students

In the wake of September 11, the U.S.'s universities have successfully fought off efforts to suspend the F-1 visa program for international students. Congress, however, has insisted that the USCIS move forward on plans for increased record keeping and reporting. The USCIS has been trying to monitor international students since 1979. Now a sophisticated reporting program, already mandated by Congress, is operative.

The new tracking system is called the Student and Exchange Visitor Information System (SEVIS). Under SEVIS, the USCIS has created an Internet-based record-keeping system for all international students and scholars. Campus advisors input each student's data once the student is admitted to the school. The information is available both to the USCIS and to U.S. consulates abroad. United States consuls issue the student a machine-readable document containing his or her key personal information, photograph, and fingerprints. As the student progresses through his or her education, the college must enter data about the student into the database. Thus the USCIS and the U.S. Department of State can monitor the student's location and academic progress. For more on SEVIS, see Chapter 13.

New Nonimmigrant Visa Procedures

All male nonimmigrant visa applicants (and some women) between the ages of 16 and 45, regardless of nationality, are being asked to submit a new form (DS-157, Supplemental Nonimmigrant Visa Application) when applying for a nonimmigrant visa. This includes visitors, students, and temporary workers. Some consulates are requiring the new form even from applicants not in this group. This new form must be filed with the usual Nonimmigrant Visa Application (DS-156). The new form asks for detailed employment, military service, and educational information, as well as information regarding your membership and/or association with professional, social, and charitable organizations. Finally, the form asks for your complete travel itinerary. The obvious purpose is to better identify terrorists.

Also new is the policy of granting the USCIS and U.S. consulates access to the FBI's National Crime Information Center (NCIC) database. The consulates and USCIS will check this database to determine whether an applicant for a visa or for entry into the United States is wanted by the FBI.

US VISIT: Controlled Departure

The U.S. Department of Homeland Security is implementing a new program for monitoring visitors to the United States. Under the United States Visitor and Immigrant Status Indicator Technology program, US VISIT, the DHS has begun monitoring entries and exits at airports and seaports; land checks are in the works as well. This means border officers collect digital fingerprints and a digital photograph of every visitor. The DHS includes such information in a database with other data about the visitor. Visitors are then required to check out at kiosks prior to leaving the country.

Previously, the DHS inspected nonimmigrants (for example, students and visitors) only when they first entered the country. The agency didn't inspect nonimmigrants when they left. With a controlled entry/exit program, the government will know when someone has overstayed. U.S. border states have opposed controlled departure as a threat to tourism and commerce, fearing long delays, particularly at land borders. The DHS claims that the new procedures add just seconds to entry and exit processes.

Traveling to Canada, Mexico, and Adjacent Islands

Usually a nonimmigrant needs a valid visa to enter the United States. For years, an exception to this rule allowed a nonimmigrant with a valid I-94 (but expired visa) to travel to Canada or Mexico for up to 30 days, and those in F-1 or J-1 status to travel to adjacent islands (other than Cuba) as well. In response to September 11, 2001, however, the government has changed this rule. Under the new rule, citizens of countries the government calls "state sponsors of terrorism" are unable to return from these countries without a valid visa, even with a valid I-94. At the time of publication, the list of "state sponsors of terrorism" include Iraq, Iran, Syria, Libya, Sudan, North Korea, and Cuba. The list is expected to expand. Check the Immigration Answers Web site at www.allanwernick.com for up-to-date information. For more on nonimmigrant visas and I-94s, see Chapter 17.

NEW BENEFITS

Following are some new benefits that may apply to you.

Preservation of Green Card Rights

Under the U.S.A. Patriot Act, enacted shortly after the events of September 11, if you are the beneficiary or fiancé(e) of any relative petition filed by someone who died in the terrorist attacks of September 11, 2001, you now qualify immediately for permanent residence. If your employer had an immigration case for you, but the employer couldn't continue the case due to the disaster, you too can get permanent residence. If you would have qualified under a family or employment preference category, your spouse and/or unmarried children under age 21 can also get immigrant status. The public charge of ground of inadmissibility (see Chapter 5) does not apply. To better understand family and employment immigration, read Chapters 1, 2, and 3.

Benefit for Grandparents

The grandparents of a child who lost both parents in the September 11, 2001 disaster may qualify for permanent residence. To benefit, one of the deceased parents must have been a U.S. citizen or legal permanent resident.

Post-September 11, 2001, we are seeing increased scrutiny of all USCIS and U.S. consulate applications, particularly those from citizens and nationals of Middle Eastern countries. Still, if you have a clean record and qualify for a benefit, you should get it based on the same rules that applied before the terrorist attacks. Let me remind you that Middle Easterners are treated unfairly, but you will still get the benefit if you rightfully deserve it.

Getting a Green Card

"Tomorrow is your green card interview, Maria. Don't forget to put our wedding pictures in your purse," said Andrew.

"Don't you worry. I packed everything. Even this photo where you are dancing with my mother," Maria said laughingly.

Andrew is a permanent resident who got his green card when his employer, a U.S. corporation, sponsored him. Andrew and Maria had been childhood sweethearts. When Andrew learned that Maria had come to the United States to study, he called her and they rekindled their romance. After just a few months, they married.

Andrew petitioned for Maria based on his status as a permanent resident. Because of the long wait in the category for the spouse of a permanent resident, Maria couldn't get her immigrant visa right away. The USCIS approved the petition immediately, but because of the long waiting list for the spouses of permanent residents, Maria had to wait until she got to the front of the line in her visa category.

It took several years, but eventually Maria became a permanent resident and then a U.S. citizen. Once she became a United States citizen, she then petitioned for green cards for her mother, Jane, and her younger brother, Chris.

Getting an immigrant visa (a permanent resident card commonly called a green card) is the goal of millions of people in the United States and around the world. In this section, I explain the entire immigrant visa process.

In Chapter 1, I give an overview of the ways that you might qualify for an immigrant visa. In Chapters 2 and 3, I give you details on the two main green card categories: Family-Based permanent residence and Employment-Based permanent residence. In Chapter 4, I explain who is eligible for the green card lottery and how you can enter. In Chapter 5, I review the bars to permanent residence (problems that could prevent you from becoming a permanent resident). Finally, in Chapter 6, I explain the procedures for preparing your immigrant visa application, offering tips on how to prepare for the all-important interview where, in most cases, the final decision to grant or deny you permanent residence will be made.

CHAPTER 1

Who Can Get an Immigrant Visa?

Most people get immigrant visas (green cards) because they are related to a U.S. citizen or permanent resident. The next largest group gets immigrant visas because they have a needed or desirable job skill or ability. Then there's a smaller group that gets immigrant visas in special ways, including a lottery. I expand on the family-based, employment-based, and lottery categories in Chapters 2, 3, and 4. For now, let's begin our search to find out if you can become a permanent resident by summarizing the categories of immigrant visa eligibility.

FAMILY-BASED VISAS

You may qualify for a Family-Based green card if you are the Immediate Relative of a U.S. citizen (a category for which there is no limit to the number of immigrant visas issued each year) or if you are in a Family-Based Preference group (for which there is a limit, or quota, of 226,000 immigrants per year divided among four preferences).

Immigration laws define family relationships in a special way. An example is the term "child," which includes not only children born to a married couple but also certain adopted children, stepchildren, and children born out of wedlock. Details on these family relationships can be found in Chapter 2.

The Immediate Relative of a U.S. citizen category includes the following:

- Spouse of a U.S. citizen.
- Unmarried child (under age 21) of a U.S. citizen.
- Parent of a U.S. citizen if the citizen is age 21 or older.
- Spouse of a deceased U.S. citizen if at the time of the citizen's death the spouses had been married at least two years and were not legally separated.

The Family-Based Preferences are:

- First Family-Based Preference. Adult unmarried sons and daughters (age 21 or older) of U.S. citizens.
- Second Family-Based Preference A. Spouse and unmarried children (under age 21) of permanent residents.
- Second Family-Based Preference B. Unmarried sons and daughters (of any age) of permanent residents.
- Third Family-Based Preference (formerly Fourth Preference). Married children of U.S. citizens.
- Fourth Relative Preference (formerly Fifth Preference). Brothers and sisters of U.S. citizens if the U.S. citizen is age 21 or older.

Note that the immigration law uses the term "child" for children under 21 years old and "sons and daughters" for children of any age.

PERMANENT RESIDENCE
BASED ON WORK, TALENT, OR INVESTMENT

U.S. immigration laws recognize the value of immigrant labor to U.S. global competitiveness and job creation. Thus, you may be able to get a green card if you have unique education and skills, outstanding talent, or even willingness to work at a particularly unappealing job. You may also qualify for a green card by investing in a business. Permanent Resident visas in this category are referred to as Employment-Based visas.

There is a limit of 140,000 visas annually for all Employment-Based immigrants, but that doesn't always mean a long wait. How fast you can get an Employment-Based immigrant visa depends on your preference category as well as on how many people are applying for Employment-Based green cards from your native country. Following I list the Employment-Based Preferences. I provide details for qualifying under these preferences in Chapter 3.

The Employment-Based Preferences are:

- First Employment-Based Preference, Priority Workers. Workers with extraordinary abilities, outstanding professors and researchers, and multinational executives and managers.
- Second Employment-Based Preference. Members of professions

holding advanced degrees or workers of exceptional ability.
- Third Employment-Based Preference. Skilled workers, professionals, and other workers.
- Fourth Employment-Based Preference Special Immigrants. This includes certain religious workers, former U.S. government employees, Panama Canal employees, and certain foreign-language broadcasters working for Radio Free Europe or Radio Free Asia.
- Fifth Employment-Based Preference. Employment creation (investor).

OTHER PEOPLE WHO CAN GET IMMIGRANT VISAS

Additional Options

Even if you do not qualify in one of the relative or employment categories, you may still be able to get an immigrant visa through one of the following categories:

1. Derivative Beneficiaries. A beneficiary is a person for whom a Family-Based or Employment-Based immigrant visa petition has been filed. A derivative beneficiary is the spouse or unmarried child of that person. The term "derivative" is used because your right to an immigrant visa derives, or comes, from your spouse or parent, who is the primary beneficiary.

Under the derivative beneficiary rule, if you're coming to the United States under one of the Family- or Employment-Based Preferences, you can bring your spouse and unmarried children under age 21 with you. Your spouse and your children don't need to have separate petitions filed for them. Your spouse and children can even follow you to the United States after you've gotten here, provided you were married to your spouse and your children were born before you got your immigrant visa.

Immediate relatives of U.S. citizens cannot bring their family members with them as derivative beneficiaries. This means that if you're getting your immigrant visa as the spouse, parent, or unmarried child under age 21 of a U.S. citizen, you cannot automatically bring your spouse or children with you to the United States. This rule doesn't make much sense, but it's the law. Once you get your immigrant visa in the Immediate Relative category, you can then petition for your spouse and children.

Kim's and Jimmy's stories illustrate the law regarding derivative beneficiaries.

————— *Kim's Story* —————

Kim's mother, a U.S. citizen, petitioned for Kim to become a permanent resident. Kim is married to Harry. They have three children: Bertha, age 18 and married; Aaron, age 19 and single; and Cathy, age 23 and single.

Kim will get her immigrant visa under the Family-Based Third

Preference as will Harry and Aaron. Harry is Kim's spouse, so he is automatically a derivative if Kim gets a green card. Aaron is still a "child" (under 21) and single. He, too, is a derivative. Harry and Aaron can get green cards when Kim does even if no one files petitions for them. Cathy and Bertha, however, cannot get immigrant visas at the same time as Kim, Harry, and Aaron because children must be under 21 and unmarried to be derivative beneficiaries. Once Kim and Harry become permanent residents, either one can petition for Cathy under the Family-Based Preference 2B, provided she stays single. Unless she becomes "unmarried" through divorce or the death of her husband, Bertha must wait until one of her parents becomes a U.S. citizen, and then the parent can petition for her under the Third Family Preference.

Jimmy's Story

Jimmy is a 22 year-old U.S. citizen. His mother married his stepfather when Jimmy was just ten years old. Jimmy could petition for his mother and stepfather for permanent residence. However, he only petitions for his mother because he doesn't like his stepfather. Can Jimmy's mother bring the stepfather along as a derivative beneficiary? No. Jimmy's mother qualifies for an immigrant visa under the Immediate Relative of a U.S. citizen category. An immigrant visa applicant in that category can't bring family members along. Once the mother gets her residence, she can petition for her husband under the Family-Based Preference 2A.

Derivative Beneficiaries and the Child Status Protection Act

Some children of preference Permanent Residence applicants may benefit from a law enacted on August 2, 2002 called the Child Status Protection Act (CSPA). The purpose of the law is to protect certain children of U.S. citizens and permanent residents who may lose benefits because of long USCIS processing delays. For derivative beneficiaries, the law provides that the age of a child who is a derivative beneficiary of a preference green card applicant is fixed on the date a priority date becomes "current" for the primary beneficiary minus the time it takes the USCIS (or took the INS or BCIS) to approve the petition. The qualifying derivative child must begin processing for permanent residence within one year of qualifying.

Simone's story illustrates how The CSPA might benefit a derivative beneficiary.

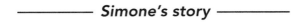

Simone's story

Simone's mother Migdalia was petitioned for by Migdalia's U.S. citizen sister, Cecilia. Cecilia filed the petition for Migdalia to become a permanent resident on January 2, 1993. On that date, Simone was age 11. Migdalia qualifies for residence in the Fourth Family Preference category, with its long wait. The INS (now USCIS) approved the petition on January 2, 1995, two years later. Then eight years later, in January 2003, just after Simone's twenty-first birthday, her mother Migdalia's priority date became current.

Despite having turned 21, Simone can still get her immigrant visa as a derivative beneficiary of her mother. That's because her age was fixed on the date her mother's priority date became current, minus the two years it took for the USCIS to decide the petition. Under prior law she would have had to wait until her mother became a permanent resident and petitioned for her, a process that would have taken many years.

2. Visa Lottery Winners. Each year the U.S. Department of State holds a green card lottery through which they give out 55,000 permanent resident visas. The visas are for natives of countries with low levels of immigration during the previous five years. In some years the number of visas will be reduced to 50,000, with 5,000 visas going to NACARA (Nicaraguan Adjustment and Central American Relief Act) visa applicants. NACARA provides special opportunities for permanent residence for certain natives of Nicaragua, Cuba, El Salvador, Guatemala, and former Soviet Bloc countries. The filing dates for NACARA have passed. If you think you may have qualified for a NACARA green card, see an immigration law expert for advice. See Chapter 4 for more on the visa lottery.

3. Asylees and Refugees. Asylees and refugees can apply for permanent residence after one year in that status. Becoming an asylee or refugee is not always easy, as I discuss in Section IV.

4. Registry. If you entered the United States before January 1, 1972, and you have resided in the United States continuously since you entered, you may qualify for permanent residence just because of your many years in the United States. Many of the usual requirements for a green card, like proving that you don't need welfare, do not apply to registry applicants.

5. Special Immigrants. The Special Immigrant category includes certain religious workers, juvenile dependents of a court who are eligible for foster care, some dependents of diplomats, certain long-term employees of the U.S. government working in foreign countries, holders of S (informers on terrorists, or criminals), I (victims of trafficking), and U (victims of other crimes) visas, and persons who have served in active duty in the U.S. armed services for 12 years or 6 years for those who reenlist for 6 additional years.

6. Family Unity Visas. The spouse and unmarried children under 21 of "legalized" immigrants qualify for permanent residence under special rules. A legalized immigrant is one who got residence under one of the amnesty programs I discuss here.

7. Unusual or Difficult Categories. The immigration laws provide a few unusual and especially difficult ways to become a permanent resident. You shouldn't try to get a green card in one of the following listed ways until you speak to an immigration law expert. These ways include:

Cancellation of Removal

If you have resided continuously in the United States for ten years, you may be eligible for "cancellation of removal." For a battered spouse, child, or parent of a battered child, you need only continuously reside in the U.S. for three years.

The law provides different kinds of cancellation of removal. For the basic kind of cancellation of removal, you must prove "exceptional and extremely unusual hardship" to your spouse, parent, or child. Hardship to yourself is not good enough. Also, for you to qualify, your spouse, parent, or child must be a U.S. citizen or permanent resident. Cancellation of removal used to be called suspension of deportation and was far more generous than cancellation of removal is now.

Be warned: You can only apply for cancellation of removal in an immigration court. Cancellation of removal can only be granted by an immigration judge in removal proceedings. If you apply for cancellation of removal and the judge grants your application, you become a permanent resident right then and there. If the judge denies your application, the judge may order you deported. If you think that you qualify for cancellation of removal, don't just walk into a USCIS office. They might detain you on the spot and deport you right away. If you want to apply for cancellation of removal, you should get advice from an immigration attorney or accredited not-for-profit representative before trying anything.

The law also provides for specialized forms of cancellation of removal. If you are a battered spouse or child, or the parent of a battered child, you can apply for cancellation of removal if you have been in the United States for at least three years. To successfully apply for this kind of cancellation of removal, you should seek the help of an immigration attorney or accredited not-for-profit representative.

Private Bills

A Private Bill is an act of Congress granting permanent residence to an individual. Congress very rarely passes Private Bills. You need a member of Congress to sponsor the bill and push it through both the Senate and the House of Representatives. In order to get a green card based on a Private Bill, you would have to show an extraordinary humanitarian reason why you should get a visa.

Special Rules for Special Nationalities

Over the years, Congress has seen fit to make green cards available to immigrants from certain countries, outside the normal immigrant visa system. In recent years, Nicaraguans, Cubans, Haitians, Salvadorans, Guatemalans, natives of former Soviet Bloc countries, and Syrian Jews have benefited from nationality-specific laws.

Amnesty and "Late Amnesty"

In 1986 Congress passed a legalization or "amnesty" law. Under this law, people who had lived in the United States continuously, but unlawfully, since before 1982 could get permanent residence. Amnesty visas also were given to certain agricultural workers. The deadline to apply for amnesty was May 4, 1988.

After the deadline, many amnesty applicants complained that the USCIS unlawfully turned them away. In some famous court cases, sometimes referred to as CSS/LULAC cases after the organizations that represented many of the late amnesty applicants, the USCIS was forced by the federal courts to accept some late amnesty applications. To qualify for late amnesty you must have been in the United States since before January 1, 1982, but failed to file for amnesty because the USCIS unlawfully discouraged you from filing. Some people think that the late amnesty was a new amnesty because applicants are allowed to file so long after the original deadline. Many of those who filed late got USCIS work permission. But if you came to the United States after January 1, 1982, and you filed for amnesty, your amnesty application is a fraud.

The CSS/LULAC cases did not end the amnesty controversies, but there is new hope. Late amnesty applicants have a new chance to apply for permanent residence. On March 23, 2004, the USCIS announced filing procedures based on a settlement of the CSS/LULAC federal court cases. The USCIS will accept applications from May 24, 2004 to May 23, 2005.

The hardest part in getting late amnesty is proving that you came to the United States prior to January 1, 1982, and that you lived here unlawfully until at least May 4, 1988. The best way to prove you've been in the U.S. is to keep all documents issued by federal, state and municipal institutions. Examples are INS entry stamps, public school records, a driver's license, and income tax filings. Next best are leases, utility bills, and bank records. Even postmarked letters can help. Maybe a relative back home saved some of your letters from the United States. If you don't have an institutional document or postmarked letter, you might win using affidavits (sworn statements) from religious leaders, friends and relatives.

Even if you have a weak case, it can't hurt for you to apply. Unless the government finds fraud, your legalization application is confidential and a denial won't lead to deportation. For more information and the necessary forms, visit the USCIS website at http://uscis.gov/graphics/lawsregs/settlement.htm, or call the Center for Human Rights at (213) 388-8693.

MAINTAINING YOUR PERMANENT RESIDENCE

Making the United States your primary home is a requirement for permanent residence. You can lose your permanent resident status if you spend too much time outside the United States. If you plan to spend a great deal of time abroad, get a reentry permit before you leave the United States. A reentry permit is a USCIS travel document valid for entry into the United States after absences of up to two years. If you will be out of the country longer than two years, you must come back to the United States and apply for a new reentry permit. You file for a reentry permit using USCIS Form I-131, Application for Travel Document. When applying for the reentry permit, you must explain why you need to be abroad for so long. People get reentry permits for a variety of reasons, including to temporarily work abroad, to care for a relative who is sick, and to study.

Maintaining Your Residence

If an inspector at a port of entry believes that you have abandoned your U.S. residence, the government can try to take away your immigration status. Usually, stays abroad of less than six months are not a problem. If you are abroad for more than six months, you should be prepared to explain to a border officer why you were out of the country for so long. Evidence that you have maintained your residence includes having a bank account, paying U.S. taxes, and having a place to live in the United States. If you get a reentry permit before you leave the United States, an inspector is more likely to admit you into the United States after a long absence.

If an inspector believes that the United States is not your primary country of residence, the inspector can deny you entry. If that happens, you have a right to a hearing before an immigration judge, who will decide whether you have really abandoned your residence.

Trips Abroad of More Than One Year

After one continuous year abroad, your permanent resident card is not valid for reentry. If you plan to be out of the United States for more than one year, apply to the USCIS for a reentry permit before you leave.

If you are outside the United States for more than one year without having first gotten a reentry permit, you can get a returning resident visa to ease your reentry into the United States. You can apply for the visa at a U.S. consulate. You'll need to prove that you haven't abandoned your U.S. residence. If you return to the United States after 365 days abroad without getting a returning resident visa, you may be detained at a port of entry or denied entry.

Proving that you are a returning resident after spending a year or more abroad can be difficult. Be very careful when planning long-term travel abroad.

The stories of Conrad, Danielle, Suresh, and Tony illustrate the issue of maintaining residency

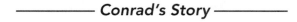

—————— *Conrad's Story* ——————

Conrad's wife, Mariel, a U.S. citizen, petitioned for him to become a permanent resident. Two years after he became a resident, his wife's employer transferred her temporarily to the French branch of the company. It was a five-year assignment.

Conrad and Mariel planned to spend the Christmas holidays in New York with their families. But they were going to give up their New York apartment and rent an apartment in Paris.

Conrad is not abandoning his U.S. residence. He should submit USCIS

Form I-131 with a letter from his wife's company explaining that they have sent her abroad to work. Conrad can then get a reentry permit, which is valid for only two years. He must return to the United States within two years to apply for a new reentry permit. He cannot apply for a new permit from abroad.

—————— Danielle's Story ——————

Danielle, an actress, became a permanent resident so that she'd be ready to work when she got her big break and became a Hollywood movie star. Meanwhile, she lived in Sweden until she got the call to stardom.

Danielle traveled to the United States frequently for auditions but did most of her theatrical work in Europe. For several years, she made three trips a year to the United States. She was never in the United States for more than a couple of weeks at a time. Five years after she became a permanent resident, an inspector noticed the many entry stamps in Danielle's passport and asked her where her residence was. Danielle claimed that her residence was in the United States, but her only proof was a small bank account she maintained in Los Angeles. The inspector at the airport made an appointment for Danielle for an interview with a USCIS inspector. She was allowed to enter as a parolee (see the Introduction for a definition of parolee status).

At the interview with the inspector, Danielle claimed that she was residing in the United States, but she still had no proof. The inspector told her she had two choices: to leave the country or to try to convince a judge that she was residing in the United States.

Whether Danielle can keep her permanent residence will depend on the evidence that she presents at her hearing. If she gives up and goes home, she can become a permanent resident later if a relative or employer petitions for her.

—————— Suresh's Story ——————

Suresh works for a large American computer company, which sponsored him for his permanent residence. Suresh was promoted to International Sales Director, a job that required extensive trips outside the United States, and stays in hotels while abroad.

Though Suresh is spending most of his time outside the United States, he should have no problem convincing an inspector that he has not abandoned his residence. His job is in the United States, his home is in the United States, and he is only out of the country for lengthy periods because of his job.

Tony learned that his father, in the Dominican Republic, was ill and went to visit him. When Tony got there, he found out that things were worse than he'd thought. His father needed constant care, and Tony was the only one in the family available to help. Tony wrote back to his employer, a small U.S. law firm, and quit his job. Sadly, a year and a half after Tony had left the United States, his father died. Tony stayed another six months in the Dominican Republic to sell his father's business and then decided to return to the United States.

Since Tony did not get a reentry permit before he left for the Dominican Republic and he had been abroad for more than one year, he must apply for a returning resident visa from the U.S. consulate. He will have to explain to a consular officer why he spent so much time out of the United States. He'll need evidence that he didn't intend to abandon his U.S. residence.

The fact that Tony maintained a bank account and a mailing address in the United States is helpful. Most important will be letters from his father's doctor and family business documents. This evidence shows that Tony didn't intend to abandon his U.S. residence. He was only in the Dominican Republic so long because he had to care for his father.

Green Card Expiration and Renewal

At one time, green cards (the official name is "permanent resident" card — and they're not green) were issued without an expiration date. You only needed a new one if you lost your card, or you got your card as a child and an inspector insisted that you get a new card with an updated photo. Cards issued now are valid for ten years.

When your card expires, you don't lose your permanent residence. That's a myth. It is just your card that expires, not that your legal status as a permanent resident expires.

In 1994, the government required that certain permanent residents get new cards, even if their cards had not expired. Most of these cards were issued prior to 1979. Here's how to tell if you need a new card: If your card is one with a ten-year expiration date, you of course need to replace the card when it expires. If you have one of the older cards, you must replace the card unless it has the notation "I-551" on it.

CHAPTER 2

Family-Based Immigration

Under what is called **Family-Based** immigration, you may qualify for an immigrant visa if you are the spouse, parent, or child of a U.S. citizen or you are the spouse or unmarried son or daughter of a permanent resident.

U.S. immigration law divides Family-Based immigration into two groups: the Immediate Relatives of U.S. citizens and the four Family-Based Preferences. Note one important difference between Immediate Relatives of U.S. citizens and preference applicants: A preference applicant can bring his or her spouse and/or unmarried child under 21 as accompanying family members. Immediate Relatives cannot. This illogical rule is called the **"derivative beneficiary"** rule. For more on derivative beneficiaries, see Chapter 1.

When discussing family-based immigration, we call the U.S. citizen or permanent resident filing for a relative (petitioning for the relative) the **petitioner**. We call the relative trying to get an immigrant visa (who benefits from the petition) the **beneficiary**. The form a petitioner files for a beneficiary is USCIS Form I-130, Petition for Alien Relative (see Appendix B). Before I explain how U.S. immigration laws define family relationships, let's review the family immigration categories.

THE IMMEDIATE RELATIVE CATEGORY

You are an Immediate Relative of a U.S. citizen if you are one of the following:

- Spouse of a U.S. citizen.
- Unmarried child (under 21) of a U.S. citizen.
- Parent of a U.S. citizen where the citizen is 21 or older.
- Spouse of a deceased U.S. citizen, where at the time of your spouse's death, you had been married at least two years and were not legally separated, you self-petitioned within two years of your spouse's death, and you have not remarried.

If you qualify for the Immediate Relative category, you don't need to worry about a quota or waiting list. You can get a green card as soon as your papers are processed. That's because the number of visas available to Immediate Relatives is unlimited.

Some children of United States citizens may benefit from a law enacted on August 2, 2002, the Child Status Protection Act (CSPA). The purpose of this law is to protect certain children of U.S. citizens and permanent residents who may lose benefits because of long USCIS processing delays.

Under the CSPA, when a U.S. citizen petitions for his or her unmarried child under 21, the child's age is "fixed" on the date the USCIS receives the petition.

Ida's story illustrates how an under 21 unmarried child of a U.S. citizen can benefit from the CSPA.

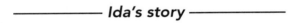
Ida's story

Ida was 20-years-old and unmarried when her U.S. citizen mother petitioned for her. Ida remains qualified as the immediate relative of a U.S. citizen regardless of how long it takes the USCIS or U.S. consulate abroad to process her permanent residence application. This is true even if Ida turns 21 while waiting. Prior to the enactment of the CSPA, once she turned 21, she would have moved to the first family preference category, with a long wait for permanent residence.

Family-Based Preference Categories

Under the four Family-Based Preference categories, you are subject to a yearly quota. For some preference categories the wait can be many years.

If you get an immigrant visa under a Family-Based Preference, your spouse and your unmarried children under age 21 can follow or accompany you to the United States as derivative beneficiary immigrants. (For more information on derivative beneficiaries, see Chapter 1.) Note that immigration law uses the term "child" to refer to a child under 21. A "son or daughter" is a child of any age.

The preference categories for the relatives of U.S. citizens and permanent residents are:

- **First Family-Based Preference:** Adult unmarried sons and daughters (age 21 or older) of U.S. citizens.

You qualify as an unmarried son or daughter if you have never married or you are divorced or widowed. However, you cannot get a divorce for the sole purpose of getting a visa. You can expect the USCIS to be suspicious if you get a divorce and then shortly thereafter your mother or father sponsors you for a First Family-Based Preference visa.

- **Second Family-Based Preference A:** Spouse and unmarried children under age 21 of permanent residents.
- **Second Family-Based Preference B:** Unmarried son or daughter of any age of permanent residents.

Family Preference Beneficiaries and the Child Status Protection Act

Some of family preference immigrant visa applicants may benefit from the Child Status Protection Act (CSPA). The purpose of the law is to protect certain children of U.S. citizens and permanent residents who may lose benefits because of long USCIS processing delays. For Second Family Preference A children, the law provides that the age of a child is fixed on the date the child's priority date becomes "current" minus the time it takes the USCIS (or took the INS or BCIS) to approve the petition. The child must begin processing for permanent residence within one year of getting to the front of the line under the quota system and thus qualifies for permanent residence.

Carol's story illustrates how the CSPA might benefit a child of a permanent resident under the Second Family Preference A.

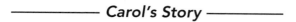

———————— *Carol's Story* ————————

Carol's mother, a permanent resident, petitioned for Carol to become a permanent resident on January 2, 2003. Carol, as an unmarried daughter of a permanent resident age 15, qualified for residence in the Second Family Preference A category. On January 2, 2004, the USCIS approved the petition. Five years later, just after her twenty-first birthday, Carol's priority date became current. Despite having turned 21, she can get her immigrant visa under The Second Family Preference A category. That's because her date was fixed on the date her priority date became current, minus the one year it took for the USCIS to decide the petition. Under prior law she would have moved to the Second Family Preference B category, where the wait is longer.

If you are applying in the Second Family-Based Preference A category as a unmarried child, you must remain unmarried until you become a permanent resident. I must mention again that you cannot get a divorce for the sole purpose of getting a visa.

Mario's story illustrates that in order to get a green card under the Second Family-Based Preference, you must remain single until you become a permanent resident.

Mario's Story

Mario, a citizen of Ecuador, was single when his mother, a permanent U.S. resident, petitioned for him for a green card. Four years later a U.S. consular officer called Mario in for his final immigrant visa interview at the U.S. consulate in Guayaquil.

All went well at Mario's interview; the consular officer approved his case and gave Mario his immigrant visa. Mario would become a permanent resident upon his first entry into the United States. When Mario told his girlfriend, Maria, that the consular officer had given him an immigrant visa, she was very excited for him. However, Maria was concerned that Mario would forget her once he got to the United States. Mario and Maria decided to get married right away, before Mario left for his new home in New York. When Mario arrived at JFK Airport, the USCIS inspector asked him if he was married, and Mario answered yes. The USCIS did not allow Mario to enter the United States, and he was forced to go back to Ecuador. That's because Mario no longer qualified for a green card as the unmarried son of a permanent resident as required by the petition filed for him by his mother. When his mother becomes a U.S. citizen, he will be eligible to get a green card under the Third Family-Based Preference as a married son of a U.S. citizen.

Had Mario waited until he had entered the United States at least once before he got married, his entry would have made him a permanent resident. He could have flown home right away, married Maria, and then returned to the United States to petition for her.

- **Third Family-Based Preference (formerly Fourth Preference):** Married sons and daughters of U.S. citizens.
- **Fourth Family-Based Preference (formerly Fifth Preference):** Brothers and sisters of U.S. citizens where the U.S. citizen is 21 years of age or older.

Under the fourth preference, the U.S. citizen petitioner must be 21 years of age or older. This preference has long waiting lists. Some experts estimate that new cases will take 20 years or longer.

FAMILY RELATIONSHIPS

U.S. immigration laws are very specific in defining family relationships. In this section, we look at how the law defines husband and wife, child and parent, and brother and sister relationships.

HUSBAND OR WIFE

In order to get a green card based on a petition filed by your spouse, you must prove that you didn't get married just to get a green card. If you or your spouse were previously married, you must prove that your and/or your spouse's prior marriages ended either through divorce or death.

Real Marriages Versus Green Card Marriages

The USCIS will not recognize a marriage as bona fide or "real" if you got married just to get a green card. If you try to get a green card using a phony marriage and get caught, you risk being permanently barred from becoming a permanent resident.

George's story illustrates what can happen if you try a "green card" marriage.

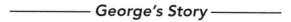
——————— *George's Story* ———————

George ran away from his home in London when he was 14. After several years of trying to make it on his own in Liverpool, he came to the United States, supposedly just for a visit. In reality he hoped to get work here as a welder. He went to live with a friend, Frank, in Los Angeles, California. Despite his skills, George found it almost impossible to find work because he didn't have work permission from the USCIS. Employers were afraid to hire him because of the employer sanctions law (see section V). Frank's girlfriend, Ginny, offered to marry George to help him get a green card. When the couple went to George's green card interview, Ginny was very nervous. When the examiner questioned her about the marriage, Ginny broke down and cried, admitting that she only married George to help him get legal papers. The USCIS examiner denied George's green card application.

Some time later, George got a notice to appear for a removal hearing. By that time he had married Sharon, a U.S. citizen, who was already pregnant with George's child. George really loved Sharon, but because the USCIS had earlier caught George in a phony marriage scheme, he cannot get a green card by a petition filed by Sharon, another relative, or an employer.

To make sure that the USCIS approves your marriage petition, your spouse should present proof that your marriage is bona fide. Evidence of a real marriage includes:

- Photographs of your wedding, of your reception, or of you and your spouse together before or after you were married.
- Records of a joint bank account.
- A lease for an apartment or a mortgage agreement for a home containing both your and your spouse's name.
- Letters from third parties addressed to you and your spouse at the same address.
- Health and other insurance policies with the names of you and your spouse.
- Affidavits from friends, relatives, or religious leaders as to the

honesty of the marriage.

- Personal records showing your spouse as your emergency contact.
- Joint tax returns.
- Joint credit cards.
- Utilities and phone bills with both names.

You should attach the evidence to the USCIS-130 petition when you submit it to the USCIS. By providing lots of evidence that yours is a real marriage, you may avoid further inquiry from the USCIS about whether your marriage is bona fide. Plan to bring additional supporting documents when you have your green card interview.

The Marriage Fraud Interview

If you and your spouse are both living in the United States, the USCIS may interview you about your life together. This may happen as part of your adjustment of status interview (see Chapter 6) or in a separate **marriage fraud interview**. Actually, the USCIS approves many I-130 petitions filed by U.S. citizens and permanent residents without a marriage fraud interview.

You may bring an attorney or an accredited not-for-profit representative to a marriage fraud interview. At the interview, the USCIS examiner may separate you and your spouse and ask the two of you the same questions, such as whether you have ever met each other's relatives, the color of the walls in your apartment, when you met, what vacations you have taken together, if any, and whether you have a television. The purpose of the questions is to see if you and your spouse give the same answers. No matter how much you prepare, you'll find it difficult to pass the interview if yours is a phony marriage.

The story of Susan and Tom gives you a sense of what happens at a marriage fraud interview.

—— The Story of Susan and Tom ——

Tom and Susan were truly a couple in love. Tom was a U.S. citizen. Susan, an Australian, had come to the United States on a visit and, after meeting Tom, decided to stay. When Tom and Susan appeared for Susan's interview, they presented no evidence other than their marriage certificate to prove that their marriage was real. No photos, no letters, nothing. The USCIS examiner decided to interview Tom and Susan separately to make sure that they didn't get married just so that Susan could get a green card.

The USCIS examiner asked Susan what Tom had given her for her birthday. The truth was that Tom had forgotten all about Susan's birthday and had not given her a gift. Susan was afraid that if she told the interviewer the truth, the examiner would think they weren't really a couple. So Susan answered, "A red sweater." Later when the examiner asked Tom the same question, he told the truth, saying that he had not gotten Susan a present. Whoops!

Tom and Susan had forgotten the main goal of a USCIS marriage fraud interview: to see if the husband and wife say the same things.

Fortunately for Tom and Susan, their examiner was especially nice. She asked Tom and Susan about the different answers to the question about the birthday gift and Susan explained the reason for her answer. Since Susan and Tom had given the same answer to so many questions, the USCIS examiner gave them a day to bring in additional evidence that they were living together. Tom and Susan submitted the evidence that afternoon, and the USCIS interviewer approved the case.

If the USCIS examiner believes that your marriage is real, the examiner will approve the I-130 petition. If the examiner believes that your marriage is not bona fide, the examiner will deny the petition or ask the petitioner (your spouse) to withdraw it. This means that the USCIS is asking your spouse to stop the case. If your spouse withdraws the petition, you will not get a permanent residence from that petition. Often, whether the petition is denied or withdrawn, the USCIS will start proceedings to remove you from the United States.

A third possibility is that the examiner will not decide right away but will send the case out for a field investigation. A USCIS officer may visit your home. USCIS field investigations of marriages are less common than people think, but they do happen. If the examiner sends your case to the investigations department, at some point in the future (sometimes several months after your initial interview), a USCIS investigator may appear at the residence you listed on the I-130 petition. The investigator is looking for evidence that you and your spouse are living together, such as men's and women's clothes, two toothbrushes, shaving cream, and perfume. The investigator may also talk to neighbors.

A USCIS investigator doesn't have the right to enter your house without either a warrant or your permission. Nevertheless, it is up to the two of you to prove that you are eligible for permanent residence. If you do not let the investigator in to look around, the USCIS may deny the marriage petition.

It's easy to see: You want to do all that you can to keep your case from being sent out for an investigation. Even if the investigator ultimately finds that your marriage is a valid one, the investigation itself can take weeks or months. If you want to avoid a long and nervous delay in your case, be sure to document your marriage well.

Self-Petitioning—Abused Spouse or Child

If you or your child has been physically or mentally abused by your U.S. citizen or permanent resident spouse, you may be able to **"self-petition"** for a green card. That means you don't need a sponsor. You can file by yourself for a green card without your spouse's help.

In order to qualify to self-petition, you or your child must have either been battered or subjected to extreme cruelty by your spouse. You must be living in the United States and at some time must have lived with your spouse. But you don't have to be living together at the time that you file the petition. The abuse must have happened sometime during your marriage. Abuse that takes place after you are legally divorced is not enough, although it might help prove that abuse took place during your marriage. You need not be married to your spouse at the time that you file your petition if the reason for the divorce was battery or extreme mental cruelty. However, if you are divorced, the divorce must have occurred within two years of filing the petition.

An abused child of U.S. citizen or permanent resident parents may also self-petition. To prove that you are an abused spouse, an abused child, or a parent of an abused child, you will need some evidence of the abuse, such as a record of having called the police, a family court protection order, or a letter from a psychiatrist, psychologist, or social worker who has assisted you or your child. Because the USCIS has a strict standard for extreme hardship, you should get the help of an immigration law expert before filing a battered spouse petition.

Once the USCIS approves your petition as an abused spouse, an abused child, or a parent of an abused child, the USCIS will allow you to remain in the United States until you become a permanent resident.

If You and Your Spouse Are Living Apart

What if you and your spouse are not living together? Can your spouse's petition for you be approved?

If the separation has nothing to do with your intentions to be together as husband and wife, the USCIS should approve the petition, if you can satisfy any doubts about the validity of your marriage.

If your marriage is in trouble and you and your spouse are living apart but you have not taken steps to legally separate or end the marriage, the USCIS can still approve the I-130 petition. However, if the two of you are living apart, it may be more difficult to establish that your marriage is bona fide.

If you or your spouse has filed a separation agreement or divorce action with a court, as far as the USCIS is concerned, the marriage is over. In some U.S. states, merely signing a separation agreement may be enough for a marriage to be considered ended.

The stories of Jim and Martha and of Jaime and Altagracia show that even if a husband and wife are living apart, the couple can still show that their marriage is real.

—— *The Story of Jim and Martha* ——

Jim, a U.S. citizen, and Martha, a citizen of Mexico, met when they were both students at the University of Chicago. Upon graduation, Jim got accepted to a law school in San Francisco and Martha got accepted to a medical school in Los Angeles. They decided that they would have to be apart. To express their commitment to each other, they got married.

By the time that the USCIS interviewed Jim and Martha about Martha's permanent residence, they were already living in different cities. Jim and Martha brought evidence of their continuing relationship to the interview. This evidence included phone bills showing that they spoke every night, letters, and photographs of the two of them together in Niagara Falls on their honeymoon. They also gave the USCIS photos taken on their visit to Martha's family in Mexico City. Martha had no problem becoming a permanent resident.

– The Story of Jaime and Altagracia –

Jaime and Altagracia had known each other for many years before they got married. Jaime was a citizen of Costa Rica who was studying architecture at the University of California at Los Angeles (UCLA). Altagracia, a U.S. citizen of Mexican ancestry, was also a student at UCLA. She and Jaime were college sweethearts from their freshman year. After graduation they decided to marry. Altagracia then petitioned for Jaime to become a permanent resident.

Jaime and Altagracia found that there was a big difference between being married and being boyfriend and girlfriend. They didn't like being married so they decided to separate. While they were living apart, the USCIS called them to come in for the interview regarding Jaime's application for permanent residence.

Even though they admitted that they were living apart and conceded that information immediately when they began their interview, Altagracia was able to prove that she had been Jaime's girlfriend and that the marriage was bona fide. She explained that neither had begun divorce proceedings, that they were truly a couple, and that this was not a business marriage. They had several albums full of photographs taken together on trips and at parties. And they had a photo from their lavish wedding, when 20 of Jaime's relatives had flown in from Costa Rica just for the ceremony. The USCIS examiner was convinced that the marriage between Jaime and Altagracia was a real marriage and granted Jaime his permanent residence.

Prior Marriages

If your former spouse has died, you must present a death certificate when submitting the petition. If your or your spouse's prior marriage ended in divorce, you should submit the divorce judgment (not just a certificate of divorce).

If the divorce took place in a foreign country, the USCIS checks to see that the divorce was proper under the laws of that country. The USCIS also checks to make sure that the divorce is valid under the laws of the state or country where the marriage ceremony between you and your spouse took place.

Evaluating whether a marriage has been properly ended can be difficult. An example is the case of Tomas, Sally, and Wilma.

– The Story of Tomas, Sally, and Wilma –

Tomas is a naturalized U.S. citizen living in New York City. He was born in the Dominican Republic. Tomas would like to marry and file an I-130 petition for his girlfriend, Wilma, who is also from the Dominican Republic. Wilma is living in New Jersey, studying for her master's degree at New Jersey State University. She is legally in the United States in F-1 foreign student status (see Chapter 13 for more on student visas).

Tomas was previously married to Sally, a U.S. citizen born in Kansas City, Missouri. Tomas and Sally had no children and no property to divide. The most important thing to them at the time was to get a divorce as soon as possible.

Tomas and Sally agreed through attorneys to file for divorce in the Dominican Republic. The divorce was granted. Neither Tomas nor Sally appeared at the divorce proceedings, although they had lawyers represent them in court.

Some states, for instance New Jersey, recognize "mail order" divorces, that is, divorces where neither party appeared at the proceeding. Other states do not recognize all "mail order" divorces but may recognize some. New York State does not recognize "mail order" divorces in the circumstances described in Tomas and Sally's case. New Jersey does. Thus under New Jersey law, Tomas and Sally are divorced and free to remarry. New York law still considers Tomas and Sally to be husband and wife, despite the divorce in the Dominican Republic.

If Tomas marries Wilma in New York State, his marriage will not be considered valid and he cannot petition for her. If he marries her in New Jersey, the marriage will be valid under New Jersey law. Both the USCIS and New York State will recognize the marriage. This makes no sense to Tomas and Wilma. But to avoid getting a new divorce from Sally, he and Wilma will marry in New Jersey. After the marriage, Tomas will file a petition for Wilma. When the USCIS approves the petition, Wilma will become a permanent resident based on Tomas's petition.

Conditional Residence

If you get an immigrant visa based on a marriage that is less than two years old at the time you become an immigrant, you are a **conditional permanent resident.** Being a conditional permanent resident means that you get a temporary green card, which expires in two years. You and your spouse must file an application called a joint petition (USCIS Form I-751, Petition to Remove the Conditions on Residence) to make your permanent residence truly permanent. You must file the joint petition in the 90 days prior to the second anniversary of your becoming a permanent resident. If you became a permanent resident more than two years after your marriage, the conditional residence rule does not apply. If you get divorced before the USCIS removes the condition, or your spouse refuses to sign the joint petition, you must apply for a waiver of the joint petition requirement as discussed in the following text. Except for the need to remove the condition, a conditional permanent resident has the same rights as other permanent residents. Time in conditional permanent resident status counts toward U.S. citizenship.

The stories of Carlos and Juanita and of Yoko and Yoshi illustrate the conditional residence rule.

— The Story of Carlos and Juanita —

Carlos, a citizen and resident of Barcelona, met Juanita, a U.S. citizen, when Juanita was studying Spanish in Barcelona. Shortly after Juanita and Carlos met, they got married. Since Carlos had a good job as a language instructor, they decided to live in Barcelona, despite objections from Juanita's parents. Three years later, Juanita filed a relative petition for Carlos. Several months later, Carlos became a permanent resident without condition. That's because he had already been married to Juanita for more than two years when he became a permanent resident.

—— The Story of Yoko and Yoshi ——

Yoko, a U.S. citizen, met Yoshi, an exchange student from Japan, in Aspen, Colorado. Both were in Aspen on ski vacations. Yoko, although of Japanese descent, could speak very little Japanese, and Yoshi could speak very little English. Nevertheless, they fell head over heels for each other and flew to Las Vegas to get married. They began living together in Los Angeles, and Yoko immediately filed papers for Yoshi. Yoshi became a conditional permanent resident about three months later. Because he became a permanent resident within two years of his marriage to Yoko, Yoshi's permanent residence was conditional.

But when the time came for Yoshi to apply to have the condition removed from his permanent residence, he and Yoko had been living apart for well over a year. Because Yoko wanted Yoshi to get his green card, she agreed not to divorce him until the USCIS removed the condition from Yoshi's permanent residence. On the joint petition to remove the condition, Yoko and Yoshi gave separate addresses. The USCIS called them in for an interview. At the interview, they presented evidence, including photos from their many trips together, to show that they had not gotten married just so Yoshi could get a green card. The USCIS examiner believed their story and ruled that the USCIS should remove the condition from Yoshi's permanent residence. He became a permanent resident without condition. After Yoshi became a permanent resident without condition, Yoko divorced him.

Removing the Condition Without Your Spouse's Signature

If your marriage has been terminated by the death of your spouse or by annulment or divorce, or your spouse refuses to sign the joint petition, you may still apply to have the conditional status removed. We call this "applying for a waiver" of the joint petition requirement. You file the same form, USCIS Form I-751, with the USCIS. For the USCIS to remove the condition from your residence without the signature and cooperation of your spouse, you must show one of the following:

- Yours wasn't a "sham marriage" and deportation (called "removal" as of April 1, 1997) will cause you extreme suffering and hardship.
- You entered the marriage in good faith, and the marriage ended by divorce or annulment.
- You were the victim of domestic violence.
- Your spouse is deceased.

Under the USCIS interpretation for the second ground, that you entered the marriage in good faith and the marriage ended by divorce or annulment, your divorce must be complete before you can file the petition. Under prior interpretations, you could apply before your two years expired, and if your divorce was pending, the USCIS would not decide on your petition until the divorce was complete. Now, if you are not divorced, the USCIS will deny your joint petition. You can, however, renew your request to remove the petition in what's called "removal proceedings" (formerly called deportation proceedings).

If the USCIS denies your application to remove the condition from your residence, you may be placed in **removal proceedings**. If you can convince the immigration judge that your marriage was valid, the immigration judge can reverse the USCIS's decision.

Jimmy's story and Karen's story both illustrate the effect of a divorce in a conditional residence case.

 *Jimmy's Story*

Jimmy came to the United States from Ireland as a drummer in a rock-and-roll band. Partying after one of his concerts, he met Susan, a U.S. citizen. They were soon married. Susan petitioned for Jimmy. Three months later, he became a conditional permanent resident. Unfortunately for Jimmy, his new wife fell in love with the band's lead singer and filed for divorce. Jimmy agreed to the divorce. Twenty-one months after Jimmy became a permanent resident, he applied to have the condition removed from his permanent residence. Since his wife had divorced him, he had to file for a waiver of the joint petition requirement. He submitted the divorce papers and explained in an affidavit (a sworn statement) exactly what had happened. He provided lots of evidence that he and Susan had been together as husband and wife. The evidence included a photo of them together at the MTV Video Awards ceremony published in *Rolling Stone* magazine. Jimmy convinced the USCIS examiner that the marriage was bona fide and that the divorce was not Jimmy's fault. The examiner granted the waiver, and the USCIS removed the condition from Jimmy's permanent residence.

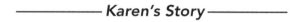
Karen's Story

After a long courtship, Harry, a U.S. citizen, married Karen, a Canadian citizen. Unfortunately, shortly after their marriage (but after Karen had become a conditional permanent resident), Harry lost his job and developed a drinking problem. He became very abusive around the house, screaming and yelling and threatening to hurt Karen. Although he never hit her, he often threatened to do so, and when he came home drunk, he would throw furniture, dishes, and other items around the apartment. Often Karen had to call the police. Eventually, she obtained a protection order from a court banning her husband from their apartment and ultimately divorced him.

When Karen applied to remove the condition from her residence, she brought in copies of the police reports (which, in addition to showing spousal abuse, proved that she and her husband were living together) as well as a copy of the protection order. She included a letter from a psychiatrist who explained how Harry's abuse had inflicted psychological trauma upon Karen. Based on the evidence presented, the USCIS examiner removed the condition from Karen's permanent residence.

Getting Divorced and Filing for a New Spouse—The Five-Year Rule

If you became a permanent resident based on marriage to a U.S. citizen or permanent resident, you cannot remarry and petition for your new spouse unless you can prove one of the following:

- The death of your spouse ended the prior marriage.
- You didn't enter the prior marriage only to become a permanent resident.
- Five years have passed since you first became a permanent resident.

Some people think that a person cannot remarry and petition for a new spouse for five years after they become a permanent resident. That's not true. The law only makes it more difficult because you must show that not just one but two marriages were bona fide: the one where you got the green card and the new one, the one that the USCIS is now considering.

Kitty's story illustrates the five-year rule.

Kitty's Story

Kitty, from England, became a permanent resident when her husband, Henry, sponsored her. Henry was born in California. Henry and Kitty had met at a friend's house, fallen in love, and within two months of their meeting decided to marry. Three months later Kitty became a permanent resident.

Shortly after the wedding, Kitty and Henry began having marital problems. They tried to make their marriage work, but after three years, they divorced. When Kitty went home to England for Christmas, she bumped into her high school sweetheart, Sam, and decided to give marriage another chance. Though she had become a permanent resident just three years before and the five-year rule applies, she can petition for Sam immediately after their marriage.

Kitty has a lot of evidence that her marriage to Henry was bona fide. They traveled together, and she has photographs from trips with Henry before and after their wedding. Kitty and Henry had lived in the same apartment for more than two years, and both their names were on their apartment lease. Henry had been the beneficiary on Kitty's pension plan, and both their names were on a family health insurance policy.

Kitty can prove that her relationship with Sam is bona fide as well. Kitty and Sam had been corresponding for many years, and she had Sam's letters and records of their phone calls. They had a big wedding, they invited both of their families, and they took lots of pictures. Of course, since Sam is eligible under the Second Family-Based Preference, he must wait several years before he can become a permanent resident. That's because of quota backlogs. Nevertheless, because Kitty can prove that her marriages to both Henry and Sam were bona fide, she can file the petition and the USCIS can approve it. Sam can obtain his priority date and begin his wait for a green card.

Self-Petitioning for a Widow(er)

If you are the widow(er) of a U.S. citizen, you can petition for a green card for yourself. You must have been married to the U.S. citizen for at least two years. You must file the petition within two years of your spouse's death, and you must not have remarried at the time that you become a permanent resident. If you were legally separated or divorced from your spouse at the time of death, you don't qualify. To qualify for a green card as a widow(er), you must file USCIS Form I-360, Petition Widow/Special Immigrant.

The Parent-Child Relationship

You must prove a parent-child relationship when you are filing for a parent or a parent is filing for you.

Mother-Child

You are considered the son or daughter (child) of your natural mother, regardless of whether your mother and father were married. The only exception is for adopted children who on adoption no longer have a mother-child relationship with their natural mother.

Father-Child

For immigration purposes, a person is considered the child of a natural father if one of the following conditions is met:

1. The child was born to married parents.
2. The child was legitimated before the age of 18.
3. The country of nationality does not distinguish between legitimate and illegitimate children.
4. The parent-child relationship was established prior to the child's 21st birthday.

To claim a father-child relationship under number 4 in the previous list, the father need not have legally recognized his relationship with the child as long as the father can show an act of concern for the child's "support, instruction, and general welfare." The story of Timothy and his son, Tony, illustrates the rule regarding father-child relationships where the child was not legitimate or legitimated.

— *The Story of Timothy and Tony* —

Timothy was a permanent resident of the United States. On one of his visits back home, he spent time with his old high school girlfriend and she became pregnant with his child. Timothy did not know he was the father of Tony until 15 years later when Tony's mother wrote to Timothy asking if he would help Tony, his son, with his college expenses. Timothy was shocked to learn that he had a 15 year-old son, but he decided that he wanted to help Tony out.

On his next trip to his country, Timothy spent time with Tony and began a regular correspondence with him. Every month, he sent Tony $100 to help him pay for his expenses, and once or twice a year, he visited Tony.

Ten years later, when Tony was 25 years of age, he decided that he wanted to become a permanent resident of the United States himself. Timothy petitioned for Tony, and Tony came into the United States as the adult unmarried son of a permanent resident under the Second Family-Based Preference B, although Timothy had never legally recognized Tony as his son and had never married Tony's mother. The fact that Timothy established a relationship with Tony that was typical of a father-son relationship was enough for Tony to qualify for a permanent resident as the unmarried son of Timothy.

Stepparent-Stepchild

U.S. immigration law recognizes a stepparent-stepchild relationship if the stepchild is less than 18 years old at the time of the marriage between the natural parent and the stepparent. This parent-child relationship remains regardless of the child's age when the petition is filed. Even if the natural parent and stepparent divorce, the USCIS will sometimes recognize the parent-stepchild relationship. Finally, the USCIS recognizes the relationship between a child and the child's natural parents, even after a stepchild-stepparent relationship is created.

The stories of Michael, Martha, and their children and of Karen, Steve, Sally, and their children illustrate the stepparent-stepchild rule.

— *The Story of Michael, Martha, and Their Children* —

Michael is a U.S. citizen who married Martha, a citizen of Venezuela. At the time of her marriage to Michael, Martha had two children, Charlie (14 years of age) and Carmen (19 years of age). They are all living in Venezuela, but Michael would like them to come to live in the United States as soon as possible.

Martha and Charlie can become permanent residents in a short time as Immediate Relatives of a U.S. citizen. That's because Martha is Michael's spouse and Charlie is his stepchild, since Charlie was less than 18 when Martha and Michael married. Martha and Charlie can become permanent residents when their papers are processed because of the unlimited number of green cards available for Immediate Relatives of U.S. citizens.

Since Carmen was 19 at the time of Martha and Michael's marriage, the USCIS does not consider her a stepchild of Michael. Carmen cannot become a permanent resident based on a petition filed by Michael. Carmen must wait until Martha becomes a permanent resident and then can petition for her. Then she must wait until her priority date (see Chapter 6 for more on priority dates) is reached before she can get an immigrant visa under the Second Family-Based Preference B.

—*The Story of Karen, Steve, Sally, and Their Children*—

Karen and Steve, natives and residents of Australia, had both been married and divorced before they met, fell in love, and married. Steve had a child, Chris, from his marriage with his first wife, Sally. At the time of the marriage of Karen and Steve, Chris was 12 years old. Under U.S. immigration laws, Chris is Karen's stepchild. When Chris was 25 years old, he became a U.S. citizen. He then petitioned to bring Karen and Steve from Australia. Though Chris is over 18, the stepchild-stepparent relationship created by the marriage of Karen and Steve lasts throughout both their lives. Even if Karen and Steve had divorced, Chris could petition for Karen, provided that he could show a continuing relationship with her. And he could petition for Sally as well, since she is his natural mother.

Adopted Child

A child adopted before the age of 16 who has lived in the same household with and has been in the legal custody of his or her adopted parent for two years is considered by the USCIS to be a child of that parent.

Some countries still have informal or "customary" adoptions. In the case of customary adoptions, the USCIS will look to the laws of the country where the adoption took place. The USCIS will recognize the customary adoption if the adopted child has rights equal to a child formally adopted.

Orphan Child

A U.S. citizen can petition for an orphan child who is under the age of 16 at the time the adoptive parent files the petition. Death or disappearance of or abandonment by his or her parents must have been the cause of the child becoming an orphan. "Abandonment" may include a situation where a parent or parents are incapable of caring for the child. To petition for an orphan, a U.S. citizen must be married or at least 25 years-old. The adoptive parents must have adopted the child abroad, or the petitioner must prove that he or she will adopt the orphan child when the child comes to the United States. The adoptive parent(s) can do this by meeting the preadoption requirements in the state where the orphan will be residing.

Brother or Sister

To establish a sibling relationship, you must prove one parent in common under the rules for the parent-child relationship as discussed above. A U.S. citizen must be more than 21 years of age to petition for a brother or sister.

If siblings have the same parents and those parents were married, proving that they have a brother-sister relationship is easy. Birth certificates are usually enough to prove the sibling relationship. But suppose they have only one parent in common. What happens then is illustrated by the story of Miguel, Sonia, and Reynaldo.

— The Story of Miguel, Sonia, and Reynaldo —

Sonia and Reynaldo have the same father, Miguel, but different mothers. Sonia, a 25-year-old U.S. citizen, wants to petition for her half brother, Reynaldo.

Sonia is the legitimate child of Miguel, having been born to Miguel's wife, who passed away shortly after Sonia's birth. Reynaldo was born out of wedlock to Miguel and his girlfriend, Virginia. Under the laws of the country where Reynaldo was born, he was considered "illegitimate." However, Miguel had raised Reynaldo since his birth and had been Reynaldo's sole means of financial support and fatherly guidance. Thus Reynaldo is Miguel's child under the law, and Sonia can successfully petition for Reynaldo.

Miguel is clearly Sonia's father because she was his legitimate daughter. Miguel is also Reynaldo's father since he established a father-son relationship with Reynaldo before Reynaldo's 21st birthday. Therefore, since Sonia and Reynaldo have one parent in common, Sonia and Reynaldo are sister and brother.

CHAPTER 3

Employment
Based Immigration

Whether you're a housekeeper, gardener, designer, or scientist, you may be able to get an immigrant visa based on an offer of employment. In most cases, your employer must prove that no qualified U.S. worker is immediately available to do the job. Sometimes you can get an immigrant visa simply because of the value of your skills, knowledge, or experience to U.S. society.

In this chapter, I offer you an overview of how you can get an immigrant visa based on your work, talent, or investment. These categories are called **Employment-Based Preferences**. In most Employment-Based categories, there's no quota backlog (for more on quotas, see Chapter 6). Your only wait in getting the green card is for the processing of the papers. For some categories the wait can be lengthy.

If your employer must show that no qualified U.S. worker is available to do the job, the employer must get a **labor certification** from the U.S. Department of Labor. The labor certification will confirm the unavailability of U.S. workers for this position. Getting a labor certification can take anywhere from many months to more than two years. It depends on the state and region of the country where you'll be working.

To get an immigrant visa based on employment, you must be the beneficiary of a USCIS-approved petition, USCIS Form I-140, Immigrant

Petition for Alien Worker. Where the law requires a labor certification, it must be presented with the petition. Where the law doesn't require a labor certification, you file the petition with supporting documents showing your qualifications under a particular Employment-Based visa category. You or your employer file the petition at one of four USCIS regional offices (see Appendix C, "USCIS National and Regional Offices").

Under new laws, you sometimes can change jobs and then continue with your Employment-Based case without filing a new labor certification and immigrant visa petition. For more on this portability rule, see "Petition Portability for Employment-Based Cases," later in this chapter. Also new is the right to file your I-140 petition with your application for adjustment of status, form I-485. For information on whether you qualify for adjustment of status, the process of getting permanent residence without leaving the United States, see Chapter 6.

YOUR EMPLOYMENT-BASED PRIORITY DATE

When a labor certification must support a petition, your **priority date** is the date when the State Department of Labor in your employer's state first receives your labor certification application. Your priority date is your place in line under the preference system (for more on priority dates, see Chapter 6). Where no labor certification is required, your priority date is the date that the USCIS receives your petition. Proof of your education and/or experience must accompany the petition. Unless a well-known company is sponsoring you, your employer must submit proof of the company's ability to pay the offered salary.

MUST YOU STAY AT YOUR JOB
AFTER YOU GET YOUR IMMIGRANT VISA?

Just because your employer sponsored you doesn't mean you must stay with that job forever. However, if you quit soon after getting your immigrant visa, the USCIS may someday check whether the job offer was genuine.

Christine's and Joan's stories illustrate the rule about changing jobs for Employment-Based green card holders.

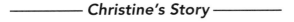
———— Christine's Story ————

Christine was working as a physical therapist in Holland when a hospital in Houston, Texas, offered her a job. She came to work at the hospital in H-1B professional worker status (see Chapter 14 for more on H-1B status). After Christine spent a year on the job, the hospital agreed to sponsor her for permanent residence. One year later, she became a permanent resident. Unfortunately for Christine, two weeks after becoming a permanent resident, the hospital replaced her supervisor. Christine began having a miserable time at her job. She quit her position at the hospital and went to work teaching pottery making to nursery school children. It was something she'd always wanted to do.

Five years after becoming a permanent resident, Christine applied for U.S. citizenship. At her USCIS naturalization interview, the examiner looked over her work history. The examiner discovered that Christine had worked for her employer for only two weeks after she became a permanent resident. Christine had made very careful notes of all her experiences at the hospital. She convinced the USCIS naturalization examiner that she had not cheated when she got her green card by only pretending to work at the hospital. The examiner approved her naturalization application.

——————— Joan's Story ———————

Joan was a skilled automobile repair worker living in Germany. Through a friend in the United States, she learned about a shortage of good German car repair specialists in Los Angeles. Having always wanted to live in the city of the stars, she came to the United States on a visit. While here, she interviewed at a German auto repair shop. The owner of the repair shop agreed to sponsor her for a permanent visa. Joan would have liked to start work immediately, but she wasn't eligible for any temporary work-related visa. She could not get H-1B status because she was not considered a professional. The job wasn't temporary, so she was not eligible for the H-2 temporary work visa for skilled workers (see Chapter 11 for more on H-2 status). She returned to Germany while her employer processed her green card papers.

Two years later, the U.S. Department of Labor approved Joan's labor certification application. The employer petitioned for her, and six months after the USCIS approved the petition, the U.S. consulate called her in for her immigrant visa interview. A week before her interview, Joan got a letter from her employer saying that the job was still open. The letter stated that they were interested in employing her in a permanent position at the wage noted in the labor certification application. The U.S. consulate issued Joan a permanent visa. Before beginning her new life in the United States, she spent a month traveling in Europe. After her travels, she came to the United States and went right to Los Angeles to begin working at her new job.

Unfortunately, the night before Joan arrived in Los Angeles, the repair shop burned down. The employer did not have insurance, and Joan had no job. Though Joan had never worked for the employer who sponsored her, her permanent residence status is valid. If anyone from the USCIS ever questions Joan about how she got her green card, she would have to show that she intended to work for the company when she entered the United States. If asked for proof, she might submit to the USCIS a fire department report about what happened. She could also submit a letter from the employer who had originally sponsored her, explaining about the fire. She may also be asked for documentation that shows the company was financially healthy at the time of petitioning.

THE EMPLOYMENT PREFERENCES

If you get an Employment-Based immigrant visa, your spouse and unmarried children under 21 can accompany or follow you. They qualify for immigrant visas as your derivative beneficiaries (see Chapter 1 for more on derivative beneficiaries).

Let's review the Employment-Based immigrant visa preferences.

FIRST EMPLOYMENT-BASED PREFERENCE —PRIORITY WORKERS

The term priority worker reflects the intent of the U.S. Congress to make green cards easily available for certain businesspeople, professors and researchers, and people with special talents. If you qualify in this category, you don't have to show that no U.S. workers are available to do your job. No certification is required from the Department of Labor.

The law divides priority workers into three subcategories: aliens with an extraordinary ability, outstanding professors and researchers, and multinational executives and managers.

Aliens with an Extraordinary Ability

To apply in this category, you must show extraordinary ability in the sciences, arts, education, business, or athletics. You must show sustained national or international acclaim with recognized achievements. To win an extraordinary ability case usually requires extensive documentation. You should be able to show at least *three* of the following:

- Receipt of a national or international award in your field.
- Membership in an association that requires outstanding achievement as a condition of membership.
- Published material about yourself in professional, trade, or major media publications.
- Reviews or discussions of your work in a major publication or other major media.
- Your participation as a judge of the work of others in the same or a related field.
- Original contributions, usually through publication, of major significance in your field.
- Authorship of scholarly articles.
- Display of your work at significant exhibitions.
- Performance in a significant role for organizations or establishments that have a distinguished reputation.
- Receipt of a higher salary than is usual in the field.
- Commercial success in the performing arts as shown by box office receipts or sales records.

While the law does not require a specific job offer in this category, you must present some evidence that you intend to continue work in your field. Examples are a contract with an agent or publisher. Ying Shu's and Chudi's stories provide examples of workers of extraordinary ability.

Ying Shu's Story

Ying Shu is one of the world's leading Chinese zither players. Although little known in the United States, hers is a household name in China and in Chinese-speaking communities throughout the world. On her yearly visits to the United States, she plays to packed houses in New York and San Francisco, and she has several bestselling albums. She has received many awards and is a member of the prestigious International Society of Musicians. Though most people in the United States do not know Ying Shu, she is nonetheless an individual of extraordinary ability in her musical specialty.

To get a green card, Ying Shu filed an I-140 petition supporting a documentation of her achievements. She included a letter from experts on Chinese music, many album covers, and articles about her in both American and Chinese newspapers. Her application included a letter from her agent showing that she had several performances scheduled for the next year. Once the USCIS approved her I-140 petition, she applied to become a permanent resident. She did not need an employer to sponsor her.

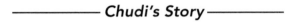

Chudi's Story

Chudi is a citizen of Nigeria. He came to the United States after several years of writing for Nigeria's leading national paper. He has been working for the last five years in H-1B temporary professional worker status at the Los Angeles Gazette, that city's leading daily paper. (For more on H-1B status, see Chapter 14.) The Gazette is recognized as one of the outstanding daily newspapers in the United States. The managing editor promoted Chudi to chief international reporter. Chudi has won national and international awards, and his articles have been published in national and international publications. He files an I-140 petition and includes letters from journalists, professors, and the editors of three leading newsmagazines in the United States. The letters state that he is recognized as a leading writer on the topic of international events. Chudi will have no problem becoming a permanent resident. He can petition for himself without the help of his employer.

Outstanding Professors and Researchers

To qualify in this category, you must show international recognition as being outstanding in a specific academic area. You must have at least three years of experience in teaching or research in the area. While this category doesn't require a labor certification showing the unavailability of U.S. workers, you must have a job offer from a college, university, research institute, or private company. For a college or university teacher, the job must be for a tenured or tenure-track position.

To qualify as an outstanding professor or researcher, you must meet at least two of the following criteria:

- Receipt of a major award for outstanding achievement in your field.
- Membership in academic associations that require outstanding achievements as a condition of membership.
- Published discussions of your work in professional journals.
- Participation as a judge of the work of others in the same or a related field.
- Original scientific or scholarly research.
- Authorship of scholarly books or articles.
- Three years' experience as a teacher or researcher.

The stories of Suzanne and Julie help us understand the outstanding professors and researchers category.

Suzanne's Story

The Southern San Diego Research Institute in California offered Suzanne employment as a researcher in biomedics. For the last four years, she had been working for the Institute in H-1B temporary professional worker status. Prior to that, she had worked for four years in a similar institute in her home country, France. Though she held only a master of science in biology, she had coauthored several reports in the nationally recognized Journal of Biological Medicine. Her years of experience (which are over the minimum required) and her publications in a national journal qualify her as a priority worker under the outstanding professors and researchers category

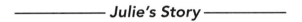
Julie's Story

Julie was not as fortunate as Suzanne. Julie was trying to get a green card as a professor of economics at Valley State University in California. She had been a professor at the college for three years working in H-1B status. However, other than the three years' experience, she couldn't qualify as an outstanding professor. She was in a tenure-track position and she was considered the best teacher in the entire college, but she had not achieved much in other areas of professional activity. Julie always believed that her primary role as a professor was to teach and enlighten her students. But her excellent teaching wasn't enough to make her qualified for an immigrant visa as an outstanding professor and researcher. She had published many articles in popular newspapers and magazines but nothing in a professional journal. She had even written a book, Making Money in America, which was published by a small press, but this still was not enough.

Julie can become a permanent resident as an employee of the college, but she will need to apply for a labor certification. If the employer files a labor certification within 18 months of the college having hired her, Julie can get a labor certification without her employer having to show that no U.S. workers are available to fill the position. The employer need only show that the search was fair and that they chose the person they believed was best for the position.

Multinational Executives and Managers

This category eases the transfer of international personnel. Prior to filing the papers, a branch, subsidiary, parent, or affiliate of the sponsoring company must have employed you abroad as a manager or executive for at least one of the previous three years. The U.S. company must have been doing business for at least one year. Most important, you must be coming to the United States to work as a manager or executive.

The stories of Katherine and Wei provide examples of getting a green card as an intracompany transferee.

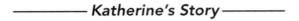
Katherine's Story

Katherine works for a British bank with a branch office in New York. Her company transferred her to the United States to manage the international investment division of the company's New York branch. She entered the United States on an L-1 international transferee temporary visa. Katherine answers directly to the president of the bank's U.S. operations. She has several professional and nonprofessional employees working under her. These employees include investment advisors, financial analysts, and secretaries.

After two years of working in the United States, Katherine wanted to become a permanent resident. She wrote to the home office asking the company to sponsor her. The home office agreed to help Katherine become a permanent resident. The president of the New York branch of the bank filed an I-140 petition for her, and she became a permanent resident.

Wei's Story

Wei had been president of his own import-export company, Wei's Imports Ltd., in Taiwan for more than 20 years. He did business around the world, but he had not seen the need to establish a branch office in the United States.

Wei grew concerned about the long-range future of Taiwan and considered applying for a business investor visa. After speaking to several business and legal experts, he decided that the laws and regulations regarding permanent visas for international investors would interfere with his investment plans. Applying for a green card based on an investment was not worth the trouble, particularly considering the other options proposed by his advisors.

Wei decided instead to expand his New York operations. He opened an office there and hired two executives to help him run the business. His company, Wei International Ltd., which was incorporated under the laws of Taiwan, wanted to transfer him to New York to manage and run the new operations. Rather than bothering with a nonimmigrant visa such as an L-1 for intracompany transferees, he decided to have the company petition for him for permanent residence. After submitting detailed documentation regarding the development of the new office, he entered the United States as a permanent resident. His case took just over six months. He continued to manage the New York operations of the business and traveled to Taiwan one month out of every three to supervise the Taiwan business.

SECOND EMPLOYMENT-BASED PREFERENCE— MEMBERS OF PROFESSIONS HOLDING ADVANCED DEGREES OR ALIENS OF EXCEPTIONAL ABILITY

In this category you must be either (a) a member of the professions holding an advanced degree (or have the equivalent in education and experience) or (b) a person of exceptional ability. The term "member of the professions" means that to do your job a person would need at least a bachelor's degree or higher. Examples are teachers, engineers, architects, and college professors. An "advanced degree" is the equivalent of a U.S. master's degree or higher. A bachelor's degree followed by five years of experience may be considered to be the equivalent of a master's degree.

The fact that you hold an advanced degree in the category is not enough. Your job must also require the degree you hold. Rachel's and Paul's stories illustrate the relationship between the job and the degree for professional workers.

Rachel's Story

Rachel studied mathematics in her home country of Poland. Her English was excellent. Rachel had her transcripts evaluated by a professional credential evaluation company in the United States. The evaluation showed that she had the U.S. equivalent of a master's degree in mathematics. A cousin in the United States told her about a job as a math teacher at a local private school, and she applied. The school got her a labor certification from the Department of Labor and then filed a petition for her in the Second Employment-Based category. The school explained that a master's degree or higher in the subject to be taught was a normal requirement for an instructor at the school. The USCIS approved the petition, and about one year later Rachel came to the United States with a permanent resident visa.

Paul's Story

Paul received his Ph.D. in art history from the University of Moscow. His father had been the manager of a large factory. While Paul had no formal business training or work experience, he was very well connected in the growing Russian business community.

When Paul came to the United States to present a paper at a conference on 20th-century Russian art, a friend introduced him to an executive of the Bulls and Bears stock brokerage firm. The firm was based in San Francisco, California. The executive offered Paul a job at $200,000 a year, plus bonuses, if Paul could help the company with business development. His main responsibility would be to introduce the Bulls and Bears company to Russian investors and to entertain Russian business executives when they came to the United States.

Paul probably can't qualify under the Second Employment-Based Preference to do the job being offered by Bulls and Bears. He has an advanced degree, but his job doesn't require that degree.

The Second Employment-Based Preference category also includes individuals who can show "exceptional ability" in the sciences, arts, or business. To qualify as a person of exceptional ability, you must show at least three of the following:

- An official academic record showing that you have a degree related to the area of exceptional ability.
- Evidence that you have at least 10 years of full-time experience in the job you are being petitioned for.
- A license to practice your profession.
- Evidence that your salary reflects your exceptional ability.
- Membership in professional associations.
- Evidence of recognition for achievements and significant contributions in your field.

In the Second Employment-Based Preference category, your employer must get you a labor certification certified by the Department of Labor unless the USCIS grants you a national interest waiver (discussed later this chapter).

THIRD EMPLOYMENT-BASED PREFERENCE— PROFESSIONALS, SKILLED WORKERS, AND OTHER WORKERS

Professionals are individuals who hold U.S. bachelor's degrees or the academic equivalent and who are members of the professions. The degree must be a normal requirement for the job. Skilled workers can perform labor requiring at least two years of education, training, or experience. Other workers perform unskilled labor requiring less than two years of training or experience. No more than 10,000 visas annually are available for the category of "other workers."

In the category of Third Employment-Based Preference, your employer must get you a labor certification.

Billy's story helps us to understand the difference between "skilled" workers and workers in the "other worker" category. The difference is important because of the particularly long wait for visas in the "other worker" category.

Billy came to the United States as a student in F-1 status. He soon tired of school and decided to go to work. He convinced an employer to hire him as a chef's assistant in a 24-hour restaurant, a job that required one year of experience. Billy worked the 12:00 A.M. to 8:00 A.M. shift in the same position for two years. His employer wanted to help and agreed to sponsor him for permanent residence. Because of the late hours, no U.S. workers with the necessary experience were ready, willing, and able to take his position. The Department of Labor approved Billy's labor certification. Billy realized, however, that it would be 15 years or longer before he would qualify for permanent residence. That's because of the backlog in the quota for less-skilled workers (other workers).

Meanwhile, in the two years that had passed since Billy's employer first filed the labor certification application, the chief chef in the restaurant had trained Billy to cook the homemade pastries that had made the restaurant famous. A different restaurant offered Billy a pastry chef position, based on his four years of experience as a chef's assistant and his two years of training as a pastry chef. Now Billy was doing a job that required at least two years of experience.

Billy's new employer filed a labor certification for him, and two years later the Department of Labor approved his labor certification. Billy was then able to file immediately for permanent residence. In contrast to the long waiting list for less-skilled workers, there was no waiting list for skilled workers from Billy's country, Trinidad.

FOURTH EMPLOYMENT-BASED PREFERENCE— RELIGIOUS WORKERS AND CERTAIN SPECIAL IMMIGRANTS

Religious workers with two years of experience, ministers, religious professionals, some religious nonprofessionals, and certain foreign-language broadcasters working for Radio Free Europe or Radio Free Asia can get green cards as special immigrants.

The Fourth Employment-Based Preference special immigrant category also includes juvenile dependents of a court who are eligible for foster care, some dependents of diplomats, employees of the American Taiwan Institute for at least 15 years, and persons who have served in active duty in the U.S. armed services for 12 years or after 6 if they have reenlisted for 6 additional years.

FIFTH EMPLOYMENT-BASED PREFERENCE —EMPLOYMENT CREATION (INVESTOR)

You can get an employment creation immigrant visa if you have invested, or are in the process of investing, a minimum of one million dollars in a new or existing business. The minimum is $500,000 if the investment is in a targeted employment area, that is, an area that has experienced unemployment of at least 150 percent of the national average or a rural area with a population of less than 20,000. The enterprise must create full-time employment for at least ten U.S. citizens or permanent residents. If you are investing in an existing enterprise, your investment must produce ten *new* jobs. Of the 10,000 visa numbers available in this category, 3,000 are set aside for aliens who establish enterprises in a targeted employment area.

If you get your green card under the investor provisions, you become a conditional permanent resident. You must apply to the USCIS to have the condition removed within the 90-day period preceding the second anniversary of your having become a permanent resident.

To get the USCIS to remove the condition, you must prove that a commercial enterprise was established, that you actually made the investment, and that you are sustaining the investment as a commercial enterprise.

THE LABOR CERTIFICATION REQUIREMENT

As noted above, some Employment-Based green card categories require certification from the Department of Labor. The Department of Labor certifies that no lawful U.S. worker is ready, willing, and able to fill the job offered. "Lawful U.S. workers" include U.S. citizens, permanent residents, asylees, and refugees. The labor certification is, in most cases, a prerequisite for applying for permanent residence.

Many people have the mistaken impression that in order to get a labor certification, you must be an internationally renowned scientist or a famous rock singer, or that you must speak several languages or have advanced technical skills. True, outstanding ability or fame is important in some cases. However, you will find that you can establish unavailability of lawful U.S. workers in most jobs that require a substantial amount of experience. You can prove unavailability even in some selected job categories requiring little experience, such as live-in domestic household workers.

The stories of Melissa and Johnny provide examples of workers who qualified for labor certifications.

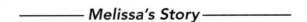

——————— *Melissa's Story* ———————

Melissa came to the United States from Ireland on a visitor's visa. Though she had no children of her own, Melissa loved kids and began working as a housekeeper and child care attendant for a young couple. The children's parents both worked as lawyers, and they needed somebody like Melissa to live in their home to help them with running the household and caring for the children. Melissa had her own room with a separate bathroom in the house. After a year working for the family, Melissa and her employer decided that they would begin the process of getting Melissa a green card. Though Melissa's job does not require a large amount of experience and training, finding housekeepers and child care workers willing to live in is hard. Melissa's employers applied for a labor certification for her and it was approved.

The problem for Melissa is that under current law the waiting list for a lesser skilled worker is more than 15 years. Melissa has her labor certification, but that does not give her the right to work. Melissa may never get a green card based on this labor certification. By the time her number comes up under the quota system, 10 to 15 years from now, the family may not even need a housekeeper or child care attendant.

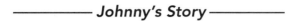
Johnny's Story

Johnny is the assistant manager in a supermarket in a largely Chinese community. He speaks Cantonese and Mandarin, two of the most common Chinese dialects. He learned the business of supermarket management in Hong Kong, where he lived until he was 25 years of age. Johnny is responsible for maintaining inventory, hiring and firing, and managing the supermarket when the senior manager is not available. Because of his skills and his language ability, Johnny can do a job that few Americans are ready, willing, and able to perform. His employer can probably get a labor certification for him. If the employer can convince the Department of Labor and the USCIS that his job requires at least two years of experience, he will be eligible under the skilled worker category and he will not have a long wait for his immigrant visa. His big problem will be overcoming the bar to residence for people out of status (see Chapter 5).

You Can't Tailor the Job

The Department of Labor will be careful to ensure that your employer doesn't tailor job requirements to your particular experience. Your employer must justify any unusual job requirement based on a business necessity, not just a personal preference.

Jim's story shows how the Department of Labor may deny a labor certification application if they believe that the employer is tailoring the job requirements to a particular employee.

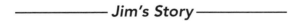
Jim's Story

Jim came to the United States from England on a visit. Jim asked his employer to sponsor him for permanent residence. Jim had studied languages in school in England, and he was fluent in French, Italian, and Spanish. To keep other qualified workers from applying, Jim's employer included in his recruitment ad the requirement that the receptionist/secretary speak French, Italian, and Spanish. Nobody else applied for the position.

When Jim's employer submitted the labor certification application, the New York State Department of Labor wrote back asking for documentation as to the employer's need for a secretary/receptionist who spoke French, Italian, and Spanish. Unfortunately for Jim, no such need existed. None of the other employees or the firm's clients or business associates spoke foreign languages. Since Jim's employer could not prove the need for the foreign language requirement, he had to readvertise the position using the genuine job requirements: "word processing skills, secretarial/receptionist skills, two years' experience." Whether the Department of Labor will approve the labor certification will depend on whether qualified people apply for the position. That in turn will depend on the market forces in existence at the time the ad appears. If many qualified people in the area have the skills required, Jim cannot get a labor certification. If no qualified applicants are ready, willing, and able to take the position, Jim can get the labor certification. There may be many secretaries in New York City with the skills that are required for the position. However, if they are all working and not looking to change jobs and thus no qualified people apply, then Jim can get the labor certification.

Advertising

An employer usually establishes the unavailability of U.S. workers through advertising in a newspaper or professional journal. The employer must also place a job order for the position at the offices of the State Department of Labor in the nearest city. Additionally, the Department of Labor requires that your employer place a public notice at the place of employment for 10 days to notify existing employees of the job opening.

The Prevailing Wage Requirement

In a case requiring a labor certification, your employer must offer the job to U.S. workers at the prevailing (normal) wage for the job. The prevailing wage is based on the geographic area of employment and on the job duties and requirements.

The State Department of Labor in the state where you will be employed determines the prevailing wage. Your employer usually may offer the job at 5 percent less than the prevailing wage determined by the Department of Labor. If your employer disagrees with the prevailing wage determination by the Department of Labor, he or she can submit evidence, such as an independent survey, to challenge the Department of Labor prevailing wage determination.

Special Labor Certifications

An exception to the requirement that the employer prove unavailability of U.S. workers is made for nurses, physical therapists, and some university professors. It is also made for some exceptional workers who can show widespread acclaim and international recognition. The exceptional ability standard in this category is something less than the extraordinary ability standard for priority workers.

Employer Sanctions and the Labor Certification Process

Employer sanctions created a new wrinkle in the process of becoming a permanent resident based on an offer of employment. Employer sanctions penalize employers who hire people not authorized to work by the USCIS. While you don't have to be working for an employer at the time that the employer sponsors you, many employers want to see employees on the job before sponsoring them for permanent residence.

If the Department of Labor receives a labor certification application that indicates that the employee is not lawfully working for the employer, they may turn that information over to the USCIS. The USCIS may do nothing, they may write a letter about the matter to your employer, or they may go visit your employer. Unless you qualify for a temporary work visa or you have USCIS employment authorization, you have only three possible solutions to this problem:

1. Your employer can decide not to sponsor you at all.
2. Your employer can sponsor you but not employ you until you get your permanent visa.
3. Your employer can employ you, violating employer sanctions, and take the risk of being sanctioned by the USCIS.

For more on employer sanctions, see Section V.

National Interest Waivers

If you are coming to the United States to do work that will benefit the national interest of the United States, you might qualify for an immigrant visa without a labor certification. You don't even need an employer to sponsor you; you can sponsor yourself. You will need to prove that you will work in the United States in your field. To get a national interest waiver, the USCIS usually (but not always) requires you to have at least the equivalent of a U.S. master's degree. It's gotten very, very hard to get a national interest waiver. Still, if your work is exceptionally important, it can't hurt for you to try.

PETITION PORTABILITY FOR EMPLOYMENT-BASED CASES

If you change jobs while your application for adjustment of status (application for permanent residence filed in the United States) is pending, your Employment-Based petition may still be valid. That means that the USCIS will continue to process your permanent residence application based on sponsorship from your new employer. You'll keep the priority date that you were assigned based on your old job. Your new employer need not file a new I-140 petition. To qualify for this portability, the following must be true:

1. You applied for adjustment of status based on an approved Employment-Based petition.
2. You filed for adjustment of status (see chapter 6), and your application has been pending for 180 days when you change jobs.
3. The new job is in the same or a similar occupation to the job for which your original petition was filed.
4. You are applying for permanent residence in the First, Second or Third Employment-Based Preference category.

CHAPTER 4

Lottery Green Cards

One of the more unusual (some say bizarre) ways that the United States hands out immigrant visas is the Diversity Visa, or, as people commonly call it, "the green card lottery." Each year, the U.S. government gives 55,000 visas to applicants who are natives of low-admission countries. Low-admission countries are countries where fewer than 50,000 people have immigrated during the preceding five years. For the next few years, the government will give only 50,000 visas. Of the usual 55,000, 5,000 will go to NACARA applicants. For more on NACARA, see Chapter 1.

No matter where you are currently residing, if you are a native of a qualifying country, as the law defines "native" under the lottery rules, you may win the lottery. You may be living in the United States, your native country, or any other country in the world. If after reading this chapter you are still not sure whether you qualify, go ahead and enter. The entry procedure is very simple. As this book went to press, no fee was required to enter the lottery, although that may change. If you win, you'll pay the same fees as other immigrant visa applicants. You can worry about the fees once you've won.

The U.S. Department of State runs the green card lottery. Each year they publish a list of the countries whose natives are eligible. The natives of most countries of the world qualify for the lottery. The list changes every year, so you must check every year to see if they include your country.

Among those countries whose natives have been excluded from the lottery in past years are India, South Korea, the People's Republic of China, the Republic of China (Taiwan), the Philippines, Vietnam, Canada, Colombia, the Dominican Republic, El Salvador, Jamaica, Poland, Haiti, and Mexico. However, some of these countries may be included in the future.

Lottery entry rules change every year. The U.S. Department of State usually issues the new rules in August. You can get the latest lottery info at the Department of State Web site, www.travel.state.gov/visa_services.html, or at the Immigration Answers Web site, www.allanwernick.com.

IF YOU DON'T WIN,
WILL THE USCIS DEPORT YOU?

Some people living in the United States are afraid to apply for the lottery. They think that if they don't win, the USCIS will arrest and deport them. You don't need to be afraid to apply for the lottery. First, you don't even have to put your own address on the lottery application or on the envelope you use to send in the application. You just need to give the Department of State a mailing address so that they can notify you if you are a winner. Even if you were to put your home address, it is unlikely that the USCIS will come looking for you.

THE FAMILIES OF LOTTERY WINNERS

If you win the lottery, your spouse and any of your children who are under age 21 and unmarried when you become a permanent resident can get lottery green cards when you do.

The USCIS and U.S. consuls will deny some lottery green card applications if you don't list your spouse and/or children on your lottery entry. That rule does not apply if your children left out are U.S. citizens or over 21. If you left out children over age 18 but under 21, the government will excuse your omission only if you can successfully argue that you thought children over 18 were excluded from getting a lottery green card as your dependent.

Some unmarried minor children of DV lottery winners will benefit from the Child Status Protection Act (called CSPA and enacted on August 2, 2003). For "Diversity Lottery" purposes, the CSPA fixes the age of a DV lottery derivative beneficiary as the date the primary lottery applicant becomes eligible for permanent residence *minus* the time between the first day that applicant can enter the lottery and the date on the applicant's "congratulatory" letter. The congratulatory letter is the letter an applicant receives notifying him that he is a lottery winner.

Rosemary's story illustrates how the CSPA might benefit a child of a DV lottery winner.

——————— *Rosemary's Story* ———————

Rosemary's mother entered the DV lottery for 2005. For the 2005 lottery, the first day you could send in your entry was November 1, 2003. On that date, Rosemary was exactly twenty years and five months old, having been born on May 1, 1983. Her mother was a lucky winner. The congratulatory letter notifying her that she had won the lottery was dated August 1, 2004. Rosemary's age will be fixed nine months earlier (the period between November 1, 2003 and August 1, 2004) than the date her mother becomes eligible for a lottery green card. The lottery has a waiting list, so despite the fact that the government began approving lottery green card applications on October 1, 2004, Rosemary's application wasn't approved until January 1, 2005. Though Rosemary turned 21 on June 1, 2004, if she is still single, she qualifies for a derivative DV lottery visa. That's because deducting nine months from her mother's eligibility date on January 1, 2005 gives us a date that Rosemary's age was fixed on April 1, 2004. Since Rosemary was not yet 21 on that date, she can get a lottery green card when her mother does.

Suppose that Rosemary's mother didn't qualify under the lottery quota until September 1, 2005. In that case Rosemary WOULD NOT qualify for a lottery green card. That's because even if she deducts nine months from September 1, 2005, her birthday is fixed at December 1, 2004. She had already turned 21 on that date. Once Rosemary's mother gets permanent residence the mother can petition for her under the Second Family Preference. Rosemary can get her green card, but it will take several years.

WHO IS ELIGIBLE TO WIN THE GREEN CARD LOTTERY?

To qualify to win the green card lottery, you must be a native of a country with low immigrant admission over the past five years. You must also have at least a high school education or its equivalent or have worked in an occupation requiring at least two years of training or experience.

Who Is a Native?

You are a native if you meet one of the following requirements:

- You were born in the qualifying country.
- Your husband or wife was born in the qualifying country.
- You are under 21 and unmarried, and one of your parents was born in a qualifying country.
- One of your parents is a native of a qualifying country, and your parents didn't reside in your country of birth.

If you are not sure whether or not you are a "native" of a qualifying country, go ahead and enter the lottery anyway.

The stories of Claudette, Jason, and William illustrate how the law defines the term "native" for the purposes of the lottery.

Claudette's Story

Claudette was born in Canada. The year she entered the lottery, Canada was not considered to be a low-admission country. So she herself was not a qualifying country native. However, Claudette was married to George, who was born in Sweden, which was a qualifying country. Claudette and George lived together in Canada, where George was a landed immigrant, the Canadian equivalent of a permanent resident. Because George is a native of a qualifying country, Claudette and George can each make separate entries in the visa lottery. If either George or Claudette wins the lottery, the other can get an immigrant visa at the same time as the winner.

Jason's Story

Jason is 17 years old and single. He was born in the People's Republic of China (not a qualifying country the year that he wanted to enter the lottery). However, Jason's mother was born in Laos, which was a qualifying country that year. Thus Jason qualifies as a "native" because his mother is a native of a qualifying country and Jason is under 21 and single. Of course, his mother can also apply separately and if she wins, then Jason can get an immigrant visa when she does. However, if Jason wins, he cannot get an immigrant visa for his mother at that time.

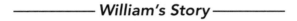

William's Story

William was born in Egypt to Canadian parents. His parents were in Egypt working on a short-term assignment from a Canadian bank. Though Canadian natives were not eligible to win the lottery the year William entered, he nonetheless qualified. He benefited from the rule that says that a person who is born in a country where his parents weren't residing qualifies as a native of his or her country of birth.

The Education/Work Experience Requirement

Once you win the lottery, you must prove that you meet the education/work requirements. You can meet the requirements in one of two ways. One way is by having at least a high school degree (or higher) or its foreign equivalent. The second way is by proving that you have worked for two of the past five years at a job that requires at least two years of training or experience. You don't have to prove that you meet the education requirement until you win the lottery and apply for your immigrant visa.

If you have completed high school in the United States, your diploma is enough evidence. A "foreign equivalent" of a high school diploma is proof that you have completed a 12-year course of elementary and secondary education that is similar to a high school degree in the United States. The USCIS view is that a high school equivalency diploma, which is valid to enter college in some states, does not meet the education requirement for the lottery. For a list of high school education documents equivalent to a high school diploma from outside the United States, see Appendix D.

If you don't have a U.S. high school diploma or the foreign equivalent, you must have worked two out of the past five years in a job in a job that requires two years of experience. Even if you have more than two years of work experience during the last five years, the two years' experience must have been in a job that required two years' experience. The U.S. Department of State uses the U.S. Department of Labor's O*NET OnLine online database, www.onetcenter.org/, to determine which jobs require two years' experience.

The stories of Karen, Constantine, and Susan illustrate the lottery work experience requirement.

—————— *Karen's Story* ——————
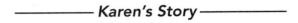

Karen came to the United States from the former Soviet Union ten years ago on a visitor's visa to visit her sister, who was attending school in the United States. Karen was 16 years old when she came to the United States. She had not yet finished high school and had no work experience. She ended up staying in the United States, working for various employers as a housekeeper or child care worker. She wanted to become an artist, so she took various painting and drawing classes, but she never made much money in that field. Natives of all the countries of the former Soviet Union qualify for the lottery, but Karen is not eligible for a lottery visa. Though she has more than five years' work experience, she has never worked in a job that requires at least two years of experience. Housekeepers and child care workers, according to the U.S. Department of Labor, can do their job with only three months' experience.

—————— *Constantine's Story* ——————

Constantine's situation is a lot more complicated than Karen's. Constantine has never been in the United States. He was born and has spent his entire life in Greece. He dropped out of school when he was 15, and for the last 28 years he has worked at many different jobs. Most of his work has been in restaurants and cafés. During the last five years, he has worked in a variety of cooking jobs. For instance, he worked as a cook in a fast-food restaurant, preparing sandwiches and salads. That's a job that the U.S. Department of Labor says requires no more than one year of experience. He has also been the kitchen chef in a fancy French-style restaurant, a job that the U.S. Department of Labor says needs from two to four years of experience. In order for Constantine to get a lottery immigrant visa, he must show that over the last five years he has worked more than two years total in the chef position. Even if he worked a few days at a time in each restaurant, if he can prove that he has worked a total of two years in the chef position, he can get a lottery green card. He should be prepared to show letters from his employers, pay stubs, or other documentation. Constantine should enter the lottery. He can worry about whether he meets the lottery requirements if he is chosen as a winner.

—————— *Susan's Story* ——————
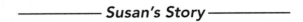

Susan had been an electrician in Israel before she came to the United States to study electrical engineering at the University of California at

Berkeley. While studying, she worked on campus 20 hours a week as an electrician. An electrician is a job that the U.S. Department of Labor says requires four years or more of training and experience. She qualifies for a lottery immigrant visa.

ENTERING THE GREEN CARD LOTTERY

The U.S. Department of State now accepts lottery green card entries only online. The application form is simple. When you complete the form, you receive an electronically generated filing receipt. You must submit a digital photo. That means you must either have your photo taken with a digital camera, or scan a photo into your computer.

There is a 60-day window (time period) in which the Department of State must receive your lottery entry. You gain no advantage by applying early or late within the 60-day window. If your application arrives too early, the Department of State will reject it. The law allows you only one entry per year. The Department of State claims it has disqualified up to 500,000 entries in the past because people send in more than one entry. Of course, each qualifying applicant can send in an entry. That means that if you, your spouse, and your children all are natives of qualifying countries and meet the education requirements, you may each submit a separate entry.

DO I NEED A LAWYER
TO HELP ME ENTER THE LOTTERY?

A lawyer can't increase your chances of winning the green card lottery. A lawyer can help you prepare your entry, but the application is very simple and the DOS provides clear instructions. A lawyer can help you figure out if you are a native of a qualifying country or if you meet the education requirement, but you can worry about this once you're a winner. If you win the lottery, you must apply for an immigrant visa by adjustment of status or consular processing (see chapter 6 for more on applying for your immigrant visa). At that point, you must prove that you are not inadmissible (ineligible) for an immigrant visa. That's the time when it's worthwhile to speak to an immigration lawyer or another immigration law expert.

WHERE DO I GET INFORMATION
ON THE NEXT GREEN CARD LOTTERY?

In the past, the U.S. Department of State, Bureau of Consular Affairs, has provided green card lottery information at the DOS website, http://travel.state.gov/. You can also get information on the lottery at my *immigration answers* Web site: www.allanwernick.com.

CHAPTER 5

Overcoming the Bars
to Permanent Residence

EXCLUSIONS AND WAIVERS

To get an immigrant visa, you must prove that you are not "inadmissible" (before April 1, 1997, the USCIS used the term "excludable" rather than "inadmissible"). Being inadmissible means that you cannot get a visa even though you qualify for one under one of the immigrant or nonimmigrant visa categories. You may be inadmissible and thus barred from permanent residence, for instance, because you have engaged in criminal activity or you have insufficient financial resources. Sometimes the USCIS will forgive, or waive, your inadmissibility, although getting a waiver is often very difficult. If the USCIS grants you a waiver, you can get your immigrant visa despite the bar.

In this chapter, I discuss the most common grounds of inadmissibility and how to overcome them. A complete list of the bars to permanent residence (grounds of inadmissibility) can be found in Appendix E, "Grounds of Inadmissibility/Exclusion." The six most common grounds of inadmissibility are:

- Having been unlawfully present in the United States.
- Likelihood of becoming a public charge (needing welfare or other public assistance).
- Criminal activity.
- Misrepresentations to the USCIS or to a U.S. consul.

- Political activity.
- Medical conditions.

UNLAWFUL PRESENCE BAR

The government may bar you from permanent residence for three years if you have been in the United States unlawfully for more than 180 continuous days, and then you leave the country. The bar is ten years if you leave after having been in the United States unlawfully for 365 or more continuous days. Days in unlawful status prior to April 1, 1997, won't count against you.

The USCIS may waive these bars (and thus you can become a permanent resident despite the bar) if you are the spouse, son, or daughter of a U.S. citizen or permanent resident.

The **unlawful presence bar** doesn't apply to applicants for permanent residence under the special rules for battered women and children and the parents of battered children if you can show that your unlawful status was related to the battering you or your child received. Nor does the bar apply if you are a family member of an amnesty permanent resident (a "Family Unity" case).

The USCIS won't count time spent in the United States unlawfully while you were under 18 years of age. Nor will the USCIS count the time your asylum application is pending, including while you are making an asylum claim to an immigration judge or appealing a denial of an asylum claim, unless you work without USCIS authorization during that time. If you file for **adjustment of status** (see Chapter 6), that stops the clock while your application is pending before the USCIS.

Finally, if you make a "timely" (before your lawful stay expires) application for a change of status or extension of stay, you don't start counting your unlawful presence unless and until the USCIS denies your application. If the USCIS approves your application, you were never unlawfully present. If the USCIS denies the application, you start counting unlawful presence from the date of the denial. To benefit from this **"tolling-until-denial"** policy, you must apply for the extension or change of status before your current status expires, and you must not engage in unauthorized employment. This USCIS policy could change. If it does, you can read about it at the Immigration Answers Web site, www.allanwernick.com.

The tolling-until-denial policy is a generous interpretation of the law by the USCIS based on the agency's inability to quickly decide cases. Actually, the law provides only a 120-day tolling based on a pending application for change of status or extension of stay. And the tolling applies only to the beginning of the count of 180 days under the three-year bar, not for the 365 days for the ten-year bar.

If you are a Canadian or Commonwealth citizen residing in Canada, a special rule applies. If you entered the United States after inspection by an USCIS officer, you are considered lawfully present for the purpose of this bar, regardless of whether you violate your status. You will only be considered to have violated the unlawful presence law if an immigration judge or immigration officer finds that you violated your status. This is similar to the rule that applies to nonimmigrants granted "duration of status," discussed in the following section.

Perhaps the most important rule regarding the unlawful presence bar is that it only applies to those who leave the United States after unlawful employment. That means that if you can get permanent residence without leaving the United States, the process we call adjustment of status, the bars don't apply. More on this later in the chapter.

What Is Unlawful Presence?

The USCIS will consider you unlawfully present if you do one of the following:

- Remain here longer than permitted on a temporary stay.
- Enter the United States without USCIS authorization.
- Enter with phony papers.
- The USCIS immigration judge finds that you violated your status.

If you are here in lawful nonimmigrant status, violating the conditions of your stay will not make you subject to the **unlawful presence bars** unless the USCIS or an immigration judge decides that you are out-of-status. So, if you work without permission, or otherwise violate your status but you don't get caught, you don't automatically become unlawfully here for the purpose of these bars. If the USCIS catches you, you could be deported for violating your status, but you can't be barred under the three- and ten-year bars. If the USCIS allowed you to remain in the United States for **duration of status** (as is commonly done in the cases of most F-1 International Students, J-1 Exchange Visitors, and I Journalists), you'll never become subject to the three- and ten-year bars unless the USCIS or an immigration judge finds you out of status. If this approach sounds strange to you, you're not alone. However, that's how the USCIS has interpreted this rule.

The cases of Dan, Tim, Liz, and Gary help us understand what the USCIS means by unlawful presence.

Dan's Story

Dan entered the United States on an F-1 visa to study engineering at San Diego State University in California. When he arrived at San Diego International Airport, the USCIS inspector at the border wrote "D/S" on his USCIS Form I-94, Arrival/Departure Document. "D/S" stands for "duration of status," meaning that Dan can stay in the United States so long as he maintains lawful student status. To maintain status, Dan must remain a full-time student and not work in violation of U.S. immigration laws. Dan decides to drop out of school and become a professional surfer. He begins working part-time in a sporting goods store.

Dan isn't subject to the unlawful presence bars, despite having violated his status. Ten years later, an employer sponsors him for permanent residence as a senior instructor in a surfing school. Because he's violated his status by dropping out of school and working, he may have to leave the United States to get an immigrant visa. (See Chapter 6 for more on who must leave the United States to get an immigrant visa.) However, because the USCIS granted him duration of status, he won't be inadmissible for having been unlawfully present in the United States.

Tim's Story

Tim entered the United States as an F-1 student to study at Iowa State University. After two years, he dropped out of school for a year to write a novel. When the year was up, he applied to New York University and was admitted. He applied to the USCIS for reinstatement of his student status, and the USCIS denied his application on August 1, 1998. Since the USCIS denied his application for reinstatement, he is now considered out of status for the purpose of the three- and ten-year bars to permanent residence. If he remains in the United States beyond 180 days from the day the USCIS denies his reinstatement and then leaves the United States, he'll face the bars. Had he not applied for reinstatement, the USCIS would never have decided that he was out of status, and he would not be subject to the bars. However, though not subject to the bars, he would have been removable.

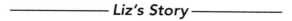
Liz's Story

Liz came to the United States in H-1B temporary professional worker status on January 1, 1998. She worked as an engineer. The USCIS admitted her for three years, until January 1, 2001, the maximum for an H-1B worker (unless she extends her H-1B status). After just one year working as an engineer, she quit her job to try a career as a lounge singer. Liz is out of status and if the USCIS catches her, they could remove her from the United States. To make sure she can stay in the United States should her singing career fail, Liz asks a company to sponsor her for permanent residence. Her green card case goes smoothly, and on December 1, 2000, Liz left the United States to apply for an immigrant visa at a consul abroad. Since Liz left the United States before her stay expired, she wasn't subject to the unlawful status bars. That's because violating status doesn't make a person subject to the bars.

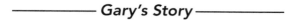
Gary's Story

Gary came to the United States to attend his sister's wedding. The USCIS inspector at the airport gave him six months to stay in the United States. He decided to stay longer, and two years later he still hasn't left. Gary is subject to the new bars for people out of status since he has overstayed the time given him by the United States by more than one year. If he leaves the United States, he'll be barred for reentry for ten years unless the USCIS grants him a waiver of the bar.

The Three-Year Bar for 180 Days in Unlawful Status

The three-year bar applies to permanent residence applicants who were in the United States unlawfully for more than 180 continuous days and then left the country. As I discuss in detail later in this chapter, if you qualify to get permanent residence without leaving the United States, this bar won't be a problem.

Under the three-year bar rule, the law says that the USCIS can excuse up to 120 days of your being out of status. The USCIS calls this a "tolling" of the unlawful status period. This law has little relevance now that the USCIS has ruled that any time you spend in the United States waiting to hear on an extension of stay or change of status won't count as unlawful presence. However, you must have been in lawful status when you applied and not have worked without authorization.

The Ten-Year Penalty for One Year in Unlawful Status

The law bars you from permanent residence for ten years if you have been here unlawfully for one year or more. Unlike the 180-day bar, the USCIS won't excuse or toll any time if you are subject to the ten-year bar.

The three- and ten-year bars apply only if you leave the United States. So if you're in the United States and can get your permanent residence status without leaving, the new bars don't apply.

Not everyone can become a permanent resident without leaving the United States, the process called "adjustment of status." In Chapter 6, I detail who can adjust status.

The stories of John, Steve, Regina, and Nilda help us understand the unlawful status exclusion.

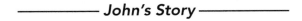

John's Story

John came to the United States from Ghana to visit his brother Paul, a U.S. citizen. He arrived on February 10, 1995, and entered on a B-2 visitor's visa. The USCIS gave him permission to visit with his family for six months. He liked life here so much that he decided he wanted to stay. In December 1995, Paul filed a family-based immigrant petition for John. Six weeks later, the USCIS approved the petition. Unfortunately, because of the long quota backlog for brothers and sisters of U.S. citizens, it will be many years before John can apply for adjustment of status. To apply he must be in the front of the line for an immigrant visa (he must have a priority date that is "current").

John can avoid the ten-year bar to permanent residence for having been in the United States unlawfully, provided he doesn't leave the country until he becomes a permanent resident. It may take many years before he can apply for adjustment of status. He has to remain here unlawfully without employment authorization until his number comes up under the visa quota system. Still, under the rules for adjustment of status, he has the right to get his permanent residence without leaving and thus can avoid the ten-year unlawful presence bar.

Steve's Story

Steve, from Moscow, entered the United States by sneaking across the Canadian-U.S. border in November 1997. He had tried to get a visitor's visa at the U.S. consul, but the consular officer denied his visa application. Steve's son, a 21-year-old U.S. citizen, filed a family-based petition for him on June 1, 2001. Though Steve is an Immediate Relative of a U.S. citizen, he must return home for his immigrant visa interview. However, if he leaves the United States to go to his immigrant visa interview, after having been here unlawfully for more than 180 days, the consul will deny him an immigrant visa because of unlawful status bars to permanent residence. Since the law does not provide a waiver for the parent of a U.S. citizen, Steve has two choices. He can remain in the United States unlawfully, unable to ever get a permanent visa (unless he marries a U.S. citizen and applies for a waiver or Congress changes the law). Or he can leave and wait three years (if he's overstayed more than 180 days) or ten years (if he's overstayed 365 days or more) before applying for an immigrant visa.

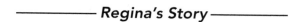
Regina's Story

Regina is a French cook. She came to the United States in 1994 on a visitor's visa and then overstayed the six months the USCIS gave her to visit. Her employer sponsored her for permanent residence. He filed a labor certification application for her on December 30, 1996. The U.S. Department of Labor certified that no U.S. workers were ready, willing, and able to do her job. On July 1, 1998, when her priority date became current under the visa quota system, she became eligible for permanent residence (see Chapter 6 for more on the quota system).

Under the rules for adjustment of status discussed in Chapter 6, she got permanent residence without leaving the United States. She didn't have to worry about the unlawful presence bar. She became a permanent resident, and she didn't need a waiver of inadmissibility. The USCIS will interview her here in the United States.

Nilda's Story

Nilda came to the United States as an H-1B temporary professional worker in March 1994. (See Chapter 14 for more on H-1B status.) She grew tired of her job and quit in March 1995 to pursue a career as an artist. Thus she fell out of status. In June 1998, she met John, a U.S. citizen, and in October 1998, they married. Nilda immediately filed for permanent residence.

Nilda didn't have a problem with the unlawful presence bar—it didn't apply to her although she has been in the United States unlawfully for more than one year. Because she entered the United States legally and she is an Immediate Relative of a U.S. citizen, she won't have to leave the United States to become a permanent resident.

Waivers of the Unlawful Presence Bars

The USCIS may waive the three- or ten-year bars to permanent residence. To qualify for a waiver, you must be the spouse, son, or daughter of a U.S. citizen or permanent resident. In addition, you must prove that your U.S. citizen or permanent resident relative will suffer extreme hardship if the USCIS or a consular officer doesn't grant you permanent residence.

LIKELIHOOD THAT YOU'LL BECOME A PUBLIC CHARGE

To get an immigrant visa, you must prove to the U.S. government that once you become a permanent resident, you won't need public assistance—in the words of the immigration law, you won't become a "public charge." Needing food stamps, Medicaid, and other "means-tested" benefits for poor or disabled people would make you a public charge. Needing public assistance is not a problem if you are applying for permanent residence based on your status as an asylee, a refugee, a Cuban Adjustment Act beneficiary, a NACARA beneficiary, a registry applicant, or a self-petitioning abused spouse, abused child, or parent of an abused child.

An **affidavit of support** is one way to prove that you won't become a public charge. An affidavit of support is a form signed by a person promising to support you, if you need support, once you become a permanent resident. Under the 1996 Immigration Act, an affidavit of support is required in Family-Based cases (except for those based on spousal or child abuse). The law also requires an affidavit of support if you are coming to the United States to work for a relative or for a business where relatives own 5 percent of the company. In other cases, the affidavit is just one of many ways to prove you won't become a public charge.

We begin by discussing the rules that apply in cases where an affidavit of support is *required*. Then we will discuss proving that you'll not be a public charge in other cases.

When an Affidavit is Required

The 1996 immigration law made an affidavit of support a required document in most Family-Based cases. Where the law requires an affidavit, the person who signs for you must prove the ability to support you at 125 percent of the federal poverty guidelines. If you are an active member of the armed forces petitioning for a spouse or child, you need only show support at 100 percent of the poverty level.

If your petitioner doesn't have enough income, he or she can get a **joint sponsor** to submit an affidavit. You or your sponsor can also use liquid assets (money in bank accounts, stocks, or mutual funds—more on the use of assets to follow) to prove you won't become a public charge. A sponsor can use income from family members living in their household to support the affidavit. The USCIS issued a new form, USCIS Form I-864, Affidavit of Support Under 213A of the Act, which you must use where the law requires an affidavit. Perhaps the most significant change in the law is that which makes affidavits of support binding contracts.

Note: A sponsor under the new rule must submit notice to the USCIS of a change of address until the sponsorship requirement expires.

Is an Affidavit of Support Absolutely Required in Your Case?

If you're getting your immigrant visa based on a petition from a family member, the law now requires you to submit an affidavit of support from that person. The USCIS calls the relative the "sponsor." The only exceptions are when the beneficiary of the petition has worked forty quarters (ten years) in the United States, the petitioner has died, or the beneficiary is self-petitioning under the special rules for a battered spouse, a battered child, or a parent of a battered child, or as the widow or widower of a U.S. citizen. Even if you're wealthy, you need someone to sign for you. There's one other situation where the law insists that you get an affidavit of support. That's the unusual situation where you're getting your immigrant visa based on an offer of employment and your employer is a relative or a company where relatives own 5 percent.

Josie's story illustrates the requirement that a family-based sponsor submit an affidavit of support.

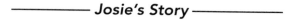

Josie's Story

Josie's mother, Marsha, is a U.S. citizen. Josie wants to become a permanent resident of the United States. Suppose Marsha petitions for Josie. Though Josie has a good job, the law requires an affidavit of support from Marsha. Marsha must prove that she can support herself, her household, and Josie at 125 percent of the federal poverty level. If Marsha doesn't have sufficient income and/or assets, she may ask a person with more resources to be a joint sponsor. If a relative of Marsha has been living with her for at least six months, Marsha can include that relative's income if she becomes a "contract sponsor."

Finally, if Marsha, Josie, or a contract sponsor have liquid assets (money in the bank, for instance), Josie can use those assets to prove she won't become a public charge. However, even if Josie's assets are enough, standing alone, to prove that she won't become a public charge, Marsha must still submit an affidavit of support.

Who Can Be a Sponsor?

Sponsors must also be U.S. citizens, nationals, or lawful permanent residents, must be age 18 or older, and must have their primary residence in one of the 50 states, Washington, D.C., or a U.S. territory or possession.

If you are a sponsor, you'll need to submit your tax returns for the past three years or prove that you weren't required to file returns.

Proving You Can Support a Relative: The 125 Percent Rule, Household Size, Income, and the Income of Household Members

Where the law requires an affidavit of support, your petitioning sponsor (or your sponsor and a cosigner) must prove that he or she can support you at 125 percent of the federal poverty guidelines. The poverty guidelines specify the maximum amount you can earn and still qualify for public assistance. The guidelines for 2004 can be found in Appendix F, "Poverty Guidelines." If you are an active member of the U.S. armed forces, your unmarried children under age 21 and your spouse need only prove that you can support them at 100 percent of the guidelines.

Mark's story illustrates the 125 percent of income rule.

———————— Mark's Story ————————

Mark is single and 25 years old. His mother, a permanent resident of the United States, petitioned for him to become a permanent resident. Though he has a good job, the 1996 immigration law requires that he get an affidavit of support from his mother. His mother is unmarried and has two other children. That means that when Mark joins the family, they will be a family of four. In 2002 the poverty line for a family of four in New York, where his mother is living, was $18,100. Mark's mother (or his mother and a cosigner) must show income of at least 125 percent of that amount ($22,625) or use her and/or his assets to supplement the income. The amount will be higher in 2003.

Under the 125 percent rule, the amount you need to show depends on the size of your household including, as illustrated above in Mark's story, the newly arriving immigrants and yourself as the sponsor. Household size also includes anyone living with the sponsor for at least six months who is related to the sponsor by birth, marriage, or adoption. Also included are dependents listed on the sponsor's federal income tax return for the most recent tax year and immigrants previously sponsored using the new affidavit of support.

Household Contract Sponsor Rule

If any of the sponsor's household members are working, sometimes you can include the household members' income with the sponsor's income to meet the "125 percent of the poverty level" standard. The household member must submit USCIS Form I-864A, Contract Between Sponsor and Household Member. This contract makes the household members jointly responsible with the sponsor to reimburse the costs of any means-tested public benefits used by the sponsored immigrants (see "Affidavit of Support as a Contract Rule" below).

A **"household contract" sponsor** must be related to the petitioning sponsor by birth, marriage, or adoption. Also, the contract sponsor must have lived in the sponsor's household for at least six months and must be living there when the sponsor submits the affidavit, or the primary sponsor must have listed the contract sponsor on his or her income tax.

The Joint Sponsorship Rule

If your petitioning relative doesn't earn enough to provide for you, then you can get another person to act as a cosponsor. Both your sponsor and cosponsor must submit affidavits of support. While relatives are often the best cosponsors, the law doesn't require that the cosponsor be a relative—of either the applicant or the primary sponsor. Joint sponsors (unlike persons living in the same household) cannot add their income to that of another sponsor to reach 125 percent of the poverty guideline. A joint sponsor, by himself or herself, must meet the full 125 percent income requirement.

Sally's story illustrates the joint sponsorship rule.

Sally's Story

Sally, a U.S. citizen, wants to bring her mother here from Italy. She and her husband both work, but they barely make enough money to support themselves and their three children. Sally petitions for her mother as an Immediate Relative of a U.S. citizen (see Chapter 2). When her mother goes to her immigrant visa interview, she must submit an affidavit of support from Sally. However, Sally doesn't have the income and assets to support her mother at 125 percent of the federal poverty level. So she must have another person, preferably a close relative, be a joint sponsor. Sally and the joint sponsor must both sign affidavits that Sally's mother can submit with her immigrant visa application. Sally asks her cousin Cathy to be a joint sponsor and sign a separate USCIS Form I-864, Affadavit of Support, for Sally's mother to submit with her application. Cathy is an executive in a bank and makes enough to support her family, Sally's family, and her aunt as well. By submitting both Sally's and Cathy's affidavits, Sally's mother can show she's not likely to become a public charge.

The Affidavit of Support as a Contract Rule

Under the 1996 Immigration Act, the new affidavit of support is now a contract between you, the government, and the person(s) who signed for you. If your sponsor won't provide you financial assistance, you can sue them. If you receive certain public benefits (benefits where your income is an eligibility factor) from a federal, state, or local government agency, the agency can collect the cost of that benefit from your sponsor. For instance, if you get food stamps, the government can try to collect the cash value of those food stamps from your sponsor.

Your sponsor's obligations continue until you become a U.S. citizen or you have worked 40 quarters (the equivalent of ten years).

The rule that makes your relative responsible for the public benefits you receive does not apply to emergency Medicaid; immunization; some testing for communicable diseases; short-term, noncash emergency relief (like shelter during a hurricane); child nutrition, including the WIC (Women, Infant & Children) program and school meals; foster care and adoption assistance; higher education loans and grants; elementary and secondary education; Head Start; the Job Training Partnership Act (JTPA); and some noncash programs such as soup kitchens.

The legal responsibility of the person who signs an affidavit of support for you applies only to public benefits, not to private debts. So if you go into debt by buying a car or an appliance, the relative signing the affidavit is not responsible for that debt.

Using Assets to Prove You Won't Become a Public Charge

If your sponsor, your cosponsor, or a household contract sponsor doesn't have sufficient income to prove that you won't become a public charge, your assets or a sponsor's assets can make up any difference between required income and the poverty guidelines. The assets must equal five times the difference between the sponsor's income and the minimum income requirement under the guidelines. You and/or your sponsor must be able to convert the assets to cash within one year. Examples of assets are money in bank savings or checking accounts, stocks or mutual funds, certificates of deposit, and real estate. The real estate *may not* be the affiant's (the person signing the affidavit) primary residence.

Scott's story illustrates how you can use assets to prove you won't become a public charge.

——————— *Scott's Story* ———————

Marsha, a U.S. citizen, petitioned for her son Scott. He and his wife, Winona, are graduate students and have no income. Marsha, the mother, is supporting herself and Scott's three brothers and sisters. Marsha inherited $100,000 when her husband died. Marsha doesn't work, but she receives income of $20,000 per year from her husband's pension. Scott's wife will immigrate with Scott as a "derivative beneficiary" (see Chapter 1 for more on derivative beneficiaries).

Scott's mother must submit an affidavit of support and show income for a family of six: herself, Scott and his wife, and her three other children. The poverty level in 1998 for a family of six when Scott and his family applied for permanent residence was $22,050—125 percent of the guideline was $27,562. Marsha's yearly income was only the $20,000 from her deceased husband's pension. The difference between the 125 percent guideline and Marsha's income was $7,562. To support an affidavit for Scott and his wife, she must have at least $37,810 in savings (five times the difference between her income and the poverty guidelines). Since she still has the $100,000 she inherited from her husband, she has sufficient assets to prove that Scott and his wife won't become a public charge.

Using Employment to Prove You Won't Become a Public Charge

If you are the beneficiary of an affidavit of support and you have lived six months with the affiant, you can use your income to make up any difference between the sponsor's income and the amount of 125 percent of the poverty level. You'll need to prove that your income is likely to continue.

The Change of Address Rule

If you are a primary sponsor, cosponsor, or household contract sponsor and you move, you must report a change of address to the USCIS within 30 days. You report the change using USCIS Form I-865, Sponsor's Notice of Change of Address. You must also report the change to the state government where you resided when you submitted the affidavit to the USCIS and to the state government where you now reside. As this book went to press, the USCIS hadn't yet provided information on how to report to state governments.

Proving That You Won't Become a Public Charge in Lottery Cases and Other Cases Where the Law Doesn't Require an Affidavit of Support

As mentioned above, not every case requires that you follow the new rules and use the new affidavit of support form. You may use the old affidavit of support, USCIS Form I-134 (and your own income and/or assets without a sponsor's affidavit), without meeting the new requirements in the following cases:

- You and your family members are applying in an employment-based case. The new affidavit *is required* if a close relative owns 5 percent or more of the business, unless the relative is a U.S. citizen or permanent resident not living in the United States.
- You are a self-petitioning widow or widower.
- You are a self-petitioning battered spouse or child.
- You are applying under the diversity visa lottery program (see Chapter 4).
- You are applying under the Cuban Adjustment Act.
- You are a returning resident.
- You are a registry applicant.
- You are an applicant under the Nicaraguan Adjustment and Central American Relief Act (NACARA) of 1997.
- You are required to present evidence that you won't become a public charge as part of a nonimmigrant visa application.
- You are applying for permanent residence based on cancellation of removal or suspension of deportation.
- You are applying for a nonimmigrant visa, including a B-2 visitor's visa or a K visa for a spouse or fiancé(e) of a U.S. citizen.

Among the ways to prove that you are not likely to become a public charge in these cases is by:

- Showing that you are ready, willing, and able to work and have an offer of employment, or if you are in the United States, that you are already working.
- Presenting affidavits, supported by tax returns from close family members, to the effect that the family members will provide you financial support if necessary.
- Showing sufficient personal assets to prove that you don't need to work.
- Showing a combination of employment, support, and assets.
- Presenting, if you are in the United States and working, a current job letter explaining the type of work you are doing, whether the job is full-time and permanent, your salary, and how long you've been employed. If available, you should present work stubs and copies of income tax forms filed with the IRS.

Even if you're working "off the books" and your boss is paying you "under the table" (meaning that your employer doesn't keep records of your wages), you can still use your work history to prove that you can support yourself. One way to do this is by filing tax returns. If you do not have a social security card, you can still file your tax return using an Individual Tax Identification Number (ITIN). An ITIN is a nine-digit number used for tax purposes by people not eligible for a social security number. You apply for an ITIN using IRS form W-7, Application for IRS Individual Taxpayer Identification Number. You can get the form by calling 800-870-3676. For information about the ITIN on the Web, go to www.irs.gov/ind_info/itin.html. If you don't have an ITIN and you want to file a tax return, include your ITIN application with your return. A consular officer or USCIS examiner is usually more concerned about whether you are likely to become a public charge than about the collection of taxes.

CRIMINAL ACTIVITY

The most difficult ground of inadmissibility to overcome involves criminal activity. Not all crimes will make you ineligible for a green card. If you have been convicted of a crime, speak to an immigration law expert before making any application to the USCIS.

Two major areas of criminal activity that may make you ineligible to become a permanent resident of the United States are crimes involving moral turpitude and crimes involving drugs. The USCIS may waive some of these grounds of inadmissibility. Other criminal activities may make you inadmissible as well. You can find a complete list of grounds of inadmissibility in Appendix E, "Grounds of Inadmissibility/Exclusion."

Crimes Involving Moral Turpitude

If you have committed or admit to a crime involving moral turpitude, you may be ineligible to become a permanent resident unless you first get a waiver of inadmissibility. **Moral turpitude** is hard to define, but generally it means a crime involving acts committed by people who are mean or evil-spirited or who cheat the government. Most crimes involving theft and violence involve moral turpitude. Simple assault often doesn't involve moral turpitude.

Drug-Related Crimes

The immigration laws are especially harsh toward the sale or use of illegal drugs. If you are convicted of any crime involving a controlled substance, you are probably barred from immigrating. A waiver is available in only one situation: a single offense of possession of 30 grams or less of marijuana. No waiver of exclusion is available for immigrant visa applicants for other crimes involving drugs. The "no waiver" rule applies to even minor drug-related activity such as more than one marijuana possession conviction, selling marijuana (even a small quantity), and possession of any amount of cocaine.

Forgiveness of Criminal Activity—Exceptions and Waivers

Under an exception for young offenders, you aren't barred from residence and do not need a waiver if (1) you were convicted of only one crime involving moral turpitude, (2) you were under 18 at the time, and (3) more than five years have passed since the time that the crime was committed or since you were released from jail. Under a petty offense exception, you are also not inadmissible for a conviction of a single crime involving moral turpitude where the maximum possible sentence is one year and you were sentenced to no more than six months in jail. This exception is available no matter your age.

Other Options

Options other than a waiver may be available to you if you are inadmissible for criminal activity. If you received a full and complete pardon (forgiveness granted by a governor or president), your conviction won't count against you. If a U.S. conviction was totally expunged from your record, the conviction may not count against you. The expungement must result in your record showing that it is as if you had never been convicted. Whether an expungement eliminates a conviction for immigration purposes is an area of law that is constantly changing. Check with a legal expert for updated information about the rules applying to expungements. Regardless of the rule applied to expungements, some drug-trafficking crimes will make you inadmissible, expunged or not.

If you're inadmissible because you committed a crime involving moral turpitude or you were convicted of only a single count of simple possession of 30 grams or less of marijuana, you may be eligible for a waiver of inadmissibility. To get the waiver, you must prove that either (1) you are the spouse, parent, or child of a U.S. citizen or permanent resident and that your relative would suffer extreme hardship if you were not admitted as a permanent resident or (2) the offense happened more than 15 years before your application, you have rehabilitated, and your admission to the United States would not be contrary to the welfare, safety, or security of the country.

To apply for a waiver of a criminal ground of exclusions, you must file USCIS Form I-601, Application for Waiver of Grounds of Excludability.

FRAUDULENT MISREPRESENTATIONS

If you have ever made a **"fraudulent misrepresentation"** (a lie or falsehood) when applying to enter the United States, for a visa or for any other immigration benefit, you may be inadmissible (ineligible for a visa or entry) because of that act. The misrepresentation must have been "knowing" (on purpose), "willful" (also, on purpose), and "material" (significant). That is, the USCIS *shouldn't* punish you for meaningless lies.

If you have made a fraudulent misrepresentation, you may be able to get an exclusion waiver. To get the waiver, you must be the spouse or child of a permanent resident or U.S. citizen, and you must be able to prove that extreme hardship would result to your spouse or parent if you don't get a permanent visa.

John's story provides an example of a fraudulent misrepresentation.

John's Story

John applied for a visitor's visa at the U.S. consulate in his country, Costa Rica. He told the consular officer that he was attending college, and he presented a student identification card (ID) with his picture on it as proof. However, the picture ID was a phony. John had substituted his picture for another student's. John had been unemployed and living on the streets for five years and had never attended college.

Obviously, John lied to the consular officer, and this lie would probably be considered a knowing, willful, and material misrepresentation. It is material because if the consular officer had known that John was not in school, he would not have granted John a visitor's visa. In order to obtain a visitor's visa, John had to prove that he had not abandoned his residence in Costa Rica. He also had to prove that he intended only to visit the United States and that he would leave the United States after his visit (for more on visitor's visas, see Chapter 12). Whether or not John is in school is important to the question of whether he will return to his country once his visit to the United States is over.

The consular officer didn't discover that John was lying and issued John a visitor's visa. Upon John's arrival in the United States, the USCIS admitted him for a six-month visit. Shortly after his arrival, he met and fell in love with Susan, a U.S. citizen. If John applies for an immigrant visa based on Susan's petition, the USCIS may discover that he lied when he got his visitor's visa. If the USCIS discovers his lie, he may still get his immigrant visa, but he probably will need a waiver of inadmissibility.

Marriage Fraud

The immigration laws are particularly harsh on people who marry just to get an immigrant visa. A person who enters into a phony marriage can never get a Family-Based or Employment-Based visa. No waiver is available—ever—for marriage fraud. If you are found guilty of marriage fraud, your only hope for getting an immigrant visa is through asylum, through cancellation of removal, as a derivative beneficiary, or through a private bill. (See Chapter 1 for an explanation of cancellation of removal and private bills.)

POLITICAL ACTIVITY

If you were a member of a totalitarian or communist party, either in the United States or abroad, you are inadmissible (with a few exceptions). Sometimes a Communist Party member can get an immigrant visa, but usually with some difficulty. If the U.S. government believes that you would be a foreign policy risk or that you participated in genocide or persecution, U.S. immigration law bars you from permanent residence without exception. Exclusions based on political activity are far less common than in the past.

Even if you were a member of a communist organization, you can still immigrate if you were age 16 or under at the time you joined the organization or if you joined the organization because you had to. You are also admissible if you have terminated your affiliation connection with the communist organization at least two years before applying for permanent residence. If your membership was in a communist party that controlled the government of your country, you must have ended your membership at least five years before making your application. These exceptions apply only if you are not a threat to the security of the United States.

Even if you're inadmissible because of membership in a communist or totalitarian organization, a waiver is available if you are the spouse, parent, child, or sibling of a U.S. citizen, or the spouse or child of a permanent resident. In order to get the waiver, your admission to the United States must serve a humanitarian purpose, assure family unity, or otherwise be in the public interest. Again, you must not be considered a threat to the security of the United States.

If your membership in a communist or totalitarian organization wasn't meaningful, willful, or voluntary, it cannot be a basis for denying you permanent residence.

You may be barred from the United States if you have engaged in terrorist activity. The law defines "terrorist" to mean either committing an act of terrorism or "affording material support" to any individual, organization, or government in conducting a terrorist activity. The law defines "material support" as, among other things, the soliciting of funds or other items of value for terrorist activities or for any terrorist organization.

Health Issues

Unless you submitted a medical exam as part of an earlier application to come to the United States, for instance as a K or V visa applicant or in USCIS refugee status, you must take a medical examination prior to becoming a permanent resident. Most refugees are examined before coming to the United States. The examination includes a chest X ray and a blood test. If you are pregnant, you may be excused from being X-rayed. You don't have to take the blood test if you can prove a legitimate religious objection to taking the test. You must also be vaccinated against communicable diseases.

The most common medical conditions that make you ineligible for residence are having infectious tuberculosis, being HIV positive, having a sexually transmitted disease (STD) like syphilis and gonorrhea, or being mentally retarded or ill.

If you are inadmissible because you test positive for tuberculosis or other treatable diseases, you will be given time to obtain treatment, take a new medical examination, and be admitted as a permanent resident.

If you test HIV positive or if you are mentally ill or retarded, you can only become a permanent resident if you first obtain a waiver of inadmissibility. The waiver is available if you are the spouse or unmarried son or daughter of a permanent resident or U.S. citizen, or if you have a son or daughter who is a U.S. citizen, who is a lawful permanent resident, or who has been issued an immigrant visa. Unlike some other waiver applications, you need not show that your relative will suffer hardship if you don't get your immigrant visa. Apply for the waiver using USCIS Form I-601 Application for Waiver of Grounds of Excludability.

If you are applying for a waiver because you have tested HIV positive, you must show the following: (1) You are receiving, or will receive upon admission, care and treatment for HIV infection; (2) You have the qualifying relationship with a U.S. citizen or lawful permanent resident; (3) You have sufficient financial resources or insurance to meet the medical care and cost for treatment of HIV infection, and you are not likely to become a public charge; and (4) You have been counseled or educated about how HIV is transmitted.

In the United States, only an USCIS -authorized physician can do the medical exam. Abroad, the physician must have been authorized by the U.S. Department of State. You can obtain a list of doctors from your local USCIS district office or a U.S. consulate. Under the 1996 immigration laws, you must present proof that you have been vaccinated against vaccine-preventable diseases, which include mumps, measles, rubella, polio, tetanus and diphtheria toxoids, pertussis, influenza type B, and hepatitis B. You can be exempt from the vaccine requirement if getting the vaccine would not be medically appropriate.

Other Grounds of Exclusion

On the application for permanent residence, whether it is USCIS Form I-485, Application for Adjustment of Status, or the final package from the U.S. consulate, Form OS-230, Part II (Application for Immigrant Visa and Alien Registration), many questions relate to inadmissibility. Read the list carefully, and if you must answer "Yes" to any of these questions, contact an immigration law expert before submitting the application form.

CHAPTER 6

Applying for an Immigrant Visa

When You File, Where You File,
Preparing for Your
Immigrant Visa Interview,
Your Right to Appeal

In this chapter, I review the filing procedures for an immigrant visa. Once you know that you qualify for an immigrant visa based on your family ties or work, you need to know when and where you can get your visa. I explain how to know if you qualify for a visa immediately or if you must wait for a visa under the quota system. I then explain your options as to where you can be interviewed for the visa followed by tips on preparing for that interview. Finally, I explain your right to appeal or seek review of a denied application.

WHEN YOU QUALIFY TO GET YOUR IMMIGRANT VISA —THE PREFERENCE, OR "QUOTA" SYSTEM

As I explained in Chapters 2 and 3, in order to get a Family-Based or Employment-Based immigrant visa, the USCIS must approve a petition filed by you or on your behalf. But that doesn't mean that you can always get an immigrant visa immediately. Under the preference, or "quota," system, an immigrant visa may not be available right away.

If you are an Immediate Relative of a U.S. citizen, you don't come under the quota system. With no limit on the number of immigrant visas available, you can get your immigrant visa as soon as your papers are processed.

However, in many preference categories, more people want visas than are available in a given year for a given country. If that's true in your case, even if the USCIS has already approved a petition for you, you can't get your immigrant visa immediately. You'll have to wait your turn. Your place in line to get a preference immigrant visa is called your priority date. Some preferences have a long waiting list. Some categories have no wait. Whether you must wait and for how long depends on your native country and your preference category.

In a Family-Based Preference case, the date your relative files the petition establishes your priority date. It doesn't matter how long the USCIS takes to process the petition—the priority date is set when the USCIS receives the petition. Sometimes, when there is no waiting list, you can file your petition and application for permanent residence at the same time (see Chapter 5).

In an Employment-Based Preference, you establish your priority date, usually when your employer files a labor certification application with the U.S. Department of Labor. The time it takes to process the application has no effect on your priority date. (For more on the question of labor certifications, see Chapter 3.) Where the law doesn't require a labor certification, the filing of an I-140 petition with the USCIS establishes your priority date. The USCIS has implemented a promised program of allowing applicants (with current priority dates) in employment-based cases to file I-140 petitions simultaneously with applications for permanent residence.

If you are a preference applicant, you must look to the current USCIS Visa Bulletin to learn if a visa is immediately available for you. If a visa is available, we say that your priority date is current.

How do you know if your priority date is current? Around the 11th or 12th of every month, the Department of State issues a Visa Bulletin with the cutoff dates for the following month. You can find out the cutoff dates for each category yourself by calling the Department of State at 202-632-2919. By Internet, you can get the Department of State Visa Bulletin at the Consular Affairs Web site at www.travel.state.gov/visa_bulletin.html. Using fax, the Visa Bulletin is available by dialing 202-647-3000. To be placed on the Department of State's Visa Bulletin mailing list, write to Visa Bulletin, Visa Office, Department of State, Washington, DC 20522-0113. They will put only U.S. addresses on the mailing list. Finally, you can also access and download the Visa Bulletin from the Consular Affairs electronic bulletin board at 202-647-9225.

Reading the Visa Bulletin

Let's look at the immigrant visa cutoff dates in the Visa Bulletin for July 1996 and see how to read the Visa Bulletin. A recent Visa Bulletin can be found in Appendix G. I use the July 1996 bulletin below for illustration because it shows the full range of possibilities regarding the preference cutoffs. Preference applicants whose priority date was before the date listed in the Visa Bulletin qualified for immigrant visas in July 1996. The Department of State issued this bulletin in June 1996.

	ALL CHARGEABILITY AREAS EXCEPT THOSE LISTED	INDIA	MEXICO	PHILIPPINES
1st	C	C	U	01 May 86
2A	22 Dec 92	22 Dec 92	15 May 92	22 Dec 92
2B	01 Mar 91	01 Mar 91	01 Mar 91	01 Mar 91
3rd	01 Aug 93	01 Aug 93	15 Oct 87	01 Apr 85
4th	15 Feb 86	08 Oct 84	01 Jul 85	08 Oct 77

Employment-Based Preferences

	ALL CHARGEABILITY AREAS EXCEPT THOSE LISTED	INDIA	MEXICO	PHILIPPINES
1st	C	C	C	C
2nd	C	U	C	C
3rd	C	U	C	01 Feb 95
Other Workers	08 May 87	U	08 May 87	08 May 87
4th	C	C	C	08 Mar 95
Certain Religious Workers	C	C	C	08 Mar 95
5th	C	C	C	C
Targeted Employment Areas/ Regional CentersTargeted	C	C	C	C

To use the Visa Bulletin to figure out if you could get an immigrant visa in July 1996, you must know what preference category you are in. Suppose you are in the First Family-Based Preference. That means that you are over 21 and your mother or father, a U.S. citizen, has petitioned for you. Except for Mexico and the Philippines, you find a "C" under the countries listed for the First Family-Based Preference for July 1996.

The "C" means "current," a way of saying that in July 1996 a visa was immediately available for First Family-Based Preference applicants born in all countries except Mexico and the Philippines. Only applicants born in Mexico and the Philippines have to wait. For Mexico, you find a "U." The "U" means that until October 1, 1996, when the new USCIS fiscal year begins, no visas at all will be available for First Family-Based Preference applicants born in Mexico. For the Philippines, an unmarried child of a U.S. citizen who had a parent file for them before May 1, 1986, got immigrant visas in July 1996.

If the Visa Bulletin doesn't mention your country by name, you come under the all chargeability category. Notice that in July 1996 in the Fourth Family-Based Preference (the brothers and sisters of U.S. citizens) for the Philippines, the U.S. citizen would have to have filed the petition prior to October 8, 1977. At the time the Visa Bulletin came out, these applicants had already been waiting more than 17 years.

The stories of Aida, Tomas, Marcia, and Pilaf illustrate how the Visa Bulletin works.

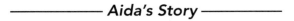

Aida's Story

Aida came to the United States on the F-1 student visa. She is a citizen of Mexico. While studying at the University of California, Los Angeles, she met Ruben, a U.S. citizen of Mexican ancestry. Ruben and Aida married, and he petitioned for her permanent residence. As the spouse of a U.S. citizen, Aida doesn't have to check the Visa Bulletin since she has an immigrant visa immediately available to her. Since the law places no limit on the number of Immediate Relatives of U.S. citizens who can come to the United States every year, they are not part of a preference category. The Visa Bulletin is irrelevant to the right of Immediate Relatives of U.S. citizens to apply for a permanent residence.

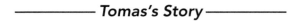

Tomas's Story

Tomas lives in the Dominican Republic, where he was born. He is 22 years old and married. His mother came to the United States many years ago and is now a U.S. citizen. Tomas wanted to come to live in the United States, so on July 31, 1993, his mother filed a relative petition for him. By reading the Visa Bulletin for July 1996, we can see that in that month he had a current priority date and could get an immigrant visa immediately. Any Third Family-Based Preference applicant whose petition in the all chargeability category was filed before August 1, 1993, was eligible for permanent residence in July 1996.

Marcia's Story

Marcia, a native of Venezuela, worked in New York as a live-in domestic household worker. Her job required only one month's experience. Marcia's employers wanted to petition for her for a green card. They filed a labor certification for her on January 15, 1992. Because finding live-in help is hard, the employer could prove that no qualified U.S. workers wanted the job. The Department of Labor approved the labor certification application. On February 1, 1994, the employer filed a petition for her with the USCIS . The USCIS approved the petition on October 1, 1994.

Marcia didn't yet qualify for an immigrant visa in July 1996. Her priority date was January 15, 1992. When an Employment-Based Preference case requires a labor certification, the priority date is the date the Department of Labor receives the petition. Applicants born in Venezuela whose labor certifications the Department of Labor received before May 8, 1987, were at the front of the line to get immigrant visas in July 1996. Marcia still has a long wait before she qualifies for an immigrant visa. At the time her priority date becomes current, her employer will need to prove that he or she still needs a live-in housekeeper. Otherwise, Marcia won't qualify for an immigrant visa.

Pilaf's Story

Pilaf is a citizen and a native of France. She has a sister in the United States who is a U.S. citizen. In the hope that Pilaf would join her in the United States, the sister petitioned for Pilaf. The USCIS received the petition on January 15, 1989. Pilaf's priority date is January 15, 1989, and she is eligible for a permanent residence under the Fourth Family-Based Preference. By July 1996, Pilaf had been waiting to become a permanent resident for almost seven years, and she may still have a long wait before she'll get an immigrant visa. She can get her immigrant visa when French natives whose petitions were received by the USCIS before February 15, 1986, are current. Since the Visa Bulletin doesn't move one month every month it is hard to tell how long Pilaf must wait, but it could be many more years.

Cross-Chargeability:
Qualifying Under the Country of Your Spouse or Parent

Sometimes you can claim an immigrant visa under the country of birth of your spouse or parent. If you are a Preference immigrant visa applicant, your unmarried children and your spouse can get an immigrant visa when you do. We call your children or spouse derivative beneficiaries. If your derivative beneficiary spouse is a native of a different country, you can claim eligibility from that country. If you are accompanying your parent, your visa may be changed to either parent. Note that a parent cannot charge his or her visa to the country of a child. If you were a U.S. citizen but lost your citizenship, your visa may be charged to country of current citizenship or, if citizenship is nonexistent, to country of last residence. Finally, if you were born in a country where neither of your parents was born or had residence (for instance, your parents were studying in that country), you may be charged to the country of either parent.

Migdalia's story provides an example of how cross-chargeability works.

Migdalia's Story

Migdalia was born in Mexico. When she was 20, she married David, who was born in the Dominican Republic. Migdalia's father immigrated to the United States, and when he became a U.S. citizen on July 31, 1993, he petitioned for her under the Third Family-Based Preference. Looking at the July 1996 Visa Bulletin, we see a long wait under the Third Family-Based Preference for citizens of Mexico. However, since David will be immigrating to the United States with Migdalia, she can claim her immigrant visa under the quota for the Dominican Republic. The Dominican Republic is current under the Third Family-Based Preference for applicants whose petitions were filed for them before August 1, 1993. The Dominican Republic is in the all chargeability areas category for July 1996. Migdalia and David can get their green cards as soon as the U.S. government can process the papers.

Can You Wait in the United States Until Your Priority Date Becomes Current?

If you don't have a visa immediately available, can you wait here until your priority date is reached? If you're in lawful nonimmigrant status, you can stay in that status until your status expires. Even if you are not here legally, in most parts of the country, the USCIS won't come looking for you while you wait for your priority date to become current. In some USCIS districts, the USCIS does investigate people if the Department of Labor denies their labor certification application. Though the USCIS may try to remove you if you come to the attention of the USCIS in a factory raid, you commit a serious crime or you get caught up in an "anti-terrorist" investigation. The USCIS will almost certainly try to remove you if you apply for asylum and the USCIS doesn't approve your application. Of course, the policy described here could quickly change if public sentiment or public policy turns against all, or a specific group of, immigrants.

WHERE TO APPLY FOR YOUR IMMIGRANT VISA

If you are in the United States, in some cases you can get immigrant status without leaving the United States. This process is called adjustment of status. If the law doesn't allow you to adjust status, you must apply at a U.S. consulate abroad, a procedure called consular processing. If you are in the United States and qualify for adjustment of status, you may still choose to apply at a U.S. consulate abroad, but I advise most people to apply in the United States if they can.

Getting Your Green Card Here Is Usually Best

If you are in the United States, adjustment of status is almost always the best way to become a permanent resident. Adjustment of status is more convenient than consular processing. It is also safer. If you are applying for adjustment of status and a problem arises in your case, or the USCIS denies your application, you can often remain in the United States while you try to solve the problem. And if the USCIS tries to remove you, you can renew your application with the immigration judge. If you are trying to get a visa at a U.S. consulate, you have little right to review if a consular officer denies your application. Your options are more limited, and any problems you face are harder to solve. Also, certain grounds of inadmissibility apply only if you leave the United States (see Chapter 5).

If you go home for an interview at a U.S. consulate and a problem arises with your case, you may have to remain outside the United States until you can resolve the problem.When you apply for adjustment of status, you can get USCIS permission to work while your application is pending. And in most cases, you can travel abroad and return to the United States while your application is pending. We call this permission to travel advance parole. If your are unlawfully in the United States, don't travel abroad without speaking to an immigration law expert, even if the USCIS has granted you travel permission. Despite the USCIS having granted you advance parole, a person unlawfully here who travels abroad may have problems getting permanent residence.

The stories of Barbara and Arthur show why it is usually best to apply for your green card here in the United States through the adjustment of status process.

Barbara's Story

Barbara applied for adjustment of status based on her marriage to Roberto, a U.S. citizen. Roberto had been married once before in his native country, the Dominican Republic, but he had gotten a divorce.

When Roberto and Barbara went to Barbara's adjustment of status interview, they brought Roberto's certificate of divorce, but they did not have the complete divorce judgment. The USCIS examiner who interviewed them insisted that she could not approve the case until she saw the actual divorce judgment with a translation. When Roberto took too long to get it, the examiner denied Barbara's adjustment of status application, and the USCIS sent her a letter saying that she had 30 days to depart the United States. The USCIS usually does not try to enforce an applicant's departure in a situation like that faced by Barbara and Roberto. Roberto got the divorce judgment and Barbara applied again for adjustment of status. The USCIS approved the new application.

If Barbara had applied for her immigrant visa at the U.S. consulate abroad, she would have had to wait outside the United States until Roberto obtained the documents. Because she applied for adjustment of status, she could wait in the United States and stay with her husband.

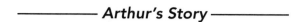

Arthur's Story

Arthur applied for adjustment of status based on sponsorship by his employer. Arthur had been arrested when he was 17 years old for demonstrating against the Italian government. He had been a member of a socialist student group, and the police had charged and convicted him of disorderly conduct for assaulting a police officer. Arthur answered the questions on the application honestly, admitting that he had been arrested. He believed that he would have no problem becoming a permanent resident. His lawyer told him that since simple assault is not a crime involving moral turpitude and he was under 18 at the time of his conviction, he could become a permanent resident despite the conviction. He was never a member of a communist party. He told his story to the USCIS examiner at his adjustment of status interview, but still the examiner denied his application, claiming that Arthur was barred from permanent residence under the law that makes Communist Party members inadmissible. When the examiner denied the application, Arthur was placed in deportation (called "removal" as of April 1, 1997) proceedings. For more on inadmissibility for political activity, see Chapter 5.

Arthur has a right to present evidence at his deportation hearing about the student organization he belonged to in Italy. He can bring witnesses to testify, such as university professors who are knowledgeable about the political system in Italy. He can testify himself about his beliefs and the beliefs of the organization as he understood them. If the immigration judge does not agree with Arthur's analysis and upholds the decision of the USCIS , Arthur can appeal to the Board of Immigration Appeals and remain in the United States while the appeal is pending. On the other hand, if Arthur had applied at a U.S. consulate abroad and they denied his application, his only right to review would be a nonbinding advisory opinion by the U.S. Department of State in Washington, D.C., a slow and unreliable process. He would not have the right to appeal the denial nor could he come and live in the United States pending a favorable decision on his case.

WHO CAN GET AN IMMIGRANT VISA WITHOUT LEAVING THE UNITED STATES?

Not everyone in the United States who qualifies for permanent residence can get their immigrant visa without leaving the country. Some people who qualify to have the USCIS interview them in the United States have to pay $1,000 for the privilege. With the following exceptions noted, you qualify to become a permanent resident without leaving the United States if you meet one of the following criteria:

- You were inspected upon entry by an USCIS officer, you were never out of status, and you never worked without permission.

- You were inspected upon entry by an USCIS officer and you are applying for permanent residence as an Immediate Relative of a U.S. citizen. If you are in the Immediate Relative category and the USCIS inspected you at entry, you can adjust status even if you are in the United States unlawfully. The immediate relative category includes the spouse of a U.S. citizen, unmarried children under age 21 of U.S. citizens and the parents of U.S. citizens who are over age 21, and the spouse of a deceased U.S. citizen where, at the time of your spouse's death, you had been married at least two years and were not legally separated.
- You are applying based on your status as a refugee or asylee.
- You are an employment-based immigrant visa applicant or a special immigrant religious worker, you entered the United States lawfully, and you were not out of status more than 180 days since your last lawful nonimmigrant entry.

Or, under what many refer to as the "245(i) grandfather clause," you can adjust status if you pay a $1,000 filing penalty and meet one of the following criteria:

- You're applying as a family-based immigrant and your relative petitioned for you by January 14, 1998.
- You are an employment-based visa applicant and your employer filed a labor certification for you with the State Department of Labor, or you or your employer filed a petition with the USCIS by January 14, 1998.
- A relative petitions for you or you start an employment-based case on or before April 30, 2001, and you were in the United States on December 21, 2000.
- You are a derivative beneficiary of a "245(i) grandfathered" individual. See Chapter 1 for the definition of derivative beneficiary.

Note that the "physical presence in the United States on December 21, 2000," rule applies only if the petition or labor certification was filed for you after January 14, 1998, but on or before April 30, 2001. If your family- or employment-based papers were filed by January 14, 1998, the physical presence rule doesn't apply. Note also that once you get grandfathered under 245(i), you can adjust status regardless of whether you qualify for your immigrant visa through your original papers or in another category.

On January 26, 2001, the USCIS issued a memorandum explaining how to prove physical presence in the United States on December 21, 2000. The USCIS prefers that you submit a federal-, state-, or city-issued document. However, the memorandum instructs USCIS officers to accept other documentation as well, including letters and affidavits. The USCIS recognizes that sometimes several documents taken together may prove physical presence on December 21, 2000. The memorandum gives the example of a person who makes a mortgage payment on December 1, 2000, and another on January 1, 2001.

Now is the time to gather proof that you were here on December 21, 2001. It may take years before you can file your 245(i) application. Keep copies of the proof (and all other important documents) in a very safe place.

The USCIS memorandum clarifies also that dependent (derivative) spouses and children need not prove physical presence on December 21, 2001, to qualify for 245(i). Suppose that you qualify for permanent residence as the married daughter of a U.S. citizen. You were here on December 21, 2001, having entered as a visitor in 1999. Your U.S. citizen mother files for you on April 30, 2001. It may take five or more years for you to qualify for permanent residence under the preference quota system. When you do qualify, the USCIS will interview you here. The USCIS will also interview here your spouse and your unmarried under-21 children, regardless of whether they, too, were here on December 21, 2001.

Exceptions: If you entered in C or D crew member status, or with permission to enter in Transit Without Visa status, you can only adjust status if you are 245(i) grandfathered. If you came here with a K visa, you cannot adjust status except through marriage to the U.S. citizen who petitioned for you to get K status. If you qualify for an immigrant visa other than through that petitioner, you must return home for the immigrant visa interview. The 245(i) grandfather clause won't help you.

The stories of Timothy, Sharon, Katy, Ruth, Manuel, and Samson illustrate who can get an immigrant visa without leaving the United States.

——————— Timothy's Story ———————

Timothy came to the United States in August 1995 on an F-1 student visa to study at a community college. He did well and continued his studies through college and law school. He worked part-time on campus with the permission of his international student advisor. After law school, he got USCIS permission to work for one year under the practical training program for F-1 students. His employer liked him and sponsored him for an H-1B temporary professional work visa. Three years later, his employer sponsored him for an immigrant visa. Timothy can become a permanent resident without leaving the United States. He can adjust status. He never worked without permission, and he was never unlawfully here.

——————— Sharon's Story ———————

Sharon entered the United States using a phony passport. She married Jim, a U.S. citizen, on February 1, 1998. Jim immediately petitioned for her to become a permanent resident. Sharon may have to go home for her permanent resident interview. Though she qualifies for an immigrant visa as an immediate relative of a U.S. citizen, the fact that she entered unlawfully may result in the USCIS finding that she's ineligible for adjustment of status. Still, some applicants in Sharon's situation have successfully adjusted status, though they need the USCIS to grant them a fraud waiver and they need to pay the $1,000 filing penalty. For more on fraud waivers, see Chapter 5.

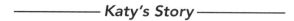
Katy's Story

Katy and her husband came to the United States from the Philippines with tourist visas and decided to stay. Katy's mother is a U.S. citizen, and on January 5, 1997, Katy's mother petitioned for Katy. Katy qualifies for permanent residence under the Third Family-Based Preference for the married sons and daughters of U.S. citizens. Her husband will get his immigrant visa as a derivative beneficiary of Katy. Because of the long wait in the third preference for nationals of the Philippines, it may be ten years before Katy and her husband get to the front of the immigrant visa line. Still, the USCIS will interview them here if they each pay a $1,000 penalty. Though they overstayed the time the USCIS granted to them, Katy's mother petitioned for Katy before the January 14, 1998, cutoff.

Ruth's Story

Ruth entered the United States on December 1, 2000, on a visitor's visa. The USCIS gave her permission to visit for six months, but she decided to stay. She was an experienced engineer, and she was offered a good job here. The company filed a labor certification application for her on April 30, 2001. Since Ruth was physically present in the United States on December 21, 2000, and her employer petitioned for her on or before April 30, 2001, she can adjust status once the U.S. Department of Labor approves her labor certification and the USCIS approves an employment-based petition for her. To adjust status, she'll need to pay the $1,000 filing penalty.

Manuel's Story

Manuel entered the United States on December 22, 2000. He came here from Mexico without being inspected by an USCIS officer. He entered at night undetected by the USCIS . In January 2001, he married a U.S. citizen. His wife petitioned for him on February 1, 2001. Though Manuel is married to a U.S. citizen, he must return to Mexico to process for permanent residence. He cannot adjust status because he entered without inspection. He cannot benefit from the 245(i) law because he was not physically present in the United States on December 21, 2000. If he remains in the United States 180 days after his initial entry and then leaves to process at a U.S. consulate in Mexico, he'll face the three-year bar to admission. He'll only get his permanent residence if the USCIS grants him a waiver. For more on these waivers, see Chapter 5.

Samson's uncle Alfred, a U.S. citizen, petitioned for Samson's mother. Samson's mother was Alfred's sister. Samson was 15 years old when Alfred filed the petition on January 14, 1998, and thus was 245(i) grandfathered as a derivative beneficiary of his mother. Samson and his mother had come to the United States in visitor's status and then overstayed. The wait is so long under the category for the brothers and sisters of U.S. citizens, the Fourth Family-Based Preference, that when Samson turned 21, his mother's priority date was not yet current. Under USCIS law, Samson at age 21 lost his right to immigrate as a derivative beneficiary. However, he did not lose the right to interview here under the 245(i) rule. Suppose that five years later, an employer gets a labor certification approved for Samson. He can adjust status under the 245(i) rule. His rights that he earned as a derivative beneficiary under 245(i) remain with him for the rest of his life.

WHO MUST PAY AN EXTRA FEE FOR ADJUSTMENT OF STATUS?

Some people qualify for adjustment of status only because relatives or employers began cases for them by January 14, 1998, or because the papers were filed by April 30, 2001, and they were in the United States on December 21, 2000. These applicants must pay a $1,000 penalty for the right to have the USCIS interview them in the United States.

If you're applying for permanent residence as the immediate relative of a U.S. citizen and you entered legally, you don't have to pay the penalty. That's true even if you're not now in legal status. You can also adjust status and avoid the penalty if you entered lawfully, you are applying in an employment-based category, and you weren't in the United States unlawfully for 180 days since your last entry. If you are applying in a family preference category, you can avoid the penalty if you entered the United States lawfully, you never worked without permission, and you were never out of status.

If you're a crew member of a ship and the USCIS gave you a pass to come ashore while your ship docked here, or you were admitted to the United States on a C or D visa to join a ship, you must pay the $1,000 penalty to adjust status. The same is true if you were admitted to the United States on the way to another country and you entered with Transit Without Visa (TWOV) permission.

Refugees, asylees, and some Chinese, Cubans, Haitians, and others applying under special adjustment acts don't have to pay the extra fee. You are also exempt from paying the extra fee if you are under 17 years of age at the time the USCIS decides your application for adjustment of status.

The stories of Javier, Lloyd, Marla, Wanda, and Priscilla show how the adjustment of status penalty rule works.

Javier's Story

Javier, a native of Haiti, entered the United States from Canada. He had lost his passport and U.S. visa, so he entered by evading U.S. border officers. On January 1, 1998, he married a U.S. citizen. She petitioned for him on January 13, 1998. Javier can adjust status, but because he entered the United States without inspection, he must pay a $1,000 penalty for the right to have his interview here.

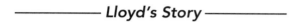

Lloyd's Story

Lloyd came to the United States on an F-1 student visa in 1995. He finished his four years of college and worked for one year as an F-1 practical trainee. After he finished his F-1 trainee status, he decided to spend a year traveling around the United States. He was out of status, but he guessed that the USCIS wouldn't catch him. He did not have to work because he had a rich uncle who sent him a check every month.

After his one year of fun on the run, Lloyd wanted to start his career as an industrial designer. Lloyd found an employer who successfully sponsored him for a permanent visa based on a labor certification (see Chapter 3). The employer filed the labor certification application on April 30, 2001. Even if it takes two years to process his labor certification application, Lloyd can apply to become a permanent resident without leaving the United States. That's because he began his case before the April 30, 2001, cutoff. He must pay the $1,000 penalty because he had been out of status in the United States.

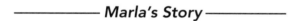

Marla's Story

Marla entered the United States using a phony passport and visa on December 21, 2001. Her mother, who was already in the United States, got her permanent residence on June 1, 2001. Marla was 25 years old at the time. Marla's mother petitioned for her on April 30, 2001. Once Marla's number comes up under the Second Family-Based Preference B category for the sons and daughters of permanent residents, she can adjust status, but she must pay the $1,000 filing fee. She was physically present in the United States on December 21, 2000, and her mother petitioned for her on or before April 30, 2001.

Wanda's Story

Wanda came to the United States from Poland on a B-2 visitor's visa, telling the consular officer who issued her visa that she wanted to visit colleges in the United States, intending to continue her studies in economics. The University of Texas accepted her in their graduate economics program, she changed status to F-1 student, and she began her studies. She graduated and began work in H-1B status. In December 1997, Wanda's employer filed a labor certification application for her to begin the process of making her a permanent resident. While she was still in lawful status, the U.S.

Department of Labor approved the labor certification application, and she applied for adjustment of status. Wanda was never out of status and never worked without permission. The USCIS will interview her in the United States, and she need not pay the $1,000 penalty.

Priscilla came to the United States on an "I" visa for international journalists. Le Monde sent her here to write about the 1992 presidential elections. In the excitement of the campaign, she met and fell in love with Jay, a U.S. journalist. They married, but they were too busy covering the campaign to file papers with the USCIS so that Priscilla could become a permanent resident. Priscilla quit her job with Le Monde and began doing freelance work for several U.S. newspapers. Eventually, her husband petitioned for her and she applied for adjustment of status.

Because she qualifies for permanent residence as an Immediate Relative of a U.S. citizen and she entered the United States legally, she doesn't have to pay the $1,000 penalty. The fact that she violated her status by working for U.S. newspapers doesn't disqualify her from adjusting status.

Consular Processing for People in the United States

If you're in the United States, you may want to consider **consular processing**. While sometimes risky, consular processing can be faster than adjustment of status. Assuming you have a current priority date, consular processing takes nine months to one year. In some parts of the United States, adjustment of status takes more than 24 months. Of course, if you are not eligible to adjust status, you have no other choice than to apply for your immigrant visa at a U.S. consulate.

APPLYING FOR ADJUSTMENT OF STATUS

You apply for adjustment of status using USCIS Form I-485. You can find a sample I-485 in Appendix H. If you are age 14 or older, you must also submit USCIS Form G-325A, Biographic Information, and two photographs. Note that the photos must be special three-quarter profile photos with your right ear showing. You no longer submit fingerprints with your application. You must pay a separate fingerprinting fee, and the USCIS will notify you when to appear so they can take your prints.

Usually, you must also file your birth certificate with the I-485 application, along with a translation, if necessary. An applicant under 14 may have a parent or a guardian sign the form.

Filing Your I-485 Adjustment of Status Application

If you are an Immediate Relative of a U.S. citizen, you may file your USCIS Form I-130 and USCIS Form I-485 applications simultaneously. You may also file petitions and I-485 applications simultaneously in Family-Based cases if your priority date is current. In Family-Based cases, once your priority date is current, you are at the front of the line and you may then file your adjustment of status application. In Employment-Based cases, the USCIS must approve a petition for you and you must have a current priority date before you file your adjustment of status application at an USCIS regional processing center. As we go to press, the USCIS has yet to implement a promised program of allowing applicants (with current priority dates) in employment-based cases to file I-140 petitions simultaneously with applications for permanent residence. Once the USCIS implements that policy, you can read about it at my Immigration Answers Web site, www.ilw.com/wernick/.

The stories of Frieda, Sherman, Jeremy, and Sean illustrate when you may file your application for adjustment of status.

Frieda's Story

Frieda came to the United States on a student visa. While here, she fell in love with and married Tom, a student at her college. After the wedding, she filed her application for adjustment of status using USCIS Form I-485. She attached a petition signed by her husband. She may file her application with the petition, although the USCIS has not approved it, because she is an Immediate Relative of a U.S. citizen. Since the law doesn't limit the number of Immediate Relatives of U.S. citizens who can adjust status each year, Frieda doesn't have to worry about a priority date. A visa for her is immediately available. That's why the USCIS allows her to file the petition and application simultaneously.

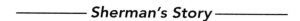

Sherman's Story

Sherman is an unmarried 25-year-old South African engineer. His mother recently became a U.S. citizen. Sherman came to the United States to visit his mother and decided that he wanted to stay. At the time that he decided to become a permanent resident of the United States, his preference category, the First Family-Based Preference, was current for South Africans. Because Simon had a visa immediately available for him, he could file his application for adjustment of status simultaneously with his mother's petition.

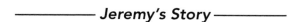

Jeremy's Story

Jeremy and his wife came to the United States from their home country of Sweden. They came to work for a computer design firm. Jeremy's mother was a U.S. citizen. Jeremy liked the United States so much that he decided to make it his home. Jeremy's mother was willing to petition for Jeremy. At the time Jeremy decided to become a permanent resident, the Third Family-Based Preference was backlogged several years. That's the preference for the married sons and daughters of U.S. citizens. Therefore, though Jeremy's mother filed a petition for him, Jeremy could not file his application for adjustment of status since no visa was immediately available in his preference category. Three months after Jeremy's mother filed the petition, the USCIS approved it. Every month, Jeremy checked the Visa Bulletin (discussed earlier in this chapter) until finally his priority date became current. He was then able to file his application for adjustment of status. He included a copy of the USCIS notice of approval of the petition his mother had filed for him.

————————— *Sean's Story* —————————

Sean, from Scotland, was in the United States working in New York as an architect in H-1B temporary professional worker status. He came to the job with a master's degree and two years' experience in indoor swimming pool design. His company agreed to sponsor him for an immigrant visa and filed a labor certification application for him. Two years later, the U.S. Department of Labor certified that no U.S. worker was ready, willing, and able to do the job that Sean was doing. They also certified that his employer had offered the job at the prevailing wage. Sean's immigrant visa category (Third Employment-Based Preference) had no backlog, but before he could file his I-485 adjustment of status application, his employer had to get the USCIS to approve an I-140 employment petition for him. Once the USCIS approved the petition, Sean filed his application for adjustment of status.

Agency Check

The USCIS will send your fingerprints and one page from USCIS Form G-325A (Biographical Information) for a Federal Bureau of Investigations (FBI) "agency check." Normally, the FBI will report within 60 days as to whether you have an arrest record in the United States. However, the fingerprint clearance won't be considered late until 120 days after the USCIS sent your prints to the FBI. The USCIS will often also check with the Central Intelligence Agency (CIA) and the U.S. consul in your country of last residence and/or other countries where you have lived.

Other government agencies are not usually contacted, but they may be. For instance, if an USCIS examiner suspects that you have received Medicaid or some other form of public benefit that will make you inadmissible (see Chapter 5 for more on inadmissibility), they may check with the relevant government agency.

Medical Exam

Unless you had a medical exam as part of your refugee application, you must submit a blood test, a chest X ray, and proof that you have been vaccinated against certain diseases as part of your adjustment of status application. For information on medical conditions that could result in your being denied permanent residence, see Chapter 5. The X ray will sometimes be waived for pregnant women. Or sometimes a pregnant woman must wait until she gives birth and then take the X ray. The blood tests may be waived if you have a legitimate religious objection to your blood being drawn. The vaccination requirement can be waived if getting vaccinated would be contrary to your religious beliefs or moral convictions, or if getting vaccinated would not be medically appropriate.

The Final Step: USCIS Interview for Adjustment of Status

Your final step as an applicant for adjustment of status is usually an interview with an USCIS examiner. The USCIS usually waives interviews in cases involving applications for adjustment of status based on an I-140 petition (a petition based on an offer of employment) or a petition for a parent or minor unmarried child of a U.S. citizen.

If your case is based on an I-130 petition filed by your spouse, and the USCIS calls you for an interview, they will want your petitioning spouse to appear at the interview with you. Sometimes you can get your immigrant visa in a marriage case without your spouse appearing, but that is highly unusual. This is different from interviews for permanent residence at U.S. consulates abroad. There, a consular officer does not expect your petitioning spouse to appear, unless the officer specifically requests your spouse to do so.

If all goes well at your adjustment of status interview, the USCIS examiner may grant you immigrant status that day. "Going well" means that your priority date is current (or you are an Immediate Relative of a U.S. citizen), the agency check revealed no damaging information, and you are not found inadmissible. The examiner stamps a temporary approval of permanent residence onto your passport or onto a separate approval notice. You can use the stamped passport or stamped notice to travel in and out of the United States as a permanent resident. You can also use the stamped passport or approval notice to petition for relatives and as evidence of USCIS authorization to work. Keep in mind that if you have derivative beneficiaries, they can apply simultaneously with you for permanent residence.

Sometimes an USCIS examiner defers a final decision on an adjustment of status application. This is likely to happen in cases in which the USCIS examiner requests further information or documentation—for instance, a document such as a passport or birth certificate, which would normally be presented at an adjustment interview—that you forgot to bring. The examiner might like to see more evidence about whether you are inadmissible for criminal activity or as a person likely to become a public charge. Or the examiner may believe that an investigation of some aspect of your case, such as whether yours is a real marriage, is required. A deferred decision may also result from bureaucratic error, such as a lost agency check. If you have another USCIS file, sometimes the delay is due to problems locating that file.

In cases where the USCIS waived your interview, you'll get an answer by mail. If your application is approved, you'll receive a notice to appear at an USCIS District Office for processing of your green card.

If the USCIS denies your application, you may challenge that decision in deportation (called "removal" as of April 1, 1997) proceedings or on rare occasions in federal court. In that case, you will almost certainly need the help of an immigration law expert.

Adjustment of Status of Asylees and Refugees

If you were admitted as a refugee or the USCIS granted you asylum, you may apply for adjustment of status after one year in refugee or asylee status.

If you had a medical exam prior to admission as a refugee, the USCIS will usually not require a further medical examination. If you are an asylee, a medical examination is required.

For both the asylee and refugee, certain grounds of exclusion, including the public charge exclusion, do not apply. Waivers are available for all other grounds of exclusion unless you are inadmissible as a subversive, former Nazi or Nazi collaborator, or trafficker in narcotics. If you are an asylee or refugee, your spouse and unmarried children under 21 are also eligible for adjustment of status. Your relationship with them must predate your becoming a refugee or asylee.

If you are an asylee, the USCIS will backdate your permanent residence to one year before the adjustment application was approved. If you are a refugee, the USCIS will backdate the approval to your date of entry into the United States.

CONSULAR PROCESSING

As explained earlier, immigrant visa applicants usually use consular processing if they are already outside the United States. Consular processing is similar for all consulates, although each has its own forms and/or local procedures.

The process begins when the NVC, or Department of State National Visa Center (32 Rochester Avenue, Portsmouth, NH 03801-2909; 603-334-0700), receives your approved I-130 or I-140 petition from the USCIS. If your priority date is current or you are the immediate relative of a U.S. citizen, the NVC sends you (or your representative) an Instruction Package for Immigrant Visa Applicants (formerly called "Packet III") containing Department of State forms. If your visa category is backlogged, the NVC will send you a notice that they have received the petition. Write down your case number (it is different from the number on your USCIS petition filing receipt) and keep it in a safe place. Check the NVC notice to make sure your immigrant visa classification (how you qualify for an immigrant visa) and your priority date are correct. The NVC will send you the application forms within three months of your priority date. The forms ask for biographical information and give you a checklist of documents you will need to become a permanent resident. Return the forms as instructed on the packet. Next, you should receive a notice to appear for your immigrant visa interview at the U.S. consulate.

The Visa Application

After the consulate receives the forms in the Instruction Package for Immigrant Visa Applicants and a visa becomes available, the consul will send the visa application (formerly called "Packet IV"), to you or your representative. This is the final set of documents that must be prepared for submission at the time of the final visa interview. This visa application package includes information concerning the medical examination and the time and location of your interview.

At your interview, a U.S. consular officer will review all the documents that make up your case, including the petition filed by your relative or employer. If the officer has any doubts about the petition, the officer may defer a decision while the consulate investigates your case. If the officer believes that you don't qualify for an immigrant visa, the officer will deny your application. Your only chance then is to ask the officer to reconsider or write to the U.S. Department of State for an Advisory Opinion asking that they reverse the officer's decision. The Department of State sometimes reverses the decision of a consular officer on a question of law, but rarely on a question of fact. To get an advisory opinion, contact the Advisory Opinion Division, U.S. Department of State, 2401 E Street, NW, Washington, DC 20522-0113, 202-663-1225.

The stories of Jeff and Mandy help us understand the review process when a consular officer denies an immigrant visa application.

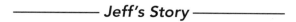

Jeff's Story

Jeff's mother, a permanent resident of the United States, petitioned for him. Jeff's mother was receiving public assistance, but Jeff had an uncle who was very successful in the United States. The uncle and Jeff's mother each signed an affidavit of support for him, but Jeff couldn't convince the U.S. consular officer who interviewed him that he was not likely to be a public charge. The officer denied Jeff's immigrant visa application. Jeff would be wasting his time if he wrote for an Advisory Opinion from the Department of State regarding the consular officer's denial. Deciding whether Jeff is likely to become a public charge is something left to the discretion of the consular officer. Jeff must just keep trying to provide further evidence that he can support himself if he wants to become a permanent resident of the United States.

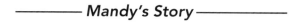

Mandy's Story

Mandy had a rough time growing up and had been in and out of trouble. She had only one criminal conviction, however, and that was for possession of a small amount of hashish when she was 18 years old. Mandy eventually fell in love with a U.S. citizen who was traveling throughout the world, and he petitioned for her for permanent residence. Mandy was convinced that she qualified for permanent residence despite her criminal conviction because under the law of her country, the conviction had been entirely expunged.

When she went to her immigrant visa interview, she admitted that she had been arrested and brought the papers from the court explaining the expungement. The consular officer's view was that under immigration laws, the expungement was not sufficient to eliminate the exclusion by drug-related offense, and the officer denied Mandy an immigrant visa.

If Mandy believes she deserves to become a permanent resident and the consular officer disagrees, she can seek an Advisory Opinion from the Department of State. The Department of State Advisory Opinion Division will write to the consular officer, and the officer will abide by that decision. If Mandy is successful, the U.S. consul will issue her an immigrant visa.

OTHER THINGS TO KNOW
ABOUT YOUR FINAL IMMIGRANT VISA INTERVIEW

Here are some other things to consider as you prepare for your immigrant visa interview.

Review of Petition

Even if the USCIS has approved a petition filed by you, a relative, or your employer, the examiner may review the petition as part of the USCIS review of your right to become a permanent resident. If you filed the petition at the same time as your application for adjustment of status, the USCIS examiner will certainly review it.

If an USCIS examiner or consular officer believes that the documents establishing a brother-sister, parent-child, husband-wife, or employee-employer relationship are questionable, the officer can request a field investigation. For a Family-Based Preference case, an investigator may go to the area where the beneficiary and petitioner were born, or where their relationship developed, in order to learn whether the relationship is real. In parent-child or sibling cases, the consul may request that the petitioner and beneficiary take a blood test to verify the relationship.

If you are applying for permanent residence based on marriage to a U.S. citizen or permanent resident, the consular officer or USCIS examiner may investigate the relationship or may examine previous divorces to ensure they are valid.

At the final interview, the USCIS examiner or consular officer is going to want to see all original documents. This includes birth certificate and marriage certificates, as well as job letters and other proof of income.

Do You Need a Lawyer?

Though many people get permanent residence without the help of a lawyer, I recommend that you have a lawyer or other immigration expert help you prepare for your final visa interview. At an adjustment of status interview, you have the right to have a lawyer or accredited representative attend the interview with you. At a consular interview, while you do not have a right to have a lawyer, most consular officers will allow a lawyer to attend the interview or be available to answer your questions.

Naturalization
and Citizenship

"Mom, you'll never become a citizen. You've been in this country 20 years, and you still don't speak or read English," complains Maria

"But I don't need to speak English to live in this neighborhood," Maria's mother, Jane, explains. "Anyway, I don't need to become a U.S. citizen. I'm happy the way I am."

"But Mom, what if you retire back home in the old country? You may not be able to come back and visit us," Maria responds.

Maria would like her whole family to become U.S. citizens. That way they can be assured of the right to come back to the United States even after spending years abroad. She's already a U.S. citizen. Her brother, Chris, has been a permanent resident for ten years, but he is afraid to apply to be naturalized because of his criminal record. Chris got arrested for a minor shoplifting offense ten years ago when he first came to the United States. It was his first and only arrest.

Jane and Chris may both qualify for U.S. citizenship. As you will learn in this section, Jane may be excused from the English language requirement because of her age and long residence here. As for Chris, since he has had a clean record for five years, he, too, has a good chance of becoming a U.S. citizen. But because of his criminal record, Chris should speak to an immigration law expert before filing his naturalization application.

This section will help you with the last step in the immigration journey: Naturalization, the process of becoming a U.S. citizen. I begin in Chapter 7 by discussing the advantages of becoming a U.S. citizen as well as the risks and pitfalls of the naturalization process. In Chapter 7, I also discuss dual citizenship. In Chapter 8, I explain the requirements for naturalization. In Chapter 9, I provide step-by-step instructions on how to complete USCIS Form N-400, Application for Naturalization, and provide practical hints for getting through the naturalization process. Finally, in Chapter 10, I discuss children and naturalization: how a person becomes a citizen by birth and how your children may become citizens upon your naturalization.

Of course, the first step toward naturalization is to become a permanent resident. If you are not already a permanent resident, you should read Section I to find out how you can become one.

CHAPTER 7

Do You Want to Become a U.S. Citizen?

In this chapter, I discuss the advantages of becoming a U.S. citizen, consider the risks of the naturalization process, and explain dual citizenship. I also discuss whether you will need a lawyer to help you become a naturalized U.S. citizen.

WHY BECOME A U.S. CITIZEN?

Let's look at the reasons why a permanent resident might want to become a U.S. citizen. As compared to a permanent resident, a U.S. citizen can:

1. **Vote and hold public office.** The right to vote is usually reserved for U.S. citizens. Some cities allow permanent residents to vote in local school board and community board elections, but those are rare exceptions. If you become a naturalized citizen, you can hold all public offices except President and Vice President of the United States.

2. **Be employed in government jobs not available to permanent residents.** Most federal jobs and some state and municipal jobs (such as firefighter and police officer) require U.S. citizenship as a condition of employment.

3. **Live outside the United States without losing permanent residence.** Unlike a permanent resident, a U.S. citizen does not have to worry about the right to return to the United States after a lengthy absence abroad. If you are a permanent resident and you spend too

much time abroad, you may be considered to have abandoned your U.S. residence. You may lose your right to return.

John's story illustrates why a person who plans to live abroad for a long time may want to become a U.S. citizen.

────────── *John's Story* ──────────

John had been a permanent resident for 20 years when he retired from his job at age 65. A native of Greece, he wanted to live out his final years at home, so he sold his house in the United States, closed his bank account, and moved to Athens.

Every Christmas, John came back to the United States to spend time with his son, his daughter-in-law, and his grandchildren. Though John was not living here, he used his green card to enter the United States. For several years, he had no problem at the airport. USCIS inspectors didn't question him about his permanent resident status. Finally, five years after John had moved to Athens, the USCIS inspector at JFK Airport in New York City noticed that John came into the United States every Christmas. The inspector asked John how long he was planning to stay. John told the truth, answering "one month." The inspector questioned John further and learned that John was not really living in the United States but in Athens. The inspector told John that he was not eligible to come into the United States as a permanent resident. The USCIS inspector gave him two choices. He could return home immediately to Greece and thus give up his permanent residence, or he could ask for a hearing and try to convince an immigration judge that he hasn't abandoned his U.S. residence. If John had become a U.S. citizen, he could have lived in Athens as long as he liked and returned to the United States anytime.

4. **Avoid danger of being removed for events occurring after naturalization.** If you are a U.S. citizen, you cannot be removed for violations of law or public policy that occurr after you became a U.S. citizen. A permanent resident can be removed for a number of reasons, including criminal activity, smuggling, and political activity. Once you become a U.S. citizen, you cannot be removed from the United States unless you didn't have the right to become a U.S. citizen in the first place. In that case, the USCIS will have to take your citizenship away before they can remove you.

Jean's and Gary's stories illustrate this benefit of becoming a U.S. citizen.

────────── *Jean's Story* ──────────

The day after Jean was naturalized as a U.S. citizen, she was on her way to a party in New York City with three of her friends. Jean was unaware that her friend Tom, who sat next to her in the back seat, had brought an ounce of cocaine with him, which he had put under the seat. When the driver of the car ran a red light, the car was stopped by the police. It turned out that the driver had an outstanding arrest warrant, and the police, after a search, discovered the cocaine under the seat. Jean and her friend Tom were both indicted and charged with possession of cocaine with intent to sell. If Jean goes to trial, she may be able to convince the jury that she didn't know that the cocaine was there. However, if the jury doesn't believe her, they may find her guilty. Even though Jean has been a U.S. citizen for only a couple of days, she cannot be removed. The United States is her new country and—while she might face jail time—she has the right to remain in the United States even if she is convicted of a serious crime.

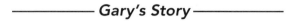

Gary's Story

When Gary applied to become a permanent resident of the United States, he stated on his application for permanent residence that he had never been arrested by the police either in the United States or his country of origin. That was not true. Gary had been convicted of armed robbery in his home country, but by bribing a court officer he managed to get documentation proving that he had never been arrested. He became a permanent resident. When he applied for naturalization, he again lied and said that he had never been arrested. After he became a citizen, a scandal broke out in the U.S. consulate that had processed his immigrant visa application. Every application that had been processed in the month that Gary had been interviewed for his immigrant visa was carefully investigated. The investigators found out that Gary had been arrested and convicted of a serious offense and had lied about the events on his immigrant visa application. The USCIS may try to denaturalize Gary.

The denaturalization process is very complicated and difficult. The U.S. government will evaluate Gary's case and decide whether to try to denaturalize him. If he is denaturalized, he might be removed from the United States.

5. **Get a U.S. passport.** Sometimes a U.S. citizen can visit countries that citizens of other countries cannot. Some permanent residents become U.S. citizens so that they can travel easily to countries where previously they needed a visa or were forbidden to go.

6. **Have the right to public benefits.** The 1996 welfare reform law took away the right of some permanent residents to get many public benefits. If you become a U.S. citizen, you'll feel better knowing that if you need help from the government, you'll be able to get it.

RISKS OF THE NATURALIZATION PROCESS

When you apply for naturalization, you give the USCIS the opportunity to review your immigrant history. If you have committed an act that may make you removable, consult an immigration law expert before filing your application. Be especially careful if you have been convicted of a crime or if the USCIS may think that you obtained your permanent resident status improperly. Michael's and Sharon's stories illustrate the risks of applying for naturalization.

Michael had been a permanent resident for just two years when he was caught selling a small amount of cocaine in New York City. Since it was his first offense and since the cocaine was under a gram, the judge sentenced Michael to five years' probation. He did not go to jail. After his probation was over, thinking that his record was clean, Michael applied for naturalization. Not only was Michael not naturalized, but the USCIS began deportation (called "removal" as of April 1, 1997) proceedings against him, as a person convicted of a drug-related offense. He may have a defense to removal, and he may ultimately get U.S. citizenship. Almost certainly, he'll have to defend himself before an immigration judge.

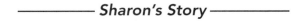 *Sharon's Story*

Sharon became a permanent resident when her mother petitioned for her. After her interview at the U.S. consulate in Trinidad, when the consul had given her an immigrant visa, she decided to marry her high school boyfriend, Billy. She married Billy before she made her first entry into the United States as a permanent resident. She got married, came into the United States, but did not tell the inspector at the airport that she had married. This is considered visa fraud and a removable offense.

Five years later, when she applied for U.S. citizenship, the USCIS examiner noticed that Sharon's marriage had taken place before she entered the United States. Since a person immigrating as the daughter of a permanent resident must be unmarried, Sharon didn't deserve to become a permanent resident. Fortunately, her mother had become a U.S. citizen. Her mother then petitioned for her as the married child of a U.S. citizen. Several months later, Sharon got a new immigrant visa and began the wait all over again to become a U.S. citizen. Sharon was lucky.

CITIZENSHIP: IF YOU NATURALIZE, WILL YOU LOSE YOUR FOREIGN CITIZENSHIP?

If you become a naturalized U.S. citizen, do you have to give up your citizenship in other countries? That depends on the laws of the other country. When you become a U.S. citizen, the U.S. government asks that you renounce all other citizenship. Some countries do not recognize this renunciation and will consider you, a naturalized U.S. citizen, to be a citizen of both countries. Among the many countries that allow for dual citizenship are Colombia, the Dominican Republic, France, Israel, and Mexico. (For a list of countries that allow dual citizenship, see Appendix I.) If you are worried that you will lose citizenship in another country, check with that country's consulate before you naturalize.

If you are already a U.S. citizen and want to become a citizen of another country, you probably can do so without jeopardizing your U.S. citizenship. You can lose your U.S. citizenship, however, if you commit an act of expatriation, such as joining a foreign army or participating in a foreign government.

CHAPTER 8

Requirements
for Naturalization

If you are a permanent resident, you can become a U.S. citizen through the process called naturalization. To be naturalized, most applicants must meet the following requirements:

1. You have resided in the United States as a permanent resident continuously for five years. (You can qualify after only three years of permanent residence if you were married to, and living with, the same U.S. citizen spouse during those three years or your became a permanent resident under the special rules for a victim of domestic abuse.

2. You have been physically present in the United States for half of the five- (or three-) year period.

3. You are a person of good moral character.

4. You have a basic knowledge of U.S. government and history (the civic knowledge requirement).

5. You are able to read, write, and speak simple English (with exceptions for some older, longtime permanent residents).

6. You are at least 18 years of age.

7. You express your allegiance to the U.S. government.

As you will learn, the law provides exceptions to many of these requirements.

CONTINUOUS RESIDENCE REQUIREMENT

To become naturalized, you must have resided continuously in the United States as a lawful permanent resident for at least five years before being naturalized. If you are the spouse of a U.S. citizen, you may be naturalized three years after you become a permanent resident if you have been married to and living in marital union with a U.S. citizen for the entire three years. The USCIS says that you must be married to and living with your U.S. citizen spouse both at the time you file your naturalization application and at the time of your naturalization interview. You may also qualify after only three years if you self petitioned for permanent residence and became a permanent resident under the special rules for the victims of domestic abuse. The five or three years required is sometimes referred to as the statutory period. You may file your application 90 days before you have met the continuous residence requirement. If you file your application more than 90 days before you have the necessary five or three years, the USCIS will deny your application as prematurely filed.

The three-year rule for the spouse of a permanent resident is illustrated by the stories of Maria, Joseph, Louisa, and Karen.

Maria's Story

Maria became a permanent resident on January 2, 1992, when she was sponsored by her mother. On January 1, 1993, she married John, a U.S. citizen. Maria was first eligible to become a U.S. citizen on January 2, 1996. At that time, she had been married to a U.S. citizen for three years while a permanent resident.

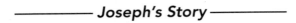

Joseph's Story

On January 2, 2002, Joseph became a conditional permanent resident when he was sponsored by his wife, Susan, a U.S. citizen. If Joseph and Susan stay married and living together, Joseph can become a U.S. citizen on January 2, 2005. If they divorce, Joseph must wait until 2007 to qualify for citizenship.

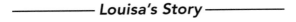

Louisa's Story

Louisa became a permanent resident when she was sponsored by her U.S. citizen husband. She was married on January 2, 1998, and she became a permanent resident on January 2, 1999. Two and a half years after she became a permanent resident, she and her husband separated. Louisa cannot become a U.S. citizen using the three-year rule because she is no longer living with her U.S. citizen husband, although she is still married to him. To take advantage of the three-year rule, Louisa has to have been married to and living with a U.S. citizen for those three years. Louisa will have to wait until January 2, 2004, when she has five years of permanent residence, in order to become naturalized as a U.S. citizen.

———— Karen's Story ————

Karen became a permanent resident on January 2, 1991. She was sponsored by her brother. Four years later, on January 2, 1995, she married Tom, a U.S. citizen. She became eligible for U.S. citizenship herself on January 2, 1996, five years after she became a permanent resident. The fact that she married a U.S. citizen does not speed up her eligibility for naturalization. She qualified after having acquired five years of continuous residence separate and apart from having married a U.S. citizen.

Continuous residence doesn't mean that you must have been in the United States without ever leaving for the statutory period. It does mean, however, that during the five (or three) years before naturalization:

1. You did not abandon your permanent residence.

2. The United States was your principal residence.

3. And, most important, you have not been out of the country for more than one year at a time, or 365 consecutive days straight. An absence of more than a year breaks the continuity of your residence. The USCIS gives you one full year for the first day of your return. Then you need four more years (two more if you are married to and living with a U.S. citizen) before you can naturalize.

If you are going abroad on business, to do religious work, or to work for the U.S. government, you may be absent for more than a year without breaking your continuous residence if you get approval to do so from the USCIS (see "Exceptions to the Continuous Residence Requirement" below).

Sonia's story illustrates how absence abroad for more than one year breaks the period for continuous residence.

———— Sonia's Story ————

Sonia became a permanent resident on January 1, 1989. She was sponsored by her mother, a U.S. citizen. On January 1, 1991, Sonia left the United States to study for two years in Spain. Because Sonia was going to be out of the United States for so long, she applied for a reentry permit. (See chapter 1 for more on reentry permits.) The USCIS granted the reentry permit, and when Sonia completed her studies, she entered the United States on January 2, 1993. Because Sonia was out of the United States for more than one continuous year, she had to wait four years and one day from her last entry—or until January 3, 1997—before she could become a U.S. citizen. If she had been married to and living with a U.S. citizen, she could have become a citizen after two years and one day.

If you have been outside the United States for more than six months, but less than a year in several of the years just prior to your applying to be naturalized, the USCIS examiner may think that you have abandoned your residence. Much will depend on the reason or reasons you left the country. If you have a reasonable explanation for having spent so much time outside the United States, the examiner can be convinced that you kept your residence here. Common reasons why people spend a lot of time abroad are illness in the family, attendance at a school or university, or business affairs. Trips abroad of less than six months are usually not a problem unless you have so many of them that it looks like you are living outside the United States.

EXCEPTIONS TO THE CONTINUOUS RESIDENCE REQUIREMENT

Certain businesspeople, religious workers, government employees, researchers for a U.S. research institution recognized by the USCIS, and sea men and women may be out of the United States for more than one year and still meet the continuous residence requirement. To apply for this exception, you must file USCIS Form N-470, Application to Preserve Residence for Naturalization Purposes. Special continuous residence rules also apply to applicants who have served in the U.S. military (see "Special Naturalization Qualifications—Veterans and Those in Military Service"). Your spouse and dependent children residing abroad in your household are also entitled to this benefit.

Business Workers

To qualify for the exception for business workers, you must have been physically present in the United States for an uninterrupted period of at least one year after becoming a permanent resident and one year prior to filing USCIS Form N-470. You must be employed by, or under contract with, the government of the United States; an American institution of research recognized by the Attorney General; a U.S. firm or corporation, or a subsidiary of a U.S. firm or corporation (more than 50 percent of the subsidiary must be owned by the American company), engaged in developing the trade and commerce of the United States; or a public international organization of which the United States is a member. The USCIS publishes lists of research institutes and public international organizations whose employees qualify under Title 8 of the Code of Federal Regulations (CFR).

A business worker whom the USCIS grants an exemption from the continuous residence requirement is not exempt from the physical presence requirement discussed below.

Religious Workers

Religious workers, like people abroad on business, must have been physically residing in the United States after being granted permanent residence for at least one year before the applicant files for the exemption using USCIS Form N-470.

To qualify for a religious worker exemption, you must be authorized by a U.S. religious denomination to perform ministerial or priestly functions or be engaged solely as a missionary, brother, nun, or sister by a U.S. religious denomination or an interdenominational missionary organization.

Unlike business workers, religious workers whose Form N-470 applications are approved may count periods outside the United States performing religious duties toward satisfaction of the physical presence requirement (discussed below) for naturalization.

Sea Men and Women

You may be exempted from both the continuous residence and physical presence (see the next section) requirements if you have served on a U.S. vessel. A U.S. vessel is one that is operated by the U.S. government or whose home port is the United States. This rule applies as well to those who work on vessels registered in the United States or owned by U.S. companies. You must have been a permanent resident for the statutory five- (or three-) year period, but time spent outside the United States won't be held against you.

PHYSICAL PRESENCE REQUIREMENT

In order to be naturalized, you must have been physically present in the United States for half of the required five- (or three-) year statutory period of continuous residence. The USCIS counts back from the day they receive your naturalization application.

Tom's and Marie Jean's stories illustrate the physical presence requirement.

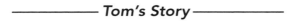

Tom's Story

Tom became a permanent resident on January 2, 1992. On a trip to the Dominican Republic, he fell in love with a college student, Sandra. He was a professor at the University of Miami, and he took advantage of every school break to spend time with Sandra in the Dominican Republic. He spent every January, June, July, and August in the Dominican Republic with Sandra. Tom will have no trouble becoming a U.S. citizen once he has five years' permanent residence. Since Tom was out of the United States for only four months out of every 12 months, he will have met the physical presence requirement. He also maintained his residence here as shown by his keeping his job at the university.

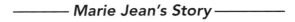

Marie Jean's Story

Marie Jean became a permanent resident on January 1, 1996. On January 1, 1997, she began traveling regularly to France as part of her job as an international financial advisor to a U.S. bank. While she maintained a home in the United States, she only spent one week out of every month here, spending the other three weeks in France. She will probably not lose her permanent residence status so long as she maintains an apartment, a bank account, and other ties to the United States and is employed by a U.S. company. As long as she spends so much time in France, she will never fulfill the physical presence requirement. On January 2, 2001, she had five years' continuous residence, but she had not spent half of her time in the

United States during the five-year period.

GOOD MORAL CHARACTER REQUIREMENT

Good moral character does not mean moral excellence. If you have a record of criminal activity; have failed to pay required family support; have had problems with alcohol or drugs; have been involved in illegal gambling, prostitution, or procuring; have failed to pay your taxes; have failed to register with the selective service; or have lied to the USCIS to gain immigration benefits, you may fail the good moral character requirement. Parking tickets, disorderly conduct convictions, and many other minor offenses usually will not prevent you from proving that you have good moral character. However, the USCIS may contend that you don't have good moral character if you have repeated convictions for minor violations.

The question of who has "good moral character" under U.S. laws is not easy to answer. If you have any doubts, particularly regarding a criminal record, you should speak to an immigration law expert before filing your naturalization application.

Generally, good moral character must be shown only for the statutory period of five (or three) years. Except for **aggravated felonies**, crimes committed before the statutory period, either in the United States or abroad, will not affect your right to become a citizen unless they reflect on your present character. Although, if you are still on probation or parole for a crime, the USCIS may deny your naturalization until your parole or probation has ended.

An aggravated felon convicted on or after November 29, 1990, is permanently barred from naturalizing. An aggravated felon is a person who has been convicted of one of several serious crimes, especially crimes involving drugs and violence. (For a clearer idea of what constitutes an aggravated felony, see Appendix J, "List of Aggravated Felonies.") The 1996 immigration law expanded the definition of aggravated felony. If you were convicted of an aggravated felony before November 29, 1990, you may be able to show good moral character, but at the same time you may be deportable. If you have ever been convicted of a crime, even a minor one, you would be foolish to apply for naturalization without speaking to an immigration law expert.

The stories of Sam, Tim, and Jane show the complexity of the good moral character requirement.

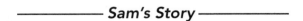 *Sam's Story*

Sam had been involved in a number of illegal gambling operations. He had been arrested several times, and each time he had pled guilty to minor gambling charges. Since a person who makes a living from illegal gambling cannot be naturalized, when Sam went to his interview, he was questioned about whether he had continued his gambling. Even though he had not been arrested at any time during the last five years, the USCIS naturalization examiner noted that Sam lived in a very expensive neighborhood and wore very expensive clothes. Sam had been employed during the last five years as a clerk in a small neighborhood store. The examiner wanted to know how Sam could afford his high lifestyle on his low salary; he suspected that perhaps Sam was involved in illegal gambling. Fortunately for Sam, he had inherited a million dollars from a rich uncle just about five years before his interview.

Tim's Story

Tim became a permanent resident on January 1, 1980. He had been arrested on numerous occasions for illegal horse race bookmaking. His last arrest was in 1984. Nevertheless, Tim was denied naturalization as a U.S. citizen in 1990. When he went for his interview, the USCIS examiner noticed that although he had not been employed for the last five years, he lived in a mansion in Beverly Hills, traveled to Europe regularly (the examiner noticed the foreign entry stamps in Tim's passport), and was wearing a gold watch. Having reason to believe that Tim earned a living from illegal gambling, the examiner denied the application, since a person who makes a living from illegal gambling is precluded from establishing good moral character. The examiner's decision was based on Tim's many arrests and the fact that he had no visible means of support.

Jane's Story

Jane became a permanent resident in January 1985. In January 1989, she was caught stealing a purse from a fancy boutique. She pled guilty to a theft in February 1990. Her crime was not an aggravated felony. In February 1995, when her probation ended, she was interviewed regarding her naturalization as a U.S. citizen. During those five years, she had led an average life and had no run-ins with the law. Jane was able to establish good moral character for the previous five years and had no problem becoming a U.S. citizen.

GOOD MORAL CHARACTER AND CRIMINAL ACTIVITY

You cannot prove good moral character if, during the five- (or three-) year period prior to your naturalization, you have been convicted in the United States or abroad of one or more of the following:

- A crime involving moral turpitude.
- Two or more gambling offenses.
- A narcotics offense.
- Two or more nonpolitical offenses for which you were sentenced to five years' imprisonment or more.
- Any crime for which you were confined to prison for more than 180 days.

- Any aggravated felony.

You can also be denied naturalization if you have admitted committing a crime involving moral turpitude or the USCIS believes that you have been involved in drug trafficking, even if you have never been convicted of these crimes.

Not all criminal activity, even where a felony conviction is involved, will necessarily result in the USCIS denying your naturalization application. An example of a conviction that would not be a bar to naturalization would be a conviction for vehicular manslaughter.

Since conviction of a single crime involving moral turpitude can be a bar to naturalization, let's consider how the law defines these terms. Moral turpitude is conduct or behavior that is reprehensible in its own right. It is an indication of inherent baseness or depravity of character. Good people may break the law, but good people don't commit crimes involving moral turpitude.

A crime involving fraud or dishonesty will usually be considered to involve moral turpitude. Among crimes considered by the immigration laws to involve moral turpitude are arson; assault with intent to kill, commit rape, rob, or inflict serious bodily harm with a dangerous or deadly weapon; bigamy; blackmail; bribery; bad check convictions; burglary; counterfeiting; embezzlement; forgery; larceny; manslaughter; murder; pandering; perjury; prostitution; receiving stolen goods; robbery; and sexual offenses.

Crimes not generally considered to involve moral turpitude include simple assault, breaking the peace, drunkenness, disorderly conduct, a single gambling offense, or violations of government regulations that do not require intent to defraud as an element of the crime.

CHILD SUPPORT REQUIREMENT

If you willfully fail to meet your child support obligations, you do not have good moral character for naturalization purposes. Child support refers to financial support that you provide your children when they are not living with you.

How does the USCIS know whether you are meeting your child support obligations? On USCIS Form N-400, you are asked whether you are separated or divorced and whether you are living with or apart from your spouse. Sometimes an interview notice will advise you to bring in your divorce decree and any papers relating to the divorce. At the interview, the USCIS examiner may ask about the child support obligation and whether it has been met. You may be required to produce documentation that you have met your obligations, such as canceled checks. The USCIS may check with the person caring for your children or ask you to get a letter from them confirming that you are supporting your children.

SELECTIVE SERVICE REGISTRATION

It is the USCIS view that failing to register reflects on your moral character and your adherence to the U.S. Constitution.

The United States is not presently drafting men or women into the armed forces. Still, U.S. Selective Service laws require that all men, U.S. citizens, permanent residents, and undocumented immigrants register with Selective Service.

The registration requirement applies to men only if they were in the United States between the ages of 18 to 25 and were born after January 1, 1960. The requirement ends once you reach the age of 26. Persons born before January 1, 1960, are not required to register. The registration requirement does not apply to men here in lawful nonimmigrant status, such as with F-1 student or H-1B temporary worker visas.

If you are not yet 26 years old, you can register late with the Selective Service. You can get a registration form at your local post office. You can bring proof of your late registration with you to your naturalization interview, and the USCIS examiner may excuse your failure to register.

Some men were unaware of their obligation to register and didn't get a notice to register from either the Selective Service or the USCIS. If this describes your situation, try submitting an affidavit (a sworn statement) to the USCIS examiner explaining that you didn't willfully and knowingly fail to register. The examiner may approve your application.

If you are found to have knowingly and willfully failed to register, you must wait until you are at least 31, five years after your obligation to register ended, before you can become a U.S. citizen. If you're married to and living with a U.S. citizen, you can be naturalized when you reach the age of 29, three years after your obligation to register ended.

If you did register with Selective Service, but you don't know your registration number, you may call Selective Service toll free at 888-655-1825. Have your date of birth and social security number ready when you call. You may also write to the Selective Service asking for your number at Selective Service, P.O. Box 94636, Palatine, IL 60094-4636. Include your name, date of birth, and social security number.

TAXES

If you were required to file a federal tax return but failed to do so, your naturalization application will be denied. Many people are not required to file tax returns because their income is less than the amount for which filing is required. Don't be afraid to answer "No" to this question if you earned so little money in a particular year or years that you were not required to file a return.

Usually, the USCIS will want to see your last five years' tax returns, or they will want an explanation as to why you didn't file returns.

Richard's story illustrates how a person may be naturalized without having filed tax returns.

Richard's Story

Richard always had a hard time making money. Ever since his permanent resident mother got him an immigrant visa, he has worked only part-time, if at all. Sometimes he survived on welfare. Never did he make more than $4,000 in a single year. In 1996, Richard applied to become a U.S. citizen. He can truthfully answer that he never failed to file a federal tax return—because he earned so little, filing a return wasn't required. At his naturalization interview, he presented an affidavit from his mother explaining that she had supported him for the last five years. He also brought along stubs from his welfare checks. Richard passed his naturalization interview.

OTHER COMMON INDICATIONS OF A LACK OF GOOD MORAL CHARACTER

A habitual drunkard or a user or dealer of drugs is not a person of good moral character. The same is true if you earn income from illegal gambling, prostitution, or drug dealing. If you have been arrested for one of these activities and currently have no visible means of support, the USCIS may wonder if you are still engaging in illegal activity.

If you are a polygamist or have ever smuggled aliens into the United States for economic gain, you will fail to meet the good moral character requirement.

CIVICS KNOWLEDGE REQUIREMENT

In order to be naturalized, you must have a basic understanding of the history and government of the United States. You must correctly answer questions from a list of 100 questions provided by the USCIS. If you are more than 65 years of age and you have been a permanent resident for 20 years, you need to answer only six out of 10 simple questions from a list of 25. You can find these lists at the end of this chapter. The civics knowledge requirement, like the English reading and writing requirement, can be met by passing a test before the interview. If you cannot learn due to a documented mental or physical disability, you are exempt from having to pass a test of civics knowledge.

ENGLISH LANGUAGE REQUIREMENT

With limited exceptions, every naturalization applicant must pass an English speaking, reading, and writing test. If you can answer orally the questions on the application form (such as "Where do you live?" and "Where were you born?"), you can probably pass the English oral comprehension and speech test.

If a question arises at the interview that needs to be discussed in detail—for instance, whether you made required child support payments—

you have the right to have that discussion in your native language.

You are exempt from the English language requirement if you have been a permanent resident for more than 20 years and you are older than 50 or you have been a permanent resident for more than 15 years and you are older than 55. If you qualify for this exemption, you must still pass a civics and history test, but you can be tested in your native language. If you are incapable of writing, reading, or speaking because of a documented mental or physical disability, you may apply to be exempted from the English language requirement. You are also exempt from taking an English language test if you take a similar test as part of the process of getting permanent residence through the amnesty program. Finally, Hmong immigrants who fought in the CIA's war in Laos during the Vietnam War era are exempt from the English language requirement. To be eligible for this exemption, Hmong veterans must have served with a special guerrilla unit or irregular force operating in or from Laos in support of the U.S. military anytime between February 28, 1961, and September 18, 1978.

AGE REQUIREMENT

In order to be naturalized, you must be at least 18 years old. You may not file your application prior to your 18th birthday. Children of applicants for naturalization who are under 18 years of age sometimes may acquire citizenship through their parents (see chapter 10).

COMPETENCY REQUIREMENT

To naturalize, you must be legally competent. That is, you must have the mental capacity to take an oath of allegiance to the United States. The USCIS can waive the oath requirement if the applicant is unable to understand, or communicate an understanding of, the oath's meaning because of a physical or developmental disability or mental impairment. Even severely disabled people, unable to understand the oath, qualify for naturalization.

ALLEGIANCE TO THE U.S. GOVERNMENT

To become a U.S. citizen, you must express your allegiance to the United States and our form of government. As part of the naturalization process, you must take an oath of allegiance to the United States. You can find the Oath of Allegiance in Appendix K. You must be willing to either bear arms on behalf of the United States or perform some form of military service or civilian work of national importance. As mentioned under "Competency Requirement," the USCIS can waive the oath for the disabled.

You may be denied naturalization if you are, or have been, a member of or connected to a communist party or a similar organization during the ten years prior to filing your naturalization application. You may also be barred from naturalization if you have been connected with an organization that believes in anarchy, the overthrow of organized government, sabotage, injury, or assassination of U.S. government officers.

If your membership in one of the groups described above was more than ten years prior to your filing for naturalization you may still be naturalized. Your political activity may be forgiven as well, if your membership in the organization ended before you were 16 years of age or if your membership was involuntary. Involuntary means compelled by law or for the purposes of getting the necessities of life.

SPECIAL NATURALIZATION QUALIFICATIONS —VETERANS AND THOSE IN MILITARY SERVICE

Special rules apply to active duty veterans of World War I, World War II, the Korean War, the Vietnam War, and the Persian Gulf War. Special rules also apply to Filipinos who served in the military during World War II and for people who are, or have been, in the U.S. armed services for three years or more.

If you are a Filipino World War II veteran or a Gulf War veteran, you may be naturalized. You need not have ever been a permanent resident. You are also exempt from the English language, civics knowledge, and good moral character requirements.

Filipino war veterans must have served honorably in the U.S. military anytime during the period beginning September 1, 1939, to December 3, 1946. You must have been in active duty status under the command of the U.S. military in the Far East or within the army of the Philippines, the Philippine Scouts, or a recognized guerrilla unit. Finally, you must have resided in the Philippines prior to your military service.

Persian Gulf veterans may be naturalized if they served honorably in active duty status between August 2, 1990, and April 11, 1991. The Persian Gulf veteran law applies to all aliens in active service during the period August 2, 1990, to April 11, 1991, not just those who participated in the Gulf War conflict.

If you are a permanent resident who has served honorably for three years in the U.S. military, regardless of whether your service was continuous, you may be naturalized. In most cases, you are exempt from the continuous residence and physical presence requirements. If you don't apply while in the service or within six months after your discharge, you must have resided in the United States during your periods of nonservice, going back five years. You are not exempt from the good moral character, English language, or civics knowledge requirements.

List of 100 Questions Used by USCIS Naturalization Examiners

1. What are the colors of our flag?
2. How many stars are there on our flag?
3. What color are the stars on our flag?
4. What do the stars on the flag mean?

5. How many stripes are there in the flag?

6. What color are the stripes?

7. What do the stripes on the flag mean?

8. How many states are there in the union?

9. What is the Fourth of July?

10. What is the date of Independence Day?

11. Independence from whom?

12. What country did we fight during the Revolutionary War?

13. Who was the first president of the United States?

14. Who is the president of the United States today?

15. Who is the vice president of the United States today?

16. Who elects the president of the United States?

17. Who becomes president of the United States if the president should die?

18. For how long do we elect the president?

19. What is the Constitution?

20. Can the Constitution be changed?

21. What do we call a change to the Constitution?

22. How many changes or amendments are there to the Constitution?

23. How many branches are there in our government?

24. What are the three branches of our government?

25. What is the legislative branch of our government?

26. Who makes the laws in the United States?

27. What is Congress?

28. What are the duties of Congress?

29. Who elects Congress?

30. How many senators are there in Congress?

31. Can you name the two senators from your state?

32. For how long do we elect each senator?

33. How many representatives are there in Congress?

34. For how long do we elect the representatives?

35. What is the executive branch of our government?

36. What is the judiciary branch of our government?

37. What are the duties of the Supreme Court?

38. What is the supreme law of the United States?

39. What is the Bill of Rights?

40. What is the capital of your state?

41. Who is the current governor of your state?

42. Who becomes president of the United States of America if the president and the vice president should die?

43. Who is the chief justice of the Supreme Court?

44. Can you name the 13 original states?

45. Who said "Give me liberty or give me death"?

46. Which countries were our enemies during World War II?

47. What are the 49th and 50th states of the union?

48. How many terms can a president serve?

49. Who was Martin Luther King, Jr.?

50. Who is the head of your local government?

51. According to the Constitution, a person must meet certain requirements in order to be eligible to become president. Name one of the requirements.

52. Why are there 100 senators in the Senate?

53. Who nominates Supreme Court justices?

54. How many Supreme Court justices are there?

55. Why did the pilgrims come to America?

56. What is the head executive of state government called?

57. What is the head executive of city government called?

58. What holiday was celebrated for the first time by the American colonists?

59. Who was the main writer of the Declaration of Independence?

60. When was the Declaration of Independence adopted?

61. What is the basic belief of the Declaration of Independence?

62. What is the national anthem of the United States?

63. Who wrote "The Star-Spangled Banner"?

64. Where does freedom of speech come from?

65. What is the minimum voting age in the United States?

66. Who signs bills into law?

67. What is the highest court in the United States?

68. Who was the president during the Civil War?

69. What did the Emancipation Proclamation do?

70. What special group advises the president?

71. Which president is called the "Father of Our Country"?

72. What Immigration and Naturalization Service form is used for applying to become a naturalized citizen?

73. Who helped the pilgrims in America?

74. What is the name of the ship that brought the pilgrims to America?

75. What were the 13 original states of the United States called?

76. Name three rights of freedoms guaranteed by the Bill of Rights.

77. Who has the power to declare war?

78. Name one amendment that guarantees or addresses voting rights.

79. Which president freed the slaves?

80. In what year was the Constitution written?

81. What are the first 10 amendments to the Constitution called?

82. Name one purpose of the United Nations.

83. Where does Congress meet?

84. Whose rights are guaranteed by the Constitution and the Bill of Rights?

85. What is the introduction to the Constitution called?

86. What is one benefit of being a citizen of the United States?

87. What is the most important right granted to U.S. citizens?

88. What is the U.S. capitol?

89. What is the White House?

90. Where is the White House located?

91. What is the name of the president's official home?

92. Name one right guaranteed by the first amendment.

93. Who is the commander in chief of the U.S. military?

94. Which president was the first commander in chief of the U.S. military?

95. In what month do we vote for the president?

96. In what month is the new president inaugurated?

97. How many times may a senator be reelected?

98. How many times may a congressman be reelected?

99. What are the two major political parties in the United States today?

100. How many states are there in the United States?

Answers

1. Red, white, and blue

2. 50

3. White

4. One for each state in the Union

5. 13

6. Red and white

7. They represent the original 13 states

8. 50

9. Independence Day

10. July 4

11. England

12. England

13. George Washington

14. [insert current information]

15. [insert current information]

16. The electoral college

17. The vice president

18. Four years

19. The supreme law of the land

20. Yes

21. An amendment

22. 27

23. Three

24. Legislative, executive, and judiciary

25. Congress

26. Congress

27. The Senate and the House of Representatives

28. To make laws

29. The people

30. 100

31. [insert current information]

32. Six years

33. 435

34. Two years

35. The president, Cabinet, and departments under the Cabinet members

36. The Supreme Court

37. To interpret laws

38. The Constitution

39. The first 10 amendments of the Constitution

40. [insert local information]

41. [insert local information]

42. The Speaker of the House

43. William Rehnquist

44. Connecticut, New Hampshire, New York, New Jersey, Massachusetts, Pennsylvania, Delaware, Virginia, North Carolina, South Carolina, Georgia, Rhode Island, and Maryland

SECTION II: NATURALIZATION AND CITIZENSHIP

45. Patrick Henry

46. Germany, Italy, and Japan

47. Hawaii and Alaska

48. Two

49. A civil rights leader

50. [insert local information]

51. Must be a natural born citizen of the United States; must be at least 35 years old by the time he/she will serve; must have lived in the United States for at least 14 years

52. Two from each state

53. The president

54. Nine

55. For religious freedom

56. Governor

57. Mayor

58. Thanksgiving

59. Thomas Jefferson

60. July 4, 1776

61. That all men are created equal

62. "The Star-Spangled Banner"

63. Francis Scott Key

64. The Bill of Rights

65. 18

66. The president

67. The Supreme Court

68. Abraham Lincoln

69. Freed many slaves

70. The Cabinet

71. George Washington

72. Form N-400, Application for Naturalization

73. The American Indians (Native Americans)

74. The Mayflower

75. Colonies

76. a. The right to freedom of speech, press, religion, peaceable assembly, and requesting change of government

   b. The right to bear arms (the right to have weapons or own a gun, though subject to certain regulations)

   c. The government may not quarter, or house, soldiers in a person's home during peacetime without a person's consent

d. The government may not search or take a person's property without a warrant

e. A person may not be tried twice for the same crime and does not have to testify against himself or herself

f. A person charged with a crime still has some rights, such as the right to a trial and to have a lawyer

g. The right to trial by jury in most cases

h. Protects people against excessive or unreasonable fines or cruel and unusual punishment

i. The people have rights other than those mentioned in the Constitution

j. Any power not given to the federal government by the Constitution is a power of either the state or the people

77. The Congress

78. 15th, 19th, 24th, and 26th

79. Abraham Lincoln

80. 1787

81. The Bill of Rights

82. For countries to discuss and try to resolve world problems; to provide economic aid to many countries

83. In the Capitol in Washington, DC

84. Everyone (citizens and noncitizens living in the United States)

85. The Preamble

86. Obtain federal government jobs; travel with a U.S. passport; petition for close relatives to come to the United States to live

87. The right to vote

88. The place where Congress meets

89. The president's official home

90. 1600 Pennsylvania Avenue, NW, Washington, DC

91. The White House

92. Freedom of speech, press, religion, peaceable assembly, and requesting change of the government

93. The president

94. George Washington

95. November

96. January

97. There is no limit

98. There is no limit

99. Democratic and Republican

100. 50

SECTION II: NATURALIZATION AND CITIZENSHIP

65/20 QUESTIONS AND ANSWERS

These are citizenship questions for applicants older than 65 who have been permanent residents for more than 20 years. You must answer six out of 10 questions selected by an USCIS examiner.

Questions

1. Why do we celebrate the Fourth of July?
2. Who was the first president of the United States?
3. Who is the president of the United States?
4. What is the Constitution?
5. What are the first 10 amendments to the Constitution called?
6. Who elects Congress?
7. How many senators are there in Congress?
8. For how long do we elect each senator?
9. For how long do we elect the representatives in Congress?
10. Who nominates judges to the Supreme Court?
11. What are the three branches of our government?
12. What is the highest court in the United States?
13. What major river running north to south divides the United States?
14. The Civil War was fought over what important issue?
15. What are the two major political parties in the United States?
16. How many states are in the United States?
17. What is the capital of the United States?
18. What is the minimum voting age in the United States?
19. Who is Martin Luther King, Jr.?
20. What nation was the first to land a man on the moon?
21. What is the capital of your state?
22. What is it called if the president refuses to sign a bill?
23. What two oceans bound the United States?
24. What famous American invented the electric light bulb?
25. What is the national anthem of the United States?

Answers

1. Independence Day
2. George Washington
3. George W. Bush
4. The supreme law of the land
5. The Bill of Rights
6. The people

7. 100

8. Six years

9. Two years

10. The president

11. Executive, legislative, and judicial

12. The Supreme Court

13. The Mississippi River

14. Slavery or states

15. Republican and Democratic

16. 50

17. Washington, DC

18. 18

19. A civil rights leader

20. The United States of America

21. [insert local information]

22. A veto

23. The Atlantic and Pacific Oceans

24. Thomas Edison

25. "The Star-Spangled Banner"

CHAPTER 9

Getting Naturalized:

Completing the Naturalization Application,
Filing for Naturalization,
Preparing for the Final Interview,
Your Right to Appeal

In this chapter, I provide detailed advice on how to complete USCIS Form N-400, Application for Naturalization, and all of the supporting forms and documents. I also provide practical hints on getting through the naturalization process. I prepare you for your naturalization interview and explain your right to appeal if the USCIS denies your application.

COMPLETING USCIS FORM N-400

Most of USCIS Form N-400 is very straightforward, but some questions require care in answering. You can find a sample form in Appendix L. You should type your answers into the form if possible, but you can fill it out by hand, making sure that you print clearly.

You can get USCIS Form N-400 and other USCIS forms by calling 800-870-3676 or from the USCIS Web site, http://uscis.gov/. The Web version is available in an easy-to-use "fillable" format. You can complete the form on your computer, print it out with your information, and mail it to the USCIS. You can't yet file online, but hopefully that's coming in the future.

Tips on Completing USCIS Form N-400

Note that I haven't described every part of the form, but only certain parts I thought may need additional explanation. **When you fill out the form, use black or blue ink**.

Part 1. Your Name (The Person Applying for Naturalization)

A. Your current legal name.

Write your name as you would like it to appear on your naturalization certificate.

C. If you have ever used other names, provide them in the following space.

Include here your maiden name and other names you may have used on official documents, if any.

D. Name change (optional)

You may use the citizenship process to legally change your name. When you go to your naturalization interview, the USCIS examiner should ask you whether you would like to be sworn in by a federal judge or magistrate or by the USCIS. If you want to legally change your name, you may have to be sworn in by a federal judge or magistrate.

Part 2. Information About Your Eligibility (Check Only One)

Check "A" if you, like most naturalization applicants, qualify because you have been a permanent resident for five or more years. Check "B" if you have been married to, and living with, a U.S. citizen for three years while a permanent resident. (See chapter 8 for more on the three-year rule.)

Part 3. Information About You

F. Are either of your parents U.S. citizens? (if yes, see Instructions)

If one or both of your parents naturalized before you turned 18, you may already be a U.S. citizen. For more on derivative citizenship, see chapter 10.

G. What is your current marital status?

Your marital status is important to the USCIS for several reasons. For more on this issue, see Part 8. If you are applying under the three-year permanent resident rule for the spouse of the U.S. citizen, you must be currently married to and living with your U.S. citizen spouse. For more on the three-year rule, see chapter 8.

H. Are you requesting a waiver of the English and/or U.S. History and Government requirements based on a disability or impairment and attaching a Form N-648 with your application?

If you are unable to either speak or learn to speak English and/or learn U.S. history and government, based on a physical or mental disability or impairment, you may qualify for a waiver of these requirements. To apply for a disability exemption, submit USCIS Form N-648, Medical Certification for Disability Exceptions.

Some applicants need not have the ability to read/write and speak English. Some are eligible for testing based on a simpler list of history and government questions. For more on the English and U.S.

history and government requirement, see chapter 8.

I. Are you requesting an accommodation to the naturalization process because of a disability or impairment? (See Instructions for some examples of accommodations.)

If you are unable to fully participate in the naturalization process because of a disability, the USCIS will make special accommodations. They will even in some cases send an officer to a household or rest home to interview an applicant. This section is where you let the USCIS know that you will be needing this special accommodation.

Part 4. Addresses and Telephone Numbers

The USCIS asks you to designate both your residence and your mailing address. The latter is the address where the USCIS will send your notice to appear for fingerprinting and for your naturalization interview. If you think you'll be moving in the next couple of years, use the mailing address of a friend or relative. If you change your address, call 800-375-5283 to notify the USCIS.

Part 5. Information for Criminal Records Search

If you have had any run-ins with the police or other governmental authorities, speak to an immigration law expert before filing your naturalization application.

Part 6. Information About Your Residence and Employment

If you weren't employed over the last five years, you should feel free to say so. You won't be kept from naturalizing just because you weren't employed. If you are receiving public benefits, that, too, is okay. You can still become a U.S. citizen.

If you have been employed, the USCIS will ask that you present your tax returns. Failure to report income may be a ground for denying you U.S. citizenship. Unless you earned so little income that you were not required to pay taxes, the USCIS will not naturalize you until you have complied with Internal Revenue Service (IRS) reporting regulations.

Suppose your employer petitioned for you for permanent residence and you left the employment shortly after becoming a permanent resident. The USCIS naturalization examiner may want to know why you left the job with your sponsor. The law doesn't require that you remain employed with a sponsor for any particular period of time. However, the examiner may want you to explain what happened if you left very soon after you got your green card. (For more on your right to leave an employer who sponsored you for a green card, see chapter 3.)

Part 7. Time Outside the United States (Including Trips to Canada, Mexico, and the Caribbean Islands)

The section dealing with absences from the United States is particularly important. Very few people have no absences, although if this is the truth, you should put "No." If your country of birth or your last residence is near the United States, the USCIS examiner may be skeptical about your claim that you've never left the country. However, if that is the truth, of course you should answer "No."

If you have traveled a great deal, the USCIS will look at your absences to detect whether you have met the physical presence requirement. If you have long absences, the USCIS may question you about whether you have abandoned your permanent residence. The USCIS will want to make sure that you have met the continuous residence and physical presence requirements. If you were outside the United States for more than one continuous year of the last five (or three) years, you have broken your continuous residence requirement. If you were out more than six months but less than a year, the USCIS examiner may want to know why you were abroad for so long.

You must have also been physically present in the United States for at least half of the time during the past five years (three years if you are applying under the three-year rule for the spouse of a U.S. citizen). The law allows exceptions to some of these rules for some businesspeople, religious workers, sea men and women, and people serving in the military and people working for the U.S. government abroad.

Part 8. Information About Your Marital History

If you got your permanent residence based on a spouse petition, and you divorced or separated from your spouse shortly after you got permanent residence, the USCIS may question whether yours was a "real," or bona fide, marriage. For more on spouse petitions, see chapter 2. The USCIS examiner may be interested in your marital status also to make sure you were honest in applying for public benefits and/or completing tax returns.

Jeremy's story illustrates one reason why an USCIS examiner may carefully question a naturalization applicant about marital history.

———— Jeremy's Story ————

Jeremy got his green card by marrying Jenny, a U.S. citizen. He and his wife were married three years. Jeremy had been married once before, to Rachel. Just two months after Jeremy got his permanent residence, he and Jenny divorced. Jeremy then married Rachel for a second time and petitioned for her for a green card. The fact that Jeremy remarried his ex-wife doesn't prove that his marriage to Jenny was a green card marriage. After all, the actress Elizabeth Taylor married Richard Burton twice. However, to become a U.S. citizen, Jeremy may have to present proof to the USCIS naturalization examiner that he didn't marry Jenny just to get a green card.

Part 9. Information About Your Children

List information about all of your children, even children who are U.S. citizens. The USCIS is not asking you to "include" your children in your application; rather, it is asking for simple information about them. Failure to provide accurate information here may lead to problems later. Some of your children may get U.S. citizenship automatically when you naturalize. For more on the naturalization of children, see chapter 10.

Part 10. Additional Questions

Answer these questions carefully. In order for you to be naturalized, you must be a person of good moral character and you must be attached to (or devoted to) the principles of the United States. Part 10 is designed to help the USCIS determine whether you meet these criteria. If you answer "Yes" to any of the questions, make sure you consult an immigration law expert before you submit your naturalization application. Your "Yes" answer may adversely affect your eligibility for citizenship.

Note: The USCIS sometimes takes the position that if you make a statement that is not true, even if it is meaningless, it is grounds for denying your application for having lied on the application itself.

A. General Questions

- Questions 1, 2, & 3.

    1. **Have you ever claimed to be a U.S. citizen *(in writing or any other way)?***

    2. **Have your ever registered to vote in any Federal, state, or local election in the United States?**

    3. **Have you ever voted in any Federal, state, or local election in the United States?**

These questions are designed to determine whether you ever made a false claim to U.S. citizenship or improperly registered to vote or voted unlawfully in an election. Sometimes people honestly believing that they were U.S. citizens have registered and voted in elections. Even if you answer "Yes" to this question, you still may qualify for naturalization. Sometimes even people who made false claims to U.S. citizenship did not do so in a manner that would make them ineligible for citizenship. An immigration law expert can better advise you.

In some cities, even undocumented immigrants can vote in school board and community elections. If local law allowed you to vote, your having voted won't bar you from naturalizing.

- Question 4.

    4. **Since becoming a Lawful Permanent Resident, have you ever failed to file a required Federal, state, or local tax return?**

If you were required to file a federal return, but failed to do so, your naturalization application will be denied. Many people are not required to file tax returns. For instance, some people don't have to file because their income is less than the amount for which filing is required. Don't be afraid to answer "No" to this question if you earn so little money in a particular year or years that you are not required to file a return.

Usually the USCIS would want to see your tax returns from the last five years (three years if you qualify under the three-year rule for the spouse of a U.S. citizen), or they would want an explanation as to why you didn't file returns. For more information on tax and citizenship, see chapter 8.

- Question 5.

   5. Do you owe any Federal, state, or local taxes that are overdue?

Owing taxes is not an absolute bar to becoming a U.S. citizen. It is a factor that may be taken into consideration by the naturalization examiner.

- Question 6.

   6. Do you have any title of nobility in any foreign country?

A title of nobility is inconsistent with U.S. citizenship. If you hold a title of nobility, you must renounce the title prior to being naturalized.

- Question 7.

   7. Have you ever been declared legally incompetent or been confined to a mental institution within the last 5 years?

This question was designed to help the USCIS decide whether you are capable of understanding the Oath of Allegiance to the United States. In 2000, a law went into effect allowing the USCIS to waive the oath requirement for applicants who are mentally or physically disabled. Answering "Yes" to this question will not bar you from naturalizing.

Still, if you were legally incompetent at the time you became a permanent resident, the USCIS might challenge your permanent resident status. Having been declared legally incompetent or having been confined to a mental institution in the last five years does not mean that you will necessarily be barred from becoming a naturalized U.S. citizen.

- Question 8.

   8a. Have you ever been a member of or associated with any organization, association, fund, foundation, party, club, society, or similar group in the United States or in any other place?

   8b. If you answered "Yes," list the name of each group in the space provided. If you need more space, attach the names of

the other group(s) on a separate sheet of paper.

If the true answer to this question is none, write "None." Otherwise, include the name of the organization as requested. You should include religious, social, and athletic clubs. The examiner is trying to learn whether you are ineligible for naturalization because of certain political activities, such as membership in a communist or pro-communist organization.

- Question 9.

   9. Have you ever been a member of or in any way associated (either *directly* or *indirectly*) with:

   a. The Communist Party?

   b. Any other totalitarian party?

   c. A terrorist organization?

   If you were associated with a communist organization or what the law calls a "totalitarian party," you may not file for naturalization for at least ten years after you left the organization. The USCIS may make an exception if you became a member of the party involuntarily, such as to get a better job, or because of some other economic or physical pressure. The USCIS may naturalize a person who was a member of a communist organization if the person ended their party membership before the age of 16. Terrorists are barred from naturalizing.

- Question 10.

   10. Have you ever advocated (either directly or indirectly) the overthrow of any government by force or violence?

   If you are ineligible under the provision for those who advocated the overthrow of a government, you may still be naturalized under the rules that apply to members of "communist" or "totalitarian" organizations described under question 9 above.

- Question 11.

   11. Have you ever persecuted (either directly or indirectly) any person because of race, religion, national origin, membership in a particular social group, or political opinion?

   A person who has persecuted any person because of race, religion, national origin, membership in a particular social group, or political opinion may not become a naturalized U.S. citizen.

- Question 12.

   12. Between March 23, 1933, and May 8, 1945, did you work for or associate in any way (either directly or indirectly) with:

   a. The Nazi government of Germany?

b. Any government in any area (1) occupied by, (2) allied with, or (3) established with the help of the Nazi government of Germany?

c. Any German, Nazi, or S.S. military unit, paramilitary unit, self-defense unit, vigilante unit, citizen unit, police unit, government agency or office, extermination camp, concentration camp, prisoner of war camp, prison, labor camp, or transit camp?

Former Nazis may not become naturalized U.S. citizens no matter how much time has elapsed since party membership.

C. Continuous Residence

• Questions 13–14.

Since becoming a Lawful Permanent Resident of the United States:

13. Have you ever called yourself a "nonresident" on a Federal, state, or local tax return?

14. Have you ever failed to file a Federal, state, or local tax return because you considered yourself to be a "nonresident"?

If you claimed an exemption from having to pay federal taxes because you do not consider yourself to be a resident of the United States, you may be ineligible for naturalization. The same is true if you did file tax returns as a nonresident. In either case, the USCIS may consider you to have abandoned your residence or interrupted the statutory period of five (or three) years of continuous residence.

D. Good Moral Character

• Questions 15–21.

15. Have you ever committed a crime or offense for which you were NOT arrested?

16. Have you ever been arrested, cited, or detained by any law enforcement officer (including USCIS and military officers) for any reason?

17. Have you ever been charged with committing any crime or offense?

18. Have you ever been convicted of a crime or offense?

19. Have you ever been placed in an alternative sentencing or a rehabilitative program (for example: diversion, deferred prosecution, withheld adjudication, deferred adjudication)?

20. Have you ever received a suspended sentence, been placed on probation, or been paroled?

21. Have you ever been in jail or prison?

If you have committed certain criminal acts, even if you were never convicted of the crime, you may be ineligible to be naturalized. If the act occurred before five years of your interview (three years if you were married to and living with a U.S. citizen), you may still be naturalized in some cases. For a discussion of the naturalization implications of criminal activity, see chapter 8.

The USCIS takes the position that if you are arrested and never charged with a crime or if your record was entirely expunged, you have to answer "Yes" to the relevant questions on this form. The immigration law impact of a criminal act or your being accused of having committed a criminal act is one of the most complicated areas in immigration law. If you have any questions about this matter, see an immigration law expert.

- Question 22.

If you answer "Yes" to any of the subsections of question 22, it's possible that you cannot prove good moral character. The USCIS may deny your naturalization application. However, if the act occurred prior to the five years (three if you are married to and living with a U.S. citizen) you've lived in the United States as a permanent resident, you may still be able to show good moral character.

22. Have you ever:

a. been a habitual drunkard?

A chronic alcoholic is a habitual drunkard. The USCIS examiner may question you about your drinking if you have several arrests for driving while intoxicated (sometimes called "driving under the influence") or you have been charged with disorderly conduct for incidents arising out of alcohol abuse.

b. been a prostitute, or procured anyone for prostitution?

A professional prostitute is not eligible for naturalization. The law defines a professional prostitute as someone who has engaged in prostitution over a period of time. Having been convicted of a single act of prostitution will not necessarily make you ineligible for citizenship. The same is true for a single conviction for soliciting a prostitute.

c. sold or smuggled controlled substances, illegal drugs or narcotics?

Most drug offenses make a person ineligible for naturalization. The only exception is for a person who has been convicted of a single offense of simple possession of 30 grams or less of marijuana. Some drug offenses are only temporary bars to naturalization, but even offenses that bar you temporarily from naturalizing may make you subject to removal proceedings.

d. been married to more than one person at the same time?

This question seeks to identify individuals who practice or advocate polygamy. The USCIS takes the position that even a person who has practiced polygamy in the past is barred from establishing good moral character. Still, if you have practiced polygamy in the past outside the United States and did not come to the United States to practice or advocate polygamy, you might qualify for naturalization. An immigration law expert can help you argue your case.

e. helped anyone enter or try to enter the United States illegally?

You may be barred from naturalization if you smuggled someone into the United States. You need not to have been convicted of a smuggling crime. Even without a conviction, you may be barred. The smuggling provisions of the immigration law that would make you ineligible for citizenship are relatively new. It is unclear whether a person who smuggled a relative into the United States would be barred from naturalizing.

f. gambled illegally or received income from illegal gambling?

This clearly does not apply to a person who is involved in legal gambling activities, such as an employee in a Las Vegas casino. Nor will you be barred from naturalizing simply because you were convicted of a single act of illegal gambling. The bar from naturalization applies to you if gambling activities are a principle source of your income or if you were convicted of two or more gambling offenses during the statutory period of five (or three) years for which you must prove that you had good moral character. Some gambling offenses are considered aggravated felonies and would permanently bar you from establishing good moral character necessary to become a U.S. citizen. And conviction of an aggravated felony would make you removable (deportable) from the United States.

g. failed to support your dependents or to pay alimony?

Failure to support your dependents or to pay alimony shows a lack of good moral character. If you have children who are not living with you or a spouse who is not living with you, be prepared to answer questions as to whether you are required to support them or whether you are doing so. Particularly if you have children who are not living with you, be prepared to establish to satisfaction of the naturalization examiner that you are contributing to the support of your children. If you are not required to support your children, you will need to prove that to the examiner.

23. Have you ever given false or misleading information to any U.S. government official while applying for any immigration

benefit or to prevent deportation, exclusion, or removal?

If you have given false testimony trying to get an immigration benefit, you are barred from establishing good moral character. This bar is not permanent but applies only to the statutory period of five (or three) years for which you must prove good moral character.

24. Have you ever lied to any U.S. government official to gain entry or admission into the United States?

This question simply brings out information that would make you ineligible under the same rules that apply in question 23 above.

E. Removal, Exclusion, and Deportation Proceedings

If you are presently in removal proceedings, the USCIS will put off a decision on your naturalization application until an immigration judge decides your case. If you were ever ordered removed, excluded, or deported from the United States and manage to resolve that problem prior to becoming a permanent resident or after becoming a permanent resident, you may still be eligible to become a U.S. citizen.

F. Military Service

29. Have you ever served in the U.S. Armed Forces?

If you have served in the U.S. armed forces, the USCIS will check your armed services records as part of their investigation into your background and character. You will need to submit USCIS Form G-325B, Biographic Information, with your naturalization application.

30. Have you ever left the United States to avoid being drafted into the U.S. Armed Forces?

Vietnam War era "draft dodgers" may be naturalized because of a pardon granted by former U.S. President Jimmy Carter. The pardon benefits men who left the country to avoid being drafted into the U.S. armed services between August 4, 1964, and March 28, 1973.

31. Have you ever applied for any kind of exemption from military service in the U.S. Armed Forces?

If you were drafted, but claimed an exemption from military service because you are not a U.S. citizen, you may be permanently barred from becoming a U.S. citizen. But if you weren't obligated to serve and you didn't need the exemption, you may naturalize despite your having claimed an exemption. You also may be naturalized if you can show that you didn't knowingly request the waiver or that you didn't understand the consequences of applying for the waiver. Having made a claim for conscientious objector status will not bar you from becoming a U.S. citizen.

32. Have you ever deserted from the U.S. Armed Forces?

Wartime deserters from the military may be ineligible for U.S. citizenship. Some military deserters from the Vietnam War era, between August 4, 1964, and March 28, 1973, may benefit from a pardon granted by former U.S. President Jimmy Carter.

G. Selective Service Registration

33. Are you a male who lived in the United States at any time between your 18th and 26th birthdays in any status except as a lawful nonimmigrant?

If you answered "NO", go on to question 34.

If you answered "YES", provide the information in the space provided.

If you answered "YES", but you did NOT register with the Selective Service System and are still under 26 years of age, you must register before you apply for naturalization, so that you can complete the following information:

Date Registered (Month/Day/Year) _____ Selective Service Number ___/___/___

If you answered "YES", but you did NOT register with the Selective Service and you are now 26 years old or older, attach a statement explaining why you did not register.

It is the USCIS view that failing to register reflects on your moral character and your adherence to the U.S. Constitution. The United States is not presently drafting men or women into the armed forces. Still, U.S. Selective Service laws require that all men register with the Selective Service if they are (1) U.S. citizens, permanent residents, or undocumented immigrants, (2) in the United States, and (3) 18 to 25 years of age.

The registration requirement applies to men only who were born after January 1, 1960. The requirement ends once you reach the age of 26. The registration requirement does not apply to men here on lawful nonimmigrant status, such as with B-2 visitor, F-1 student, or H-1B temporary professional worker visas.

If you are not yet 26 years old, you can register late with the Selective Service. You can get a registration form at your local post office. You can bring proof of your late registration with you to your naturalization interview, and the USCIS examiner may excuse your failure to register.

Some men were unaware of their obligation to register and didn't get a notice to register from either the Selective Service or the INS. If this describes your situation, try submitting an affidavit (a sworn statement) to the USCIS examiner explaining that you didn't willfully and knowingly fail to register. The examiner may approve your application.

If you are found to have knowingly and willfully failed to register, you must wait until you are at least 31, five years after your obligation to register ended, before you can become a U.S. citizen. If you're married to and living with a U.S. citizen, you can be naturalized when you reach the age of 29, three years after your obligation to register ended.

If you did register with the Selective Service but you don't know your registration number, you can get your number by calling or writing to the Selective Service Administration. You can call their machine-operated toll-free number at 888-655-1825. Have your date of birth and social security number ready. To reach a Selective Service representative, call 847-688-6888 or write to the Selective Service at P.O. Box 94636, Palatine, IL 60094-4636. Be sure to include your name, date of birth, and social security number.

H. Oath Requirements (See Part 14 for the text of the oath)

Answer questions 34 through 39. If you answer "No" to any of these questions, attach (1) your written explanation why the answer was "No" and (2) any additional information of documentation that helps to explain your answer.

34. Do you support the Constitution and form of government of the United States?

To be naturalized, you must believe in the U.S. form of government and our Constitution. If you advocate totalitarianism or the overflow of our government, you might be ineligible for naturalization. The law allows no exemption from the requirements that you believe in the U.S. form of government.

35. Do you understand the full Oath of Allegiance to the United States?

This is a new question that has not been asked on previous forms. I assume that the question goes to two issues: (1) to determine if you have the mental capacity to understand the oath and (2) to make sure that at a later time, should you complain that you didn't fully understand the oath, your statement on the form can be used against you.

- Questions 36–39.

  ### 36. Are you willing to take the full Oath of Allegiance to the United States?

  ### 37. If the law requires it, are you willing to bear arms on behalf of the United States?

  ### 38. If the law requires it, are you willing to perform noncombatant services in the U.S. Armed Forces?

  ### 39. If the law requires it, are you willing to perform work of

national importance under civilian direction?

To be naturalized, you must be willing to take an oath of allegiance to the United States. You may omit that part of the oath relating to bearing arms or performing attendance in military service. If you want to omit part of the oath, answer "No" to question 36.

The Oath of Allegiance is printed on USCIS Form N-400. You must agree to be willing to bear arms, perform some form of military service, or do civilian work of national importance. If you meet conscientious objector standards, you can take an abbreviated form of the oath saying that you are willing only to perform civilian service. You must, however, be willing to perform some form of government service.

Part 11. Your Signature

I certify, under penalty of perjury under the laws of the United States of America, that this application, and the evidence submitted with it, are all true and correct. I authorize the release of any information which USCIS needs to determine my eligibility for naturalization.

If you are physically able to write, you must sign here. If you are physically unable to write, the person who helped you complete the form signs Part 12.

Part 12. Signature of Person Who Prepared This Application for You (if applicable)

The law does not require any individual who helps another complete USCIS Form N-400 to sign Part 12. Only if you are physically unable to write must the person who helped you complete the form sign here.

Parts 13–14.

Do Not Complete Parts 13 and 14 Until an USCIS Officer Instructs You To Do So

You will complete these parts at the interview, when instructed by an USCIS officer.

NATURALIZATION PROCEDURES AND TIPS

Filing USCIS Form N-400

You must file your application in the USCIS service center office for the geographic area where you reside. You must have resided in your state for 90 days. Mail your application by certified mail with return receipt requested. You should keep a copy of your proof of filing in a safe place in case the original is lost or destroyed. You may file your application three months before you meet the continuous residence requirement.

File USCIS Form N-400, Application for Naturalization, with an application fee, at the time of this writing, of $260 plus $50 for USCIS fingerprinting, for a total of $310. Applicants age 75 and over need not be

SECTION II: NATURALIZATION AND CITIZENSHIP

fingerprinted. Check the Immigration Answers Web site, www.ilw.com/wernick/, before filing your application to make sure the fee hasn't changed. A copy of the form can be found in Appendix L. Use a personal check or money order to pay the filing fee; that way you'll have proof that the USCIS received your payment.

Fee Waiver Applications

The USCIS will waive the $260 naturalization application filing fee for those who can prove they can't afford to pay it. Unlike most applicants for permanent residence, you can naturalize even if you are receiving public assistance. However, the USCIS may not waive the $50 fingerprinting fee.

If you want a fee waiver, you'll need to prove your inability to pay the fee. Here are some factors that the USCIS will consider:

- Whether you qualified for or received a "federal means-tested public benefit," such as food stamps, Medicaid, Supplemental Security Income, and Temporary Assistance of Needy Families within the last 180 days.

- Whether the income you reported to the Internal Revenue Service (IRS) for the most recent tax year is at or below the poverty level. See Appendix F for recent poverty guidelines.

- Whether you are elderly (age 65 or over) at the time you submit the fee request.

- Whether you are disabled. The disability should have been previously determined by the Social Security Administration (SSA), Health and Human Services (HHS), the Veteran's Administration (VA), the Department of Defense (DOD), or another federal agency.

- Humanitarian or compassionate reasons, either temporary or permanent, that justify granting a fee waiver request. Here, the USCIS gives the examples of applicants who are temporarily destitute; applicants who do not own, possess, or control assets sufficient to pay the fee without causing substantial hardship; or applicants on fixed incomes and confined to a nursing home.

- Any other evidence or factors that establish your inability to pay the required filing fees.

If you are applying for a fee waiver, include a cover sheet with your application with the words **"FEE WAIVER REQUEST INCLUDED"** in red letters.

Photos and Fingerprints

You must also submit two photographs with your application. The photos must be three-quarter profile photos with your right ear showing. Print your name on the back of each, and below your name, write your "A" number—the number on your permanent residence card. You do not submit fingerprints with your application. The USCIS will notify you when to appear at a fingerprinting center.

Name Changes

You can change your name as part of the naturalization process. To change your name, you may have to be sworn in as a U.S. citizen by a federal court. If your naturalization interview goes well, you may choose to be sworn in by the USCIS or by a federal judge or magistrate. In some parts of the country, you can get an USCIS swearing-in faster than the court procedure. The only other difference is that only the court can change your name. If you wish to begin using a name different from the name on your alien card, or a name changed as a result of marriage or divorce, you must request a court swearing-in.

Do You Need a Lawyer in Order to Naturalize?

Most people become citizens without the help of a lawyer. Of course, if you can afford a private lawyer, you may want to hire one to help you. You may just want someone to help you feel comfortable throughout the process. Some naturalization cases are complicated and require the assistance of an immigration law expert. If you cannot afford a lawyer, there are many organizations throughout the United States that help people with naturalization applications for little or no cost. I've provided a list in Appendix M.

Consider consulting with an immigration law expert if you are concerned that the USCIS may discover that you have done something that makes you removable. (See "Risks of the Naturalization Process" in chapter 7.) If you believe that you will have a problem at your interview, you may want an attorney to attend the interview with you.

The USCIS Interview

Sometime after you file your application, you will receive a notice to appear for an interview. At the interview, the USCIS requires that you show that you can read, write, and speak English; the USCIS examiner reviews your application; and you are questioned orally as to your knowledge of the government and politics of the United States. As discussed earlier, some older, longtime resident applicants are not required to read, write, and speak English in order to become U.S. citizens. A waiver of the English language requirement may be available to you if you have a mental or physical defect.

At the start of your interview, the USCIS examiner will ask you to swear that all the information you are about to give is true. After you have taken this oath, the USCIS examiner will go over your application to make sure that your statements there are accurate. The examiner will ask that you present tax returns or that you explain why you didn't need to file the returns.

Witnesses—No Longer Required

Up until 1981, the USCIS required naturalization applicants to bring two character witnesses to the naturalization interview. This is no longer the case. You can bring a witness if you need a witness to help you prove that you are eligible to be naturalized.

After the Interview

If the USCIS approves your naturalization application, the examiner should give you the choice of being sworn in at an USCIS ceremony or taking an oath given by the federal court. The USCIS ceremony is usually faster, but if you want to legally change your name as part of the naturalization process, you must request a court ceremony. At the time of the swearing-in ceremony, you will take the Oath of Allegiance to the United States and become a naturalized citizen.

If the USCIS denies your application because you could not prove the ability to read, write, or speak English, you will get two more chances to try to pass the test without having to pay another fee. You may apply for naturalization as often as you like.

The USCIS examiner usually decides a case at the interview, but not always. The USCIS must decide in 120 days, or you will have the right to file an application with the federal district court to get your case resolved.

Appealing a USCIS Denial of Your Naturalization

If the USCIS denies your application, the USCIS examiner must inform you that you have 30 days to request a hearing before an immigration officer. If you are unsuccessful at that hearing, you may seek a review of the decision in federal court. The court will make an independent decision and can overturn the USCIS decision.

How Children Become U.S. Citizens:

Birth in the United States, Birth Abroad, and Naturalization

You may not know it, but you may already be a U.S. citizen. You may have been born a U.S. citizen either because you were born in the United States or because you were born to a U.S. citizen abroad. Or you may have become a U.S. citizen at the time of one of your parents' naturalization.

BIRTH IN THE UNITED STATES

Unless your parents were foreign diplomats, if you were born in the United States, you are a U.S. citizen. Even if your parents were undocumented immigrants, you are still a U.S. citizen. You are also a U.S. citizen if you were born in Puerto Rico, the U.S. Virgin Islands, Guam, or the Mariana Islands. If you were born in American Samoa or Swain's Island, you are a U.S. national and you are eligible for a U.S. passport. François's story shows how a person can be a U.S. citizen and not even know it.

——————— François's Story ———————

François was 25 years old when he tried to get a visa to leave Haiti for the United States. He loved a young woman, Marcia, who was a U.S. citizen. Marcia had met François while in Haiti on business. When François was fired from his job, he decided to visit Marcia, who had returned to the United States, so he applied for a visitor's visa. The U.S. consular officer denied his application because François could not establish that he had not abandoned his residence in Haiti.

François and Marcia wrote letters to each other regularly, and he was anxious to join her in the United States. Marcia loved François but did not want to marry him until they had spent time together. She was desperate to find a way to get him to America and even considered arranging for a smuggler to bring him in with phony papers. Finally, she visited an immigration lawyer who discussed the many options, including a K-1 fiancé visa. Finally, near the end of the interview with the lawyer, Marcia mentioned that François had been born in the United States but had never bothered filing for citizenship. His parents had been studying at New York University when François was born. He and his family left the United States when he was nine months old. François and Marcia had not known until she talked to the lawyer that his U.S. birth meant he was a U.S. citizen.

Marcia obtained François's birth certificate and sent it to him. He came to the United States the next day, using the birth certificate as proof of his U.S. citizenship.

BIRTH ABROAD TO A U.S. CITIZEN PARENT OR PARENTS

If you were born outside the United States and one of your parents was a U.S. citizen, you may have automatically become a U.S. citizen at birth. A child born abroad today to U.S. parents is a U.S. citizen if one of the following requirements is met:

- Both parents were U.S. citizens, the parents were married, and one parent had resided in the United States.
- The parents were not married and the U.S. citizen mother had been physically present in the United States for at least one year before the child's birth.
- The parents were not married and the U.S. citizen father (1) legitimated the child before the child's 18th birthday or acknowledges paternity in writing under oath, (2) agreed in writing to provide financial support until the child reaches the age of 18 (unless the father is deceased), or (3) had been present in the United States for at least one continuous year before the child's birth.
- The parents were married but only one parent was a U.S. citizen, and the U.S. citizen parent had been physically present in the United States or a U.S. possession for five years prior to the child's birth, at least two of which were after the parent turned 14.

CITIZENSHIP CHARTS FOR CHILDREN BORN ABROAD

The current rules I just described apply to children of U.S. citizens born abroad on or after November 14, 1986. The rules may be different if you were born before November 14, 1986. To help you figure out if you are a U.S. citizen, I've provided charts that outline the citizenship rules which apply to births outside the United States. Which rule applies to you depends on the date of your birth. The charts at the end of this chapter will help you to decide if you became a U.S. citizen at the time of your birth.

Michelle's story gives us an example of how the charts can help us determine whether a child born abroad is a U.S. citizen at birth.

Michelle's Story

Michelle was born in Italy in 1960, and she lived in Italy her entire life, having never been to the United States. Her father, Frank, was a 20-year-old U.S. citizen who had grown up in New York City. He left New York for his first trip abroad when he was 19, going to Italy to study Italian architecture. Michelle's mother was an Italian citizen. Michelle's mother and father were married at the time of her birth. Shortly after Michelle was born, her parents separated and Frank returned to the United States. They divorced two years later.

Michelle is a U.S. citizen. Since she was legitimate at birth, we look to Chart A under the section for children born on or after 12/24/52. We see that a child born abroad to one citizen with five years of prior physical presence in the United States, at least two of which are after age 14 (for births on or after 11/14/86), is a U.S. citizen at birth. Frank had lived more than ten years in the United States, five of those years after age 14.

The chart also shows no retention requirement for Michelle, a child born in 1960. Michelle is a U.S. citizen though she has never set foot in the United States.

If you are a U.S. citizen at birth because you were born abroad and one or both of your parents were U.S. citizens, you don't need to claim your U.S. citizenship by any specific time. If you are a citizen but were not born in the United States, you can apply for a U.S. passport at a post office, passport office, or U.S. consulate. Or you may apply to the USCIS for a certificate of citizenship using USCIS Form N-600, Application for Certificate of Citizenship. Applying for a U.S. passport is usually easier and faster.

DERIVATIVE CITIZENSHIP

If one of your parents is a U.S. citizen, you may be a derivative citizen. Derivative citizenship happens automatically by what we call **operation of law.** That means that if certain acts occur, you get U.S. citizenship, whether you know it or not. You don't fill out an application, it just happens.

On February 27, 2001, a law went into effect that changed the rules for who gets derivative citizenship. The law applies to natural born children and adopted children. It does not apply to stepchildren unless the stepparent legally adopts the child. Under this law, called the Child Citizenship Act of 2001, a child born outside the United States automatically becomes a U.S. citizen when all of the following conditions have been fulfilled:

1. At least one parent of the child is a citizen of the United States,

whether by birth or naturalization.

2. The child is under the age of 18 years.

3. The child is residing in the United States in the legal and physical custody of the citizen parent.

4. The child is a permanent resident, pursuant to a lawful admission for permanent residence.

Note that if the child is born illegitimate, the naturalization of the father will not automatically result in the child gaining derivative citizenship. For a child born illegitimate to acquire derivative citizenship from his or her father, the child must be legitimated under the laws of the country of birth. In some countries, all that is required is the father putting his name on the child's birth certificate. Your consul in the United States may be able to help you with questions about the legitimation rules in your country. If you are relying on legitimation to claim derivative citizenship, the legitimation must take place before the child's 18th birthday.

The order of events makes no difference. If your child is a permanent resident, under 18, and then you naturalize, your child gets automatic citizenship. If you naturalize and then your child gets permanent residence, the child becomes a U.S. citizen the moment he or she becomes a permanent resident, so long as that happens before the child is 18.

The stories of Suki and Yoichi, Carina, and Juanita illustrate derivative naturalization under the new law.

——— *Suki and Yoichi's Story* ———

Suki, Yoichi, and their parents moved to the United States from Japan in 1990 when Suki was 10 and Yoichi was 12. The whole family came to the United States with immigrant visas. In 1997 their father naturalized. Suki became a U.S. citizen upon the naturalization of her parents. She was 17 and a permanent resident when her father naturalized. Suki can get a U.S. passport. To get the passport, she must take her father's naturalization certificate, her parents' marriage certificate, her birth certificate, and her foreign passport showing legal permanent resident entry or a resident alien card to a U.S. passport office. Yoichi had already reached the age of 18 at the time his father was sworn in as a U.S. citizen. To become a U.S. citizen, Yoichi must file his own naturalization application.

——— *Carina's Story* ———

Carina was the child of Jean-Pierre, a French citizen. She was born in France in 1990. Jean-Pierre wasn't married to Carina's mother. When Carina was still an infant, her father came to work in the United States as a chef in a gourmet French restaurant. The restaurant sponsored him for a permanent resident visa. Carina got her permanent residence when her father did because she was a derivative beneficiary of a preference petition. If Jean-Pierre becomes a U.S. citizen before Carina's 18th birthday, Carina will automatically become a U.S. citizen. French law considers children born out of wedlock to be legitimate at birth. Jean-Pierre need not take any action to make Carina a U.S. citizen, other than to be naturalized, before Carina turns 18 years old.

Suppose Jean-Pierre naturalizes when Carina is 17, and the next month Carina returns to France, not knowing that she is a U.S. citizen. She can return to the United States as a U.S. citizen anytime. If she presents her birth certificate identifying Jean-Pierre as her father with a copy of his naturalization certificate to a U.S. consular officer, Carina can get a U.S. passport. The fact that she didn't know she was a U.S. citizen and left the United States so soon after her father's naturalization is irrelevant.

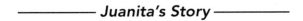

Juanita's Story

Juanita's parents, Juan and Carmen, were living in Venezuela when Juanita was born. They were citizens of Venezuela. When Juanita was four years old, her parents decided to move to the United States and became permanent residents. They left Juanita in Venezuela with her grandmother while they established themselves in the United States. When Juanita was 12 years old, her mother naturalized. When Juanita was 13, her father petitioned for her and she came to the United States as a permanent resident. Since Juanita's mother is a U.S. citizen, upon her entering the United States with an immigrant visa, Juanita automatically got derivative naturalization. She may immediately apply for a U.S. passport.

Children who are automatically naturalized don't have to pass any tests. If you want proof that your child was automatically naturalized, you may get a certificate of citizenship or U.S. passport for your child. To get a certificate of citizenship, file USCIS Form N-600. Getting a U.S. passport is faster, cheaper, and easier.

Children Who Turned 18 Before February 27, 2001

Prior to February 27, 2001, permanent resident children derived citizenship under rules different from those that apply today. Children who turned 18 prior to this date automatically became U.S. citizens only if one of the following conditions is met: (1) a parent naturalized before the child turned 18, (2) the child became a permanent resident before turning 18, or (3) the child was unmarried, and one of the following requirements was met:

- The other parent was or became a U.S. citizen.
- The child was born out of wedlock and the parent naturalized was the mother.
- The child's other parent was deceased.
- The parents were divorced or separated and the parent being naturalized had legal custody of the child following the divorce or separation.

Jerold's story illustrates the pre-February 27, 2001, derivative citizenship rule.

Jerold was ten years old when his mother, Betty Ruth, was naturalized as a U.S. citizen. Jerold and his parents had immigrated to the United States from Poland. They all entered with permanent resident visas. Jerold's father, Ralph, was so busy building his career as an engineer that he didn't bother to apply to be naturalized. Finally, in 2000, when Jerold was 17, his father naturalized. Jerold became a derivative U.S. citizen on the day his father naturalized. He could get proof of U.S. citizenship by applying for a certificate of citizenship using USCIS Form N-600 or by applying for a U.S. passport. Or he could do nothing.

Had Betty Ruth wanted Jerold to become a U.S. citizen before Ralph was naturalized, she could have applied for him to get a certificate of citizenship using USCIS Form N-600. Jerold would have become a U.S. citizen when the USCIS approved the N-600 application. Unlike the case of a derivative citizen, he could not have gotten a U.S. passport until the USCIS approved the N-600. Derivative naturalization is automatic. Citizenship by application by a parent required USCIS approval. Under the current law, the N-600 procedure described in Jerold's case is irrelevant.

Citizenship by Application for Children Born Abroad

Some children born abroad who do not acquire citizenship at birth or who do not acquire derivative citizenship may get U.S. citizenship through an application by a parent. The parent must apply for a certificate of citizenship for the child using USCIS from N-600K. To qualify, one parent must be a U.S. citizen, the child must be legally present in the United States, the child must be under 18, and the child must be in the legal and physical custody of a U.S. citizen parent who has been in the U.S. five years, two of which were after his or her 14th birthday. If the child is adopted, the child must have been adopted prior to age 16 (unless the child was a natural sibling of an adopted child and was adopted while under 18) and must meet all the requirements for an adopted child or orphan. A citizen parent who has not been physically present in the U.S. for five years, two of which were after his/her 14th birthday, may also obtain a certificate for his or her child if the child is under 18, is present in the U.S. pursuant to a lawful admission, and a grandparent (parent of the USC parent) has been physically present in the U.S. for five years, two of which are after the grandparent's 14th birthday.

Chart A

Birth Outside of U.S. to Citizen Parent(s)—Legitimate Births

Date of Birth of Child	Residence Required of Parent(s) to Transmit Citizenship	Residence Required of Child to Retain Citizenship
Before 5/24/34	Either your father or mother is a citizen who resided in the U.S. before birth.	None
On or after 5/24/34 and before 1/13/41	a. Both parents are citizens, one with prior residence. b. One parent is citizen with prior residence.	None
On or after 1/13/41 and before 12/24/52	a. One parent is citizen with 10 years of prior residence in U.S., at least 5 of which were after age 16. (If citizen parent had honorable military service between 12/7/41 and 12/31/46, sufficient if the 5 years were after age 12. If military service was between 12/31/46 and 12/24/52, parent needs 10 years of physical presence, at least 5 yearsof which were after age 14.)	Same as immediately below 2 years continuous presence in U.S. between ages 14 and 28 except no retention requirement if born on or after 10/10/52. (Exception: No retention requirements if citizenparent was employed by certain U.S. organizations at time of birth. This exception does not apply if citizenship is transmitted under military service exemptions in column to the left.)
	b. Both parents are citizens, one with prior residence in U.S.	None
On or after 12/24/52	a. Both parents are citizens, one with prior residence in U.S.	None
	b. One citizen parent with 10 years of prior physical presence in U.S., at least 5 of which were after age14 (for births 12/24/52 to 11/13/86). OR One citizen parent with 5 years of prior physical presence in U.S., at least 2 of which were after age 14 (for births on or after 11/14/86).	None. The retention requirement was abolished effective10/10/78. Persons still citizenson that date have no retentionrequirements.

Chart B
Birth Outside of U.S. to Citizen Parent(s)—Illegitimate Births

Child Not Legitimated

Date of Birth of Child	Requirements for Transmission of Citizenship
Before 12/24/52	Mother was a U.S. citizen who had resided in the U.S. or its outlying possessions before birth of child. A child born after 5/24/34 acquired U.S. citizenship when the Nationality Act of 1940 bestowed citizenship retroactive to date of birth.
On or after 12/24/52	Mother was a U.S. citizen who had been physically present in the U.S. or its outlying possessions for a continuous period of 1 year before birth of child.

Child Legitimated by Alien Father

The general rule is that citizenship acquired by an illegitimate child through its citizen mother is not affected by later legitimation by an alien father. The only exception is that citizenship is not transmitted by a U.S. citizen mother if an illegitimate child is legitimated by an alien father and all three of these conditions are met: (1) the child was born before 5/24/34, (2) the child was legitimated before age 21, and (3) the legitimation was before 1/13/41.

Child Legitimated by U.S. Citizen Father

Legitimation makes a child legitimate at birth. Therefore, the transmission and retention requirements applicable to legitimate children born outside the U.S. (Chart A) apply. In other words, if the child did not acquire citizenship through the mother but was legitimated by a U.S. citizen father under the following conditions, apply the appropriate provisions of Chart A. No legitimation at all is required for children of certain veterans of World War II.

Date of Birth of Child

Before 1/13/41	1. Child legitimated at any time after birth under law of father's domicile.
	2. Father had the required residence at time of child's birth.
	3. No residence required for child to retain U.S. citizenship.
On or after 1/13/41	1. Child legitimated before age 21 under law of father's domicile.and before 12/24/52
	2. Father had the required residence at time of child's birth.
	3. Child complies with residence requirements for retention.
On or after 12/24/52	1. Child legitimated before age 21 under law of father's domicile.
	2. Father had the required residence at time of child's birth.
	3. Child must be unmarried.

Child Legitimated or Acknowledged by U.S. Citizen Father

Child born on or after after 11/15/68 and - relationship established on or after-11/14/86.	1. Child-father blood relationship established.
	2. Father, unless deceased, must provide written statement under oath that he will provide financial support for child until child reaches age 18.
	3. Child must be legitimated under law of child's residence or domicile, or father must acknowledge paternity of child in writing under oath, or paternity must be established by competent court.
	4. Father must have been a U.S. citizen and met the required residence requirements at time of child's birth.
	5. Child must be under age 18 when legitimated or acknowledged. (Child of age 15–18 on 11/14/86 may elect to acquire citizenship under prior law.)

CHAPTER 10: HOW CHILDREN BECOME U.S. CITIZENS

Nonimmigrant Visas

Andrew, cousin Jerry just called. He won't be coming this summer. He didn't get his visitor's visa." Maria was upset that her favorite cousin wouldn't be coming to her son's high school graduation ceremony.

"Did he do what I told him? Did he show the U.S. consul the bank statement, the title to his house, and the letter from his employer?" asked Andrew.

"No, he just attached our invitation to the application. He thought that would be enough. I guess that wasn't enough," Maria said, disappointed.

"Don't worry, Maria," Andrew responded. "Jerry can still get the visa if he does what I told him. He still has enough time to get here for the graduation ceremony, and while he's here, let's talk to him about going back to college. I spoke to the foreign student advisor at State Technical College. Jerry might qualify for a student visa."

Most foreign nationals come to the United States as nonimmigrants. Examples of nonimmigrants are tourists, students, temporary workers, and business visitors. A nonimmigrant visa limits what you, as a nonimmigrant, can do in the United States and, in most cases, it limits the length of your stay.

A nonimmigrant visa is a stamp put in your passport, usually by a U.S. consular officer, that allows you to enter the United States for a nonimmigrant purpose. Nonimmigrant status refers to your legal status while in the United States on a nonimmigrant visa.

In Chapter 11, I provide a list, with a brief explanation, of all nonimmigrant visas. In Chapters 12, 13, 14, 15, and 16, I provide detailed information and practical advice about the most common types of nonimmigrant visas. In Chapter 12, I discuss the B-1/B-2 visitor's visa (and the Visa Waiver Program, which allows some visitors to enter without a visa). I devote Chapter 13 to the F-1 student visa, used by more than 500,000 people every year. In Chapter 14, I explain the H-1B visa for temporary professional workers and the special rules for Canadian and Mexican professionals based on the North American Free Trade Agreement (NAFTA). I expanded Chapter 14 for this edition to include detailed information on how to apply for H-1B status. In Chapter 15, I discuss the K visa for the spouse or fiancé(e) of a U.S. citizen, and in Chapter 16, the new V visa for certain spouses and children of permanent residents.

In Chapter 17, I review general concepts that apply to nonimmigrants coming to the United States. I also provide hints on how to make a successful nonimmigrant visa application, including how to prove nonimmigrant intent.

CHAPTER 11

Types of Nonimmigrant Visas

Here's a list, with short explanations, of all nonimmigrant visas:

A-1 *Ambassador, Public Minister, Career Diplomat, or Consular Officer and Members of Immediate Family*

A-2 *Other Foreign Government Official or Employee and Members of Immediate Family*

A-3 *Attendant, Servant, or Personal Employee of A-1 and A-2 Classes, and Members of Immediate Family*

Applications for A-1, A-2, and A-3 visas are handled on a country-to-country basis through the U.S. Department of State.

B-1 *Temporary Visitor for Business*

B-2 *Temporary Visitor for Pleasure*

B-1 visas are for individuals coming to the United States for business purposes. Examples include setting up a new enterprise, taking orders, or providing other services for a foreign company, or attending a professional conference. A B-1 business visitor cannot receive a salary from a U.S. employer.

B-2 visas are for individuals coming to the United States on vacation, to attend a family event such as a wedding or funeral, and for other noncommercial activities. They also are available to prospective students coming to the United States to investigate colleges or universities for possible future attendance.

The B-1/B-2 visas do not allow you to work for a U.S. employer, but you may be able to change to an employment status. (For more on B-1/B-2 status, see chapter 12.)

C-1 *Continuous Transit*

The C-1 visa is for entry into the United States in transit to another country or, if a crew member, to join a ship. It is for people passing through the United States with a stopover of no more than 29 days.

C-2 *Travel to UN Headquarters*

The C-2 visa is for travel to the United Nations in New York. C-2 visa holders may travel only within the 25-mile radius of Columbus Circle, New York, New York.

D-1 *Crewman's Visa*

The D-1 visa is for crew members landing temporarily in the United States, who will depart on a vessel from the same transportation line.

D-2 *Crewman's Visa*

The D-2 visa is for ship crew members intending to depart on a vessel from a different company than the one used to travel to the United States.

E-1 *Treaty Trader*
E-2 *Treaty Investor*

E-1 and E-2 visa status is based on treaties between the United States and an alien's country of nationality. Not all foreign countries have trader or investor agreements with the United States that qualify their nationals for E-1 or E-2 status. Some countries have either E-1 or E-2 eligibility, but not both.

E-1 treaty status is for managers and essential employees of foreign companies. The company must be engaged in trade with the United States. The trade must represent at least 51 percent of the company's business activities. To get an E-1 visa, the company must be at least half owned by nationals of the treaty country. You, the treaty trader, must be a national of the same treaty country. To get an E-1 visa, you must be entering the United States to serve as a manager or your work must involve skills essential to the company's operations.

E-2 investor status requires an investment by one or more nationals of a treaty investor country. As with the E-1, the U.S. organization must be at least half owned by nationals of the treaty country. The investment cannot be passive (for example, bank accounts or undeveloped land).

An investment that only supports you and your family is considered marginal and will not qualify you for E-2 status. E-2 status is available to the investor to direct and develop the enterprise. It is also available to essential employees of the investor, who will function in a managerial capacity or who have special skills necessary to the development of the investment.

Presently, E-1 treaty trader status is available to nationals of Argentina, Australia, Austria, Belgium, Bolivia, Bosnia-Herzegovina, Brunei, Bulgaria, Canada, Chile, China (Taiwan), Colombia, Costa Rica, Croatia, Denmark, Estonia, Ethiopia, Finland, France, Germany, Greece, Honduras, Iran, Ireland, Israel, Italy, Japan, Jordan, Korea, Latvia, Liberia, Luxembourg, Macedonia, Mexico, the Netherlands, Norway, Oman, Pakistan, Paraguay, the Philippines, Singapore, Spain, Suriname, Sweden, Switzerland, Thailand, Togo, Turkey, and the United Kingdom.

E-2 treaty investor status is available to nationals of Argentina, Australia, Austria, Bangladesh, Belgium, Bosnia-Herzegovina, Bulgaria, Cameroon, Canada, Chile, China (Taiwan), Colombia, Congo (formerly Zaire), Costa Rica, Croatia, Czech Republic, Egypt, Ethiopia, Finland, France, Georgia, Germany, Grenada, Honduras, Iran, Ireland, Italy, Japan, Jordan, Kazakhstan, Korea, Kyrgyzstan, Liberia, Luxembourg, Macedonia, Mexico, Moldova, the Netherlands, Norway, Oman, Pakistan, Panama, Paraguay, the Philippines, Poland, Romania, Senegal, Singapore, Slovakia, Spain, Sri Lanka, Suriname, Sweden, Switzerland, Thailand, Togo, Tunisia, Turkey, and the United Kingdom.

The spouse of an E-1 or E-2 status holder is eligible for USCIS employment authorization.

F-1   *Status for Students*

You can get F-1 status to attend school at any level, from grade school to graduate school. The USCIS must have accredited the school to issue Form I-20, a document you use to prove that the school has accepted you. Under limited circumstances, an F-1 student may work. (For more on F-1 student status, see chapter 13.)

G-1, G-2, G-3, G-4   *Individuals Coming to Work for International Organizations and Their Employees and Families*

G visas allow United Nations (UN) employees, World Bank employees, employees of other international organizations, and members of nongovernmental organizations affiliated with the UN to work in the United States.

H-1A   *Professional Nurses*

H-1A status, which was a category exclusively for licensed nurses, was eliminated September 1, 1995. Nonimmigrant, professional nurses must now meet the qualifications for H-1B, H-1C, or TN status (see the following list).

H-1B *Professional Workers*

H-1B status is for the temporary professional worker. I devote chapter 14 to this popular status. H-1B status allows a specialty worker (defined as a person doing a job for which the employer requires at least a four-year college degree or the equivalent) to live and work in the United States for up to six years straight. Unlike some nonimmigrant categories, to get H-1B status, you need not prove that you have a residence abroad. Nor must you show that it would be hard to find a U.S. worker to do your job.

H-1C *Nurses in Health Professional Shortage Areas (HPSAs)*

H-1C status is available for nurses working in Health Professional Shortage Areas (HPSAs) for a period of three years. This law sunsets (automatically ends) in 2003 but may be extended. Nurses with bachelor's degrees working in jobs that normally require a bachelor's degree in nursing can get H-1B status.

H-2A *Temporary Agricultural Worker*

H-2A is for temporary agricultural workers. The employer must get a certification from the U.S. Department of Labor that no qualified U.S. workers are available and the employee must be paid the prevailing wage.

H-2B *Other Temporary Workers*

This status allows you to work for an employer in a temporary position. Short-term and start-up projects often have positions considered temporary. H-2B status requires proof of the unavailability of lawful U.S. workers. You may get an H-2B visa for a period up to one year at a time with a three-year time limit. Obtaining H-2B status is often very difficult, and it's even more difficult to extend your stay beyond one year. Gregory's story illustrates H-2B status.

—————— *Gregory's Story* ——————

Gregory, from Athens, Greece, is a skilled artisan. He has ten years' experience making marble tabletops with complicated engravings. A U.S. company would like him to come to the United States for one year to help in developing their new line of marble tabletops. The project will involve the making of the tabletops and training American workers. The employer anticipates that within the year, the table production unit of the U.S. company will be on its feet and will no longer need Gregory's services. Gregory's U.S. employer, with the help of a lawyer, advertises the job offer at the prevailing wage in a local paper. The employer learns that no qualified individuals apply for the job that the company would like to offer Gregory. The Department of Labor grants the employer a labor certification valid for one year. The employer files an H-2B petition with the USCIS, and they approve it. The USCIS forwards the approved petition to the U.S. consulate in Athens, where Gregory obtains an H-2B visa valid for one year.

H-3 *Trainee*

H-3 status is available for you to receive income for work in a training program if the training is not available in your home country. H-3 status has a two-year limit. To get an H-3 visa, you need not have a college degree. Your employer may pay you a salary, and the amount may be less than the prevailing wage. You must provide details about the training program, and your employer must prove that you will not be displacing a U.S. worker. Your employer must also show that any productive work that you perform will be secondary to the training you receive.Vanessa's story illustrates the H-3 trainee visa.

────── *Vanessa's Story* ──────

Vanessa, from Venezuela, wants to participate in a two-year training program for account executives in a major international stock brokerage company. The company is based in the United States. Vanessa doesn't have a college degree. The company will pay her $40,000 a year during the training period. Vanessa needs an H-3 visa to participate in the program. To get her H-3 status, Vanessa's employer/trainer must establish that she will participate in an organized training program. The employer/trainer must provide a detailed explanation to the USCIS as to the reading materials required, the subjects that will be considered, and the process for evaluation. It is not enough to say that Vanessa will learn on the job during those two years.

Vanessa's employer will also have to prove that the training she will receive is unavailable in Venezuela and that the primary purpose of Vanessa's employment is training, not creating immediate profits for the company. Since she is learning American stock and commodities training, this should be no problem. In fact, the purpose of the program is to train people for employment in the foreign offices of the U.S. company.

H-4 *Spouse or Dependent of H-1A, H-1B, H-2, or H-3 Workers*

The spouse and dependents of individuals in H status can be in the United States in H-4 status. A person in H-4 status cannot legally work in the United States. But there is nothing to stop an H-4 applicant from getting his or her own H-1, H-2, or H-3 visa. A person in H-4 status can attend school without changing to F-1 status.

I INTERNATIONAL JOURNALIST

To qualify for I visa status a foreign newspaper, magazine, television station or network, or other mass media organization must be employing you. You may remain in the United States for as long as your employment continues, but you can only work for your foreign employer.

J-1 *Exchange Visitor*
J-2 *Spouse and Dependent Children of J-1*

J-1 exchange visitor status is used primarily to bring students, scholars, and researchers to the United States. It is also available to some businesspeople, high school exchange students, college graduates, nannies, and international camp counselors. You get a J-1 visa by participation in a program administered through the United States Information Agency (USIA) of the Department of State.

J-1 exchange visitors commonly receive financial support from the U.S. government, from their own government, or from the college or university they attend in the United States. Some, but not all, J-1 exchange visitors are subject to a two-year home residence requirement. Compliance with this requirement means returning to your home country for two years after the J-1 visa expires. If you are subject to the requirement, you cannot change status to temporary worker or permanent resident until you have satisfied the requirement or you have gotten a waiver of the requirement. If you are subject to this requirement, you must comply with the condition or get a waiver of the requirement in order to change status to H-1B temporary professional worker, H-2 temporary worker, H-3 trainee, L-1 intracompany transferee, F-1 student, or permanent resident. Waivers are often difficult to obtain.

Not every J-1 exchange visitor is subject to the two-year requirement. You are subject to the two-year foreign residence requirement only if:

- Your participation in the program was funded in whole or part, directly or indirectly, by a U.S. government agency or an agency of your home country.
- An agency of the government of your home country says that they need the skills you developed as an exchange visitor.
- You are a foreign medical graduate.

For you to qualify for J-1 status, a J-1 program must accept you. The program sponsor then issues Form DS-2019 (formerly) IAP-66 confirming your acceptance. You present the DS-2019 to a U.S. consular officer abroad to get the J-1 visa. As a prospective J-1, you can sometimes get a B-2 visitor's visa to come to the United States. To get a J-1 visa, you must have a residence abroad that you do not intend to abandon.

Your spouse and unmarried minor children may accompany you to the United States and may remain with you while you are in lawful J-1 status. Unlike the F-2 dependent or the F-1 student, J-2 dependent spouses may get USCIS work authorization. They must show that they are working to meet the financial needs of themselves and/or their children and not to support the J-1 visa holder.

K-1 *Fiancé or Fiancée Visa*

K-2 *Minor Unmarried Children of K-1 Visa Holders*

K-3 *Spouse of a U.S. Citizen*

K-4 *Minor Unmarried Children of K-3 Visa Holders*

K visas are available for a fiancé(e) or spouse of a U.S. citizen and for the unmarried children under age 21 of the fiancé(e) or spouse. You can usually get a K visa more quickly than an immigrant visa. For more on K visas, see chapter 15.

L-1 *Intracompany Transferee*

L-2 *Spouse and Dependents of L-1*

To qualify as an L-1 transferee, you must have been employed abroad as an executive, as a manager, or in a position requiring specialized knowledge. You must have been employed in that capacity for one continuous year out of the three years prior to your being transferred to the United States. The required period of one year of continuous employment is reduced to six months in some cases where the employer has filed a blanket L-1 petition.

The work you will do in the United States must be for the same company or an affiliate or a subsidiary of that company. The USCIS approves L-1 status for initially up to three years, one year if you are coming to work in an office that is new or has been open for less than one year. You can then apply for extensions of up to two-year intervals for a total of seven years as a manager or an executive but only five years in a position that requires specialized knowledge.

The spouse of an L-1 status holder may apply for USCIS employment authorization.

M-1 *Technical or Vocational School Student*

M-2 *Spouse and Dependents of M-1*

You may get M-1 status to attend schools offering technical or vocational education. Programs include such subjects as auto mechanics, paralegal studies, secretarial skills, beauty and cosmetics, keyboard operation, and computer programming.

M-1 students are barred from changing to F-1 status while in the United States and can only change to H-1B status if the student did not get the qualifying education through M-1 status. An M-1 student who wants to become an F-1 student has to leave the country and apply for an F-1 visa at a U.S. consulate abroad.

M-1 students may sometimes work, but the options are very limited. Your foreign student advisor can advise you about your work options.

N-1 *The Parent of Certain Unmarried Minors Who Are Special Immigrants*

N-2 *The Unmarried Minor Child of an N-1 and the Unmarried Minor Child of Certain Special Immigrants*

Certain G-1 nonimmigrants qualify for permanent residence as Special Immigrants. If you are under 21 and you get permanent residence as a G-1 special immigrant, you can bring your parents here as N-1 nonimmigrants until you reach the age of 21. If you are a G-1 special immigrant, you may also bring your unmarried children under the age of 21 to the United States as N-1 nonimmigrants. Finally, if you bring your parents here as N-1 nonimmigrants, they may bring with them their unmarried children under 21. The N visa is available to the parents of G-1 special immigrants, where the N nonimmigrant is under 21, and to the children and parents of N visa holders.

NATO-1 THROUGH NATO-7

NATO visas are for people coming to the United States under the NATO treaty and their dependents and personal employees.

O-1 *Individuals of Extraordinary Ability*

O-2 *Spouse and Dependents of O-1*

The O-visa category is for individuals with extraordinary ability in the sciences, the arts, education, business, or athletics, shown by sustained national or international acclaim. You can get an O-visa even if you are not extraordinary, if you accompany an O individual to the United States to help in an artistic or athletic performance. You must be an integral part of the performance and have critical skills and experience that others cannot perform.

P-1 *Internationally Recognized Athletes and Group Entertainers*

P-2 *Entertainers Coming Through an Exchange Program*

P-3 *Artists and Entertainers Coming to Give Culturally Unique Group Performances*

P-4 *Spouse and Dependents of P-1, P-2, and P-3 Visa Holders*

The P-1 visa category allows you to enter the United States to perform as an athlete at an internationally recognized level of performance. You can also get a P-1 visa as part of an entertainment group recognized internationally as outstanding in the field. You, as an individual, need not be internationally recognized if your team or group is.

P-2 status is to come to the United States to participate in an international cultural exchange. P-3 status allows you to come here to give a culturally unique performance. For P-2 and P-3 status, you and your group need not be internationally recognized as outstanding in your field.

Admission in P status can be for an initial period of up to five years with an extension for up to five years.

Q-1 *Cultural Exchange Visitors*

Q-2 *Spouse and Dependent Children of Q-1 Exchange Visitors*

The Q-1 visa allows you to come to the United States for up to 15 months to participate in an international cultural exchange program.

The USCIS must approve the program. The program's purpose, and your purpose in coming to the United States as a Q exchange visitor, must be to help the U.S. public learn about foreign cultures. You may be paid for work you do in Q status.

Q(ii) *Irish Peace Process Cultural and Training Program*

In late 1998, Congress added this new visa category for nonimmigrants from Northern Ireland and surrounding counties. The law allows 4,000 visas to be issued per year for each of three years. To qualify, you must be 35 years old or younger (you can bring your spouse and dependent children with you). The visas are for the purpose of providing practical training, employment, and the experience of coexistence and conflict resolution in a diverse society. For each visa issued under this program, there will be one less visa issued for H-2B temporary nonimmigrant workers. That category has an annual ceiling of 66,000.

R-1 *Status for Religious Workers*

R-2 *Spouse and Dependent Children of R-1 Religious Workers*

You can get an R visa if you are coming to the United States to do religious work as a minister, a professional religious worker, or a person in a religious vocation or occupation such as a liturgical worker, cantor, or missionary. To qualify for an R visa, you must have been a member of the religious denomination making the application for at least two years immediately preceding the application for admission. In addition, you must show that you are qualified in the religious occupation or vocation. The initial period granted to an R worker is for a maximum of three years. You can apply for an additional two years.

S-1 *Criminal Informants*

S-2 *Informants on Terrorism*

Every year, the USCIS may admit up to 200 people to help in criminal prosecution and 50 more to provide information on terrorist activities. The spouse and children of S nonimmigrants can also come to the United States as S nonimmigrants. Some S nonimmigrants qualify to become permanent residents.

T *Victims of Trafficking*

Victims of international smuggling.

TN *NAFTA Professionals*

The TN visa is available to Canadian and Mexican nationals coming to the United States in order to do professional work. (For more on the TN visa, see chapter 14.)

U-1 *Victim of Criminal Activity*

U-2 *Spouse, Child, or Parent of a U-1*

Victims of physical or mental abuse and their families may qualify for a U visa. An applicant must file a petition with the USCIS and prove that he or she has suffered substantial physical or mental abuse as a result of having been a victim of any one of a list of 26 criminal activities. The list includes rape, torture, domestic abuse, and enslavement prostitution.

V   *Spouses and Minor Children of Permanent Residents*

The V visa allows certain spouses and children of legal permanent residents to come to the United States while waiting to get permanent residence. I discuss the V visa in detail in chapter 16.

CHAPTER 12

Visitor for Business
or Pleasure
and the B-1/B-2
Visa Waiver Program

Every year, millions of people come to the United States to visit or do business. Tourists and others coming for personal reasons need B-2 visas. Business visitors use B-1 visas. Often a visitor's visa will be noted as B-1/B-2, which means you can use it for either business or personal visits.

In this chapter, I explain who is eligible to visit the United States and provide practical hints for getting a visitor's visa. Citizens of some countries can visit the United States without a visa under the Visa Waiver Program, and I also explain this program. Canadians may also visit without first obtaining a visitor's visa.

B-1 VISITOR FOR BUSINESS

You qualify for a B-1 visa if you are coming to do business in the United States, but you will not be employed by a U.S. company. Examples of situations where you may qualify for a B-1 visa are:

- You are a representative of a foreign company coming to the United States to take sales orders.
- You are coming to organize trade for a foreign company.
- You are coming to the United States to investigate investment possibilities.
- You are coming to the United States to speak at a conference and you are receiving only expenses rather than a salary.

- You are an athlete coming to the United States to participate in athletic events where your only earnings will be either because of success in those events (such as prize money in a prize fight or golf tournament) or for endorsement activities (such as a tennis player receiving money for a shoe contract).
- You are coming to negotiate a contract for a foreign company.
- You are coming because you are involved in a legal proceeding.
- You are coming to do independent research.
- You are coming to engage in academic activity and you are receiving an honorarium. The activity may not last more than nine days at a single academic USCIS institution. The activity must be sponsored by a USCIS institution of higher education or affiliated nonprofit entity or a nonprofit or governmental research organization. You may not accept honoraria from more than five USCIS institutions or organizations within a six-month period.

To get a B-1 visa, you must provide evidence of the purpose of your trip to a U.S. consular officer. You should be able to explain your goals and your plan of activities while in the United States. The more specific you can be, the better. You should have enough personal financial resources or support from your company so that you won't have to work for a U.S. company to support yourself while in the United States. To get a B-1 visa, you must have a residence abroad that you have not abandoned. Consular officers may ask you to provide evidence of your ties to your country. For example, bring with you a letter from your school or employer or proof that you own a business.

Normally, when you enter the United States on a B-1 visa, you will be admitted for 90 days. The USCIS may grant you an extension of your stay if you can establish a need. Or, if you have proof as to why you will need to be in the United States on business for more than 90 days, you can ask the USCIS inspector at your port of entry to admit you for a longer period. Virginia's and Jorge's stories provide examples of legitimate B-1 activities.

—————— *Virginia's Story* ——————

Virginia owns a small shoe manufacturing company in Bogota, Colombia. She recently developed a new shoe line and wants to present her company's new designs to wholesalers and retailers in the United States. When she applies for her B-1 visa, she takes a copy of her company's incorporation papers, a letter from her bank showing the resources of the company, and a list of her appointments in the United States. Virginia has no problem getting a B-1 visa.

—————— *Jorge's Story* ——————

Jorge, from Mexico, has a Ph.D. in biology. He is a world-renowned expert on infectious diseases. He recently developed a new test to determine if a person is HIV positive. He has been invited to be the keynote speaker at a three-day national health conference in Philadelphia, Pennsylvania. His out-of-pocket expenses are covered by the conference planning committee; they are giving him a $2,000 honorarium. Jorge can prove to the consular officer who interviewed him that if someone hired him to work three days in the United States, his fee would be thousands of dollars more than the honorarium. Jorge qualifies for a B-1 visa. If Jorge wanted to work temporarily in the United States for a U.S. company, he could get an H-1B visa (see chapter 14 for more on H-1B status).

B-2 TEMPORARY VISITOR FOR PLEASURE

A B-2 visa allows you to come to the United States for personal reasons other than work or study. Examples are:

- You are coming as a tourist.
- You are coming for medical treatment.
- You are coming to attend a funeral.
- You are coming to attend a wedding, graduation, baptism, or bar mitzvah.
- You are coming to visit friends or relatives.

To get a B-2 visa, you must have a residence abroad that you have not abandoned. This is often difficult to prove if you are a resident of a developing country. U.S. consular officers in developing countries often suspect that an individual seeking a B-2 visa would like to stay and work in the United States. If you believe that a consular officer may be suspicious about your intentions, you should plan to show that you have reasons to want to go home at the end of your visit to the United States. You should document your ties to your country. Examples are a letter from your employer if you are working, a letter from your school if you are studying, proof of family ties, and proof of any property you hold.

A consular officer is likely to be more sympathetic if you can show that you are coming for a specific event such as a wedding or college graduation. You should be prepared to explain in detail what you will be doing in the United States, whom you will be staying with, and how you will pay for your trip. It is better if you have a round-trip ticket.

With a B-2 visa, the USCIS usually admits you to the United States for six months. You may apply for extensions after that. It is unusual for the USCIS to give a B-2 visa holder more than one six-month extension. Joyce's story gives us an example of how to get a B-2 visa.

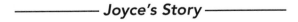
——————— *Joyce's Story* ———————

Joyce, from Jamaica, wants to visit New York. During the visit, she would like to attend her sister's wedding. She also wants to visit several colleges to see if studying in New York is best for her. She explains all of this to the consular officer, who then denies her application. The officer is sure that Joyce will not come back to Jamaica if she gives her a B-2 visitor's visa.

Joyce returns to the U.S. consulate the next week with an old passport showing that she has been to the United States several times and each time returned within the time allowed by the USCIS. She also brings a letter from her high school showing that she only has to complete one more semester to get her diploma. Finally, she presents an invitation to her sister's wedding three months away, where they list her as a bridesmaid. This time Joyce convinces the consular officer that she will return after her visit, and the officer grants her a B-2 visa.

VISA WAIVER PROGRAM

Under the Visa Waiver Program (VWP), the citizens of some countries don't need B-1 or B-2 visas to visit the United States for business or pleasure. These countries are Andorra, Australia, Austria, Belgium, Brunei, Denmark, Finland, France, Germany, Iceland, Ireland, Italy, Japan, Liechtenstein, Luxembourg, Monaco, the Netherlands, New Zealand, Norway, Portugal, San Marino, Singapore, Slovenia, Spain, Sweden, Switzerland, and the United Kingdom. If you come from one of these countries, you can enter the United States without a B-1 or B-2 visa and remain here for no longer than 90 days. The Department of State puts countries on the list for the VWP after it's been established that their citizens are rarely refused visitors' visas at U.S. consulates. Canadians may also enter without a visa for a 90-day visit.

If you enter the United States under the VWP, you cannot extend your stay past 90 days except in very unusual circumstances, and you cannot change to another nonimmigrant status while in the United States. And VWP entrants who overstay or otherwise violate their status cannot reenter under the VWP. To reenter as a visitor, the USCIS says you'll need a B-1 or B-2 visa.

Occasionally countries are added or deleted from the VWP list. Check the Immigration Answers Web site at www.ilw.com for updated information.

CHAPTER 13

F-1 Student Status

To get an F-1 student visa, a school, college, or university that has been accredited by the USCIS to admit foreign students must accept you. Though it is far less common, you can also get an F-1 visa to attend a grammar school, junior high, or high school. You must show that you have enough money or financial support to study in the United States without working, and you must prove that you do not intend to immigrate to the United States.

THE STUDENT AND EXCHANGE VISITOR INFORMATION SYSTEM (SEVIS)

In response to the events of September 11, 2001, the USCIS implemented regulations to better monitor international students in the United States. Those regulations included an internet-based tracking system, the Student and Exchange Visitor Information System (SEVIS). SEVIS regulations require schools to regularly report to the USCIS changes in a student's academic standing, address, and immigration student status. Both the USCIS and U.S. consulates abroad have access to your SEVIS information. Among other things, your FSA must now report to the USCIS the following information:

- Start date of the student's next term or session
- Student's failure to enroll
- Student dropping below a full course of study without prior

authorization by the DSO

- Any failure to maintain status or complete the program
- Change of the student's or dependent's legal name or U.S. address
- Any disciplinary action taken by the school against the student as a result of the student being convicted of a crime
- Date of the student's enrollment in an approved institution or exchange program
- Student's degree program and field of study
- Student's graduation prior to the program end date listed on the Form I-20
- Within 21 days of a change in the name, U.S. address or curriculum of a school, an FSA must update SEVIS with the current information
- Within 30 days, the FSA must report the failure of the student or exchange visitor to enroll or commence study
- Date of the termination of enrollment and the reason for termination

You can see that the SEVIS monitoring requirements and the other new regulations necessitate a higher degree of understanding and compliance by international students.

ACCEPTANCE BY A SCHOOL, COLLEGE, OR UNIVERSITY

As a prospective student, you must meet the standards set by the institution for the admission of international students. Some schools are easy to get into. For others, particularly prestigious universities, it's much harder. You should call or write to any school that you are interested in attending, read their catalog, and follow their application procedures carefully.

Many schools require a foreign student to take the Test of English as a Foreign Language (TOEFL) as part of the application process. The school usually waives the test if the student is from a country where most residents speak English. For example, a school won't require the test of students from Australia and Great Britain, but they may require it of students from India or Kenya. Schools that offer classes in the student's own language or that offer classes in English as a Second Language (ESL) do not usually require the TOEFL.

Form I-20

Once a school accepts you for admission and evaluates your ability to pay for your education, the schools FSA issue you Form I-20, Certificate of Eligibility for Nonimmigrant F-1 Student Status. Before issuing Form I-20 to you, the school must make sure that you have sufficient financial resources to study full-time without working illegally.

Evidence of Financial Support

An F-1 student can only work in the United States under limited circumstances (see "Working While Studying for the F-1 Student" below).

So to get an F-1 visa, you must show that you can support yourself, paying for both your tuition and living expenses. You'll present evidence that you can pay your education first to your school. The money can be from your own funds or those of close family members. Since living and studying in the United States can be expensive, an important part of applying for F-1 status is providing evidence of financial support.

Your Form I-20 will note the estimated cost of one year's study at the school. If you apply for F-1 status, you must show that you have the money to pay the cost of your first year of study in the United States. You must also have dependable financial resources for the rest of the educational program. You can show proof of financial capability in several ways.

One way of proving the ability to pay for your education and living expenses is through an Affidavit of Support. Someone in your immediate family, like a parent, brother, or sister, usually completes the Affidavit of Support. It should be dated less than six months from the date of submission.

Besides the Affidavit of Support, you will need letters from a bank, tax records, or other evidence confirming the financial resources of whoever signs your Affidavit of Support. You may present an Affidavit of Support from someone other than a member of your immediate family, but it's often not very helpful.

If you have the personal resources to pay for your own education, you don't need an Affidavit of Support. However, you'll need to show that you can maintain yourself throughout your course of study. You must present evidence of bank accounts, a trust, or similar income.

If a distant relative or friend will be supporting you, it's best for that person to put the money directly into your personal bank account because an Affidavit of Support may not be enough to convince a consular officer. Any factors that will reduce your expenses, such as free room and board, should also be presented in order to establish your ability to support yourself without working.

Martin's and Yoshi's stories provide examples of how to prove you can support yourself as a college student.

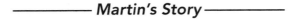

——————— Martin's Story ———————

Martin, from Ireland, wants to study in the United States. A very prestigious public university in Texas with reasonable tuition fees has accepted him. Despite the relatively low cost for tuition, Martin's family will have great difficulty showing that they can support him without his having to work. The college figures room and board to be $7,000 per student, and tuition for nonresidents of the state is $8,000, for a total of $15,000 a year.

Although Martin's father has a good job as an engineer, $15,000 per year is just a little bit more than the family in Ireland can afford. Martin is fortunate, however. His older sister lives in the same city where the university is and has offered to let Martin stay with her throughout his college years. Martin will have his own room and free meals. Also, Martin's sister will be giving him $50 per week for transportation and entertainment expenses. The only expenses that Martin's father in Ireland must pay are his tuition fees, clothing, and books. By submitting an affidavit (a sworn statement) from Martin's sister, combined with an affidavit from his father (supported by his father's income tax records and a letter from his father's bank), Martin can establish enough financial stability to get the university to issue a Form I-20. Martin submits the documentation, and a U.S. consular officer grants him an F-1 student visa.

Yoshi's Story

Yoshi, from Tokyo, has just received his bachelor's degree in political science at the University of Tokyo. A private university in San Francisco, California, has accepted him to study in a doctoral program. The university has established that living expenses for a student are $9,000 per year and that tuition is $15,000 per year, for a total of $24,000. Neither Yoshi nor his family has anywhere near the money necessary to pay for Yoshi's education. However, Yoshi is able to acquire an F-1 visa by obtaining a letter from the college giving him a full tuition grant. To get the grant, he must teach one class per semester (see "Evidence of Financial Support" on page 155). He will also receive a scholarship to cover his living expenses. Thus, although Yoshi doesn't have much money, he will not be required to work except on campus teaching for the university.

Spouses and Children of F-1 Students

As an F-1 student, your spouse and dependent children can get a derivative status known as F-2. Your family can apply when you apply for F-1 status or at a later time. If your family members apply for their visas on a different day than you do, they will need their own Form I-20. And, they must show the additional amount of expense needed to support themselves. They'll need to supply the USCIS with strong proof of substantial resources, because your family members are not entitled to work in the United States in F-2 status.

In many developing countries, obtaining F-2 visas is very difficult for the wife and children of an F-1 student. The U.S. consul often believes that if the family of the student accompanies the student to the United States, the student will have no reason to return home.

An F-2 spouse or child may only attend college to take occasional courses for recreational or avocational purposes. F-2 children may attend school from kindergarten to grade twelve.

Working While Studying for the F-1 Student

Many foreign students wish to work to gain experience, interact with U.S. businesses, and supplement family support. Sometimes you need extra funds due to changed financial need, like having a baby. Although you had to show that you could support yourself without working to obtain an F-1 visa, the USCIS provides several possibilities for employment while in F-1 status.

On-Campus Employment

As an F-1 student, you may work up to 20 hours a week while school is in session and full-time during vacations and recess periods. You must intend to register for the next term.

On-campus employment means employment on the premises of the school or at an affiliated off-site location. It means employment on campus of a type normally performed by students. Examples are work in the school library, cafeteria, or student store, or employment that is part of a student's scholarship, fellowship, or assistantship. With off-campus locations for on-campus employment, the place of employment must be associated or educationally affiliated with the school's established curriculum. Or it must be related to contractually funded research projects at the postgraduate level.

On-campus employers usually know that as an F-1 student, you hold a valid Form I-20 that allows you to work up to 20 hours a week. Sometimes you'll need a letter from your foreign student advisor in order to prove that the advisor has authorized you to work on campus. The authorization letter from the foreign student advisor will help you to get a social security card. Students who accept on-campus employment are exempt from having to obtain an Employment Authorization Document (EAD) from the USCIS.

Off-Campus Co-Op Programs and Internships

Co-op (cooperative) training programs and internships are called curricular practical training by the USCIS. You can get curricular practical training only by participating in a work-study program that is a part of a degree requirement or regular course of study. You cannot qualify for curricular practical training until you have been enrolled in the school for at least nine months. The USCIS rules provide an exception to the nine-month rule if you are enrolled in graduate studies that require immediate participation in curricular practical training.

Your foreign student advisor must give you permission to engage in curricular practical training.

Pre-Completion Practical Training

You can work off campus in a field related to your studies if you work no more than 20 hours a week while school is in session. You can work full-time during vacations and recess periods so long as you intend to register for the next term. Time spent in pre-completion practical training will be deducted from the 12 months of full-time employment available for post-completion practical training (see "Post-Completion Practical Training," below).

For example, if you work 20 hours per week for 6 months, you would have 3 months deducted from the 12 months allowed you for post-completion practical training.

Permission for pre-completion practical training requires only that your foreign student advisor certify, by signing Form I-538, that the employment is directly related to your major area of study and consistent with your educational level.

Employment Authorization Based on Severe Economic Hardship

Where unforeseen circumstances lead to a change in your economic situation, you can obtain permission to work off campus in any job of your choosing. You can work 20 hours per week while school is in session and full-time during vacation periods. Examples of a change in circumstances include the loss of your financial aid or on-campus employment through no fault of your own, an unexpected increase in your cost of living or tuition, large medical expenses, a decrease in the value of currency from your country, or an economic loss affecting your sponsor. Employment based on economic necessity is not deducted from time allowed for post-completion practical training. To qualify, you must have completed one academic year in F-1 status and be in good academic standing.

———— *Yoshi's Story Continues* ————

After Yoshi's first year of graduate studies, an economic crisis at the university resulted in his losing his scholarship. They also cut back his on-campus teaching.

To prove his new financial need, Yoshi got a letter from the university's financial aid officer explaining about the loss of the scholarship. He also got a letter from the dean of faculty as to the loss of part of his teaching income. He submitted these letters to the USCIS with an affidavit regarding his financial situation and Form I-538, which had been certified by his foreign student advisor. The USCIS granted him employment authorization to work off campus, part-time. Yoshi got a job as an international commodities trader and became rich overnight.

Post-Completion Practical Training

F-1 students are entitled to up to 12 months of post-completion practical training. However, as explained above, if you have received 12 months or more of full-time curricular practical training, you are ineligible for post-completion practical training. Time spent in pre-completion practical training also is deducted from the 12-month maximum.

You must complete your 12 months of post-completion practical training within a 14-month period following the completion of your studies. You get 12 months of practical training for each higher degree you obtain. That includes separate 12-month periods for Associate, Bachelor, Masters, and other graduate degrees.

———— Martin's Story Continues ————

Martin successfully completed his studies for a bachelor's degree in political science. He then obtained permission to engage in post-completion practical training and applied to the USCIS for an Employment Authorization Document (EAD). He had no offer of employment when he received the EAD, but the EAD was valid for 14 months. It took six months for Martin to find a job teaching American history at a community college. While his studies were in political science, teaching American history is close enough to his area of study to qualify as practical training. Martin can teach for eight months (fourteen months minus six months) in F-1 status as a practical trainee. If he wants to continue to work beyond those eight months, he must change to another status, such as H-1B temporary worker or permanent resident.

Changing to F-1 Status/Getting an F-1 Visa

Once your school's FSA issues you USCIS form I-20, your next step is to apply for F-1 status. If you entered the United States with a nonimmigrant visa and you are still in legal status, you may apply for a change from your current status to F-1 status. You do this by filing USCIS form I-539, Application to Extend/Change Nonimmigrant Status. You MAY NOT attend college in B-1/B-2 visitor status or F-2 dependent status while waiting for the USCIS to consider your change to F-1 status. This rule applies only to B-1/B-2 visitors and F-2 dependents. Other lawful nonimmigrants may attend school while waiting to hear on a change of status application. You must wait until the USCIS approves your change of status before attending school. H-1B, G and other nonimmigrants will not be penalized for beginning classes before getting approved to change to F-1 status.

Sometimes it is difficult for a B-1/B-2 visitor to change to F-1 student status. If you apply within 60 days from the time you arrive in the United States, the USCIS may think that you hid your plans to study in the United States, or might be trying to avoid the possible difficulties of applying for a student visa at the U.S. consulate in your home country. Wherever you apply, it is wise to include with the application for a change of status to F-1 student status, an explanation, in the form of an affidavit, as to why the change is sought and why no F-1 visa application was made in your home country. The affidavit should also explain why you are seeking to study in the U.S. If your desire to study developed after you entered the United States, explain how that happened. If you have concrete plans about how your education will benefit you when return to your home country, mention that as well.

You should NOT have a problem changing from B-1/B-2 status to student status if, at the time you got your B-1/B-2 visa or at the time you entered the United States, a government official noted "intending student" or similar language on your passport or I-94 Arrival/Departure form.

You must submit your change of status application before your visitors' status expires, unless you have a particularly good reason why you couldn't do that. For more on changing status, see Chapter 17.

TRAVEL ABROAD

With security tight at all U.S. ports of entry, you need to take particular care when traveling abroad. Before you leave, check with your FSA to make sure you have (or will be able to get) all the documents you will need to be readmitted to the United States. These documents include:

1. Valid SEVIS Form I-20 with a signature from your international student advisor. The document must have been issued no more than six months earlier than the time you will return to the United States.

2. Passport valid for at least six months beyond the anticipated return date.

3. Unexpired F-1 visa stamp in your passport. Note that Canadians do not need a visa to enter the United States. In some circumstances, discussed below, you may travel to Canada, Mexico, and islands adjacent to the United States for up to 30 days even if your visa has expired.

4. Evidence of financial support. See "Proving You can support Yourself Without Working" above.

5. Proof that you are enrolled at your college. An official transcript or letter from your international student advisor.

If Your F-1 Visa Stamp Has Expired

If your F-1 visa stamp has expired, to return to the United States after travel abroad, you'll need a new visa stamp in your passport. While U.S. consuls usually grant new visas to students who have maintained status, there is no guarantee. If a U.S. consular officer refuses to issue you a new visa, you may get stuck abroad. **IF YOUR VISA HAS EXPIRED DO NOT TRAVEL ABROAD WITHOUT FIRST SPEAKING TO YOUR INTERNATIONAL STUDENT ADVISOR.**

If on your form I-94, Arrival/Departure, the USCIS has granted you the right to be in the United States for Duration of Status, usually indicated by D/S or, until the date on your form I-94 has not expired, you may travel to Canada, Mexico, and islands adjacent to the United States for up to 30 days. However, if you apply for a new visa while aborad and a U.S. consul denies your visa application, you MAY NOT reenter the United States using your unexpired I-94.

CHAPTER 14

H-1B, H-1B1 and TN Status
for Temporary
Professional Workers

In this chapter, I discuss H-1B status, H-1B1, and TN status. H-1B, H-1B1 and TN status are available to temporary workers in professional positions. H-1B1 status is for nationals of Chile and Signapore. TN status is available only to Canadians and Mexicans under the NAFTA treaty. Unlike most permanent employment visas, you can get H-1B or TN status even if many U.S. workers can do the job. In part I of this chapter, I explain the rules that apply to H-1B status. In part II, I provide detailed procedural information on getting H-1B status.

PART I: RULES FOR H-1B STATUS

You can get H-1B status if you have a four-year college degree or the equivalent in education and experience. You may have obtained your education and experience either here or abroad. If the job has a license requirement, you must have that license, unless the only bar to getting a license is getting a social security card.

If you have been in the United States illegally, you still might get H-1B status, although you may have to leave the country and get a visa before you can work here. You can even get H-1B status if you have started a permanent residence case, a rule that makes the H-1B different from many nonimmigrant classifications.

You can't petition for yourself for H-1B status; your employer must petition for you. The employer must offer you a position where your degree is necessary to do the job. An H-1B employer can be an individual, a partnership, or a corporation. Even if you are the sole owner of a corporation, that corporation may petition for you.

To get H-1B status, your employer must pay you the prevailing wage for the position or the wage paid to workers in similar positions in the company (called the **actual wage**), whichever is greater. Employers must also offer H-1B workers the same benefits they offer other workers. These benefits include health, life, disability, and other insurance plans, retirement and savings plans, bonuses, and stock options.

The USCIS will approve an H-1B petition in intervals of up to three years at a time, up to a maximum of six years. Then, in limited circumstances (discussed later), the USCIS may extend your H-1B status beyond six years in one-year intervals.

TN status allows Canadian professionals to work here without the employer first getting a petition approved by the USCIS. Mexican nationals need an approved petition. The main benefit of Canadian and Mexican TN status is that some workers without a four-year college degree or the equivalent may qualify. For more on TN status, see the section "TN Status for Canadian and Mexican Nationals" later in this chapter.

You Don't Have to Be Special, Just Qualified

U.S. immigration law calls H-1B jobs **specialty occupations**. But you don't have to be "special" to get H-1B status—you just have to have a four-year degree or the equivalent and a job offer that requires a degree in your specific field. And, unlike most immigrant (permanent) employment-based visa applications, your employer need not prove that no U.S. workers are ready, willing, and able to do your job. Even if hundreds of U.S. workers qualify for the position, your employer can choose you for the job and petition for you for H-1B status.

James's story illustrates how a person with the minimum qualifications can get H-1B status despite there being qualified and lawful U.S. worker applicants for the position.

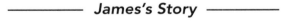
——————— *James's Story* ———————

James, from England, managed to get a degree in business management from the University of California at Los Angeles, but just barely. He spent most of his time in college going to parties. As a result, his grades suffered. He did graduate, but he was near the bottom of his class.

James had difficulty getting a job offer after graduation. Finally, through a friend of his uncle, he found a position as a junior hotel executive. The job required a college degree in business administration or hotel management but did not require experience. Although the employer had not been advertising, he routinely got 30 to 40 letters per week from qualified applicants looking for a position. Nevertheless, because the employer was a friend of James's uncle, he offered James the position and petitioned for him for H-1B status. James applied to change from F-1 to H-1B status and was successful. That's despite the large number of qualified workers applying for the position. The USCIS approved his change of status for a period of three years.

The Degree Requirement

A key element in getting H-1B status is proving that the job the employer offers you customarily requires a relevant four-year college degree as a condition of employment. Even if you have a degree, you cannot get an H-1B visa if your degree isn't typically required for the job.

Some professional positions almost always require a bachelor's degree or higher. Examples are schoolteacher, college or university professor, engineer, and architect. Some positions are not so obvious. The position of manager of a small shoe store would not normally require a specific bachelor's degree. You would have great difficulty getting H-1B status to be a shoe store manager. The position of accountant, on the other hand, would usually require a degree in accounting and would support an application for H-1B status.

Take the example of a small manufacturing company that employs a secretary, a sales representative, a buyer, a manager, and an engineer.

The secretary would probably not be considered to be in a specialty occupation. The position rarely requires a four-year degree. The sales representative and buyer might be considered professionals, but only if the buying and selling require expertise normally acquired through a college education. An example would be a job selling or buying engineering products or chemicals.

The position of manager may or may not be a specialty occupation. If the manager must understand finance or law, and the volume of business justifies the manager spending most of his or her time using this knowledge, this may be an H-1B position. The manager's job will be considered a specialty occupation if the job requires special knowledge normally acquired through a college education. If the manager's job generally requires less than a college degree, the position will not be considered a specialty occupation. The position of engineer is usually considered a specialty occupation, since to be an engineer, you usually need a four-year college degree in engineering.

The stories of Tommy, Mary, and Carson illustrate the importance of showing the relationship between an H-1B applicant's education and the job duties.

Tommy's Story

Tommy, from Thailand, had studied engineering in his country and wanted to come to the United States to work as an engineer. He had his school records evaluated by a professional academic evaluation service in the United States. The service reported that, indeed, his education was the equivalent of a U.S. bachelor of science degree in engineering. Though he had no work experience, a recruiter from Silicon Valley Engineering Associates, a U.S. company, offered him a job as an engineer.

Tommy's is an easy H-1B case. A degree in engineering is a customary degree for a position as an engineer.

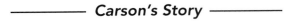

Mary's Story

Mary, from Ethiopia, received a bachelor's degree in political science from a university in her country. Her concentration was in international relations. While in New York on holiday, she began looking for a job that would qualify her for H-1B status based on her new degree. She looked for teaching jobs in a variety of subjects, including social science in a high school and history and political science in colleges. She even tried to get a job teaching in a private elementary school. She also looked for a job as a researcher in the field of government or political science. Finally, she obtained a job as an editor for a publication that wrote and distributed high school textbooks about the United Nations and international relations.

While Mary had no experience in this area, her bachelor's degree in political science and the fact that she took several courses in international relations qualified her for the position. Her employer explained in a letter to the USCIS that Mary was doing more than just correcting grammar and spelling. She was editing the text for factual accuracy. Her job also required research on world history and government. The USCIS decided that her degree qualified her for the position of editor.

Carson's Story

Carson received his degree in anthropology, studying at City College in New York City in F-1 international student status. His best friend, John, a U.S. citizen, introduced Carson to John's father, John Sr., a frozen food manufacturer and distributor. John Sr. was planning to begin a major campaign to develop, market, and distribute frozen foods worldwide. His thought was to develop special products and special marketing efforts for each country in the market. Though Carson had never studied business, let alone marketing, he was trained in researching and analyzing national and regional cultures. John Sr. felt these skills would be useful to his marketing efforts, and so he sponsored Carson for H-1B status. Though at first the USCIS questioned whether Carson's education qualified him for the job, eventually the USCIS approved the petition. The USCIS had inquired about Carson's qualifications, so John Sr. submitted letters from an anthropology professor and a business school professor confirming the important role played by anthropologists in modern product development and marketing strategies.

The Prevailing and Actual Wage Requirement

For you to get H-1B status, your employer must agree to pay you at least the prevailing wage for the position in the geographic area where you'll be working. If the actual wage, the wage paid to other workers doing your job, is higher, then the employer must pay you the higher wage. Also, the employer must offer you the same benefits offered to other workers. USCIS regulations provide several ways for your employer to decide the prevailing wage. If the position is covered by a union contract, the contract wage is the prevailing wage. The prevailing wage in cases where the work is done under federal contract is set by federal law. In other cases, the employer can use a wage determined by a state employment agency, or use a professional survey referred to as **"independent authoritative source"** or "other legitimate source," including a survey done by the employer. For jobs at institutions of higher education, or affiliated or related nonprofits, or a nonprofit research organization or governmental research organization, you can use the prevailing wage determination at similar institutions.

The Attorney Fee as Part of the Prevailing Wage

A U.S. Department of Labor rule requires that an employer pay the legal fees and costs to obtain H-1B status for the worker. If the employer does not pay the fees and costs, then the wage paid to the worker, minus the legal fees and costs, must be within five percent of the prevailing wage. Many immigration lawyers are very critical of this rule and are hopeful that the Department of Labor will eventually change it; however, such a change seems unlikely. Many attorneys simply ignore the rule, but that puts the employer at risk. If the employer is found to have paid less than the required wage for the position, the U.S. Department of Labor could impose penalties including fines and limitations on employing H-1B workers in the future.

You Must Have an Offer of Employment

The USCIS will not approve an H-1B petition unless a U.S. employer or agent petitions for you. Your employer may be an individual, a partnership, or a corporation. Sometimes a corporation, solely or majority owned by one individual, will petition for that same individual, claiming that he or she is also an employee of the corporation. This is acceptable if the business is properly incorporated, the job offer is bona fide, and the individual meets all other requirements for an H-1B petition. The USCIS sometimes scrutinizes petitions by new corporations with limited capital to ensure that someone didn't create the corporation solely to provide employment for an H-1B worker.

The Labor Condition Application for H-1B Workers

H-1B employers must get a Labor Condition Application (LCA) certified by the U.S. Department of Labor before filing an H-1B petition with the USCIS. In the LCA, the employer attests that the job is being offered at a wage higher than the prevailing or actual wage for the position, that the employer is offering the job at the prevailing working conditions for all other workers in the same job category at the facility, and that the employer has posted a notice of filing the H-1B attestation in two conspicuous locations at the place of employment or has notified the employees' bargaining representative. The notice must be posted for ten days, but the employer may file the LCA immediately after posting the notice. The employer must also keep records proving that the statements made in the LCA are true. For more on the LCA, see part II of this chapter.

How Long Can You Work Here in H-1B Status?

The USCIS can approve an initial H-1B petition for up to three years. At that point, you become eligible for one three-year extension. The USCIS will extend your status beyond six years only if you have had a labor certification or I-140 employment-based petition pending for 365 days. Then you can apply for extensions of one year until a final decision is made on your permanent residence case. The I-140 petition, labor certification application, or adjustment of status application must have been filed before the end of five years after the change of status to, or entry as, H-1B worker.

Changing Employers, Adding Employers, and the Portability Rule

H-1B status is employer-specific. That means that to work for an employer, the USCIS must have approved an H-1B petition allowing you to work for that particular employer. If you want to change employers, the new employer must first petition for you. If you want to work for two employers at the same time, each must have an H-1B petition approved for you.

Jaime's story illustrates the rule that applies if you have two H-1B employers.

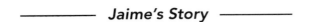

—————— *Jaime's Story* ——————

Jaime is a professor at California State College in Northridge. He holds a master's degree in mathematics, which he received from a Mexican university. He is studying for his Ph.D. in mathematics at the University of California at Los Angeles. Jaime is a part-time, or adjunct, professor. He teaches two classes each semester at California State College. Jaime wants to teach a third class at Los Angeles Community College. Because H-1B status is employer-specific, that college must first have an H-1B petition approved for Jaime. Los Angeles Community College must get an LCA certified and file the new petition. Once Los Angeles Community College files an H-1B petition for Jaime, he may begin teaching classes there. He need not wait for the USCIS to approve that petition, nor must he get a new visa.

Under the H-1B portability rule, if you are already in lawful H-1B status, you can start work for a new or second employer without the USCIS having approved the second employer's petition. To benefit form this rule, the second employer must have filed a nonfrivolous petition before your H-1B stay with the first employer expires. A nonfrivolous petition is one that has some basis in law or fact. At a minimum, this means that the second petition is filed with a certified LCA.

If you have a visa issued based on the first H-1B petition, you may continue to travel on that visa until your stay on that visa expires, plus ten days. Once the USCIS approves the second petition, you can get a new visa.

Jill's story illustrates the H-1B portability rule.

Jill's Story

Jill, a citizen of Italy, came to the United States to work for a U.S. bank as a financial analyst. She holds a degree in economics from the University of Turin, Italy. Her employer petitioned for her to work for three years in H-1B status. The USCIS approved the petition, and Jill got an H-1B visa at the U.S. consulate in Rome. After two years, she was offered a position at a different bank, also as a financial analyst, but at a higher rate of pay. The new bank petitioned for her to work for them in H-1B status for three years. Jill may begin working at the new bank as soon as the USCIS receives the bank's petition. The new bank must get an LCA certified before filing the petition, but once the petition is filed, Jill may change jobs. She need not wait until the USCIS approves the petition. Nor does she need to get a new visa. If she stays in the United States, she can work so long as she remains in H-1B status, even if her visa expires. Her current visa is valid for one more year, and she can use it to travel in and out of the United States. If she travels outside the United States after the USCIS has approved her H-1B status for the new employer, she can get a new visa, though she need not do that until her current visa expires.

Changes in Employment Conditions

If your job responsibilities change substantially, your employer may need to file a new H-1B petition for you. The USCIS requires a new petition also if you will be working more than 90 days in three years in an area beyond commuting distance from the area used to determine the prevailing wage.

Extensions of Stay

You apply for extension of stay by filing a new H-1B petition. If your LCA has expired, you'll have to support the petition with a new LCA. Also include a letter from your employer confirming your continuing employment in the H-1B position. If you file the extension request before your H-1B expires, you may continue working for your employer while waiting for the USCIS extension approval. Caution: If you travel abroad after your H-1B visa expires, you'll need a new visa to reenter, and you can't get that visa until the USCIS approves your extension. Some USCIS documents say that you may return without a new visa within ten days after your visa expires. Nothing in the USCIS regulations supports this. Don't count on the "ten-day extension" policy.

Libby's story illustrates the extension rule.

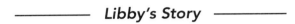

Libby's Story

Libby is an engineer at Applied Engineering Incorporated. She is working for the company in H-1B professional temporary worker status. The USCIS approved her initial H-1B status for three years. Six months prior to the expiration of the three years, the company filed an extension for Libby. The company had to first get a new LCA but then was able to file the petition requesting the extension. Six months is normally enough time for the U.S. Department of Labor to approve a new LCA and for the USCIS to approve a new petition, but in Libby's case the USCIS lost the employer's petition. Because the petition had been filed before Libby's status expired, she may continue working for the company even after her status expires until the USCIS decides the petition and extension request. If the USCIS eventually approves the petition and extension request, Libby may remain in the United States to work in H-1B status for an additional three years.

After her initial H-1B petition and change of status was approved, Libby traveled to her home country, Australia, and obtained an H-1B visa at the U.S. consulate. The visa expires at the end of the initial H-1B period authorized by the USCIS. While Libby may continue to work and live in the United States beyond the expiration of her visa, provided the employer has filed a petition and extension for her, she cannot get a new visa until the petition is approved. If the petition is not approved until after her visa and stay under the original petition expire, she will not be able to return to the United States from any travel abroad until she has the approval of the extended petition and gets a new visa.

Expedited Adjudication

H-1B petition approval usually takes 30 to 90 days, though times will vary greatly from region to region and year to year. If you want the USCIS to decide your case more quickly, you can pay a $1,000 expedite fee. You make the expedite request using USCIS Form I-907, Request for Premium Processing Service. The USCIS says that if you pay the fee, the agency will respond to the petition in 15 calendar days. Each USCIS region has a special mailing address, phone number, and e-mail address for these expedited cases. Check the USCIS Web site, www.ins.usdoj.gov/, for an up-to-date list of phone numbers and e-mail addresses. If your employer truly has an emergency need for your services and the expedited procedure won't get you H-1B status fast enough, the USCIS may process your petition even more quickly. Though to get your H-1B petition approved in less than 15 days, you'll need to prove truly exceptional circumstances.

The Number of H-1B Visas Available Each Year

The law sets an annual limit on the number of foreigners that can receive H-1B status in a fiscal year. The annual limit was 195,000 for 2001, 2002, and 2003. The USCIS fiscal year runs from October 1 to September 30. On September 30, 2003, the cap reverted back to 65,000. Congress could increase the number at any time. Check my Immigration Answers Web site, www.allanwernick.com/, for updated information on the cap. The cap of 65,000 is usually reached months before the end of the fiscal year. When that happens, no more new applicants can get H-1B status until October 1, when the new fiscal year begins. The USCIS only counts new applicants. Extension applicants are excluded from the count.

People who have H-1B status who either change jobs or apply for extensions are excluded from the count. Also excluded are employees of institutions of higher education and related or affiliated nonprofit entities and nonprofit or governmental research organizations.

If you are excluded from the count, you can get H-1B status even after the cap is reached.

Special Rules for H-1B Dependent Employers and Prior Violators of H-1B Rules

The law requires special promises, or attestations, from employers who employ a high percentage of H-1B workers. The law calls these employers dependent employers. The same rules apply to employers found to have willfully violated H-1B rules.

The law defines a dependent employer as any one of the following:

- An employer with 25 or fewer full-time employees who has more than seven H-1B workers.
- An employer with 26 to 50 full-time employees who has more than 12 H-1B workers.
- An employer with more than 50 full-time employees with 15 percent or more H-1B workers.

Dependent employers must attest that they have not displaced any U.S. worker with an H-1B worker. They must also attest that they won't displace any U.S. worker employed by them within the period 90 days before and 90 days after the filing of an H-1B visa petition. Similar requirements apply when a dependent employer places an H-1B worker to provide services in another firm. Dependent employers must also attest that they have taken good-faith steps to recruit in the United States. They must offer the position at the prevailing wage to any U.S. worker who applies and is equally or better qualified than the H-1B applicant. The employer need not recruit if the H-1B worker is a person of extraordinary ability, is an outstanding professor or researcher, or is a multinational manager or executive.

The law does not require the new attestation if a dependent employer is petitioning for an H-1B worker who holds a master's degree or higher (or the equivalent) or who receives wages at a rate of at least $60,000 per year.

No Benching Rule

If you are a full-time employee, your employer must pay you your full salary as noted on your H-1B petition, even if you don't work those hours. The only exceptions are if your employer terminates you, you are voluntarily absent, or you are unable to perform your duties. For part-time employees, the employer must pay wages for the minimum number of hours on the petition. This is called the no benching provision. It is designed to ensure that H-1B workers aren't brought in as full-time workers only to be used and paid as casual workers. Educational institutions may establish salary practices paying for work of less than 12 months if you, as an H-1B employee, agree.

Employer Obligation to Pay Travel Home

If your employer fires you before your H-1B stay expires, the law requires your employer to pay your return transportation to your home country. If your employer refuses to pay, the USCIS won't force payment, but you can sue your employer for transportation costs. The USCIS may punish the employer by restricting employment of other H-1B workers.

Your Spouse and Children

If you get H-1B status, your spouse and unmarried children, under age 21, may get H-4 status. If they are legally in the United States, they may change to H-4 status by filing USCIS Form I-539, Application to Extend/Change Nonimmigrant Status. If they are abroad, they may apply for an H-4 visa at a U.S. consulate. H-4 spouses may work in the United States after receiving USCIS employment authorization. You apply using USCIS form I-765, Application for Employment Authorization.

H-1B1 Status for Chilean and Singaporean Nationals and TN Status for Canadian and Mexican Nationals

Under various Free Trade Agreements, Chilean, Singaporean, Canadian and Mexican professionals can work in the United States under a status similar to H-1B status. For nationals of Chile and Singapore the special status is called H-1B1. For Canadians and Mexicans, it's called TN—most professionals from H-1B1 and TN countries can choose either H-1B status, H-1B1 status, or TN status. A few professionals qualify for H-1B1 or TN status but not H-1B status. Though similar to H-1B status, the H-1B1 and TN statuses include some professional positions that don't require a college degree. H-1B1 and TN professionals can renew TN status indefinitely as opposed to the six-year limit for H-1B status. Further, H-1B1 and TN applicants need not get a USCIS-approved H-1B petition before getting nonimmigrant status. Unlike H-1B status, a TN employer need not pay you the prevailing wage. H-1B1 employers, like H-1B employers, must pay the prevailing wage.

Who Is an H-1B1 and TN Professional?

A list of TN professionals can be found in Appendix N. If your work comes under a category listed, sometimes you can get TN status even if you don't have the equivalent of a U.S. four -year college degree. For instance, Canadian baccalaureate degrees, including those which require only three years of study, and Mexican postsecondary certificates, may qualify you for TN status. Management consultants often rely on experience that is less than the equivalent of a bachelor's degree to get TN status.

Chileans and Singaporeans eligible for H-1B status also qualify for H-1B1 status. In addition, Chileans and Singaporean nationals working as Disaster Relief Claims Adjusters and Management Consultants can qualify for H-1B1 status with a combination of specialized training plus three years' experience in lieu of the standard four-year degree requirement for H-1Bs. Chilean nationals only can qualify as Agricultural Managers and Physical Therapists with a combination of a post-secondary certificate in the specialty and three years' experience.

Getting H-1B1 and TN Status

TN and H-1B1 applicants do not need an approved petition to get H-1B status. If you are in the United States in lawful nonimmigrant status, you may apply to change your status to TN or H-1B while in the United States. If you are abroad, you follow the instructions below.

If you are Canadian, to get TN status you present yourself at certain U.S. ports of entry with a letter from a U.S. employer confirming the details of the position offered and proof of your qualifications.

If you are Mexican, you take your job letter and proof of your qualifications to a U.S. consulate abroad where you apply for a TN visa. Or if you are in the United States in lawful status, you may apply to change to H-1B1 status.

If you are a national of Chile or Singapore you present an offer of employment with a certified LCA to a U.S. consular officer abroad. If you are in the United States in lawful status, you may apply to change to H-1B1 status.

Even if you qualify for TN or H-1B1 status, you may prefer to get H-1B status. Workers in TN or H-1B1 status are admitted for only one year, although they have the right to reenter as often as they like during that year. At the end of the year, you must apply to the USCIS for an extension of status or reapply for status at a U.S. port of entry. You can do this indefinitely, but some professionals prefer the H-1B three-year grant of status. Further, unlike H-1B professionals, to get TN or H-1B status, you must have a residence abroad that you have not abandoned. This may cause you problems if you have begun processing for permanent residence.

Part II: Overview of H-1B Procedures

Here I describe the process of getting H-1B status from beginning to end—from finding an employer to filing a completed application. Every case is different. It's impossible to write about each and every possible situation. Still, the rules, procedures, and practical hints provided will guide you through most H-1B cases. As in all immigration cases, H-1B applicants are well advised to seek the assistance of an immigration law expert.

In part I of this chapter, I explained the rules for H-1B dependent employers and prior violators of H-1B rules. If your employer is subject to these rules, get the help of an expert. Further explanation of how to deal with these situations is beyond the scope of this book.

Finding an Employer and Convincing That Employer to Petition for You

You find most H-1B employers the same way you find any employer, by checking the want ads and applying for the job. You have no obligation to tell an employer that you need H-1B sponsorship when applying. Still, don't get pushy about sponsorship. Once an employer learns that you need sponsorship to work in the United States, the employer is free to withdraw the job offer rather than petition for you.

In speaking to the employer about sponsorship, explain clearly that unlike most employment-based permanent residence cases, an employer need not prove the unavailability of U.S. workers. Note the difference between sponsorship for H-1B status and sponsorship for employment-based permanent residence, a much more complicated procedure with very different standards. Also, explain that the H-1B process is much quicker than permanent resident visa processing. Try showing this chapter to your employer.

Some Internet sites match H-1B seeking employees with employers willing to sponsor. In Appendix O, I list some of these sites. As you do with any business relationship, be cautious when using an employment service. My listing of these services does not mean that I can vouch for their honesty or quality of services.

Notifying Workers at the Company About the LCA

Except where the position is covered by a union contract, the employer must post notice of the LCA filing for ten working days at two conspicuous spots at the place of employment. The employer need not wait until the ten working days have passed before filing the LCA. The easiest way to comply with the posting requirement is to post a copy of the LCA. Where a union contract covers the position, the employer need not post but instead need only notify the bargaining representative.

The employer must keep proof of the notice for public review. For more on the employer record-keeping requirements, see "LCA Record-Keeping Requirements."

Before the H-1B employee starts work, the employer must give him or her a copy of the certified LCA.

Completing the LCA

Getting a certified LCA isn't too difficult. The Department of Labor checks for completeness and to ensure the employer's wage scale is consistent with the prevailing wage noted on the form. The Department of Labor does not check to see that the prevailing wage is accurate. The accuracy of the employer's prevailing wage determination comes into question only if someone challenges the wage or the Department of Labor audits the employer. So the Department of Labor certification means only that the LCA has been properly completed.

You may now file an LCA using the Internet. Go to www.ows.doleta.gov/index.asp. The response is instantaneous. The Department of Labor certifies the LCA online, then you print it and the employer signs it. You can also download the form, Department of Labor Form ETA 9035, at the same site and fill it out online. For up-to-date information on LCA procedures, visit the Department of Labor's Office of Workforce Security Web site at www.doleta.gov/.

The Employer's Obligations

In part I of this chapter, I explained the employer's obligations under Department of Labor regulations. To make sure that an employer is properly informed of these obligations, a conscientious lawyer or immigration law expert will give the employer a detailed summary of the LCA rules. That protects the legal advocate and employee by giving the employer notice of the law governing H-1B employment. An excellent example is the Fact Sheet on Labor Condition Applications for H-1B Nonimmigrants (for Employers That Are Not "H-1B Dependent" or "Willful Violators") prepared by attorney Phyllis Jewell, an H-1B expert. A copy of the fact sheet can be found as sample 1 in Appendix P.

Determining the Prevailing Wage

The most complicated and important part of competing the LCA form is determining the prevailing wage. If employers err in determining the prevailing wage, the Department of Labor may still certify the LCA. Nevertheless, employers could still face penalties if they pay a wage lower than what the Department of Labor determines the prevailing wage to be. Except for positions covered by union contracts and federal statutes, employers may pay a wage 5 percent lower than the prevailing wage without incurring penalties.

The law allows institutions of higher education, nonprofit organizations, and governmental research organizations to consider only employees at such institutions (rather than the wage at all institutions, including commercial enterprises) in determining the prevailing wage.

Here are the ways to determine the prevailing wage:

Union Contract. If the job position is covered by a collective bargaining agreement (union contract), the contract wage for that position is the prevailing wage.

Federal Contractors. The wages paid by federal contractors are determined by the Davis-Bacon Act and McNamara-O'Hara Service Contract Act.

State Employment Security Agency (SESA) Wage Determination. Each state has an Employment Security Agency that you can contact to find out the prevailing wage for a position. You'll need to get the appropriate form and filing instructions from the state agency. Many employers have found the SESA wage to be unjustifiably high. Moreover, getting a SESA wage determination can add weeks to the process. Many employers, therefore, prefer to do their own surveys or rely on published studies. Nevertheless, a SESA wage is the only wage (besides union and federal contract wages) that an employer can use to be absolutely certain the offered waged is the prevailing wage. That's because if the SESA wage request accurately describes the position, the Department of Labor must accept the SESA wage as the prevailing wage.

Independent Authoritative Source. The Department of Labor allows an employer to use an independent authoritative source for the prevailing wage. These are wage surveys often published by professional organizations, governmental agencies, and professional wage consultants. To qualify as an acceptable independent authoritative source, the published salary survey must (1) provide an arithmetic mean (weighted average) of wages for workers in the appropriate occupational category in the area of intended employment, (2) be published in the last 24 months, (3) be based on data collected within 24 months of the survey's publication, and (4) be the survey that is in the most current edition of the publication. One popular independent authoritative source is the Department of Labor's own Online Wage Library at edc.dws.state.ut.us/owl.asp. What's the difference between a SESA wage and a Department of Labor online wage? For the online wage, the employer is deciding the correct job title for the position and determines the experience and education level. With a SESA wage, the employer provides the job description and the Department of Labor determines the appropriate job classification. Thus only the SESA wage provides the employer complete protection from challenge on the prevailing wage determination. Still, the Online Wage Library is a quick and useful tool for helping an employer make a wage determination. If done correctly, the wage should stand up to challenge.

Employer Survey. An employer can do its own survey. To do the survey, the employer contacts eight to ten companies or institutions with employees doing similar work. The employer adds the total wages of all the employees in the survey and divides by the number of employees.

Hints on Completing the LCA Form

The Department of Labor now provides clear and detailed information on completing the form. Read the instructions carefully. Here's my commentary on a few important items:

EIN. EIN refers to the Employer Identification Number. This is either a Federal Tax Identification Number or social security number.

Wage Rate. Here put the actual wage the employer will be paying the H-1B worker. This wage may be up to 5 percent lower than the prevailing wage noted.

Part-Time Workers. H-1B workers may be employed part-time or full-time. If you work for more than one H-1B employer, each must get an H-1B visa approved for you with a separate certified LCA.

Begin/End Date. If you'd like to begin work as an H-1B worker as soon as possible, check how long it takes to get a certified LCA and approved H-1B in your area before completing this section. Then choose a starting date on or after the date you think the USCIS will approve the petition. If you are filing to extend status to work in the same or similar job for your current employer or with a new employer, choose a date on or after the date you think the employer will file the H-1B petition. That's because you may begin working the day the employer submits the petition. You need not wait for the USCIS to approve the petition. To benefit from the extension or new employer rules, you need only apply for your new or extended H-1B status before your current status expires.

Occupational Code. The list of occupational codes is included in the instructions for the LCA form. If you are using Internet filing you'll find a link to the codes on the online form. Choose the one closest to your occupation.

Number of H-1B Nonimmigrants. You may get a certified LCA for more than one H-1B applicant. Nevertheless, a separate H-1B must be filed and approved for each H-1B employee.

Wage Source. If your wage came from the Department of Labor's Online Wage Library, enter "OES." If it was obtained from a different independent authoritative source, enter the name of the company or institution that provided the wage, or, if appropriate, "Employer-Conducted Survey."

Information for Additional or Subsequent Work Location: If the employee will be working in one or more work locations, you may have to complete this section. The prevailing wage may be different for each location. The actual wage must be within 5 percent of the prevailing wage at the new location(s). Whether or not particular work outside the primary area of employment constitutes as additional or subsequent work site is a shifting and complex area of law. You should speak to an immigration law expert if you have questions about this issue.

Public Disclosure Information. For more on employer record keeping, see "LCA Record-Keeping Requirements" below.

Contact Information. If you have a legal representative, include his or her phone number here, though the Department of Labor rarely calls.

Filing the LCA

You may mail or fax in your LCA. Most lawyers prefer the fax method. As of this writing, the fax number is 800-397-0478. The mailing address is ETA-H1B, P.O. Box 13640, Philadelphia, PA 19101. The phone number and address may change. Check the Immigration Answers Web site, www.ilw.com/wernick/, for up-to-date information.

LCA Record-Keeping Requirements

An H-1B employer must keep records proving compliance with the LCA requirements. Some records must be kept in a public access file. This file must be available to anyone who would like to see it, including other employees at the company. The file must be available for public inspection within one day after the employer files the LCA. The records must be kept for one year beyond the period noted in the LCA.

The public access file must include:

Copy of the completed LCA. Documentation that provides the wage rate to be paid H-1B nonimmigrants. A simple statement of the salary of the H-1B employee(s). See sample 2 in Appendix Q.

An explanation of the system that the employer used to set the actual wage paid in the position. A general statement of the wage range for the position and the basis for determining the H-1B employee's wage. See sample 3 in Appendix R. The employer must keep payroll records for three years for the H-1B workers and other workers doing similar work, but these records need not be part of the public access file.

A copy of the documentation used to establish the prevailing wage. The name of the source (e.g., SESA). If you use a published survey, include a copy of the relevant portions of the survey, including the survey title, date, methodology, geographic scope, and job level and description. For an employer-conducted survey, in a separate file, keep detailed information of the institutions contacted and the wages paid to the workers performing similar duties. See samples 4A and 4B in Appendix S.

A copy of the notice given to the institution's employees. This can be the LCA and information as to the dates of posting, or a copy of the notice provided to the union.

Preparing the H-1B Petition and Supporting Documents

Most H-1B petitions are easy to prepare. The two most common problem areas are proving that the position is a specialty (professional) occupation and proving that the employee has the appropriate degree for the position.

Proving That Yours Is a Specialty Occupation

As I explained in part I, a specialty occupation is one that requires a bachelor's degree or higher, or the equivalent in a particular subject. Where the link between the degree isn't obvious, the employer may need to make special effort to get the USCIS to understand why a job needs a worker with a particular degree. Examples are a stock analyst with an engineering degree or a marketing executive with an anthropology degree. In difficult cases, the employer may need to use articles from professional journals, employment records for the company showing that other employees in the same position have similar degrees, and the written testimony of experts.

Here are some criteria the USCIS uses to decide whether a particular degree is necessary for a job:

- A bachelor's or higher degree or equivalent is normally the minimum requirement for entry into the particular position.
- The degree requirement is common in the industry in parallel positions among similar organizations.
- The employer normally requires the degree or equivalent.
- The specific duties are so specialized and complex that knowledge required to perform the duties is usually associated with the worker having received the degree.

Proving You Have the Degree

Suppose the job requires a degree in civil engineering and you claim to have the degree. How do you prove it? If your degree is from a college or university in the United States or Canada, you submit a copy of an original transcript. "Original" means a transcript issued by the institution. It need not be in a sealed envelope.

If your degree is from a foreign institution, you'll need a professional evaluation to determine whether your transcript and diploma show the equivalent of a U.S. degree. Many credential evaluation services are available to analyze your documents. (A list of credential evaluation services can be found in Appendix T.)

Sometimes you can combine education with training to equal a

U.S. degree. Generally, three years of what the USCIS calls progressive experience substitutes for one year of college education. Progressive experience means that each year, you handled more difficult job tasks. The on-the-job training must include the theoretical and practical application of specialized knowledge that normally would be acquired through a college education. Some evaluation services evaluate on-the-job training as a substitute for education. You may also get a college or university professor to evaluate the experience. If the evaluator has the appropriate qualifications, the USCIS may accept the evaluation as a substitute for a degree.

Rigoberto's Story

Rigoberto attended college for two years in his home country of Venezuela. He majored in liberal arts. Because he needed to support his family, he quit college and began working as a sales clerk in Mario's Electronics, a major retailer of consumer electronic goods in Caracas. After one year as a salesperson, Rigoberto was promoted to a senior sales person for the television division.

At the end of each year's review, Rigoberto was promoted another step up in the company's ladder. After three years at Mario's Electronics, Rigoberto changed companies and began working for Crazy Jose's Retail Electronics Store. He was hired at Crazy Jose's as an assistant store manager, a position higher than the one he had held at Mario's. After three years at Crazy Jose's, Rigoberto finally became the senior store manager. All along the way in his career in the electronic retail business, he received various promotions, each one requiring more responsibility. In addition, he was occasionally sent to training programs set up by the employer to prepare him for his new and more difficult positions.

Rigoberto has an uncle with an electronics store in New York City. He would like to come work for the uncle as a store manager in H1-B status. In order for Rigoberto to prove that he qualifies for H1-B status, he will need a professional evaluation of his credentials. The credential evaluator will likely credit his two years of college. Then the evaluator will evaluate his experience to determine if the six years of experience is the equivalent of two years of education in business.

In preparing for the evaluation, Rigoberto should obtain letters from his employers explaining the responsibilities of each position he held in the two companies. The evaluator may ask for an analysis of the experience from one or more university professors, including at least one at a business school. If a professional evaluation determines that Rigoberto has the equivalent of a college degree in business management and the USCIS accepts the evaluation, Rigoberto should have no problems obtaining H1-B status to work for his uncle.

The H-1B Petition Package

The employer must file at least three USCIS forms as part of the H-1B petition package. Every H-1B submission must include Form I-129, Petition for a Nonimmigrant Worker; Form I-129 Supplement H; and Form I-129W, H-1B Data Collection and Filing Fee Exemption (you will find blank copies of the I-129 form and Supplement H in Appendix U). If your spouse and/or child is applying for a change to H-4 status, you file USCIS Form I-539, Application to Extend/Change Nonimmigrant Status. If you are applying to have the USCIS expedite your petition, you file Form I-907, Request for Premium Processing Service. Following you'll find some tips on completing Form I-129, and the I-129 Supplement H. At the end of this section I provide a checklist for filing the petition. Attorneys and accredited representatives must include USCIS Form G-28, Notice of Entry of Appearance as Attorney or Representative.

Form I-129, Petition for a Nonimmigrant Worker

Most questions on the I-129 petition are self-explanatory; therefore, I haven't described every part of the form, but only certain parts I thought may need additional explanation. A few points are worth discussing.

Part 4. Processing Information.

The USCIS wants to know where you will apply for an H-1B visa, if necessary. If you are in the United States in lawful status, in most cases you may change to H-1B status without leaving the United States. For more on changing status, see Chapter 15. You may begin working once the USCIS approves the change of status. If you leave the United States, you must get an H-1B visa at a U.S. consulate before you can return in H-1B status. In most cases, a U.S. consul will grant you a visa even without having received a copy of the notice of approval sent by the USCIS. When applying for a visa, you should present a current job letter indicating your intended or continuing employment, your salary (consistent with the wage on the petition), and your job title (also consistent with the petition). You should also present the USCIS-issued attorney or employer copy of the notice of approval.

Even if you are applying for a change of status, you should designate a consul abroad in case the USCIS denies your change of status request. If you are abroad, the USCIS will send notice of approval to the designated consulate.

Canadians don't need a visa, so instead designate an inspection facility. That's either the port of entry or the USCIS preinspection station at the airport of departure.

Have you ever filed an immigrant petition for any person in this petition? Don't be concerned if you must answer "Yes" to this question. Unlike most nonimmigrants, an H-1B worker may intend to get permanent residence and still qualify for H-1B status.

Part 5. Basic Information About the Proposed Employment and Employer.

Other Compensation: It is sufficient to put "Standard Benefits" here.

Gross Annual Income—Net Annual Income: Even companies not making a profit can sponsor H-1B workers. Many large companies show annual losses. Sometimes, but not always, the USCIS will ask a small business with little or no income to provide proof that it has enough resources to pay the H-1B worker. You need not submit this proof with your H-1B petition. If the USCIS wants this proof, they will send the employer a request for the proof. This proof could include a letter from the employer's accountant, a bank statement, or other proof that the business's owners have the resources to run the company and pay the offered wage.

Part 7. Signature of person preparing form, if other than above.

You may leave this part blank.

Form I-129 Supplement H

Section 1. Complete if filing for H-1A or H-1B classification.

The best practice is to write "see attached letter from employer" here and to attach a letter from the employer explaining the qualifications the proposed job duties and the employee's qualifications. For a sample letter, see sample 5 in Appendix V.

The Petition Package Checklist

Here's a checklist for the petition package:

____**Cover Letter:** List all forms, documents, and checks. Before you send in the package, check the enclosures against the list in the cover letter.

____**Form I-129, Petition for a Nonimmigrant Worker**

____Employer's letter explaining the job duties, the employee's qualifications, and, if necessary, why the employee's education and/or training is necessary to fulfill the job duties.

____Transcript and diploma where appropriate.

____Expert evaluation of credentials for education outside the United States and Canada and/or evaluation of experience if required.

____**Form I-129,** Supplement H

____**Form I-539, Application to Extend/Change Nonimmigrant Status:** Include this form only if your spouse and/or child is applying for a change to H-4 status or an H-4 extension. If more than one family member is applying for a change of status or extension, include Form I-539 Supplement 1.

___**Form I-907, Request for Premium Processing Service:** Include this form only if you need your case expedited and you are willing to pay $1,000 for the service.

___**Check(s):** Note that fees USCIS fees change often, so check the USCIS Web site, www.ins.usdoj.gov/, or the Immigration Answers Web site, www.allanwernick.com/, for up-to-date fee information.

___For Form I-129: $130.

___For Form I-539 (if required): $140. The fee of $140 includes all family members.

For Form I-907 (if desired): $1,000. This fee applies only if you are seeking expedited adjudication.

___**Form G-28,** Notice of Entry of Appearance as Attorney or Representative: Include this form only if the papers are submitted by an attorney or accredited representative. If Form I-539 is submitted for a change of status for a spouse and/or child, the representative must submit a separate G-28 form with the I-539.

The Final Step: Getting H-1B Status

If you are legally in the United States, you may apply for a change to H-1B status. You need not include a separate change of status application with your petition. The petition includes a change of status request. Once the USCIS approves your change to H-1B status, you apply for a visa at any U.S. consulate. Many H-1B workers apply for their first H-1B visa in Canada or Mexico.

If you are not in the United States lawfully, in most cases you must apply for your visa in your country of nationality. Unlike most nonimmigrant visa applicants, the H-1B applicant need not prove that he or she intends to return home after the stay in the United States. That means that even if you have violated your status, you still have a good chance that a U.S. consul will grant you an H-1B visa. Warning: Some out-of-status applicants who leave the United States are barred from returning for three or sometimes even ten years. If the USCIS granted you duration of status (D/S) at your last entry, the three- and ten-year bars don't apply unless the USCIS or an immigration judge finds that you violated your status. For more on the three- and ten-year bars and the D/S rule, see Chapter 5. If you come under the D/S exception, you keep the right to apply for your visa in a country other than your nationality, including Mexico or Canada. For more on getting your H-1B visa, see Chapter 17. If you have been here unlawfully, speak to an immigration law expert before traveling abroad.

CHAPTER 15

K Visas for a Fiancé(e) or Spouse of a U.S. Citizen

If you are a U.S. citizen, you may bring your fiancé(e) to the United States on a K visa. A U.S. citizen may also use the K visa to bring a spouse to the United States. The K visa is not available for the fiancé(e) or spouse of a permanent resident.

K visa holders may bring their unmarried children under the age of 21 with them to the United States.

K FIANCÉ(É) VISA

If you are a U.S. citizen intending to marry a foreigner, you may bring your fiancé to the United States for up to 90 days on a fiancé(e) visa. In most cases, you'll need to prove that you met with your fiancé(e) in the two years prior to the filing of the fiancé(e) petition. The USCIS will exempt you from this "meeting" requirement if traveling abroad will result in your suffering extreme hardship, for instance, you can't travel because of a health problem. The USCIS also can exempt you from the meeting requirement if meeting before the wedding would violate the customs of your people or those of your fiancé(e). An example is where religion prohibits the prospective bride and groom from meeting prior to the wedding day. The fiancé(e) visa is only available abroad. A person in the United States cannot change to K status without leaving the United States.

To bring your fiancé(e) to the United States, you file USCIS Form I-129F, Petition for Alien Fiancé. Once the USCIS approves the petition, the agency will send it to the U.S. consul abroad that you designate in the petition. While K visas are nonimmigrant visas, the visa interview with the U.S. consular officer is similar to an immigrant visa interview. The consular officer will carefully evaluate the authenticity of the relationship. Your fiancé(e) will be required to submit a medical exam and proof that he or she won't become a "public charge," that is, that your fiancé(e) can live in the United States without needing public assistance. In proving that your fiancé(e) will not become a public charge, you may use the nonbinding USCIS Form I-134, Affidavit of Support. (For more on the public charge issue, see Chapter 5.) If all goes well, the consular officer will grant your fiancé(e) a visa, and he or she can come to the United States for 90 days. After arrival, he or she may apply for employment authorization using USCIS Form I-765, Application for Employment Authorization. And the K visa holder can travel freely in and out of the United States.

If you marry your fiancé(e), he or she can apply for adjustment of status to permanent residence. (For more on adjustment of status, see Chapter 6.) You need not file an USCIS Form I-130, Petition for Alien Relative. Instead, include a copy of the K visa holder's Form I-94, Arrival/Departure Document.

The law limits the rights of K visa holders. They may not change to another nonimmigrant status. A K visa holder wanting to enter a different K visa status must apply for a visa at a U.S. consul abroad. Kelly's story illustrates the rule regarding change of status.

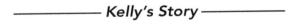

——————— *Kelly's Story* ———————

Kelly came to the United States on a K visa to marry Sean. She and Sean had fallen in love when he was studying at Oxford University in London. Sean returned to his place of birth, New York City, and petitioned for Kelly to join him in K status. Shortly after she arrived, Kelly realized that Sean was not the guy for her. Still, she liked New York, and before her 90-day stay expired, she got a job offer as an architect. Kelly qualifies for H-1B status for temporary professional workers, but despite her still being in lawful status, she cannot change from K to another status. So, for her to work in the United States in H-1B status, she must return home to apply at the U.S. consul for an H-1B visa.

Another limitation on K status is that a K fiancé(e) can only adjust status to permanent residence if he or she marries the K petitioner. If the K fiancé(e) qualifies for permanent residence in another category, he or she must leave the United States and apply for an immigrant visa at a U.S. consulate abroad. (For more on adjustment of status and consular processing, see Chapter 6.)

Simon's story demonstrates the rule that applies when a K visa holder doesn't marry his or her fiancé(e).

Simon met Sally when Sally was visiting Rome, Italy, Simon's hometown. Sally is a U.S. citizen. It was love at first sight. Simon and Sally decided to marry, but Sally wanted her fiancé to meet her family and friends and to spend some time with her in the United States. They planned to make New York City their home.

Sally filed an I-129F fiancé(e) petition for Simon, the USCIS approved the petition and sent it to the U.S. consulate in Rome. The consul granted Simon's K visa application, and he traveled to the United States. The USCIS officer at the airport granted him a 90-day stay, the maximum for a K visa holder.

Once Sally and Simon spent some time together, they realized that they were not meant to be married. Simon decided to stay in the United States. After several months, he fell in love with another U.S. citizen, Cassandra. Cassandra petitioned for Simon and the USCIS approved the petition. Simon can become a permanent resident based on Cassandra's petition, but he'll have to travel to Italy to be interviewed at a U.S. consulate for his immigrant visa. He cannot adjust status (the process of interviewing in the United States). (For more on adjustment of status and consular processing, see Chapter 6.) Depending on how long he overstayed the 90 days granted him by the USCIS, he may face the Unlawful Presence bar to permanent residence. (For more on the bar, see Chapter 5.)

K Spouse Visa

The Legal Immigration and Family Equity Act of 2000 (LIFE) made the K visa available to the spouse of a U.S. citizen. The unmarried children under age 21 of that spouse may also come to the United States in K status. To get a K visa, your spouse must be abroad. Even if your spouse is in the United States legally, he or she cannot change to K status from another nonimmigrant status. You can petition for your fiancé(e) while he or she is here, but the visa must be picked up at a U.S. consulate abroad. If the marriage took place abroad, the visa must be applied for in the country where the marriage occurred.

If your spouse is already the beneficiary of an approved USCIS Form I-130, he or she is not eligible for a K visa. The spouse must wait to apply directly for permanent residence through "adjustment of status" in the United States or for an immigrant visa at a U.S. consulate abroad.

The main advantage to the K spouse visa is that your husband or wife will come to the United States faster in K status than with an immigrant visa. However, your spouse may get permanent residence faster if he or she waits at home to get an immigrant visa. Here's why: If you file a K spouse petition, your spouse will be here in three to six months. But then to get permanent residence, your spouse must apply here for "adjustment of status," a process that could take 18 months or longer. If your spouse applies for an immigrant visa at a U.S. consulate it could take 12 months or longer for the consul to issue the visa.

To get your spouse (and your spouse's children) K status, you must first file USCIS Form I-130 for your spouse. You need not have filed Form I-130 for unmarried children under age 21. The children may accompany your spouse in K status. Still, I advise that you file for the children, assuming you are their "parent" under immigration laws. That's because the children won't get permanent residence automatically with their parent. As the spouse of a U.S. citizen, the parent of a child does not get derivative beneficiary benefits. (For more on derivative beneficiaries, see Chapter 1.) If you want the child to get permanent residence, you'll eventually want to file an I-130 petition for the child.

Warning: If your spouse is in the United States unlawfully for more than 180 days, and then leaves to get a K visa, he or she may be subject to the three- or ten-year bars to reentering the United States. That rule applies to K visa applicants as well as immigrant visa applicants. (For more on the "unlawful presence" bar, see Chapter 5.) K status works best for people already abroad.

Raphael's and Norma's stories illustrate why a person in the United States may not want to try to get K status.

Raphael's Story

Raphael's wife, Wilma, is a U.S. citizen. Raphael had come to the United States as a visitor from the Dominican Republic and overstayed his visa. Two years after he entered the United States, he married Wilma. She filed an I-130 petition for him, and he simultaneously applied for adjustment of status. He qualifies for a K visa, but it may be more trouble than it is worth. As an applicant for adjustment of status, he can work in the United States. If he travels abroad to get the K visa, he'll need a waiver of the unlawful presence bar to get the visa and return. Unless he has a serious emergency that he must tend to abroad, he's better off staying here and not trying to get the K visa.

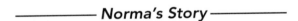

Norma's Story

Norma came to the United States in F-1 student status. She finished college and was doing her practical training when she married Howard, a U.S. citizen. (For more on student practical training, see Chapter 13.) Norma may file for adjustment of status, work permission, and travel permission with an I-130 petition filed by Howard. She can work and travel while waiting to get her immigrant visa. Getting K status isn't necessary.

As of this writing, the USCIS has yet to issue a special form for K spouse petitions. So, to get a K visa for your spouse, you file petition USCIS Form I-129F. When the USCIS issues a new form, I'll report about it on the Immigration Answers Web site, www.ilw.com/wernick/. Send your spouse

K petition to Immigration and Naturalization Service, P.O. Box 7218, Chicago, IL 60680-7218.

As is true for K fiancé(e) visas, the consul will require your spouse (and your spouse's children) to submit a medical exam and proof that he or she can live in the United States without needing public assistance. To prove that your spouse won't become a "public charge," you may follow the nonbinding affidavit support rules using USCIS Form I-134. (For more on the medical examination and the public charge rules, see Chapter 6.)

Once your spouse and your spouse's children get their K visas, they may apply for admission to the United States at a land, sea, or air port of entry. The USCIS officer will admit your spouse for two years. The USCIS will admit your spouse's children for two years as well, or until the day before the children's 21st birthdays, whichever is shorter. Your spouse and your spouse's children may then apply for USCIS employment authorization using USCIS Form I-765, Application for Employment Authorization. And they may travel freely in and out of the United States.

CHAPTER 16

V Visa for the Spouse and Unmarried Children of Permanent Residents

To help unite families during the long wait under the Second Family-Based Preference category, the U.S. Congress created a new V visa. It allows certain spouses and unmarried children under age 21 of permanent residents to live and work in the United States while waiting to get their own permanent residence. V status lasts for two years and, if necessary, can be extended. Qualifying children age 19 and older get V status valid up until the day before their 21st birthday.

REQUIREMENTS FOR A V VISA

The V visa is available to the spouse and unmarried children under age 21 of permanent residents. To qualify, your permanent resident parent or spouse must have petitioned for you on or before December 21, 2000, and you must have been waiting for permanent residence at least three years. Children eligible for V visa status include those whose mother or father petitioned for them directly (under the Second Family-Based Preference) and also children who are "derivative beneficiaries" of a spouse of a permanent resident. (For more on derivative beneficiaries, see Chapter 1.) You start counting the three years from the date the USCIS received the preference petition filed by the permanent resident spouse or parent. It doesn't matter when the USCIS approves the petition. The important date is when the USCIS receives the petition.

Violet's and Fred's stories illustrate the three-year rule.

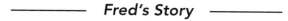
Violet's Story

Violet came to the United States on a visitor's visa in 1997. On January 2, 1998, she married a permanent resident who filed USCIS Form I-130, Petition for USCIS Relative, for her. On January 2, 2001, she had been waiting more than three years to get to the front of the line under the Second Family-Based Preference A, so she qualifies for V status.

Fred's Story

Fred's mother, a permanent resident, filed a petition for Fred on December 21, 2000. He was 12 years old at the time. The USCIS approved the petition on June 1, 2001, but because of a backlog in the quota for the unmarried sons and daughters of permanent residents, he has a five- to six-year wait to get his immigrant visa. On December 21, 2003, he will have been waiting three years and can apply for V status, since his mother petitioned for him on or before December 21, 2000.

The Benefits of the V Visa

V visa holders can live and work legally in the United States during the lengthy immigrant visa process. They can also travel in and out of the country while waiting for their number to come up under the preference quota system, though travel isn't always advisable, as explained in the following section. V status gives you the protection of lawful status and the right to apply for employment authorization using USCIS Form I-765, Application for Employment Authorization. Once the V visa holder gets to the front of the line under the preference quota system, he or she may apply for adjustment of status to permanent resident.

Travel for Those with V Status

For many V visa applicants, the right to travel is something much longed for. Many have spent years in the United States, separated from their families. For applicants unlawfully present who travel abroad, the bars to permanent residence and reentry to the United States don't apply to your right to reenter. However, if you are barred from permanent residence because you have been unlawfully present in the United States for more than 180 days, you may face these bars when you go to apply for adjustment of status. At least that's the USCIS interpretation of the law at the time this book was written. Many experts have criticized this interpretation. If the USCIS changes its position, you can read about it at the Immigration Answers Web site, www.ilw.com/.

William's story illustrates how the unlawful presence bar impacts V visa holders.

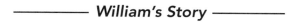
William's Story

William came from Italy to the United States on February 1, 1999. He entered using a phony passport and with a phony visa. His mother, a permanent resident, petitioned for him on March 1, 1999. On March 1, 2002, he became eligible to apply for V status. He applied for a change of status, and the USCIS approved his application. Now he has all the benefits of V status, but no V visa. Suppose he wants to travel home to Italy to see his girlfriend. If he goes abroad, he can get a V visa and the USCIS will let him enter the United States despite his having been unlawfully present in the United States for more than 365 days. Still, according to USCIS regulations, when he applies for permanent residence, he'll be barred because of the unlawful presence ground of inadmissibility. He can't get permanent residence unless the USCIS grants a him a waiver of the bar. To get the waiver, he must prove that his mother will suffer extreme hardship if doesn't get an immigrant visa. My advice would be for him to avoid travel abroad unless an expert tells him he has a strong waiver case.

For more on unlawful presence bars and available waivers, see Chapter 5.

Getting a V Visa

If you are outside the United States, you apply for a V visa at a U.S. consulate. If you are in the United States, you may apply to change to V status without returning home. If the USCIS grants your change of status, you can live and work here in V status. You don't need a V visa stamp in your passport unless you travel outside the United States.

Terry's story illustrates how a person granted a change to V status gets a visa.

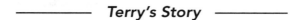

—————— *Terry's Story* ——————

Terry is an international student, here in F-1 student status. While in college, he married a permanent resident. His wife petitioned for him on May 1, 1999. On May 1, 2002, he still had not reached the front of the line under the preference quota system, so he applied for and received V status. He and his wife traveled to his home in Nigeria so his wife could meet his mother. While there, he can apply for a V visa at a U.S. consulate. Then, so long as he is in valid V status, he can travel in and out of the United States entering in V status. Once he gets to the front of the line under the quota for the spouse of a permanent resident, he can apply for adjustment of status.

Applying for a Change to V Status

If you are in the United States, you apply for a V visa by filing USCIS Form I-539, Application to Extend/Change Nonimmigrant Status, and an USCIS Form I-693, Medical Examination of Aliens Seeking Adjustment of Status. You'll pay a filing fee and a fingerprint fee. If your spouse and/or unmarried children will be applying for a change of status with you, you need file only one I-539 form for the whole family and pay only one filing fee. However, you must file separate fingerprint fees for each family member. List all for your qualifying family members (your spouse and unmarried children under age 21), on one I-539 supplement. You must also submit proof that you can support yourself without a need for public assistance. To prove you won't become a "public charge," you may follow the nonbinding affidavit support rules using USCIS Form I-134, Affidavit of Support. (For more on the medical examination and the public charge rules, see Chapter 6.) You must include a copy of the I-130, Petition for Alien Relative filing receipt, proving that a petition was filed for you by December 21, 2000. If you want USCIS work permission, you must include USCIS Form I-765, Application for Employment Authorization, with your change of status application. You submit your V visa change of status application to the U.S. Immigration and Naturalization Service, P.O. Box 7216, Chicago, IL 60680-7216.

If you live outside the United States, you apply for a V visa at a U.S. consulate. You apply at the consular post you specified on the I-130 petition (which your relative filed for you to qualify you for permanent residence) as the place you would apply for an immigrant visa. If you have relatives abroad who qualify for a V visa, send them a copy of the USCIS filing receipt. It is not necessary for the USCIS to have approved the petition. But if you have a notice of approval, send that as well. Some applicants will have received a notice from the U.S. Department of State telling them that they can apply for the V visa. Your relative can apply for the visa even without the notice.

CHAPTER 17

Nonimmigrant Status: Getting in and Staying in

Usually, to enter the United States as a nonimmigrant, you'll need a nonimmigrant visa. A nonimmigrant visa is a stamp in your passport put there by a U.S. consular officer at a U.S. consulate (in Taiwan you apply at the American Institute). You show it to an USCIS inspector at a land, air, or sea port. When you enter the United States, an USCIS inspector will stamp or write on a white card, USCIS Form I-94, the date you entered and the date your status will expire. Once you enter the United States as a nonimmigrant, we say that you are here in nonimmigrant status.

Not every nonimmigrant needs a visa to enter the United States. Under the Visa Waiver Program (VWP), the citizens of certain countries can enter the United States for business or pleasure visits without first getting a visa. (I discussed the VWP in Chapter 12.) Most Canadian nonimmigrants don't need a visa to enter the United States. The exception is Canadian treaty traders and treaty investors who do need an E visa. Canadian nonimmigrants seeking entry without a visa must meet all entry qualifications, including, in some cases, an approved petition.

WHERE TO APPLY FOR YOUR NONIMMIGRANT VISA

Most often, you must apply for a nonimmigrant visa at a U.S. consulate in the country of your current or last residence. In some countries, you can mail your application to the consulate, although often a consular officer will require a personal appearance. Since the events of 9/11, consulates have limited the number of applicants who can get a visa without a personal appearance. Now, personal appearances are required except in exceptional cases.

Some consulates, particularly in developing countries, have high refusal rates. That's why some visa applicants try to get a visa at a consulate in a country different from where they are residing. We call this third-country processing.

The 1996 immigration law took away the right to third-country process of many people unlawfully in the United States. Now you can third-country process only if you are in lawful status, if you never overstayed or were adjudicated to be out of status, if you made a timely application for a change or extension of status and that application is pending, or you can show that "extraordinary circumstances" exist in your case. If you are unlawfully in the United States, in most cases if you want a new visa, you'll have to apply at a consulate in your country of nationality.

How does the USCIS define "extraordinary circumstances?" If no consulate is operating in your country of nationality, that would almost certainly constitute an "extraordinary circumstance." Physicians who are in the United States as J-1 exchange visitors working in medically underserved areas, who are out of status for technical reasons, may also continue to qualify for third-country nonimmigrant visa processing. Extraordinary circumstances may also be shown if your employer filed a change of status application for you but the USCIS didn't approve the change until your status had already expired. You must have been in legal status when your employer petitioned for you and your stay expired only because the USCIS could not approve the change of status in time. Extraordinary circumstances exist also if you applied for an extension of stay before your current stay expired and the USCIS has not yet ruled on your extension request. Finally, A and G visa applicants can still take advantage of third-country processing.

Even if you are in the United States in lawful status, some consular officers discourage "consular shopping"—attempts to find the consulate where you think you are most likely to have your visa application approved. A third-country consular officer is most likely to favorably consider a visa application if you have a legitimate personal or business reason for being in the consular district. Some consulates, however, will accept almost any visa application if the applicant left the United States in lawful status. Consulates frequently change policy regarding whether they accept third-country applicants. Call the consul where you plan to apply to get an update before applying.

If you entered the United States on an H, L, or E visa, and your visa has expired but the USCIS has granted you an extension of stay, you can usually get a new visa by applying to the U.S. Department of State in Washington. We call this revalidating your visa.

Restrictions on Nonimmigrants from Iraq, Iran, Syria, Libya, Sudan, and Saudi Arabia.

Nonimmigrants from Iraq, Iran, Syria, Libya, Sudan, and Saudi Arabia must be fingerprinted upon arrival to the United States. A and G nonimmigrants are exempt. Thirty days after arrival, and every year thereafter, these individuals must appear in person at an USCIS field office and submit proof of residence. Nonimmigrants from the designated countries my notify an USCIS agent of their departure from the United States.

Making a Successful Nonimmigrant Visa Application

A visa applicant can do little to challenge a consular officer's denial of a nonimmigrant visa application. So it is important that you are courteous and clear in your presentation to the U.S. consular officer and that you are as prepared as you can possibly be. You should keep copies of any documents that you submit to the consul, just in case a problem develops.

If you apply for a nonimmigrant visa, you must anticipate two main issues: nonimmigrant intent and grounds of inadmissibility (a bar to an otherwise eligible applicant; formerly called a "ground of exclusion"). I discuss nonimmigrant intent in detail in the following section. In Appendix E, I list the grounds of inadmissibility. If you're inadmissible for one of the reasons listed, you may still be able to obtain a nonimmigrant visa, but you may have to apply for a waiver of inadmissibility. If you think that you may be inadmissible, speak to an immigration law expert before applying for a visa.

Proving Nonimmigrant Intent

Having nonimmigrant intent means that you plan to leave the United States when your stay expires. It also means that you're not going to use the nonimmigrant visa as a means to get to the United States so that you can live there permanently. You are most likely to have problems with the nonimmigrant intent issue if you are applying for a B, C, D, F, J, or M visa.

No problem frustrates nonimmigrant visa applicants more than having a consular officer deny their application because of a claim of immigrant intent. If you are from a developed country, you will usually not have a problem with proving nonimmigrant intent unless you have previously violated immigration laws or have had a permanent immigrant visa petition filed for you. If you are from a developing country, a consular officer may automatically assume that you have the intention of staying permanently in the United States.

In cases where nonimmigrant intent is an issue, showing the U.S. consular officer that you have strong ties to your country of residence is important. You want to show family, community, or social ties, membership in organizations and religious groups, a family business, ownership of property, and bank accounts. Mirella's and Juan's stories provide examples of nonimmigrant visa applicants confronting the issue of immigrant intent.

Mirella's Story

Mirella is from Italy and is applying for a student visa to study at Los Angeles City College, a two-year college in California. The college has accepted her, and the school's foreign student advisor sent her Form I-20. Form I-20 proves that she meets the basic qualifications for an F-1 visa.

However, Mirella's mother is a permanent resident of the United States and has petitioned the USCIS to let Mirella, too, become a permanent resident. When Mirella applies for her visa at the U.S. consulate in Milan, she notes correctly on her nonimmigrant visa application that her mother has petitioned for her. Though Mirella probably won't get her immigrant visa for four or five years, the consular officer who interviews her questions her about whether she truly has a nonimmigrant intent. Will she return to Italy when she completes her studies at Los Angeles City College? Does she plan to continue her studies at a four-year college? If she fails out of college, will she return to Italy? Is she really just planning to use the F-1 visa as a way to get into the United States while she waits to get an immigrant visa?

Consular officers rarely deny Italians nonimmigrant visas, but it happens. Whether Mirella gets a student visa depends on whether she can persuade the consular officer that she will not violate her student status. She will have to convince the officer that if she completes her studies before she qualifies for an immigrant visa, she will return to Italy until her time to immigrate.

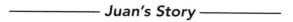

Juan's Story

Juan is a citizen of the Dominican Republic who lives in the lovely beachside town of Puerto Plata. He is 25 years old and single. He wants to attend the graduation of his sister from New York University. She is the first member of his family to graduate from a U.S. college. When he first goes to the U.S. consulate to apply for a B-2 visitor's visa, the consular officer who interviews him denies his request. The officer doesn't believe that Juan, a young man with no wife or children in the Dominican Republic, will return in two weeks as Juan has said he would.

Two days later, Juan applies again to the consular officer for a visitor's visa. This time he brings a letter from his employer, a major bank, showing his salary and explaining the fact that he is up for a promotion to vice president. Juan also brings the title to a small home that he owns in the capital of the Dominican Republic, Santo Domingo, and a copy of the graduation notice from New York University listing his sister as a commencement speaker. Based on the evidence of Juan's ties to the Dominican Republic and proof of the specific event (his sister's graduation), the consular officer approves Juan's application for a B-2 visitor's visa.

How Long and for How Many Entries May You Use Your Visa?

If a consular officer grants you a nonimmigrant visa, he or she will put a visa stamp in your passport. The stamp will contain a visa number, the location of the consulate where they issued the visa, an expiration date, and the number of times you can use the visa to enter the United States. The visa may be indefinite and valid for multiple entries, which means that you can enter and leave the United States as often as you like for as long as you live. Or the visa may be limited in time and be valid for only a limited number of entries.

For instance, if yours is a single-entry, one-year visa, you may enter the United States anytime during that year, but once you use the visa, it will no longer be valid for entry into the United States. If you leave the United States after the one entry on a single-entry visa, you will need to apply for a new visa before you return. With a single-entry visa, you may reenter without a new visa only if you are in status and you are returning from a visit of no more than 30 days to Canada or Mexico. F and J visa holders in status but with expired visas can reenter from trips of no more than 30 days from Mexico, Canada, or the Caribbean.

If you have a multiple-entry visa, you can use it to enter the United States until the visa expires. When you apply for entry into the United States, a border officer will review your documents, noting the type of visa you used to enter. The officer will also note on Form I-94 the time that you may remain in the United States.

Form I-94, then, is a document that you can use to prove your lawful entry into the United States and your status while here. The entry stamp in your passport or other travel document is also evidence of lawful entry. If you made a lawful entry, your visa may expire, but you may still be in the United States in legal status.

Ying's and Sharon's stories illustrate the difference between the validity of your visa and the lawfulness of your status.

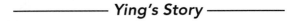

Ying's Story

A consular officer in Beijing, China, granted Ying a single-entry H-1B visa. The visa was valid for one month from the time the officer issued it. A company in Houston, Texas, had petitioned the USCIS to allow Ying to work for them for three years as a senior electrical engineer. The USCIS had approved the petition for a three-year period and sent the notice of approval to Beijing, where Ying applied for her visa.

Two weeks after the consular officer stamped the visa in her passport, on January 15, 1998, Ying arrived in New York, where she planned to stay for a week with relatives and see the sights. At the airport, an USCIS inspector stamped her Form I-94 "H-1B, valid until January 15, 2002." Thus, though her visa expired two weeks after she entered the United States, she can live legally in the United States and work for the Houston company until January 15, 2005. If the USCIS grants her an extension of stay, she can remain even longer.

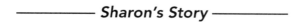
Sharon's Story

Sharon, from Costa Rica, came to the United States on an F-1 student visa to study at the University of Wisconsin. The visa was good for one year. The USCIS officer at the airport stamped her Form I-94 "D/S" (Duration of Status). The D/S stamp meant that Sharon could remain in the United States while she was pursuing a full course of study. After her third year at the university, Sharon decided on a trip to the beautiful city of Vancouver, Canada. Although her visa had expired, she was in lawful status and did not need to get a new visa. Next summer, when she goes to Costa Rica to visit her parents, she will need to get a new F-1 to reenter the United States.

If a Consular Officer Denies Your Nonimmigrant Visa Application

If a consular officer denies your application for a nonimmigrant visa, the officer will usually tell you the reasons for the denial and you will receive written notice of those reasons. Sometimes you can ask the visa officer to reconsider the denial. For instance, if the officer denied the application because you failed to show sufficient ties to your country, you may be able to return with additional proof, such as a job letter, that you are likely to return to your country. If, however, the consular officer insists on denying the application, it is very difficult to get that decision overturned.

If a consular officer denies your application or request for reconsideration, your only appeal is to seek an Advisory Opinion from the U.S. Department of State, asking them to reverse the decision of the officer. Where the officer's decision is based on a claim that you are intending to live permanently in the United States, what the law calls an "intending immigrant," it is very unlikely that the Department of State will reverse the consular officer's decision. Where an issue of law is involved, such as an interpretation of government regulations or statutes, the Department of State will sometimes reverse the consular officer's decision. To get an Advisory Opinion, write to Advisory Opinions Division for Visa Services, United States Department of State, 2401 E Street, NW, Washington, DC 20522-0113.

The Procedure at the Port of Entry

When you present yourself at an air, land, or sea port, an USCIS inspector will look at your passport, ask you about your purpose in coming to the United States, and decide whether you should be admitted. Usually the inspection is routine. Sometimes the USCIS inspector will question you carefully or check your luggage. If you have a valid, unexpired visa, the inspector will then do one of three things: (1) admit you, stamping your I-94 with the type of visa and the length of time for which you are admitted, (2) parole you in pending further proceedings (physically let you in but without legally admitting you), or (3) tell you that you are not admissible and ask you to return to where you came from.

If you are applying for entry using a valid visa, you have the right to a hearing before an immigration judge as to your right to enter the United States. If you are applying for entry under the Visa Waiver Program, you waive that right to a hearing.

Changing Nonimmigrant Status

Once you arrive in the United States using a nonimmigrant visa, you may want to change your nonimmigrant status. You might come to the United States as an H-1B professional worker and want to change to F-1 student. Or, if you are here in F-1 student status, upon graduation from college, you may want to become an H-1B temporary professional worker.

A change of status application is usually made by using USCIS Form I-539, Application to Extend/Change Nonimmigrant Status. You file the change of status application with the USCIS Regional Service Center having jurisdiction over your temporary home in the United States. When you change to H-1B, H-2, or H-3 work status, you don't need to file a separate change of status application. The change of status application is part of the petition filed by you or your employer. The USCIS is much more likely to change your status if you are in status, that is, if your authorized period of stay hasn't expired. If you are out of status, you must have an exceptionally good reason why your status has lapsed. One exception is V visa applicants, who may apply to change to V status without leaving the United States.

Extension of Stay

If you want to stay in the United States beyond the period granted to you by the USCIS inspector when you entered the country, you'll need to file for an extension of stay on Form I-539. Make sure you file your extension request before your stay expires, or you will need an extraordinarily good excuse as to why you filed late.

Asylees and Refugees

Hⁿ "ow come you got to stay in the United States?" Maria asked her friend Barbara over coffee. "You don't have any family here," she added.

"The USCIS gave me political asylum," Barbara answered. "Convincing the USCIS that I couldn't go back to my country was very hard. But I had a copy of the papers they gave me when they released me from prison, and I gave them statements from my friends from the resistance movement. That convinced them," said Barbara. "Then, one year after they gave me asylum, I applied for permanent residence. It took a while, but eventually the USCIS gave me my green card."

Perhaps the most controversial aspect of U.S. immigration law involves the treatment of those seeking asylum and refuge in the United States. Too often, foreign policy interests and racial discrimination have biased U.S. asylum and refugee policy. It is an area of law constantly debated and litigated, and therefore it is always in flux.

Let's look at the terms "asylee" and "refugee." Asylees and refugees are people who have a well-founded fear that they will be persecuted in their home country because of their race, religion, nationality, political opinions, or membership in a particular social group. Refugees apply for refugee status at an USCIS office outside the United States. If they are successful, the USCIS gives them travel documents that they can use to enter the United States. Asylees are people who are already in the United States or at a U.S. port of entry when they apply to live in the United States.

I begin in Chapter 18 by explaining how you prove a well-founded fear of persecution; I also discuss the process for filing for asylum. In Chapter 19, I explain refugee processing procedures.

These days, getting asylum or refugee status is hard. Don't try to do it on your own. If you are in the United States, talk to an immigration law expert before sending your asylum application to the USCIS. If you are abroad, talk to a representative of a voluntary (not-for-profit) agency or a United Nations High Commission on Refugees (UNHCR) representative before contacting the U.S. government.

CHAPTER 18

Proving Fear of Persecution and Getting Asylum

The USCIS radically altered the asylum process in January 1995, and the U.S. Congress changed it further in 1996. The regulations and current USCIS practice provide for a quick resolution to asylum claims. The process is designed to discourage frivolous applications, while quickly granting asylum to qualified applicants. An important result of the new regulations is that if you apply for asylum and lose your claim, the government will try to remove you.

Some criticize the USCIS for being more interested in deporting asylum applicants than in finding genuine refugees. Yet every day, people are granted asylum. Current procedures, while discouraging people with weak or nonexistent cases from applying for asylum just to get work authorization, benefit those with strong applications.

As I explain later, either an immigration judge or the USCIS may grant you asylum. In either case, you must prove that you have a well-founded fear that you will be persecuted if you return home. Sometimes you hear the term "political" asylum used to describe any kind of asylee status. However, you can be an asylee because of many types of persecution, not just political. The persecution can be based on your religion, race, nationality, membership in a particular social group, or political opinion.

If you are granted asylum, you can work in the United States and, one year after your case is approved, you can apply for permanent residence. However, you still may wait a long time before the USCIS finally grants you permanent residence.

The One-Year Rule

You must file for asylum within one year after you arrive in the United States. The only exceptions are if you can prove changed circumstances in your country or "extraordinary circumstances" prevented you from filing within the one-year limit.

Examples of changed circumstances include a change in government in your country or a recent attack on a relative or colleague. An example of a circumstance that may have prevented you from filing would be mental or physical disability.

The one-year rule does not apply to applications for Withholding of Removal or applications under the Torture Convention discussed below.

Proving a Well-Founded Fear of Persecution

Having a well-founded fear of persecution does not necessarily mean that you will be tortured, killed, or even arrested if you return home. Persecution can also mean confiscation of your property, denial of the opportunity to work, and being forced to comply with laws that go against your religious beliefs. You can show a well-founded fear of persecution by proving that you have been persecuted in the past and that conditions have not changed. Or you can give evidence of what is likely to happen to you if you return home. What constitutes "persecution" is a complicated legal question best left to an immigration law expert.

Typically, you will prove your fear of persecution through your own statements, both written and oral, and the affidavits of friends and relatives. You may also use the statements of experts who have information about conditions in your country and what has already happened and/ or what is likely to happen if you returned there, as well as newspaper articles and arrest records.

The persecution does not necessarily have to be at the hands of the government. If you are suffering persecution from a nongovernmental authority—for instance, the majority religious group is persecuting you because you are a member of a minority religious group—and you can prove that the government is unwilling or incapable of preventing the persecution, you may have a claim for asylum. The 1996 immigration law says that you may prove a fear of persecution if you can show that you are a victim of coercive population control, such as forced sterilization or forced abortion. Only 1,000 people per year can get asylum (or become refugees) under this special provision.

You cannot base a case for asylum solely on economic hardship—for example, you would starve because poverty or famine is a common condition in your country. Nor is it enough to show that war or civil strife or a repressive government makes it dangerous to everyone in your country. The persecution must be based on one of the five listed criteria: race, religion, nationality, political opinion, or membership in a particular social group.

Carmen's story illustrates that proving suffering due to war or national disaster cannot be the basis of an asylum claim.

—————— Carmen's Story ——————

Carmen was born and raised in El Salvador. Neither she nor any close members of her family were politically active. They supported neither the government nor the rebels that were trying to overthrow the government. Carmen was aware of the political conflict in her country, but she and her family did what they could to stay away from the fighting. Unfortunately, a battle between government and rebel forces broke out near her village. Her parents and her brother and sister were accidentally killed.

Left alone with no means to support herself, she decided to come to the United States to try to get a job so that she wouldn't starve. She made her way to Mexico and, eventually, with the help of friends in California, she paid a smuggler who took her across the border into the United States.

Carmen cannot get asylum based on what happened to her family in El Salvador. Though her life was in danger because of the fighting, she was never persecuted herself for her political opinion, race, nationality, religion, or membership in a particular social group.

Discretionary Denials of Asylum

Even if you can prove a well-founded fear of persecution, an asylum officer or immigration judge may deny you asylum if the officer or judge, considering all the facts in your case, doesn't think you deserve asylum because of negative factors. We call this being denied as a matter of discretion. When an officer or a judge exercises discretion, they weigh negative factors in your case against positive factors. The officer or judge can deny you asylum as a matter of discretion because you could have applied to become a refugee before coming to the United States, because you entered the United States with phony papers, or because you have a troubling criminal record (even if it is not serious enough to automatically bar you from asylum). They may also deny you asylum as a matter of discretion if you were persecuted in the past, but returning home now is safe. Immigration judges routinely deny asylum for one of these reasons. Asylum officers rarely deny asylum as a matter of discretion.

If you are denied asylum as a matter of discretion, an immigration judge may grant you withholding of deportation, now called "withholding of removal", and you may have the right to remain in the United States (see "Withholding of Deportation/Removal" below).

Uri's story helps us to understand how discretion affects asylum applications.

Uri was born in Albania and fled to Yugoslavia with his family when he was five years old. But his life in Yugoslavia wasn't easy. Since 1979 the Yugoslav police had detained, interrogated, and physically abused him on many occasions. The police insisted that he was involved in the political activities of the Albanian minority in Yugoslavia, although he denied the accusation. He left Yugoslavia in 1986 and went to Brussels, Belgium, in order to avoid further encounters with police officials.

Uri stayed in Brussels for six weeks with a man who had been a friend of his family in Albania and Yugoslavia. His friend called a refugee organization in Italy to ask about whether Uri could stay in an Italian refugee camp. The organization told Uri's friend that they couldn't help. Uri applied at the U.S. embassy in Brussels for a tourist visa, but they denied his application. A consular officer told Uri to go to Yugoslavia to apply for a visa.

One day while he was discussing his situation in an Albanian coffeehouse in Belgium, a stranger there offered to sell him a Belgian passport with a U.S. tourist visa stamped inside. Uri gave the man his photograph and paid him $1,000 for the phony passport.

Uri entered the United States in early 1987 as a visitor using the phony passport. He went to live with his uncle and cousins, who had come to the United States many years earlier. One month later, the USCIS caught him when they raided the factory where he worked. Uri asked for a hearing before an immigration judge. He immediately told the judge that he wanted to apply for asylum. After considering the evidence, including Uri's lengthy testimony, the judge decided that Uri had a well-founded fear of persecution if they returned him home. However, because he had used phony papers to come to the United States rather than applying for refugee status abroad, the USCIS argued against asylum for Uri.

In deciding whether Uri would get asylum, or the lesser benefit of withholding of removal, the judge considered the factors in favor of and against Uri. The favorable factors were the persecution he had suffered and was likely to suffer if he returned home, as well as his efforts to stay in Europe as a refugee. The negative factor was his use of a phony passport to enter the United States and his waiting until he was caught before coming forward to request asylum. The judge opted to grant Uri asylum.

Bars to Asylum

Beyond discretionary bars to asylum, there are mandatory bars as well. An asylum officer or immigration judge must deny you asylum if you have firmly resettled in a third country. A third country means a country other than the United States and the country where you fear persecution. The officer or judge must also deny you asylum if you have been convicted of committing a particularly serious crime, including any aggravated felonies, or you have persecuted others. (See Appendix J, "List of Aggravated Felonies.")

If you are ineligible for asylum because you have firmly resettled in a third country, a judge may grant you withholding of removal, and you can remain in the United States. If you are ineligible for asylum because you have committed certain serious crimes or persecuted others, the USCIS may try to deport you home, even if you might be persecuted there. However, under the Convention Against Torture discussed below, you cannot be moved to a country where you will be tortured, regardless of whether you have persecuted others or committed a serious crime. I will discuss what's deemed "torture" momentarily in The Torture Convention Defense.

Firm Resettlement

The rationale behind the firm resettlement law is that a person seeking refugee status does not have the right to choose to live in any country he or she wishes. In order for firm resettlement to be a bar to asylum, you must have had, or been offered, all the rights and benefits of a permanent resident or citizen of that third country: the right to work, the right to attend school, the right to remain indefinitely in the country, and the right to leave and return to that country. Jacobo's story illustrates the concept of firm resettlement.

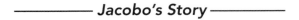

——————— *Jacobo's Story* ———————

Jacobo was a leader in a student movement in support of the Zapatistas, a militant armed group in Mexico that was challenging the authority of the government. Though he never admitted that he was a member of the Zapatista army, many believed that he had participated in armed actions. Jacobo learned through a friend in the government that the Mexican authorities would soon come to arrest him. He decided to leave Mexico for Spain. He told the Spanish authorities that he planned only to visit their country, but he ended up staying for more than a year, continuing his efforts to support the Zapatista movement. He came to the United States when a Mexican American student group invited him to speak at the University of Texas in Austin. After just a few weeks in Texas, Jacobo realized that he could do more work for his cause in the United States than in Spain, and he decided to apply for asylum.

The fact that Jacobo spent a year in Spain will not automatically disqualify him for asylum. While in Spain, he did not have legal status or permission to work. Although he was safe from persecution in Spain, he neither firmly resettled nor was offered firm resettlement.

Criminal Activity

If you are convicted of an aggravated felony or felonies and you are sentenced to an aggregate term of imprisonment of at least five years, you become ineligible for withholding of deportation/removal. Thus you will be denied both asylum and withholding of removal, and the government can send you home, unless you will face torture and you are thus protected by the Convention Against Torture.

The Torture Convention Defense

Under the United Nations Convention Against Torture and Other Crimes, Inhumane or Degrading Treatment or Punishment, (often referred to as the Convention Against Torture, CAT), you may not be returned to a country where you will be tortured.

The Board of Immigration Appeals, BIA, has defined torture as including the following: (1) an act causing severe physical or mental pain or suffering that must be "an extreme form of cruel and inhuman treatment" and not lesser forms; (2) the act must be "specifically intended" to inflict severe physical or mental pain or suffering (so an act that results in unanticipated or unintended severity of pain or suffering does not constitute torture); (3) the act must have an "illicit purpose," such as "obtaining information or a confession, punishment for a victim's or another's act, intimidating or coercing a victim or another or any discriminatory purpose;" (4) the act must be an intentional government act directed against a person in the offender's custody or control (so "negligent acts or acts by private individuals not acting on behalf of the government" are not covered); and (5) the act "does not include pain or suffering arising only from, inherent in or incidental to lawful sanctions," such as a judicially imposed death penalty.

The major benefit under the CAT appeal is that you do not have to prove that you will be persecuted for any particular reason (which is not the case when applying for a "Grant of Asylum" or a "Withholding of Deportation," where you must prove why you will face persecution if deported to a particular country). With CAT, the mere fact that you will face torture is reason enough to prevent the government from removing you.

Only an immigration judge can grant you the right to remain in the United States because you will be tortured if you are returned home. Note that relief under CAT does not make you eligible for permanent residence, nor does it make you immune to government custody. That said, unless you are a threat to the community, the government will likely release you if a judge grants you CAT relief.

Application Procedures

One aspect common to all asylum applications is that the USCIS requests an Advisory Opinion from the Department of State on each application. An asylum officer or immigration judge is not required to follow the advice of the Department of State. He or she is free to ignore the Department of State. However, the law requires that asylum officers and immigration judges make a decision independent of the Department of State Advisory Opinion.

Defensive Versus Affirmative Asylum Applications

We say you file an affirmative asylum application when you apply for asylum before the government tries to deport you. You should only file affirmatively when you are sure, after talking to an expert, that you have a very strong case. If your application is successful and the USCIS grants you asylum, you'll get work authorization and you'll qualify for permanent residence after one year. If you are here out of status and the USCIS denies your application, they will try to deport you. If you are here in status (for instance, as a legal foreign student) and the USCIS denies your application, you may have a hard time getting a nonimmigrant visa in the future.

If the USCIS denies your asylum claim, you can renew your application before an immigration judge, but, in the end, you may be forced out of the United States.

We say you are filing defensively when you file for asylum only after the government has ordered you to appear for a deportation/removal proceeding and you apply for asylum as a defense. With a defensive application, you have little to lose. You may not win asylum, but unless your application is frivolous—that is, without any merit at all—you aren't penalized for trying. If the USCIS finds that your application is frivolous, you could be barred from later becoming a permanent resident.

Affirmative Applications

You file an affirmative asylum application with the USCIS Regional Service Center for the area where you live (see Appendix C, "USCIS National and Regional Offices"). You send the application (USCIS Form I-589, Application for Asylum and for Withholding of Removal) with two three-quarter profile photos and two USCIS fingerprint charts. No filing fee is required. You should also include your own statement and the affidavits (sworn statements) of people who can support your claim. If you were arrested for your beliefs, you should include an arrest record, if you have it. You should include anything that you think will help the decide in your favor. Newspaper articles about you, your country, or your beliefs, books, medical records—it's up to you. You must submit a translation with all documents not in the English language. You can supplement your application later, but it is best if you make a strong presentation when you first file your application.

The USCIS Regional Service Center will forward your application, with supporting documents, to an USCIS asylum office. The USCIS will then schedule you for an interview with an USCIS asylum officer.

An attorney or representative of a recognized not-for-profit organization can represent you at your asylum interview. You may bring witnesses, but the interview is usually short, so it is often better to present written notarized statements than to bring witnesses.

If the decision says that the USCIS has approved your application, you can apply for employment authorization (also known as a "work card"). Your spouse and unmarried children under age 21 at the time you filed your asylum application can get asylum as well.That's true even if the child turns 21 before the USCIS approves the asylum application of the parent.

If the USCIS denies your application and you are out of status, you will recieve notice to appear for a removal hearing.

At your removal hearing, you may ask the immigration judge to grant you asylum. The judge will have your original application, and you can supplement the record with additional affidavits and documentary evidence. You may also have witnesses testify for you. The immigration judge will take into consideration your credibility (whether you should be believed), whether your statements are trustworthy and believable, and the credibility of your witnesses. USCIS rules specifically state that an applicant's asylum testimony alone may be sufficient to grant an asylum claim.

If the immigration judge grants you asylum, you'll get the same rights and benefits as any asylee. If the immigration judge rules against you, you can appeal that decision to the Board of Immigration Appeals (BIA). The government can appeal also. If the BIA dismisses your appeal, you can ask a federal court to review the BIA's decision. The government can't remove you from the United States until the BIA decides your case.

The stories of Darian and Sophie illustrate the concepts of affirmative asylum applications.

———— Darian's Story ————

Darian's family was very active in their country's politics. They were part of a growing opposition movement seeking greater democracy in their country. Darian was only 20 years old and didn't play an important role in the politics of his country, but he was outspoken against government abuses. After his first year in college, he decided to spend his summer with relatives in the United States. He came into the United States on a visitor's visa with plans to return to finish his senior year in college.

While in the United States, Darian learned that government officials had arrested his father, mother, brother, and sister. Newspaper articles in papers back home discussed how the government would try the family for treason. The articles also said that government agents were looking for Darian. Obviously, he could not return home.

Darian wasn't wealthy enough to live in the United States without working, and he didn't qualify for a work visa. After discussing his case with a representative of a not-for-profit agency that helps immigrants, he decided to apply for asylum.

Darian got an affidavit from a university professor who was an expert in his country's politics. He also got affidavits from relatives in the United States who were knowledgeable about his family's opposition to the government. When he sent in his application, he included copies of the newspaper articles about him and his family. He submitted his application with the supporting documents to the USCIS Regional Service Center. An

USCIS asylum officer interviewed him and granted him asylum. One year later, he will be eligible to apply to become a permanent resident of the United States.

Darian's application was an affirmative application because the government had not been trying to remove him from the United States at the time that he filed the application.

—————— *Sophie's Story* ——————

Sophie was from Latin America. She managed to come to the United States by crossing the Mexican-U.S. border late one night. Under U.S. immigration laws, she had no right to be in the United States. She got a job working very hard at very low wages. She knew that unless she got USCIS work permission, she would have a very hard time making it in the United States. Sophie had heard that the USCIS granted asylum to many people from her country. Sophie had never been active in any political activities, but she was desperate to get work permission. She went to an "immigration consultant" who charged her $500 and advised her to apply for asylum. The consultant who advised Sophie was neither a lawyer nor a representative of a not-for-profit organization.

With the consultant's help, Sophie applied to the USCIS for asylum. The consultant filled out the form without even asking Sophie the basis for her asylum claim, and Sophie signed it. The USCIS scheduled her for an interview with an asylum officer. At the interview, Sophie had a very hard time answering the officer's questions. She claimed that she had been very active politically in her country, but she had a hard time explaining her point of view. Under questioning from the asylum officer, she kept changing her story. She did not submit any evidence other than her own statement about why she had a well-founded fear of persecution.

The asylum officer told Sophie to come back in 30 days for the decision in her case. When Sophie returned to the asylum office, she learned that they had denied her asylum application. An USCIS officer gave her a notice to appear for removal proceedings.

Sophie had made an affirmative application for asylum. The USCIS had no knowledge that Sophie was in the United States until she filed the application. Now, because she had made a weak asylum application, she found herself in removal proceedings. Unless Sophie can figure out some legal way to remain in the United States, she will be forced to return to her country.

Defensive Applications

You file defensive applications with the immigration court after the government has already ordered you to appear for a removal hearing. At your hearing, you'll have the right to testify and present witnesses and evidence. If the immigration judge denies your application, he or she may order you to leave the country.

LaNedra's story illustrates the concepts of defensive asylum applications.

LaNedra's Story

LaNedra was a schoolteacher in a poor country. She was very popular with her students and their parents. She had a reputation as an individual who cared about other people. Often, when people in her village had problems with local authorities, they would go to LaNedra and she would speak to the authorities for them. LaNedra never thought of herself as being political, but the local government considered her a nuisance, especially after she organized a group of parents to protest poor conditions in the schools. Once, after she led a demonstration, the police chief arrested her for disorderly conduct. The police chief told her that if she didn't keep quiet, she might end up in prison.

LaNedra was making very little money. She was having great difficulty supporting herself and her two small children. Her husband had died after the birth of their second child, and she was the sole source of income for her family. Because she spoke out against local government abuses, LaNedra had trouble getting a better job. A relative in the United States encouraged LaNedra to come to New York where, he said, he could find her work. LaNedra got a visitor's visa and came to the United States.

Life in the United States was very difficult for LaNedra because she didn't have work authorization. She managed to find a job working "off the books" at a garment factory for $100 per week. One day the goverment raided the factory and arrested LaNedra. She ended up in deportation/removal proceedings.

LaNedra had little documentation about what had happened to her back home. Her case will depend primarily on her own testimony. Her claim is genuine but not very strong. But since asylum is LaNedra's only chance to stay in the United States, she has no reason not to ask the judge for asylum. LaNedra is making a defensive asylum application.

Withholding of Deportation/Removal

Even if a judge denies you asylum as a matter of discretion, you may win the right to remain temporarily in the United States under the withholding of removal law (until April 1, 1997, this was called "withholding of deportation"). Only an immigration judge can grant you withholding of removal.

The test for this relief is harder than for asylum. In order to obtain withholding of removal relief, you must show a clear probability that you will be persecuted if you are sent home. This is a higher standard than the "well-founded fear of persecution" standard used in asylum cases.

With withholding of removal, you don't qualify for permanent residence in one year as you do with asylum. However, you will get USCIS work permission. If you get withholding of removal after the judge denies your asylum application, you may get permanent residence some other way, such as through marrying a U.S. citizen or through an offer of employment.

You will have a hard time getting withholding of removal if you have been convicted of a particularly serious crime (such as an aggravated felony), you have persecuted others, you have committed a serious nonpolitical crime outside the United States, you are a danger to the security of the United States, or you are a terrorist.

Applications at Entry (or Within Two Years of Entry) into the United States

As of April 1, 1997, if (1) you arrive at a U.S. port of entry without proper entry documents, (2) you are caught trying to sneak into the United States, or (3) you have been in the United States for less than two years, you are subject to special expedited asylum processing. Under the 1996 immigration law, you can be detained until the government decides that you have proven that you have a well-founded fear of persecution and that you are eligible for either asylum or withholding of removal.

Under the new procedures, the first step is an interview by an asylum officer. If you convince the officer that you have a credible claim of persecution, you will be detained for further consideration of your application. If you can't convince the asylum officer that you have a credible claim of persecution, you have the right to a hearing before an immigration judge. The hearing must be held within seven days. If the judge denies your asylum claim, you'll be sent back to the country you were in just before you arrived in the United States.

CHAPTER 19

Refugees and Refugee Processing

Like an asylum applicant, if you want to come to the United States as a refugee, you must prove that you have a well-founded fear of being persecuted in your home country. (For an explanation of what is meant by "well-founded fear of persecution," see Chapter 18.) Refugee applicants, like asylum applicants, must prove that they face persecution based on race, religion, political opinion, nationality, or membership in a social group. And, just as in the case of asylees, you can be denied refugee status if you have firmly resettled in a third country or committed certain serious crimes. Also barred from refugee status, without the right to a waiver, are former or current members of the Nazi Party, those who have participated in genocide, and those convicted of certain serious crimes.

If the USCIS approves your refugee application, your spouse and your unmarried children under age 21 may come with you to the United States or follow you here after your arrival. One year after your admission to the United States as a refugee, you may apply for an immigrant visa (green card).

Typically, a refugee is living outside his or her home country, afraid to return home. In exceptional situations, you can apply to be a refugee without leaving your country at USCIS in-country refugee processing centers. In recent years, the USCIS has set up in-country centers in Havana, Moscow, and Ho Chi Minh City.

APPLYING FOR REFUGEE PAPERS

If you want to apply to come to the United States as a refugee, you may contact an international relief organization. You may also contact the United Nations High Commission on Refugees (UNHCR), which has offices in countries throughout the world. U.S. embassies and consulates also can provide you with refugee processing information. The refugee applications then are processed at USCIS offices outside the United States.

The yearly quota for U.S. refugee admissions is set by the President after consultation with Congress. Once you have established a well-founded fear of persecution, the USCIS will consider a number of factors in deciding whether they will admit you to the United States as a refugee. Among the factors are family and other ties to the United States, general humanitarian concerns, and the policy interests of the United States.

A refugee application is made on USCIS Form I-590, Registration for Classification as a Refugee, and is submitted with USCIS Form G-325C, Biographic Information, and a completed fingerprint chart. An USCIS officer will have the applicant make a sworn statement. The USCIS will require a medical examination that screens the applicant for tuberculosis ("TB"), HIV, and venereal diseases. Treatable diseases must be cured before a refugee is allowed to travel to the United States. People testing HIV positive need a special waiver (see "Health Issues," Chapter 5). To get refugee travel papers, you must also have a sponsor who can guarantee your transportation to the United States. The sponsor can be a person or an organization.

Once the USCIS has decided that you meet the qualifications to be a refugee, you must arrange for resettlement in the United States. The USCIS, the UNHCR, or a voluntary agency abroad will help you make contact with a U.S. resettlement agency. Before you are given refugee papers, a U.S. voluntary agency must agree to assist you upon your arrival in the United States.

Once you arrive in the United States, voluntary agencies usually provide support for your first 90 days. All refugees can get USCIS work authorization upon their arrival, and they are eligible for most public benefits, such as Medicaid and food stamps.

To travel outside the United States, a refugee can get a "refugee travel document," renewable at one-year intervals. They look like white U.S. passports.

If your spouse and/or children didn't accompany you to the United States, you can petition or sponsor them to come to the United States. The children must be unmarried and under age 21. Petition for family members using USCIS Form I-730, Refugee/Asylee Relative Petition.

Maria's story helps us to understand refugee processing.

Maria was an active member of the antigovernment movement in Poland in 1987. She often took risks, participating in illegal actions against the government. In one such action during the election, she was arrested and interrogated by police. The police took her passport away and let her go. She was stopped again immediately after she left the police station for not having an ID and was kept in jail for 48 hours. When she finally got out, she decided to leave the country. Some of her best friends from the movement had already left for the refugee camp in Latina, Italy. She decided to join her friends in Italy.

In Italy she went straight from the airport to the refugee camp in Latina and declared herself a political refugee. Maria's friends had since left for the United States. The Tolstoy Foundation, one of many U.S.-based voluntary agencies in Europe that assist refugees, helped her file an asylum application with the Italian government. The Italians denied her application, but she got an appointment for an interview with the USCIS at the U.S. consulate in Rome.

At her interview, she confirmed the facts given in the application, explaining her fear of persecution if she returned to Poland. She gave the USCIS in Rome the names of her friends with whom she had conspired in Poland, the same friends that had been admitted to the United States as refugees. She reconstructed the details of her arrest and political activity. The USCIS agreed to give her refugee status in the United States.

After one year in the camp in Latina, Italy, she was flown to the United States and reunited with the friends who had sponsored her. After one year, she applied for permanent residence.

Employer Sanctions

Mom, listen to this. I went for a job interview today, and the personnel office wanted to see my passport. I've been a citizen of this country for over 20 years, and they still want to see my working papers," Maria told her mother. "I don't even have a passport."

"Maybe you should forget about that job. Maybe they don't like people like us," Maria's mother said.

"But they pay twice as much as what I get now, and they offer much better benefits," Maria responded.

Frustrated, Maria called an immigration lawyer to find out what kind of documents she was required to show her potential employer to prove that she is authorized to work. The lawyer told Maria that an employer has the right to ask her for proof of her identity and authorization to work, but not to demand to see her passport. Maria must present proof that she is authorized to work in the United States, or the employer can't hire her.

Employer sanctions refers to the law that requires employers to check the documents of new employees to ensure that they are authorized to work in the United States. The law punishes employers who don't check employees' documents and who knowingly hire workers not authorized to work. But employers must be careful how they go about complying with the law. An employer who asks for more or different documents than the law requires or who refuses to accept documents that appear valid may face fines and other penalties. Not only can an employer be sanctioned for failing to check documents, but an employer can also be sanctioned for discriminating against a worker on the basis of that worker's citizenship or nationality.

The employer sanctions law was part of the Immigration Reform and Control Act of 1986 (IRCA). IRCA, also known as the amnesty law, gave immigrant visas to millions of undocumented persons who had been in the United States since before January 1, 1982. The employer sanctions provisions are supposed to deter new undocumented workers from coming unlawfully to the United States by limiting their access to employment. While most commentators believe that employer sanctions have been a failure, repeal efforts have yet to gain broad support in the U.S. Congress.

If you're an employer, Chapter 20 will help you understand your record-keeping responsibilities and the penalties you face for violating the law. If you are an employee, Chapter 21 will help you make sure that an employer treats you fairly when you are asked to present your work authorization documents.

The 1996 immigration laws changed the employer sanctions rules by eliminating some of the documents that may be used to prove authorization to work. The new laws also make it more difficult for workers to prove that an employer discriminated against them. Finally, the new law created a "good-faith" defense for employers accused of improper record keeping who tried to comply with the law but made an honest mistake.

CHAPTER 20

Employers' Obligations Under Employer Sanctions

The **employer sanctions law** requires employers to check Employment Authorization Documents of all the workers that they hire. To comply with employer sanctions, the employer must (1) make sure that their workers can provide documents showing that they are authorized to work in the United States, (2) keep work authorization records using USCIS Form I-9, Employment Eligibility Verification, and (3) not knowingly hire a person unauthorized to work. If as an employer you violate this law, you could face fines. For knowingly hiring 10 or more unauthorized workers in 12 months, you could face imprisonment.

The law also penalizes employers of three or more employees who discriminate against a worker based on that worker's nationality or citizenship.

You violate the law if you intentionally discriminate against workers based on their nationality by refusing to accept documents that appear valid on their face, or if you do not allow the employee to choose which documents to present from those designated as acceptable by the USCIS. If you have discriminated, you could be fined, made to pay a back-pay award, be required to pay attorney fees, and/or be required to change your hiring practices. The antidiscrimination law applies to all workers hired after November 6, 1986.

To comply with the employer sanctions law, you and your employee must complete Form I-9. This form requires both your and your employee's signatures. The employee signs to confirm that he or she is authorized to work. You sign to confirm that you have made a good-faith effort to make sure that the employee is authorized to work. You can get the form and the USCIS Handbook for Employers by calling 800-870-3676. You may also get the form at the USCIS Web site, www.ins.usdoj.gov/. You may make your own copies of the form.

Farm labor contractors must complete Form I-9 for workers recruited or referred for a fee.

THE VERIFICATION AND RECORD-KEEPING REQUIREMENTS

Even if you have only one employee, you must complete Form I-9 for that employee. Even if you are sure the employee can work legally in the United States or even if the employee is a member of your family, you must still complete Form I-9 for the employee. The only exceptions are for independent contractors, workers under your supervision but supplied by an outside company, "casual domestic hires" such as a person you occasionally hire to clean your house once or twice a week, and workers whom you have employed since prior to November 6, 1986 (regardless of temporary leaves of absence or layoffs). I recommend that employers copy and distribute both the front and back of the I-9 forms, and then direct employees to the reverse side to select possible documents.

When Must the I-9 Be Completed?

Your employee must complete Section 1 of Form I-9 at the time that he or she begins work. That's the part of the form where the employee signs confirming that he or she is authorized to be employed in the United States. You may not ask a potential employee for work authorization documents until after you have decided to hire the employee. You must complete Section 2, the part of the form that you sign, within three business days. If you are hiring the employee for only three days, Section 1 and Section 2 must be completed on the first day of employment.

Suppose that your employee claims authorization to work but doesn't have a necessary document. You may hire that employee, but within three days he or she must either produce a work authorization document or a receipt for filing to get a replacement document. If the employee shows you proof of filing for a needed document, he or she must present the document itself within 90 days.

Frank's story will help you to understand the timing of Form I-9 completion.

————— *Frank's Story* —————

Henry's Carpet was an expanding business. Henry relied on his manager,

Beatrice, to do all his hiring and firing. Thomas, his office manager, was assigned the responsibility of ensuring that new workers had proper work authorization papers and of keeping the company's Form I-9 records.

Beatrice interviewed Frank for a position as a carpet layer. As with all applicants, she made a list of his references with plans to call them to see if Frank had a good work record. She didn't ask Frank for work authorization proofs because she hadn't yet decided to hire him. If she had asked him for work authorization documents before she decided to hire him, and she did not hire him, he might charge her with discrimination. He might argue that it was only after she saw that he was not a U.S. citizen that she decided not to hire him.

A week later, after Beatrice had completed her investigation of Frank's work history, she called and offered him the job. She told him to meet with Thomas, the office manager, and to bring proof that he was authorized to work in the United States.

When Frank met with Thomas, he filled out Section 1 of the form saying that he was a permanent resident of the United States (green card holder). But Frank had forgotten to bring his social security card with him. He presented his driver's license as proof of his identity, but he couldn't prove authorization to work in the United States. Because Frank has signed Section 1 of Form I-9, stating that he is a permanent resident, Henry's Carpet can put him to work right away. However, Frank must present a social security card, permanent resident card (green card), or other acceptable proof of his own choosing, to establish that he can work in the United States within three days. If he fails to present proof that he is authorized to work (or, at least, that he has applied for a replacement document that would prove he could work), the company will be in violation of the law and could be fined for failing to comply with the inspection, verification, and record-keeping requirements.

Phony Documents

The law requires that the employer act in good faith, not that he or she be an expert in whether documents are phony. While Congress has considered a requirement that employers check employees' documents by calling a national data bank, as this book goes to press, there is no such requirement. Some employers, through their industry associations, have agreed to participate in an USCIS Employment Verification Pilot (EVP) program. These programs are voluntary, not mandatory, and are used only to verify employment eligibility for newly hired workers.

Acting in good faith means that if a document is obviously phony, is forged, is altered, is not original, or does not relate to the individual, you can't accept it. For instance, you can't accept a metal or plastic reproduction of a social security card as proof that an employee is authorized to work.

If you think that the documents a worker presents are clearly phony or belong to someone else, you do not have to hire the worker. You should document why you think the documents are not acceptable in the event of a discrimination charge. The USCIS cannot verify workers' status for employers unless you have clear and specific evidence of phony documents, or if you are participating in the USCIS EVP program.

For How Long Must You Keep Form I-9?

You must keep a copy of your employees' I-9 forms for three years after the date of hire or one year after the employment ends, whichever is later. It's best to destroy them after that date.

Copying Documents

You may keep copies of documents that your employees show you, but you aren't required to do so. Many employers choose not to make copies of documents that workers present, as the USCIS can then second-guess their conclusion of whether the documents appeared valid on their face. You should have a uniform policy. If you only make copies of documents from employees of a particular nationality group, that fact could be used against you if a worker claims discrimination. If you make copies of some, but not all, employee documents, you may lose your "good-faith" defense that you thought the documents were genuine.

The Good-Faith Defense to Record-Keeping Violations

If you make an honest effort to comply with the employer sanctions' record-keeping requirements, that's a complete defense to a charge that you failed to keep proper records. However, if the USCIS informs you that your records are deficient, you must get your records in compliance within ten days or be subject to fines.

CHECKING YOUR EMPLOYEE'S DOCUMENTS

Your employee must present both proof of identity and authorization to work. The employee can present a single document that proves both identity and work authorization, such as a U.S. passport, permanent resident card (green card), or USCIS Employment Authorization Document (with photograph). Or the employee can present a combination of documents, such as a driver's license (to prove identity) and a social security card (to prove work authorization). It is up to the employee to choose which documents to present from those types listed on the back of Form I-9. Be sure to show the employee the list and ask him or her to choose.

The USCIS Handbook for Employers outlines the documentation requirements for employer sanctions. The USCIS provides three document lists. The documents in List A prove both employment and identity. List B documents establish identity only. List C documents establish work eligibility only. To comply with the sanctions law, your employee must present either one List A document or one document from List B plus one from List C. Following are the lists of documents provided by the USCIS. (I've amended the list to comply with 1996 immigration law.) For some documents, I provide you with a brief commentary.

The USCIS has great discretion to amend the lists of documents. The lists are accurate as of the time this book went to press. The 1996 immigration laws eliminated three documents from the list to show both identity and employment authorization. The documents eliminated were Certificate of U.S. Citizenship (USCIS Form N-560 or N-561), Certificate of Naturalization (USCIS Form N-550 or N-570), and an unexpired foreign passport with an USCIS Form I-551 stamp or attached USCIS Form I-94 indicating unexpired employment authorization. However, these documents are still acceptable until the USCIS issues a new I-9 form, something not yet done at the time of publication.

List A: Documents That Show Both Identity and Employment Eligibility

1. U.S. Passport (Unexpired or Expired)

You can accept an expired U.S. passport as proof of both identity and authorization to work.

2. An Alien Registration Receipt (Permanent Resident) Card (USCIS Form I-551) with Photograph

While the term "green card" is used to describe permanent resident cards (the card given to a lawful immigrant), the card is no longer green. Recently issued cards are salmon or rose colored. If a worker presents a green or blue permanent resident card, you may want to suggest that the worker apply to the USCIS for a new one. These old-style cards have expired and are not valid to show employment authorization. You may accept an USCIS filing receipt for a new card as proof of employment authorization, or you may ask the employee to provide other documents such as a driver's license and social security card.

3. Unexpired Temporary Resident Card (USCIS Form I-688)

This is the card that the USCIS gives to a person who has applied for legalization and was granted temporary residence.

4. Unexpired Employment Authorization Card (USCIS Form I-688A, known also as an Employment Authorization Document or EAD)

This is the card given to an applicant under the "amnesty" program for legalization prior to their becoming a temporary resident of the United States. The USCIS extends these cards in one-year intervals by putting stickers on the cards. Many people applied for amnesty late, and the USCIS has renewed their cards for several years without giving them immigrant visas.

5. Unexpired Reentry Permit (USCIS Form I-327)

6. Unexpired Refugee Travel Document (USCIS Form I-571)

7. Unexpired Employment Authorization Document (USCIS Form I-

688B) with Photograph. This document is commonly called a "work card" or "EAD." It indicates temporary work status.

List B: Documents That Establish Identity (Unexpired or Expired)

1. Driver's License or ID Card

This is issued by a state or outlying possession of the United States and is acceptable to prove identification if it contains a photograph or information such as name, date of birth, sex, height, eye color, and address.

2. ID Card

Any identification card issued by federal, state, or local government agencies is acceptable provided it contains a photograph or information such as name, date of birth, sex, height, eye color, and address.

3. School ID Card with a Photograph

4. Voter's Registration Card

5. U.S. Military Card or Draft Record

6. Military Dependent's ID Card

7. U.S. Coast Guard Merchant Mariner Card

8. Native American Tribal Document

9. Canadian Driver's License

For persons under age 18 who are unable to present a document listed above:

10. School Record or Report Card

11. Clinic, Doctor, or Hospital Record

12. Day Care or Nursery School Record

List C: Documents That Establish Employment Eligibility

The 1996 immigration laws eliminated a U.S. birth certificate as a document to be used to show employment eligibility.

1. U.S. Social Security Card (except cards that state "Not for Employment Purposes")

Visitors and others legally in the United States without USCIS work permission may have social security cards. The cards are used for banking and other legitimate purposes. In recent years, the Social Security Administration added the words "Not for Employment Purposes" on cards issued to individuals who don't have work authorization in the United States. Cards with that notation cannot be used to prove authorization to work. Employers should be cautious about rejecting unfamiliar cards.

Twenty different versions of the card are in circulation.

Lots of phony social security cards are around. However, unless the card presented to you is obviously altered or forged, or you have some other reason to think it's phony (like the worker tells you it's phony), you must accept it as valid. Again, I emphasize, treat all workers the same. You would be violating the antidiscrimination provisions of the law to only question the documents of workers of a particular race or nationality.

2. Native American Tribal Document

A person with a Native American tribal document must list that document as both a "List B" and "List C" document. A tribal document is not considered a "List A" document.

3. U.S. Citizen ID Card (USCIS Form I-197)

4. ID Card for Use of Resident Citizen in the United States (USCIS Form I-179)

5. Unexpired Employment Authorization Document issued by the USCIS other than those listed under List A

The stories of Samantha, Larry, and Bertha provide examples of how the document list is used to determine employment authorization.

Samantha's Story

Samantha completes Section 1 of Form I-9 indicating that she is a U.S. citizen. She presents to her employer her driver's license and social security card. Samantha's employer can hire her and complete the I-9 form. Samantha does not have to present a U.S. passport, a birth certificate, or other proof that she is a U.S. citizen. The driver's license and the social security card show her identity and her authorization to work.

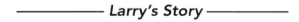
Larry's Story

Larry is a permanent resident of the United States. He presents to his employer his permanent resident card. The permanent resident card is a document that shows identity and the authorization to work. He does not have to present a social security card. His employer may hire him without violating the employer sanctions laws. The company will ask for Larry's social security number so that they can report Larry's income, but the employer can hire Larry without actually seeing the card.

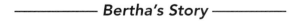
Bertha's Story

Bertha is a U.S. citizen. She presents her employer with a social security card, which proves her authorization to work. The social security card does not prove her identity because it is not on List B. To prove her identity she submits an identity card provided by her college, San Diego State

University. An identity card issued by a state agency or a school ID card and the social security card are enough to show both her identity and her authorization to work.

Don't Pick and Choose Documents

You don't have the right to require any particular document from your employees. If an employee presents any documents that the USCIS lists as acceptable, you must accept the documents so long as they appear valid on their face.

Mary's story provides an example of how important it is to accept any document that is on the USCIS-provided list.

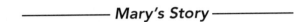
— Mary's Story —

Mary is the owner of her own business, Mary's Marketing. She has more than 50 employees who do everything from designing marketing campaigns to handing out advertising fliers on street corners.

Mary has had problems with the federal government. She was audited several times for failing to file accurate tax returns. She certainly doesn't want to violate the employer sanctions laws. So Mary has made a rule that every new employee has to present a social security card and a U.S. passport or a permanent resident card.

Sonia, from Russia, applied for a job as a computer design specialist with Mary's Marketing. Mary liked her and offered Sonia a position. Sonia is a refugee. She doesn't have a U.S. passport or permanent resident card. She shows Mary an Employment Authorization Document (with photo) that she got from the USCIS. Sonia hasn't yet received her social security card in the mail, although the Social Security Administration gave her a number. Mary decides not to employ Sonia and tells her to come back when she has a social security card and an permanent resident card or a U.S. passport. Mary is violating the law because the Employment Authorization Document is a List A document.

Reverification

If an employee's employment authorization will expire, you must reverify the employee's continued eligibility to work by the last day of authorization noted on the document. You can reverify the employee on the original I-9 form without executing a new one. You don't need to reverify employees who are permanent residents, though their "Permanent Resident" card shows an expiration date. Their status does not expire, just the card. They remain authorized to work. You do have to reverify employees who have only employment authorization cards.

For employees who must renew their employment authorization, make sure that they apply for their employment authorization extension at least 120 days before the permission expiration date. Then, if the USCIS fails to decide the case within 90 days of receiving the extension application, the employees can get an "interim Employment Authorization Document" at the local USCIS office. Since some USCIS offices don't know the rules for granting interim employment authorization, the employees should tell the USCIS they are applying under "8 CFR Sec. 274a.13(d)."

Jonathan's story provides an example to help us understand the reverification requirement.

—————— *Jonathan's Story* ——————

Jonathan has applied for late amnesty. (For more on late amnesty, see Chapter 1.) The USCIS is still considering his case. For the last four years, the USCIS has renewed his work authorization. His employment authorization card (with photo) shows that it will expire November 1, 2002. The card proves his identity and his authorization to work. Any employer who hires Jonathan must have a tickler system to check with Jonathan on November 1, 2002, to see if he continues to be authorized to work. Since his Employment Authorization Document expires on this date, if he doesn't present a List A or List C document, his employer is at risk of an USCIS fine in the unlikely event that the USCIS discovers that he was kept on the payroll. His employer does not necessarily have to see an extension of his USCIS work authorization document, so long as Jonathan shows the employer a valid List A or List C document and claims that he is authorized to work. Remember, it is up to the employee to choose which document to present to establish work authorization. The employer should list that document in Section 3 of Form I-9 and sign that section.

KNOWINGLY HIRING WORKERS NOT AUTHORIZED TO WORK

Employer sanctions are the most severe for employers who knowingly hire workers not authorized to work. You cannot be fined under this provision if you make a good-faith effort, using the I-9 completion guidelines, to check the worker's documents. If, however, the USCIS finds that you were purposely sloppy in completing Form I-9 so that you could hire unauthorized workers, you could be fined for knowingly hiring. You could also be fined for knowingly hiring if you keep a worker employed after his or her work authorization has expired. Employers whom the USCIS charges with knowingly hiring are usually those who don't complete Form I-9 and who employ large numbers of undocumented workers, but there is nothing to stop the USCIS from bringing charges against employers of only a few people.

"NO MATCH" LETTERS FROM THE SOCIAL SECURITY ADMINISTRATION

Many employers are receiving "no match" letters from the Social Security Administration (SSA) saying that the social security numbers the employer sent the SSA are not valid. The letters warn that the employer risks a fine of $50 per bad number.

The "no match" letter doesn't necessarily mean that the employee is working without authorization. Sometimes the worker changed her name when she married, or the employer put down a different name as the last name than the one in the SSA computers. Or perhaps someone just reversed a number or made a typo. In other cases, the worker just made up a number because he or she is illegal.

In a December 23, 1997, letter from USCIS General Counsel David Martin, the USCIS clarified that these SSA letters do not require the employers to reverify the employees. If you have a question about this matter, tell your lawyer that the letter was published in the newsletter "75 Interpreter Releases 203," dated February 9, 1998. Most law libraries have the publication. Nor do the letters put the employer on notice that the employee is undocumented. The SSA admits that they do not have authority to fine employers. That is only something that the IRS can do. The IRS does this only rarely. The SSA does not share the "no match" letter with the USCIS, nor does the IRS impose fines for the bad numbers.

Some employers, upon receiving the "no match" letter, post a notice to employees suggesting that they periodically check their paychecks to see that the name and SSN exactly match their SSA card. After all, if the employee later has a problem getting benefits, it is the employee's loss.

USCIS ENFORCEMENT OF EMPLOYER SANCTIONS

The USCIS can't check the records of all the businesses in the United States. Like IRS tax collection, USCIS enforcement of employer sanctions relies on voluntary compliance backed up with the threat of an audit. Companies as large as the Disney Corporation or as small as a coffee shop have been the subject of USCIS audits.

USCIS I-9 Audits

After a formal request by the USCIS, employers are permitted three days to produce I-9 forms for inspection. You should use this time, and seek an extension if necessary, to review your forms and ensure that they are complete. If you add missing information, such as the number of the driver's license that a worker showed you when he or she started work, be sure to date and initial the correction with the date when you added the information. You should not backdate forms. However, it is proof of your good faith that you made necessary corrections before presenting the forms to the USCIS. Check the forms to make sure that all the boxes are filled in and that both the employee and the employer signed and dated the forms.

Make sure that you have all the forms for all your employees by comparing your forms against your employee list or quarterly payroll report. After you have finished your review, number each form and make a copy for your records of all the documents that you give to the USCIS. The USCIS can issue subpoenas to force you to produce other evidence relevant to an investigation. If the USCIS requests your I-9 forms, immediately call an employment law or immigration law expert for advice. Don't assume an USCIS audit is easy!

USCIS Visits

Unless you consent to a search, the USCIS can't enter nonpublic parts of your premises without an arrest warrant or a search warrant. If the USCIS wants to enter your place of business without a warrant, tell them politely that they can't, no matter how friendly the agent is. Ask what the USCIS agent wants, and then call an immigration lawyer.

How the USCIS Brings Employer Sanctions Charges

The USCIS initiates legal action against an employer by the issuance of a Notice of Intent to Fine (NIF) on Form I-763. This notice must contain the employer's name, the alleged violations, and the penalty the USCIS will impose. The USCIS will usually negotiate a substantial reduction from the proposed fine in order to avoid the burden of litigating the case. You or your lawyer can negotiate this, but do not neglect to make a timely request for a hearing if you have not settled the matter within 30 days.

If you are served with an NIF, you may ask for a hearing before an administrative law judge by sending a written request to the USCIS office named on the notice. The USCIS office must receive the request within 30 days after the issuance of the NIF, or the request will be denied. You have an additional five days if the NIF was served by ordinary mail. However, the NIF is normally served by hand or by certified mail.

FINES AND PENALTIES

1. **Paperwork Violations.** You can be fined from $100 to $1,000 for each violation. This includes failing to complete Form I-9 and failing to keep Form I-9.

2. **"Knowingly Employing" Violations.** You are subject to the following penalties for employing unauthorized persons:

   - **First Violation.** $250 to $2,000 for each unauthorized person.

   - **Second Violation.** $2,000 to $5,000 for each unauthorized person.

   - **Three or More Violations.** $3,000 to $10,000 for each unauthorized person.

3. **"Pattern" or "Practice" Violations.** If you are found to have engaged in a pattern or practice of knowingly employing people not authorized to work, the USCIS can seek injunctive relief in a federal court to stop the violations. The USCIS can even criminally prosecute you with a potential sentence of six months' imprisonment and a $3,000 fine for each person unlawfully hired. USCIS regulations define a pattern or practice as "regular, repeated, and intentional" activities. "Knowingly

hired" violations are also criminal if you have hired ten employees in 12 months and you have actual knowledge that the employees were brought in illegally.

DISCRIMINATION PROVISIONS

The USCIS antidiscrimination law applies to employers of more than three workers. Under the law, you can be fined if you discriminate against employees because of their national origin or citizenship. Under the 1996 immigration law, the discrimination must be intentional. Only a person with proper work authorization documents can bring immigration discrimination charges against you. However, other discrimination laws are not limited in this way.

To avoid charges of discrimination, treat all job applicants the same and carefully follow Form I-9 completion guidelines. When you verify a worker's employment authorization status, don't ask him or her to produce more or different documents than are required by law.

Examples of discriminatory practices include:

- Firing or refusing to hire someone because he or she looks or sounds foreign.
- Hiring only citizens or imposing an across-the-board citizenship preference requirement.
- Preferring one kind of acceptable documentation over another. (A passport is no better than a social security card and a state identification card or driver's license.)
- Requiring employees always to speak English.
- Requiring English fluency where it is not legitimately job-related.
- Refusing to hire someone who has only temporary work authorization.

Penalties for Discriminating

If you are found to have intentionally discriminated against workers based on workers' nationality or citizenship, you may be required to hire (or reinstate) the workers. You may also be required to pay back salaries and attorneys' fees. In addition, you may be fined as follows:

- First Offense. Not less than $250 and not more than $2,000 for each individual discriminated against.
- Second Offense. Not less than $2,000 and not more than $5,000 for each individual discriminated against.
- Subsequent Offense(s). Not less than $3,000 and not more than $10,000 for each individual discriminated against.
- Unlawful Request for More or Different Documents. Not less than $100 and not more than $1,000 for each individual discriminated against.

Employers may also be ordered to keep certain records regarding the hiring of applicants and employees. If a court decides that the USCIS or an employee's claim against you has no reasonable basis in fact for law, the court may award you attorneys' fees.

CHAPTER 21

Your Rights As an Employee Under Employer Sanctions

When Congress first considered the "employer sanctions" law, opponents said that the law would result in discrimination against people who had foreign accents. They also said that discrimination against nonwhite people, particularly Latinos and Asians, would increase. Those critics were right. Despite the employer sanctions laws' antidiscrimination provision, U.S. government studies have proven that discrimination resulting from employer sanctions has been widespread.

The antidiscrimination provisions of employer sanctions apply to employers of three or more persons. The law gives U.S. citizens, permanent residents (who have filed for naturalization within six months of eligibility), refugees, or asylees the right to bring a complaint against an employer who discriminates against you because of your nationality or citizenship. If you win your case, you may be able to get back wages for the time you were out of work. The employer may be ordered to change his or her personnel practices to make sure the discrimination doesn't continue. But don't be angry at the employer who asks you to produce proof of your identity and your authorization to work. That's what the law requires. You must complete USCIS Form I-9, Employment Eligibility Verification, or an employer can refuse to hire you.

COMPLETING THE I-9 FORM

In Chapter 20, I listed the documents you can use to prove you are authorized to work in the United States. It is up to you to select the documents to present from the list on the back of the I-9 form (see Chapter 20). If you present the proper proof of identity and authorization to work, and an employer still asks for more proof, you may be a victim of discrimination. You'll have the right to bring charges against the employer.

Document Fraud

Beware: You may be penalized by the USCIS for using phony or forged documents when completing the I-9 form. It is also unlawful for you to present another person's document, claiming it is your own. The possible penalties include being barred from becoming a permanent resident of the United States, deportation (called "removal" as of April 1, 1997), and fines.

FIGHTING DISCRIMINATION

If you suspect at all that an employer is treating you unfairly, don't try to decide on your own if you have a good discrimination case. If you think you may have been a victim of discrimination, contact the Office of Special Counsel for Immigration Related Unfair Employment Practices (IRCA), the U.S. Department of Justice, P.O. Box 27728, Washington, DC 20038-7728, 800-255-7688, 202-616-5594, or (fax) 202-616-5509. You can also get information and a complaint form at the Office of Special Counsel Web site, www.usdoj.gov/crt/osc/. The Office of Special Counsel is the main U.S. government agency responsible for ensuring that the employer sanctions law doesn't result in discrimination against workers.

Call the Office of Special Counsel if an employer does one or more of the following:

- Refuses to hire you because you look "foreign."
- Hires only citizens (unless the employer is a city, county, or state agency hiring for a position that requires implementation of public policy, such as a police officer). Federal agencies may also limit employment to U.S. citizens.
- Insists that you provide a particular document instead of any listed document. (A U.S. passport is no better than a social security card and state identification card or driver's license.)
- Refuses to hire you solely because you have an accent.
- Requires you to speak English at all times.
- Requires English fluency where it is not legitimately job-related.
- Refuses to promote or rehire you because you are not a U.S. citizen.
- Refuses to hire you because you have only temporary work authorization.

WHO IS PROTECTED?

The IRCA antidiscrimination provisions protect everyone except persons unauthorized to work from national origin discrimination in hiring, firing, and recruitment. Citizenship status protection (discrimination against a person because he or she is a permanent resident rather than a citizen) is available to you only if you are a U.S. citizen or national, a lawful permanent resident, a lawful temporary resident, a refugee, or an asylee.

ENFORCEMENT OF THE
ANTIDISCRIMINATION PROVISIONS

If you believe you are the victim of discrimination, you must file a complaint with the Office of the Special Counsel at the Department of Justice. You must file the notice within 180 days of the act of discrimination. You don't necessarily have to file the charge or complaint yourself. Your union representative, an attorney, a friend, or a relative can file the complaint. The Special Counsel has 120 days from the time it receives your notice of claim of discrimination to decide whether there is "reasonable cause to believe" that the employer has discriminated and bring a complaint before an administrative law judge.

In some circumstances, even if the Office of Special Counsel does not agree to charge the employer, you can bring your complaint directly to an administrative law judge. If you are not happy with the decision of an administrative law judge, you have 60 days to seek review by the U.S. Court of Appeals. An employer has the same right.

An administrative law judge may penalize the employer by ordering him or her to stop the discrimination, to reinstate you, to pay you back pay, or to pay a fine. The administrative law judge may also make the employer comply with special record-keeping requirements.

Juanita's and Pierre's stories provide examples of discrimination in the I-9 completion process.

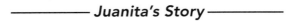

———— Juanita's Story ————

Juanita is a permanent resident of the United States, having lived here for more than 20 years. She was born in Bolivia and plans to return to Bolivia when she retires. She knows that if she becomes a naturalized U.S. citizen, she will lose her Bolivian citizenship.

Juanita applied for a job as a computer programmer in a small software development company. The company had a policy of hiring only U.S. citizens. When she was interviewed for the job, all seemed to be going well until the employer asked whether she was a U.S. citizen. Juanita answered truthfully, saying that she was a permanent resident. The employer told her she couldn't have the job if she was not a U.S. citizen.

Juanita contacted the Office of Special Counsel, and they brought a complaint against the employer. Eventually, the employer hired Juanita, and she received back pay beginning from the time she would have first begun working for the company had they not discriminated against her.

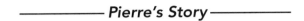

Pierre's Story

Pierre was born in Haiti but was now a naturalized U.S. citizen. Although his English was excellent, he still had a slight accent. In any event, Pierre was proud of his Haitian heritage. He never tried to hide the fact that he had not been born in the United States.

Pierre applied for a job as a cabinetmaker for a construction company. He was very skilled in his trade, and the company wanted to hire him. But because of Pierre's accent, the company's personnel director insisted that Pierre bring him proof that he was a U.S. citizen. Pierre had a social security card and a driver's license, which under the employer sanctions law is enough to prove that he was authorized to work. The driver's license proved his identity, and the social security card proved that he was qualified to work in the United States. By insisting that Pierre bring proof of his U.S. citizenship, the employer violates the employer sanctions law. Pierre can bring a complaint against the company.

Immigration Law Resources

Laws and Regulations

The following documents are available from:

Superintendent of Documents

U.S. Government Printing Office
Washington, DC 20402
202-512-1800

Title 8 Aliens and Nationality

Code of Federal Regulations (CFR)
GPO S/N 869-00075-4

Title 20 Employees' Benefits

Code of Federal Regulations (CFR)
Parts 602, 621, 655, 656
(Labor Relations)
GPO S/N 869-011-00065-7

Title 22 Foreign Relations

Code of Federal Regulations (CFR)
Parts 41-53 (Visa and Passport Regulations)
Part 514 (USIA J Visa Regulations)
GPO S/N 869-011-0075-4

General Immigration Law Treaties, Casebooks, and Other Resource Services

Immigration Business News and Comment

A twice-monthly newsletter.
Austin T. Fragomen and Steven Bell
West Group
620 Opperman Drive Eagan, MN 55123
800-328-4880

Immigration Law and Business (2001)

A concise, looseleaf treatise for business
immigration practitioners.
Austin T. Fragomen, Jr., Alfred J. Del Rey, Jr.,
and Sam Bernsen West Group
620 Opperman Drive Eagan, MN 55123
800-328-4880

Immigration Law and Crimes, (2000)

The best aid for representing immigrants
with criminal histories.
National Immigration Project of the National
Lawyers Guild West Group
620 Opperman Drive Eagan, MN 55123
800-328-4880

Immigration Law and Defense 3rd Ed. (2001)

A particularly strong treatise on deportation
defense.National Immigration Project of
the National Lawyers Guild

Immigration Law and Procedure (2001, Rev. Ed.)

The definitive treatise on immigration law–
expensive, but a must for the serious
practitioner.
Charles Gordon, Stanley Mailman, and
Stephen Yale-Loehr
Matthew Bender and Co., Inc.
1275 Broadway Albany, NY 12201
800-833-9844
212-268-6621 (fax)

Immigration and Nationality Law: Cases and Materials (2000, 3rd Ed.)

An excellent law school casebook.
Richard A. Boswell with Gilbert Paul Carrasco
Carolina Academic Press
700 Kent Street Durham, NC 27701
919-489-7486
919-493-5668

International Student Handbook: A Legal Guide to Studying, Working and Living in the United States (1992)

A popular guide for students.
Allan Wernick
Out of print

Interpreter Releases

A weekly summary of changes in immigration law policy and regulations; includes recent case summaries.
Maurice A. Roberts, Danielle Polen, and Juan Osuna, Editors
West Group
620 Opperman Drive Eagan, MN 55123
800-328-4880

Kurzban's Immigration Law Sourcebook (2000, 7th Ed.)

The best single volume summary of immigration law and procedure.
Ira J. Kurzban
American Immigration Law Foundation
1400 Eye Street, NW, Suite 1200
Washington, DC 20005
800-982-2839
202-371-9377
202-371-9449 (fax)

Citizenship and Naturalization

Naturalization: A Guide for Legal Practitioners and Other Community Advocates (2001)

A helpful how-to book.
Immigration Legal Resource Center1663 Mission Street, Suite 602
San Francisco, CA 94103
415-225-9499
415-225-9792 (fax)

Naturalization Handbook (2001)

The leading treatise on the subject of naturalization.
Daniel Levy
National Immigration Project of the National Lawyers Guild
West Group
620 Opperman Drive Eagan, MN 55123
800-328-4880

I-130 Petition for Alien Relative

U.S. Department of Justice
Immigration and Naturalization Service

OMB # 1115-0054
Petition for Alien Relative

Instructions

> Read the instructions carefully. If you do not follow the instructions, we may have to return your petition, which may delay final action.

1. Who may file?

A citizen or lawful permanent resident of the United States may file this form with the Immigration and Naturalization Service (INS) to establish the relationship to certain alien relatives who wish to immigrate to the United States. You must file a separate form for each eligible relative.

2. For whom may you file?

A. If you are a citizen, you may file this form for:
  1) your husband, wife or unmarried child under 21 years old.
  2) your unmarried son or daughter over 21, or married son or daughter of any age.
  3) your brother or sister if you are at least 21 years old.
  4) your parent if you are at least 21 years old.

B. If you are a lawful permanent resident, you may file this form for:
  1) your husband or wife.
  2) your unmarried child under 21 years of age.
  3) your unmarried son or daughter over 21 years of age.

NOTE: If your relative qualifies under paragraph A(2) or A(3) above, separate petitions are not required for his or her husband or wife or unmarried children under 21 years of age. If your relative qualifies under paragraph B(2) or B(3) above, separate petitions are not required for his or her unmarried children under 21 years of age. These persons will be able to apply for the same category of immigrant visa as your relative.

3. For whom may you not file?

You may not file for a person in the following categories.

A. An adoptive parent or adopted child, if the adoption took place after the child's 16th birthday, or if the child has not been in the legal custody and living with the parent(s) for at least two years.

B. A natural parent, if the United States citizen son or daughter gained permanent residence through adoption.

C. A stepparent or stepchild, if the marriage that created the relationship took place after the child's 18th birthday.

D. A husband or wife, if you were not both physically present at the marriage ceremony, and the marriage was not consummated.

E. A husband or wife, if you gained lawful permanent resident status by virtue of a prior marriage to a United States citizen or lawful permanent resident unless:

  1) a period of five years has elapsed since you became a lawful permanent resident; or

  2) you can establish by clear and covincing evidence that the prior marriage (through which you gained your immigrant status) was not entered into for the purpose of evading any provision of the immigration laws; or

  3) your prior marriage (through which you gained your immigrant status) was terminated by the death of your former spouse.

F. A husband or wife, if he or she was in exclusion, removal, rescission or judicial proceedings regarding his or her right to remain in the United States when the marriage took place, unless such spouse has resided outside the United States for a two-year period after the date of the marriage.

G. A husband or wife, if the Attorney General has determined that such an alien has attempted or conspired to enter into a marriage for the purpose of evading the immigration laws.

H. A grandparent, grandchild, nephew, niece, uncle, aunt, cousin or in-law.

4. What are the general filing instructions?

A. Type or print legibly in black or dark blue ink.

B. If extra space is needed to complete any item, attach a continuation sheet, indicate the item number, and date and sign each sheet.

C. Answer all questions fully and accurately. If any item does not apply, please write "N/A."

D. **Translations.** Any foreign language document must be accompanied by a full English translation, which the translator has certified as complete and correct, and by the translator's certification that he or she is competent to translate the foreign language into English.

E. **Copies.** If these instructions state that a copy of a document may be filed with this petition and you choose to send us the original, INS will keep that original for our records. If INS requires the original, it will be requested.

5. What documents do you need to show that you are a United States citizen?

A. If you were born in the United States, a copy of your birth certificate, issued by the civil registrar, vital statistics office, or other civil authority. If a birth certificate is not available, see the section below titled "What if a document is not avaliable?"

B. A copy of your naturalization certificate or certificate of citizenship issued by INS.

C. A copy of Form FS-240, Report of Birth Abroad of a Citizen of the United States, issued by an American embassy or

D. A copy of your unexpired U.S. passport; or

E. An original statement from a U.S. consular officer verifying that you are a U.S. citizen with a valid passport.

F. If you do not have any of the above documents and you were born in the United States, see instruction under 9 below, "What if a document is not available?"

6. What documents do you need to show that you are a permanent resident?

If you are a permanent resident, you must file your petition with a copy of the front and back of your permanent resident card. If you have not yet received your card, submit copies of your passport biographic page and the page showing admission as a permanent resident, or other evidence of permanent resident status issued by INS.

7. What documents do you need to prove a family relationship?

You have to prove that there is a family relationship between you and your relative. If you are filing for:

A. **A husband or wife,** give INS the following documentation:
  1) a copy of your marriage certificate.

  2) if either you or your spouse were previously marrried, submit copies of documents showing that all prior marriages were legally terminated.

  3) a color photo of you and one of your husband or wife, taken within 30 days of the date of this petition. The photos must have a white background and be glossy, unretouched and not mounted. The dimensions of the facial image should be about 1 inch from the chin to top of the hair, in a 3/4 frontal view, showing the right side of the face with the right ear visible. Using pencil or felt pen, lightly print the name (and Alien Registration Number, if known) on the back of each photograph.

  4) a completed and signed G-325A (Biographic Information Form) for you and one for your husband or wife. Except for name and signature, you do not have to repeat on the G-325A the information given on your I-130 petition.

B. **A child and you are the mother:** give a copy of the child's birth certificate showing your name and the name of your child.

C. **A child and you are the father:** give a copy of the child's birth certificate showing both parents' names and your marriage certificate.

D. **A child born out of wedlock and you are the father:** if the child was not legitimated before reaching 18 years old, you must file your petition with copies of evidence that a bona fide parent-child relationship existed between the father and the child before the child reached 21 years. This may include evidence that the father lived with the child, supported him or her, or otherwise showed continuing parental interest in the child's welfare.

E. **A brother or sister:** give a copy of your birth certificate and a copy of your brother's or sister's birth certificate showing that you have at least one common parent. If you and your brother or sister have a common father but different mothers, submit copies of the marriage certificates of the father to each mother and copies of documents showing that any prior marriages of either your father or mothers were legally terminated. If you and your brother or sister are related through adoption or through a stepparent, or if you have a common father and either of you were not legitimated before your 18th birthday, see also H and I below.

F. **A mother:** give a copy of your birth certificate showing your name and your mother's name.

G. **A father:** give a copy of your birth certificate showing the names of both parents. Also give a copy of your parents' marriage certificate establishing that your father was married to your mother before you were born, and copies of documents showing that any prior marriages of either your father or mother were legally terminated. If you are filing for a stepparent or adoptive parent, or if you are filing for your father and were not legitimated before your 18th birthday, also see D, H and I.

H. **Stepparent/stepchild:** if your petition is based on a stepparent-stepchild relationship, you must file your petition with a copy of the marriage certificate of the stepparent to the child's natural parent showing that the marriage occurred before the child's 18th birthday, and copies of documents showing that any prior marriages were legally terminated.

I. **Adoptive parent or adopted child:** if you and the person you are filing for are related by adoption, you must submit a copy of the adoption decree(s) showing that the adoption took place before the child became 16 years old. If you adopted the sibling of a child you already adopted, you must submit a copy of the adoption decree(s) showing that the adoption of the sibling occured before that child's 18th birthday. In either case, you must also submit copies of evidence that each child was in the legal custody of and resided with the parent(s) who adopted him or her for at least two years before or after the adoption. Legal custody may only be granted by a court or recognized government entity and is usually granted at the time the adoption is finalized. However, if legal custody is granted by a court or recognized government agency prior to the adoption, that time may be counted toward fulfilling the two-year legal custody requirement.

8. What if your name has changed?

If either you or the person you are filing for is using a name other than that shown on the relevant documents, you must file your petition with copies of the legal documents that effected the change, such as a marriage certificate, adoption decree or court order.

9. What if a document is not available?

If the documents needed are not available, give INS a statement from the appropriate civil authority certifying that the document or documents are not available. In such situation, you may submit secondary evidence, including:

   A. Church record: a copy of a document bearing the seal of the church, showing the baptism, dedication or comparable rite occurred within two months after birth, and showing the date and place of the child's birth, date of the religious ceremony and the names of the child's parents.

   B. School record: a letter from the authority (preferably the first school attended) showing the date of admission to the school, child's date of birth or age at that time, the place of birth, and the names of the parents.

   C. Census record: state or federal census record showing the names, place of birth, date of birth or the age of the person listed.

   D. Affidavits: written statements sworn to or affirmed by two persons who were living at the time and who have personal knowledge of the event you are trying to prove. For example, the date and place of birth, marriage or death. The person making the affidavit does not have to be a citizen of the United States. Each affidavit should contain the following information regarding the person making the affidavit: his or her full name, address, date and place of birth and his or her relationship to you, if any, full information concerning the event, and complete details explaining how the person acquired knowledge of the event.

10. Where should you file this form?

If you reside in the U.S., file this form at the INS service Center having jurisdiction over your place of residence.

If you live in Connecticut, Delaware, District of Columbia, Maine, Maryland, Massachusetts, New Hampshire, New Jersey, New York, Pennsylvania, Puerto Rico, Rhode Island, Vermont, Virgin Islands, Virginia or West Virginia, mail this petition to: **USINS Vermont Service Center, 75 Lower Welden Street, St. Albans, VT 05479-0001.**

NOTE: If the I-130 petition is being filed concurrently with Form I-485, Application to Register Permanent Residence or to Adjust Status, submit both forms at the local INS office having jurisdiction over the place where the I-485 applicant resides. Applicants who reside in the jurisdiction of the Baltimore, MD, District Office should submit the I-130 petition and the Form I-485 concurrently to the **USINS Vermont Service Center, 75 Lower Welden Street, St. Albans, VT 05479-0001.**

If you live in Alaska, Colorado, Idaho, Illinois, Indiana, Iowa, Kansas, Michigan, Minnesota, Missouri, Montana, Nebraska, North Dakota, Ohio, Oregon, South Dakota, Utah, Washington, Wisconsin or Wyoming, mail this petition to: **USINS Nebraska Service Center, P.O. Box 87130, Lincoln, NE 68501-7130.**

If you live in Alabama, Arkansas, Florida, Georgia, Kentucky, Louisiana, Mississippi, New Mexico, North Carolina, Oklahoma, South Carolina, Tennessee or Texas, mail this petition to: **USINS Texas Service Center, P.O. Box 850919, Mesquite, TX 75185-0919.**

If you live in Arizona, California, Guam, Hawaii or Nevada, mail this petition to: **USINS California Service Center, P.O. Box 10130, Laguna Niguel, CA 92607-0130.**

Petitioners residing abroad: If you live outside the United States, you may file your relative petition at the INS office overseas or the U.S. consulate or embassy having jurisdiction over the area where you live. For further information, contact the nearest American consulate or embassy.

11. What is the fee?

You must pay $130.00 to file this form. **The fee will not be refunded, whether the petition is approved or not. DO NOT MAIL CASH.** All checks or money orders, whether U.S. or foreign, must be payable in U.S. currency at a financial institution in the United States. When a check is drawn on the account of a person other than yourself, write your name on the face of the check. If the check is not honored, INS will charge you $30.00.

Pay by check or money order in the exact amount. Make the check or money order payable to Immigration and Naturalization Service, unless:

   A. you live in Guam, and are filing your petition there, make the check or money order payable to the "Treasurer, Guam" or

   B. you live in the U.S. Virgin Islands, and you are filing your petition there, make your check or money order payable to the "Commissioner of Finance of the Virgin Islands."

12. When will a visa become available?

When a petition is approved for the husband, wife, parent or unmarried minor child of a United States citizen, these relatives do not have to wait for a visa number because they are not subject to the immigrant visa limit.

However, for a child to qualify for the immediate relative category, all processing must be completed and the child must enter the United States before his or her 21st birthday.

For all other alien relatives, there are only a limited number of immigrant visas each year. The visas are issued in the order in which the petitions are properly filed and accepted by INS. To be considered properly filed, a petition must be fully completed and signed, and the fee must be paid.

For a monthly report on the dates when immigrant visas are available, call the **U.S. Department of State** at **(202) 647-0508.**

13. Notice to persons filing for spouses, if married less than two years.

Pursuant to section 216 of the Immigration and Nationality Act, your alien spouse may be granted conditional permanent resident status in the United States as of the date he or she is admitted or adjusted to conditional status by an INS Officer. Both you and your conditional resident spouse are required to file Form I-751, Joint Petition to Remove Conditional Basis of Alien's Permanent Resident Status, during the 90-day period immediately before the second anniversary of the date your alein spouse was granted conditional permanent resident status.

Otherwise, the rights, privileges, responsibilites and duties that apply to all other permanent residents apply equally to a conditional permanent resident. A conditional permanent resident is not limited to the right to apply for naturalization, to file petitions on behalf of qualifying relatives or to reside permanently in the United States as an immigrant in accordance with our nation's immigration laws.

NOTE: Failure to file the Form I-751 joint petition to remove the conditional basis of the alien spouse's permanent resident status will result in the termination of his or her permanent resident status and initiation of removal proceedings.

14. What are the penalties for committing marriage fraud or submitting false information or both?

Title 8, United States Code, Section 1325, states that any individual who knowingly enters into a marriage contract for the purpose of evading any provision of the immigration laws shall be imprisoned for not more than five years, or fined not more than $250,000, or both.

Title 18, United States Code, Section 1001, states that whoever willfully and knowingly falsifies a material fact, makes a false statement, or makes use of a false document will be fined up to $10,000, imprisoned for up to five years, or both.

15. What is our authority for collecting this information?

We request the information on the form to carry out the immigration laws contained in Title 8, United States Code, Section 1154(a). We need this information to determine whether a person is eligible for immigration benefits. The information you provide may also be disclosed to other Federal, state, local and foreign law enforcement and regulatory agencies during the course of the investigation required by INS. You do not have to give this information. However, if you refuse to give some or all of it, your petition may be denied.

16. Paperwork Reduction Act Notice.

A person is not required to respond to a collection of information unless it displays a currently valid OMB control number. Public reporting burden for this collection of information is estimated to average 30 minutes per response, including the time for reviewing instructions, searching existing data sources, gathering and maintaining the data needed, and completing and reviewing the collection of information. Send comments regarding this burden estimate or any other aspect of this collection of information, including suggestions for reducing this burden to: U.S. Department of Justice, Immigration and Naturalization Service, Room 4034, Washington, D.C. 20536; OMB No.1115-0054. **DO NOT MAIL YOUR COMPLETED APPLICATION TO THIS ADDRESS.**

Checklist.

- Did you answer each question on the Form I-130 petition?
- Did you sign the petition?
- Did you enclose the correct filing fee for each petition?
- Did you submit proof of your U.S. citizenship or lawful permanent residence?
- Did you submit other required supporting evidence?

If you are filing for your husband or wife, did you include

- your photograph?
- his or her photograph?
- your completed Form G-325A?
- his or her Form G-325A?

Information and Forms: For information on immigration laws, regulations and procedures or to order INS forms, call our National Customer Service Center at 1-800-375-5283 or visit the INS website at *www.ins.usdoj.gov.*

Form I-130 Instructions (Rev. 06/05/02)Y Page 4

APPENDIX B: I-130 PETITION FOR ALIEN RELATIVE

U.S. Department of Justice
Immigration and Naturalization Service

Petition for Alien Relative

DO NOT WRITE IN THIS BLOCK - FOR EXAMINING OFFICE ONLY

A#	Action Stamp	Fee Stamp

Section of Law/Visa Category
- [ ] 201(b) Spouse - IR-1/CR-1
- [ ] 201(b) Child - IR-2/CR-2
- [ ] 201(b) Parent - IR-5
- [ ] 203(a)(1) Unm. S or D - F1-1
- [ ] 203(a)(2)(A)Spouse - F2-1
- [ ] 203(a)(2)(A) Child - F2-2
- [ ] 203(a)(2)(B) Unm. S or D - F2-4
- [ ] 203(a)(3) Married S or D - F3-1
- [ ] 203(a)(4) Brother/Sister - F4-1

Petition was filed on: _____ (priority date)
- [ ] Personal Interview   [ ] Previously Forwarded
- [ ] Pet. [ ] Ben. " A" File Reviewed   [ ] I-485 Filed Simultaneously
- [ ] Field Investigation   [ ] 204(g) Resolved
- [ ] 203(a)(2)(A) Resolved   [ ] 203(g) Resolved

Remarks:

A. Relationship   You are the petitioner; your relative is the beneficiary.

1. I am filing this petition for my:	2. Are you related by adoption?	3. Did you gain permanent residence through adoption?
[ ] Husband/Wife [ ] Parent [ ] Brother/Sister [ ] Child	[ ] Yes [ ] No	[ ] Yes [ ] No

B. Information about you

C. Information about your relative

B. 1. Name (Family name in CAPS)   (First)   (Middle)

C. 1. Name (Family name in CAPS)   (First)   (Middle)

B. 2. Address (Number and Street)   (Apt.No.)

C. 2. Address (Number and Street)   (Apt. No.)

(Town or City)   (State/Country)   (Zip/Postal Code)

(Town or City)   (State/Country)   (Zip/Postal Code)

B. 3. Place of Birth (Town or City)   (State/Country)

C. 3. Place of Birth (Town or City)   (State/Country)

B. 4. Date of Birth (Month/Day/Year)	5. Gender [ ] Male [ ] Female	6. Marital Status [ ] Married [ ] Single [ ] Widowed [ ] Divorced

C. 4. Date of Birth (Month/Day/Year)	5. Gender [ ] Male [ ] Female	6. Marital Status [ ] Married [ ] Single [ ] Widowed [ ] Divorced

B. 7. Other Names Used (including maiden name)

C. 7. Other Names Used (including maiden name)

B. 8. Date and Place of Present Marriage (if married)

C. 8. Date and Place of Present Marriage (if married)

B. 9. Social Security Number (if any)   **10. Alien Registration Number**

C. 9. Social Security Number (if any)   **10. Alien Registration Number**

B. 11. Name(s) of Prior Husband(s)/Wive(s)   **12. Date(s) Marriage(s) Ended**

C. 11. Name(s) of Prior Husband(s)/Wive(s)   **12. Date(s) Marriage(s) Ended**

B. 13. If you are a U.S. citizen, complete the following:

My citizenship was acquired through (check one):
- [ ] Birth in the U.S.
- [ ] Naturalization. Give certificate number and date and place of issuance.

_____

- [ ] Parents. Have you obtained a certificate of citizenship in your own name?
  - [ ] Yes. Give certificate number, date and place of issuance.   [ ] No

14a. If you are a lawful permanent resident alien, complete the following: Date and place of admission for, or adjustment to, lawful permanent residence and class of admission.

14b. Did you gain permanent resident status through marriage to a United States citizen or lawful permanent resident?
- [ ] Yes [ ] No

C. 13. Has your relative ever been in the U.S.? [ ] Yes [ ] No

14. If your relative is currently in the U.S., complete the following:
He or she arrived as a::
(visitor, student, stowaway, without inspection, etc.)

Arrival/Departure Record (I-94)   Date arrived (Month/Day/Year)

| | | ▬ | | | | | | | |

Date authorized stay expired, or will expire, as shown on Form I-94 or I-95

15. Name and address of present employer (if any)

Date this employment began (Month/Day/Year)

16. Has your relative ever been under immigration proceedings?
- [ ] No [ ] Yes Where _____ When _____
- [ ] Removal [ ] Exclusion/Deportation [ ] Recission [ ] Judicial Proceedings

INITIAL RECEIPT _____ RESUBMITTED _____ RELOCATED: Rec'd _____ Sent _____ COMPLETED: Appv'd _____ Denied _____ Ret'd _____

Form I-130 (Rev. 06/05/02) Y

APPENDIX B: I-130 PETITION FOR ALIEN RELATIVE

C. Information about your alien relative (continued)

17. List husband/wife and all children of your relative.

(Name)   (Relationship)   (Date of Birth)   (Country of Birth)

_____

_____

_____

_____

_____

18. Address in the United States where your relative intends to live.

(Street Address)   (Town or City)   (State)

19. Your relative's address abroad. (Include street, city, province and country)

_____ Phone Number (if any)

20. If your relative's native alphabet is other than Roman letters, write his or her name and foreign address in the native alphabet.

(Name)   Address (Include street, city, province and country):

21. If filing for your husband/wife, give last address at which you lived together. (Include street, city, province, if any, and country):

                                                               From: **To:**

                                                             (Month) (Year)   (Month) (Year)

22. Complete the information below if your relative is in the United States and will apply for adjustment of status

Your relative is in the United States and will apply for adjustment of status to that of a lawful permanent resident at the office of the Immigration and Naturalization Service in _____. If your relative is not eligible for adjustment of status, he or she

                                (City)   (State)

will apply for a visa abroad at the American consular post in _____

                                           (City)   (Country)

NOTE: Designation of an American embassy or consulate outside the country of your relative's last residence does not guarantee acceptance for processing by that post. Acceptance is at the discretion of the designated embassy or consulate.

D. Other information

1. If separate petitions are also being submitted for other relatives, give names of each and relationship.

2. Have you ever filed a petition for this or any other alien before? ☐ Yes ☐ No

If "Yes," give name, place and date of filing and result.

WARNING: INS investigates claimed relationships and verifies the validity of documents. INS seeks criminal prosecutions when family relationships are falsified to obtain visas.

PENALTIES: By law, you may be imprisoned for not more than five years or fined $250,000, or both, for entering into a marriage contract for the purpose of evading any provision of the immigration laws. In addition, you may be fined up to $10,000 and imprisoned for up to five years, or both, for knowingly and willfully falsifying or concealing a material fact or using any false document in submitting this petition.

YOUR CERTIFICATION: I certify, under penalty of perjury under the laws of the United States of America, that the foregoing is true and correct. Furthermore, I authorize the release of any information from my records which the Immigration and Naturalization Service needs to determine eligibility for the benefit that I am seeking.

E. Signature of petitioner.

                                        Date   Phone Number

F. Signature of person preparing this form, if other than the petitioner.

I declare that I prepared this document at the request of the person above and that it is based on all information of which I have any knowledge.

Print Name _____ Signature _____ Date _____

Address _____ G-28 ID or VOLAG Number, if any.

Form I-130 (Rev. 06/05/02) Y Page 2

USCIS National and Regional Offices

USCIS Headquarters

425 Eye Street, NW
Washington, DC 20536
Phone: 202-514-4330

USCIS Regional Offices

Central Operations Regional Office

7701 North Stemmons Freeway
Dallas, TX 75247
6:30 a.m.–1:30 p.m. Monday, Tuesday, Thursday, & Friday
Wednesday by Appointment Only
Phone: 214-767-7011
Fax: 214-767-7491

Eastern Operations Regional Office

70 Kimball Avenue
South Burlington, VT 05403-6813
8:00 a.m.–4:30 p.m.
Phone: 802-660-5000
Fax: 802-660-5114

USCIS Service Center

P.O. Box 3111
Laguna Niguel, CA 92607-0111
Phone: 949-831-8427

Western Operations Regional Office

24000 Avila Road
P.O. Box 30080
Laguna Niguel, CA 92607-0080
8:00 a.m.–4:00 p.m.
Phone: 949-360-3124
Fax: 949-360-3138

USCIS Service Centers

USCIS Eastern Service Center

P.O. Box 9589
St. Albans, VT 05479-9589
Phone: 802-527-3255

USCIS Northern Service Center

850 S Street
Lincoln, NE 68501
Phone: 402-437-5218;
402-437-5900

USCIS Southern Service Center

P.O. Box 152122
Irving, TX 75015-2122
Phone: 214-767-7770

Eastern Region District Offices

Albany Sub-Office

James T. Foley Federal Courthouse
1086 Troy-Schenectady Road
Latham, NY 12110
8:00 a.m.–4:00 p.m.
Phone: 518-220-2100

Atlanta District Office

77 Forsyth Street, SW
Atlanta, GA 30303-0253
7:30 a.m.–3:00 p.m.
Phone: 404-331-0253
Fax: 404-331-7793

Baltimore District Office
Fallon Federal Building
31 Hopkins Plaza
Baltimore, MD 21201
Monday–Thursday
7:30 a.m.–4:00 p.m.
Friday 7:30 a.m.–1:00 p.m.
Phone: 410-962-2010
Fax: 410-962-7555

Boston District Office
John F. Kennedy Federal
Building
Government Center, Room 1700
Boston, MA 02203
8:00 a.m.–4:30 p.m.
Phone: 617-565-4946

Brooklyn Sub-Office
(Citizenship only for Queens, Kings, Nassau,
    Suffolk, and Richmond)
505 Fulton Street
Brooklyn, NY 11201
8:00 a.m.–4:30 p.m.
Phone: 718-330-7867

Buffalo District Office
Federal Center
130 Delaware Avenue
Buffalo, NY 14202
8:00 a.m.–3:00 p.m.
Phone: 716-551-4741

Charlotte Sub-Office
6 Woodlawn Green, Room 138
Charlotte, NC 28217
7:30 a.m.–2:00 p.m.
Phone: 704-371-6313

Cleveland District Office
Anthony J. Celebreeze Federal Building
1240 East 9th Street, Room 1917
Cleveland, OH 44199
Phone: 216-522-4766

Cincinnati Sub-Office
J. W. Peck Federal Building
550 Main Street
Room 4001
Cincinnati, Ohio 45202
8:00 a.m.–4:00 p.m. Monday, Tuesday, Thurs
    day, and Friday
Closed Wednesday
Phone: 513-684-2934

Detroit District Office
Federal Building
333 Mt. Elliott Street
Detroit, MI 48207-4381
7:00 a.m.–3:30 p.m.
Phone: 313-568-6000

Fort Lauderdale/Port Everglades Sub-Office
1800 Eller Drive, Suite 401
P.O. Box 13054
Port Everglades Station
Fort Lauderdale, FL 33316
Phone: 305-356-7298

Freeport Bahamas Sub-Office
P.O. Box F-2664
Freeport, Grand Bahama
Bahamas

Hartford Sub-Office
Ribicoff Federal Building
450 Main Street
Hartford, CT 06103-3060
8:00 a.m.–3:00 p.m.
Phone: 203-240-3050

Jacksonville Sub-Office
4121 Southpoint Boulevard
Jacksonville, FL 32216
9:00 a.m.–12:00 noon
Monday through Friday
Phone: 904-232-2164

Key West Sub-Office
301 Simonton Street,
Suite 201
Key West, FL 33040
Phone: 305-296-2233; 305-536-4274

Louisville Sub-Office
Gene Snyder Courthouse
601 West Broadway, Room 604
Louisville, KY 40202
8:00 a.m.–2:30 p.m.
Phone: 502-582-6526

Memphis Sub-Office
1341 Sycamore View Road, Suite 100
Memphis, TN 38103-3815
8:30 a.m.–2:00 p.m.
Monday through Thursday
8:30 a.m.–1:00 p.m. Friday
Phone: 901-544-0256

Miami District Office

7880 Biscayne Boulevard
Miami, FL 33138
6:30 a.m.–12:00 p.m. Monday through Friday
Phone: 305-530-7657

Newark District Office

Federal Building
970 Broad Street
Newark, NJ 07102
7:30 a.m.–4:30 p.m.
Phone: 201-645-2269

New Orleans District Office

Postal Services Building
701 Loyola Avenue, Room T-8005
New Orleans, LA 70113
7:30 a.m.–2:15 p.m. Monday through Friday
Phone: 504-589-6521

New York District Office

26 Federal Plaza
New York, NY 10278
7:30 a.m.–3:30 p.m. Monday through Friday
Phone: 212-264-3911

Norfolk Sub-Office

Norfolk Federal Building
5280 Henneman Drive
Norfolk, VA 23513
8:30 a.m.–3:00 p.m. Monday through Friday
Phone: 202-307-1557

Orlando International Airport

9403 Trade Port Drive
Orlando, FL 32827
8:00 a.m.–4:00 p.m. Monday through Friday
Phone: 407-825-4168

Philadelphia District Office

1600 Callowhill Street
Philadelphia, PA 19130
8:00 a.m.–4:30 p.m.
Phone: 215-656-7150

Pittsburgh Sub-Office

USCIS/Department of Justice
2130 Federal Building
1000 Liberty Avenue
Pittsburgh, PA 15222
8:00 a.m.–4:30 p.m.
Phone: 412-644-3360

Portland District Office

176 Gannett Drive
South Portland, ME 04106
8:00 a.m.–4:00 p.m.
Monday through Friday
Phone: 207-780-3399

Providence Sub-Office

201 Dyer Street
Providence, RI 02903
8:00 a.m.–3:30 p.m.
Monday through Friday
Phone: 401-528-5528

Puerto Rico San Juan District Office

P.O. Box 365068
San Juan, PR 00936
8:00 a.m.–4:30 p.m.
Phone: 809-766-5329

Puerto Rico District Director's Office

San Patricio Office Center
7 Tabonuco Street, Suite 100
Guaynabo, PR 00968
7:00 a.m.–4:00 p.m. Monday through Thursday
7:00 a.m.–12:00 p.m. Friday

Rochester Sub-Office

Federal Building
100 State Street, Room 418
Rochester, NY 14614
10:00 a.m.–4 p.m. Tuesday
8:00 a.m.–4:00 p.m. Wednesday
Phone: 716-263-6731

St. Albans Sub-Office

Federal Building
64 Gricebrook Road
St. Albans, VT 05478
8:00 a.m.–4:00 p.m. Monday through Friday
Phone: 802-527-3255
St. Thomas, VI, Sub-Office
Federal District Court Building
Nisky Center, Suite 1A, First Floor South
Charlotte Amalie,
St. Thomas, VI 00802
8:00 a.m.–4:30 p.m.
Phone: 340-774-1390

Syracuse Sub-Office

412 Warren Street
Syracuse, NY 13202
Phone: 315-478-1227

Tampa Sub-Office

5524 West Cypress Street
Tampa, FL 33607-1708
7:30 a.m.–4:00 p.m.
Monday through Friday
Phone: 813-637-3050

Washington District Office

4420 North Fairfax Drive
Arlington, VA 22203
7:00 a.m.–3:30 p.m.
Monday through Friday
Phone: 202-514-1900

West Palm Beach Sub-Office

301 Broadway
Riviera Beach, FL 33404
7:00 a.m.–3:30 p.m.
Phone: 407-691-9446

Central Region District Offices

Albuquerque Sub-Office

1720 Randolph Road
Albuquerque, NM 87106
8:30 a.m.–3:00 p.m.
Monday through Thursday
8:00 a.m.–12:00 p.m. Friday
Phone: 505-241-3850

Chicago District Office

10 West Jackson Boulevard
Chicago, IL 60604
7:30 a.m.–2:00 p.m.p.m.
Friday appointments only
Phone: 312-385-1500

Dallas District Office

8101 North Stemmons Freeway
Dallas, TX 75247
7:30 a.m.–4:00 p.m.
Monday through Friday
Phone: 214-655-3011

Denver District Office

4730 Paris Street
Albrook Center
Denver, CO 80239-2804
7:30 a.m.–2:30 p.m.
Monday through Friday
Phone: 303-371-0986

El Paso District Office

1545 Hopkins Boulevard
El Paso, TX 79925
8:00 a.m.–4:30 p.m.
Phone: 915-225-1749

Harlingen District Office

2102 Teege Road
Harlingen, TX 78550
8:00 a.m.–3:30 p.m.
Wednesday by appointment only
Phone: 210-427-8592

Helena District Office

2800 Skyway Drive
Helena, MT 59626
8:00 a.m.–3:30 p.m.
Monday, Tuesday, Thursday, and Friday
Closed Wednesday
Phone: 406-449-5220

Houston District Office

126 Northpoint
Houston, TX 77060
7:00 a.m.–3:30 p.m.
Monday through Thursday
7:00 a.m.–11:30 p.m. Friday
Phone: 713-847-7979

Kansas City District Office

9747 North Conant Avenue
Kansas City, MO 64153
7:30 a.m.–2:30 p.m.
Monday through Thursday
Closed Friday
Phone: 816-891-0684

Oklahoma Sub-Office

4149 Highline Boulevard, Suite 300
Oklahoma City, OK 73108
8:00 a.m.–3:00 p.m.
Monday through Friday
Phone: 405-231-5928

Omaha District Office

3736 South 132nd Street
Omaha, NE 68144
8:00 a.m.–2:00 p.m.
Monday, Tuesday, Thursday, and Friday
Closed Wednesday
Phone: 402-697-9152

St. Paul District Office

2901 Metro Drive, Suite 100
Bloomington, MN 55425
8:00 a.m.–2:30 p.m.
Monday through Thursday
Closed Friday
Phone: 612-335-2211

San Antonio District Office

U.S. Federal Building
8940 Four Winds Drive
San Antonio, TX 78239
8:00 a.m.–4:00 p.m.
Monday through Friday
Phone: 210-967-7000

Western Region District Offices

Anchorage District Office

620 East 10th Avenue, Suite 102
Anchorage, AK 99501-3701
8:00 a.m.–3:00 p.m.
Monday, Tuesday, Thursday, and Friday
8:00 a.m.–12:00 p.m.
Wednesday
Phone: 907-868-3524

Fresno Sub-Office

865 Fulton Mall
Fresno, CA 93721-2816
8:00 a.m.–2:00 p.m.
Monday through Friday
Phone: 209-487-5132

Guam

Sub-Office
Sirena Plaza
108 Hernan Cortez Avenue, Suite 801
Hagatna, GU 96910
8:00 a.m.–2:30 p.m.
Monday through Friday
Phone: 671-472-7385; 671-472-7253

Honolulu District Office

595 Ala Moana Boulevard
Honolulu, HI 96813
8:00 a.m.–3:00 p.m.
Monday through Thursday
8:00 a.m.–2:00 p.m.
Friday
Phone: 808-541-1388; 808-541-1389

Las Vegas Sub-Office

3373 Pepper Lane
Las Vegas, NV 89120
7:30 a.m.–2:30 p.m.
Monday through Thursday
Closed Friday
Phone: 702-451-3597

Los Angeles District Office

300 North Los Angeles Street, Room 1001
Los Angeles, CA 90012
6:00 a.m.–3:00 p.m.
Monday, Tuesday, Wednesday, and Friday
6:00 a.m.–12 p.m. Thursday
Phone: 213-894-2780

Phoenix District Office

2035 North Central Avenue
Phoenix, AZ 85004
8:00 a.m.–4:30 p.m.
Phone: 602-379-3114

Portland District Office

Federal Office Building
511 NW Broadway
Portland, OR 97209
7:30 a.m.–2:30 p.m.
Monday through Thursday
7:30 a.m.–12:00 p.m.
Phone: 503-326-3962

Reno Sub-Office

1351 Corporate Boulevard
Reno, NV 89502-7102
9:00 a.m.–4:00 p.m.
Monday through Friday
Phone: 702-784-5186

Sacramento Sub-Office

650 Capital Mall
Sacramento, CA 95814
700 a.m.–1:00 p.m.
Phone: 916-498-6480

San Diego District Office

880 Front Street, Suite 1234
San Diego, CA 92188
8:00 a.m.–4:30 p.m.
Closed Wednesday
Phone: 619-557-5645

San Francisco District Office

630 Sansome Street
San Francisco, CA 94111-2280
7:45 a.m.–3:00 p.m.
Monday, Tuesday, Thursday, and Friday
7:00 a.m.–2:30 p.m.
Wednesday
Phone: 415-705-3102

San Jose Sub-Office

280 South First Street, Room 1150
San Jose, CA 95113
7:30 a.m.–4:30 p.m.
Phone: 408-535-5191

Seattle District Office
815 Airport Way, South
Seattle, WA 98134
8:00 a.m.–4:30 p.m.
Monday through Friday
Phone: 206-553-0070

Tucson Sub-Office
6431 Country Club Road
Tucson, AZ 85706-5907
8:00 a.m.–2:00 p.m.
Monday through Friday
Phone: 520-620-7270

Foreign Offices

Bangkok, Thailand
Sindhorn Building
Tower Two, 15th Floor
130–132 Wireless Road
Phone: 011-66-2-252-5040 x 2471

Mexico City, Mexico
c/o American Embassy
Paseo de la Reforma
305–118 Colcuauhtemoc
2nd Floor
Mexico City, Mexico 06500
Phone: 011-52-5-211-00-42 x 2572

Rome, Italy
c/o American Embassy
Via Veneto 119A
Rome, Italy 09624
011-39-6-467-42634

High School
Equivalency Documents

Following you'll find the high school equivalency documents for countries whose nationals qualified in recent years to enter the DV Visa Lottery.

Countries	Credentials
AFRICA	
Algeria	*Baccalauréat*
Angola	Secondary School Leaving Certificate
Benin	*Baccalauréat*
Botswana	Cambridge Overseas School Certificate
Burkina Faso	*Baccalauréat*
Burundi	Diplôme des humanités complètes
Cameroon	GCE O-Levels/*Baccalauréat*
Cape Verde	Curso complementar do ensino secundario (Secondary Education Complementary Course)
Central African Republic	*Baccalauréat*
Chad	*Baccalauréat*
Comoros	N/A (secondary education is available only through grade nine)
Congo	*Baccalauréat*
Congo, Democratic Republic of the	Diplôme d'etat d'etudes secondaires du cycle long (State Diploma of Long Cycle Secondary Education)
Djibouti	*Baccalauréat*
Egypt	General Secondary School Certificate
Equatorial Guinea	Information not available
Eritrea	Eritrean Secondary Education Examination Certificate
Ethiopia	Ethiopian School Leaving Certificate
Gabon	*Baccalauréat*
Gambia,	The West African School Certificate/GCE O-Levels
Ghana	West African School Certificate/GCE O-Levels

AFRICA *(continued)*

Guinea	*Baccalauréat*
Guinea-Bissau	Information not available
Ivory Coast (Côte d'Ivoire)	*Baccalauréat*
Kenya	Kenya Certificate of Secondary Education
Lesotho	Cambridge Overseas School Certificate
Liberia	Senior High School Certificate
Libya	General Secondary Certificate
Madagascar	*Baccalauréat*
Malawi	Cambridge Overseas School Certificate
Mali	*Baccalauréat*
Mauritania	*Baccalauréat*
Mauritius	Higher School Certificate
Morocco	*Baccalauréat*
Mozambique	*Certificado de habilitacoes literarias* (Secondary School Leaving Certificate)
Namibia	Cambridge Overseas School Certificate
Niger	*Baccalauréat*
Nigeria	Senior School Certificate/West African School Certificate/GCE O-Levels
Rwanda	*Certificat des humanités*
São Tomé and Príncipe	*Certidao do ensino secundario* (Secondary Education Certificate)
Senegal	*Baccalauréat*
Seychelles	Cambridge Overseas School Certificate
Sierra Leone	West African School Certificate/GCE O-Levels
Somalia	Secondary School Leaving Certificate
South Africa	Senior Certificate
Sudan, The	Senior School Certificate
Swaziland	Cambridge Overseas School Certificate
Tanzania	National Form IV Examination/Certificate of Secondary Education
Togo	*Baccalauréat*
Tunisia	*Baccalauréat*
Uganda	Uganda Certificate of Education
Zaire	See Congo, Democratic Republic of the
Zambia	Zambia School Certificate
Zimbabwe	Cambridge Overseas School Certificate

ASIA

Afghanistan	*Baccalauria*
Bahrain	Secondary School Leaving Certificate
Bangladesh	Higher Secondary Certificate
Bhutan	Indian School Certificate
Brunei	Brunei/Cambridge GCE O-Levels

ASIA *(continued)*

Burma (Myanmar)	Basic Education High School Examination/Matriculation
Cambodia	Certificate of Completion/*Baccalauréat*
Hong Kong Region)	(Special Hong Kong Certificate of Education/ Administrative GCE O-Levels
Indonesia	*Ijazah SMA* (Senior Secondary Leaving Certificate)
Iran	Certificate of Completion of Secondary Education
Iraq	Sixth Form *Baccalauréat*
Israel	*Bagrut*
Japan	Secondary School Leaving Certificate
Jordan	*Tawjihi* (Secondary School Leaving Certificate)
North Korea	Graduation Certificate Senior Middle School
Kuwait	General Secondary School Certificate
Laos	*Baccalauréat*
Lebanon	*Baccalauréat* (Second Part)
Malaysia	SPM (*Sijil Pelajaran Malaysia*)
Maldives	N/A (secondary level education is not available)
Mongolia	School Leaving Certificate
Nepal	Proficiency Certificate
Oman	*Thanawiya amma* (Secondary School Leaving Certificate)
Pakistan	Intermediate or Higher Secondary School Certificate
Qatar	Certificate of General Secondary Education
Saudi Arabia	General Secondary Education Certificate
Singapore	Singapore/Cambridge GCE O-Levels
Sri Lanka	Sri Lankan GCE O-Levels
Syria	Secondary School Leaving Certificate
Thailand	*Mathayom suksa*
United Arab Emirates	Secondary School Certificate
Yemen	*Al thanawiya* (General Secondary Education Certificate)

EUROPE

Albania	*Deftese pjekurie* (Maturity Certificate)
Andorra	*Titulo de Bachillerato* (Title of Bachelor)
Armenia	*Attestat o srednem obriazovanii* (Certificate of Secondary Education)
Austria	*Reifeprüfung* (Maturity Certificate)
Azerbaijan	*Svidetel'stvo o srednem obrazovanii* (Certificate of Secondary Education)
Belarus	*Svidetel'stvo o srednem obrazovanii* (Certificate of Secondary Education)
Belgium	*Certificat d'enseignement secondaire* (Higher Secondary Certificate)
Bosnia and Herzegovina	*Matura*
Bulgaria	*Diplom za obrazovanie* (Diploma of Completed Education)

EUROPE *(continued)*

Croatia	*Matura*
Cyprus	*Apolytirion*
Czech Republic	*Maturutní zkouska or matura*
Denmark	*Bevis for studentereksamen/Hojere forberedelseseksamen/Hojere handelseksamen*
Estonia	Secondary School Certificate
Finland	*Lukion paastotodistus*
France	*Baccalauréat*/Brevet de technicien
Georgia	*Attestat o srednem obrazovanii*
Germany	*Abitur/Fachhochschulreife/Realschulabschluss*
Greece	*Apolytirion*
Hungary	*Erettsegi bizonyitvany*
Iceland	*Studentsprof*
Ireland	Leaving Certificate
Italy	Diploma di maturità
Kazakhstan	*Attestat o srednem obrazovanii* (Certificate of Secondary Education)
Kyrgyzstan	*Attestat o srednem obrazovanii* (Certificate of Secondary Education)
Latvia	*Atestats par visparejo videjo izgitibu* (Certificate of General Secondary Education)
Liechtenstein	*Matura*
Lithuania	Secondary School Diploma
Luxembourg	*Diplôme de fin d'etudes secondaires*
Macedonia, the Former Yugoslav Republic of	*Svidetelstov za polozen zavrsen* (Secondary School Leaving Certificate)
Malta	Matriculation/Secondary Education Certificate
Moldova	*Diploma de absolvire a invatamintuni mediu general* (Diploma of Completion of General Secondary Education)
Monaco	*Baccalauréat*
Montenegro School	*Svedocanstvo o polozenom zavrsnom* (Secondary Leaving Certificate)
Netherlands	HAVO or VWO
Northern Ireland	General Certificate of Secondary Education (GCSE)
Norway	*Vitnemal den vidergaende skole* (Certificate of Upper Secondary Education)
Portugal	*Certificado de fin de estudos secundarios* (Certificate of Completion of Secondary Education)/*Certidao de decimo segundo año* (Twelfth Year Certificate)
Romania	*Diploma de bacalaureat*
Russia	*Attestat o srednem obrazovanii* (Certificate of Secondary Education)
San Marino	*Diploma di maturità*

Serbia	*Svedocanstvo o polozenom zavrsnom* (Secondary School Leaving Certificate)
Slovakia	*Maturitna skuska* (Maturity Certificate)
Slovenia	*Matura/Spricevalo o zakljucnem izpitu* (Certificate of Final Examinations)
Spain	*Bachillerato unificado y polivalente* (BUP)
Sweden	*Avgangsbetyg* (Gymnasium)
Switzerland	*Maturity Certificate of Fahigkeitszeugnis* (Certificate of Qualification)
Tajikistan	*Attestat o srednem obrazovanii* (Certificate of Secondary Education)
Turkey	*Lise diplomasi*
Turkmenistan	Attestat o srednem obrazovanii (Certificate of Secondary Education)
Ukraine	*Atestat o protnom ovshchem srednem obrazovan*i (Certificate of Completed Secondary Education)
Vatican (Holy See)	Diploma di maturità
Yugoslavia, Republic of	Svedocanstvo o polozenom zavrsnom (Secondary School Leaving Certificate)

NORTH AMERICA

Bahamas	Bahamas General Certificate of Secondary Education/GCE O-Levels

OCEANIA

Australia	"12th Year" Certificate from any state
Fiji	New Zealand School Certificate or Fiji School Leaving Certificate
Kiribati	GCE O-Levels/Secondary School Certificate/Pacific Senior Secondary Certificate/Kiribati National Certificate
Marshall Islands	GCE O-Levels/Pacific Senior Secondary Certificate
Micronesia,	Information not available Federated States of
Nauru	GCE O-Levels/Pacific Senior Secondary Certificate
New Zealand	Sixth Form Certificate
Palau	Information not available
Papua New Guinea	Higher School Certificate
Solomon Islands	GCE O-Levels/Secondary School Certificate/Pacific Senior Secondary Certificate/Solomon Islands School Certificate
Tonga	Tongan School Certificate/Pacific Senior Secondary Certificate/Completion Form Six
Tuvalu	Tuvalu School Certificate/Pacific Senior Secondary Certificate
Vanuatu	GCE O-Levels/*Baccalauréat*
Western Samoa	GCE O-Levels/Secondary School Certificate/Pacific Senior Secondary Certificate/Kiribati National Certificate

SOUTH AMERICA/
CENTRAL AMERICA & THE CARIBBEAN

Antigua and Barbuda	Caribbean Examinations Council Secondary Education Certificate (CxC)/GCE O-Levels
Argentina	*Bachillerato*

APPENDIX D: HIGH SCHOOL EQUIVALENCY DOCUMENTS

Barbados	Caribbean Examinations Council Secondary Education Certificate (CxC)/GCE O-Levels
Belize	Caribbean Examinations Council Secondary Education Certificate (CxC)/GCE O-Levels
Bolivia	*Bachillerato*
Brazil	*Certificado de conclusao de 2 grau* (Certificate of Completion of Secondary Level)
Chile	*Licencia de educacion media* (Intermediate Education Certificate)
Costa Rica	*Diploma de conclusion de educacion diversificado*
Cuba	*Bachillerato*
Dominica	Caribbean Examinations Council Secondary Education Certificate (CxC)/GCE O-Levels
Ecuador	*Bachillerato*
Grenada	Caribbean Examinations Council Secondary Education Certificate (CxC)/GCE O-Levels
Guatemala	*Bachillerato*
Guyana	Caribbean Examinations Council Secondary Education Certificate (CxC)
Nicaragua	*Bachillerato*
Panama	*Bachillerato*
Paraguay	*Bachillerato*
Peru	*Certificado de educacion secundaria completa*
Saint Kitts and Nevis	Caribbean Examinations Council Secondary Education Certificate (CxC)/GCE O-Levels
Saint Lucia	Caribbean Examinations Council Secondary Education Certificate (CxC)/GCE O-Levels
Saint Vincent and the Grenadines	Caribbean Examinations Council Secondary Education Certificate (CxC)/GCE O-Levels
Suriname	HAVO or VWO
Trinidad and Tobago	Caribbean Examinations Council Secondary Education Certificate (CxC)/GCE O-Levels
Uruguay	*Bachillerato*
Venezuela	*Bachillerato*

Courtesy of World Edication Services, Inc.

Grounds of Inadmissibility/Exclusion

Below I list the most important reasons why you might be barred from entering the United States or getting an immigrant or nonimmigrant visa.

For some of these grounds of inadmissibility, the USCIS might waive your inadmissibility. If any of these bars apply to you, speak to an immigration law expert before applying for an immigrant or nonimmigrant visa. (For more on inadmissibility in the context of an application for an immigrant visa, see chapter 5.)

- You have a communicable disease of public health significance including HIV, tuberculosis, chancroid, gonorrhea, granuloma inguinale, infectious leprosy, lymphogranuloma, enereum, or infectious syphilis.
- You have a physical or mental disorder and a history of behavior associated with the disorder that may pose or has posed a threat to the property, safety, or welfare of yourself or others. This might include alcoholism or addiction to a noncontrolled but mind-altering substance.
- You are a drug abuser or drug addict. Usually this refers to habit-forming narcotic drugs.
- You have been convicted of, or you admit to having committed, a crime involving moral turpitude that is not a purely political offense. This includes attempts of conspiracy to commit crimes involving moral turpitude.
- You have been convicted of committing, or you admit to having committed, a violation of any law or regulation relating to controlled substances as defined in federal law. In addition to cocaine and heroin, this includes LSD, amphetamines, barbiturates, Seconal, and angel dust. This exclusion includes attempts and conspiracy to commit this crime.
- You have been convicted of two or more offenses where the total sentence of confinement actually imposed was five years or more.
- A consular or an USCIS officer has reason to believe that you have been an illicit trafficker in a controlled substance or that you have assisted, abetted, conspired with, or colluded with others in the illicit trafficking of controlled substances.
- You are a prostitute, you have committed acts of prostitution, you are coming to the United States to engage in prostitution, or you have procured or attempted to procure or import prostitutes. This ground of exclusion applies to events that occurred within ten years of your application for a visa or entry into the United States.
- An USCIS or a consular officer believes that you are coming to the United States to engage in espionage or sabotage or to try to overthrow the U.S. government by force, violence, or unlawful means, or that you are coming to engage in terrorist activities.
- The U.S. government believes that your entry or activities would have potentially serious adverse foreign policy consequences.

- You are, or have been, a member of or affiliated with a communist or other totalitarian party.
- You participated in Nazi persecutions or genocide.
- You are likely to become a public charge.
- You were previously excluded and/or deported from the United States.
- You got a visa or tried to get a visa or you entered the United States or you tried to enter the United States by fraud or willful misrepresentation of a material fact.
- You are a stowaway. However, this bar only applies if you are caught trying to enter the United States. Once you enter the United States, having been a stowaway will not bar you from becoming a permanent resident.
- You are a smuggler.
- You committed document fraud.
- You are coming to the United States to practice polygamy.
- You are permanently ineligible for citizenship.
- You are accompanying an inadmissible alien whose exclusion is due to infancy, sickness, or physical and mental disability.
- You detain, retain, or withhold custody of a child outside the United States after receipt of a court order granting custody of the child to a U.S. citizen, where the child has a lawful claim to U.S. citizenship.
- You are coming to the United States in a category which requires that you obtain a certification from the Department of Labor showing there are no U.S. workers ready, willing, and able to handle your job, and you do not obtain such certification.
- You are a medical graduate of a unapproved medical school who has not successfully completed qualifying exams and who is not competent in oral and written English and you are coming to the United States to perform services as a member of the medical profession.

- You knowingly made a frivolous application for asylum after the USCIS had advised you of the consequences of filing a frivolous application.
- You haven't been vaccinated against vaccine-preventable diseases, including at least the following diseases: mumps, measles, rubella, polio, tetanus and diphtheria toxoids, pertussis, influenza type B, and hepatitis B.
- You incited terrorist activity under circumstances indicating an intention to cause death or serious bodily harm.
- You failed to appear at your removal hearing without reasonable cause. This will bar you until you have been outside the United States for at least five years.
- You have falsely claimed U.S. citizenship to get a federal or state benefit.
- You came here as a nonimmigrant and you got public benefits for which you were ineligible. This bars you until you have been outside of the United States for five years.
- You came here as an F-1 student to attend elementary or high school and you violated your status. This bars you until you have been outside the United States for five years.
- You were removed (deported or excluded) from the United States. This bars you until you have been outside the United States for five years. If you have been removed twice or convicted of an aggravated felony, you will be barred for 20 years.
- You left the United States after having been in the country unlawfully for more than 180 days. This will bar you for three years, but you may be eligible for a waiver.
- You have been in the United States unlawfully for one year or more. This will bar you for ten years, but you may be eligible for a waiver.
- You voted unlawfully.

Poverty Guidelines and Affidavit of Support, Form I-864

U. S. Department of Homeland Security
Bureau of Citizenship and Immigration Services

OMB# 1615-0075
Poverty Guidelines

2004 Poverty Guidelines*
Minimum Income Requirement For Use in Completing Form I-864

For the 48 Contiguous States, the District of Columbia, Puerto Rico, the U.S. Virgin Islands, and Guam:

Sponsor's Household Size	100% of Poverty Line For sponsors on active duty in the U.S. Armed Forces who are petitioning for their spouse or child.	125% of Poverty Line For all other sponsors
2	$12,490	$15,612
3	15,670	19,587
4	18,850	23,562
5	22,030	27,537
6	25,210	31,512
7	28,390	35,487
8	31,570	39,462
	Add $3,180 for each additional person.	Add $3,975 for each additional person.

Sponsor's Household Size	For Alaska		For Hawaii	
	100% of Poverty Line For sponsors on active duty in the U.S. Armed Forces who are petitioning for their spouse or child	125% of Poverty Line For all other sponsors	100% of Poverty Line For sponsors on active duty in the U.S. Armed Forces who are petitioning for their spouse or child	125% of Poverty Line For all other sponsors
2	$15,610	$19,512	$14,360	$17,950
3	19,590	24,487	18,020	22,525
4	23,570	29,462	21,680	27,100
5	27,550	34,437	25,340	31,675
6	31,530	39,412	29,000	36,250
7	35,510	44,387	32,660	40,825
8	39,490	49,362	36,320	45,400
	Add $3,980 for each additional person.	Add $4,975 for each additional person.	Add $3,660 for each additional person.	Add $4,575 for each additional person.

Means-tested Public Benefits

Federal Means-tested Public Benefits. To date, Federal agencies administering benefit programs have determined that Federal means-tested public benefits include Food Stamps, Medicaid, Supplemental Security Income (SSI), Temporary Assistance for Needy Families (TANF), and the State Child Health Insurance Program (SCHIP).

State Means-tested Public Benefits. Each State will determine which, if any, of its public benefits are means-tested. If a State determines that it has programs which meet this definition, it is encouraged to provide notice to the public on which programs are included. Check with the State public assistance office to determine which, if any, State assistance programs have been determined to be State means-tested public benefits.

Programs Not Included: The following Federal and State programs are *not* included as means-tested benefits: emergency Medicaid; short-term, non-cash emergency relief; services provided under the National School Lunch and Child Nutrition Acts; immunizations and testing and treatment for communicable diseases; student assistance under the Higher Education Act and the Public Health Service Act; certain forms of foster-care or adoption assistance under the Social Security Act; Head Start Programs; means-tested programs under the Elementary and Secondary Education Act; and Job Training Partnership Act programs.

* These poverty guidelines remain in effect for use with the Form I-864 Affidavit of Support from April 1, 2004 until new poverty guidelines go into effect in the Spring of 2005.

Form I-864P (Rev. 03/08/04)N

adoption who are living in your residence, if they have lived in your residence for the previous 6 months, or who are listed as dependents on your most recent Federal income tax return whether or not they live in your residence. For their income to be considered, these household members or dependents must be willing to make their income available for the support of the sponsored immigrant(s) if necessary, and to complete and sign Form I-864A, Contract Between Sponsor and Household Member. However, a household member who is the immigrant you are sponsoring only need complete Form I-864A if his or her income will be used to determine your ability to support a spouse and/or children immigrating with him or her.

If in any of the most recent 3 tax years, you and your spouse each reported income on a joint income tax return, but you want to use only your own income to qualify (and your spouse is not submitting a Form I-864A), you may provide a separate breakout of your individual income for these years. Your individual income will be based on the earnings from your W-2 forms, Wage and Tax Statement, submitted to IRS for any such years. If necessary to meet the income requirement, you may also submit evidence of other income listed on your tax returns which can be attributed to you. You must provide documentation of such reported income, including Forms 1099 sent by the payer, which show your name and Social Security number.

You must calculate your household size and total household income as indicated in Parts 4.B. and 4.C. of this form. You must compare your total household income with the minimum income requirement for your household size using the poverty guidelines. For the purposes of the affidavit of support, determination of your ability to meet the income requirements will be based on the most recent poverty guidelines published in the Federal Register at the time the Consular or Immigration Officer makes a decision on the intending immigrant's application for an immigrant visa or adjustment of status. Immigration and Consular Officers will begin to use updated poverty guidelines on the first day of the second month after the date the guidelines are published in the Federal Register.

If your total household income is equal to or higher than the minimum income requirement for your household size, you do not need to provide information on your assets, and you may *not* have a joint sponsor unless you are requested to do so by a Consular or Immigration Officer. If your total household income does not meet the minimum income requirement, the intending immigrant will be ineligible for an immigrant visa or adjustment of status, unless:

- You provide evidence of assets that meet the requirements outlined under "Evidence of Assets" below; and/or

- The immigrant you are sponsoring provides evidence of assets that meet the requirements under "Evidence of Assets" below; or

- A joint sponsor assumes the liability of the intending immigrant with you. A joint sponsor must execute a separate affidavit of support on behalf of the intending

immigrant and any accompanying family members. A joint sponsor must individually meet the minimum requirement of 125 percent of the poverty line based on his or her household size and income and/or assets, including any assets of the sponsored immigrant.

The Government may pursue verification of any information provided on or in support of this form, including employment, income, or assets with the employer, financial or other institutions, the Internal Revenue Service, or the Social Security Administration.

Evidence of Income

In order to complete this form you must submit the following evidence of income:

- A copy of your complete Federal income tax return, as filed with the Internal Revenue Service, for each of the most recent 3 tax years. If you were not required to file a tax return in any of the most recent 3 tax years, you must provide an explanation. If you filed a joint income tax return and are using only your own income to qualify, you must also submit copies of your W-2s for each of the most recent 3 tax years, and if necessary to meet the income requirement, evidence of other income reported on your tax returns, such as Forms 1099.

- If you rely on income of any members of your household or dependents in order to reach the minimum income requirement, copies of their Federal income tax returns for the most recent 3 tax years. These persons must each complete and sign a Form I-864A, Contract Between Sponsor and Household Member.

- Evidence of current employment or self-employment, such as a recent pay statement, or a statement from your employer on business stationery, showing beginning date of employment, type of work performed, and salary or wages paid. You must also provide evidence of current employment for any person whose income is used to qualify.

Evidence of Assets

If you want to use your assets, the assets of your household members or dependents, and/or the assets of the immigrant you are sponsoring to meet the minimum income requirement, you must provide evidence of assets with a cash value that equals at least five times the difference between your total household income and the minimum income requirement. For the assets of a household member, other than the immigrant(s) you are sponsoring, to be considered, the household member must complete and sign Form I-864A, Contract Between Sponsor and Household Member.

All assets must be supported with evidence to verify location, ownership, and value of each asset. Any liens and liabilities relating to the assets must be documented. List only assets that can be readily converted into cash within one year. Evidence of assets includes, but is not limited to the following:

APPENDIX F: POVERTY GUIDELINES

- Bank statements covering the last 12 months, *or a statement* from an officer of the bank or other financial institution in which you have deposits, including deposit/withdrawal history for the last 12 months, and current balance;

- Evidence of ownership and value of stocks, bonds, and certificates of deposit, and date(s) acquired;

- Evidence of ownership and value of other personal property, and date(s) acquired; and

- Evidence of ownership and value of any real estate, and date(s) acquired.

Change of Sponsor's Address

You are required by 8 U.S.C. 1183a(d) and 8 CFR 213a.3 to report every change of address to the Immigration and Naturalization Service and the State(s) in which the sponsored immigrant(s) reside(s). You must report changes of address to INS on Form I-865, Sponsor's Notice of Change of Address, within 30 days of any change of address. You must also report any change in your address to the State(s) in which the sponsored immigrant(s) live.

Penalties

If you include in this affidavit of support any material information that you know to be false, you may be liable for criminal prosecution under the laws of the United States.

If you fail to give notice of your change of address, as required by 8 U.S.C. 1183a(d) and 8 CFR 213a.3, you may be liable for the civil penalty established by 8 U.S.C. 1183a(d)(2). The amount of the civil penalty will depend on whether you failed to give this notice because you were aware that the immigrant(s) you sponsored had received Federal, State, or local means-tested public benefits.

Privacy Act Notice

Authority for the collection of the information requested on this form is contained in 8 U.S.C. 1182(a)(4), 1183a, 1184(a), and 1258. The information will be used principally by the INS or by any Consular Officer to whom it is furnished, to support an alien's application for benefits under the Immigration and Nationality Act and specifically the assertion that he or she has adequate means of financial support and will not become a public charge. Submission of the information is voluntary. Failure to provide the information will result in denial of the application for an immigrant visa or adjustment of status.

The information may also, as a matter of routine use, be disclosed to other Federal, State, and local agencies or private entities providing means-tested public benefits for use in civil action against the sponsor for breach of contract. It may also be disclosed as a matter of routine use to other Federal, State, local, and foreign law enforcement and regulatory agencies to enable these entities to carry out their law enforcement responsibilites.

Reporting Burden

A person is not required to respond to a collection of information unless it displays a currently valid OMB control number. We try to create forms and instructions that are accurate, can be easily understood, and which impose the least possible burden on you to provide us with information. Often this is difficult because some immigration laws are very complex. The reporting burden for this collection of information on Form I-864 is computed as follows: 1) learning about the form, 63 minutes; 2) completing the form, 105 minutes; and 3) assembling and filing the form, 65 minutes, for an estimated average of 3 hours and 48 minutes minutes per response. The reporting burden for collection of information on Form I-864A is computed as: 1) learning about the form, 20 minutes; 2) completing the form, 55 minutes; 3) assembling and filing the form, 30 minutes, for an estimated average of 1 hour and 45 minutes per response. If you have comments regarding the accuracy of this estimates, or suggestions for making this form simpler, you can write to the Immigration and Naturalization Service, HQPDI, 425 I Street, N.W., Room 4034, Washington, DC 20536. **DO NOT MAIL YOUR COMPLETED AFFIDAVIT OF SUPPORT TO THIS ADDRESS.**

CHECK LIST

The following items must be submitted with Form I-864, Affidavit of Support Under Section 213A:

For *ALL* sponsors:

☐ This form, the **I-864, completed and signed** before a notary public or a Consular or Immigration Officer.

☐ Proof of **current employment** or self employment.

☐ Your individual Federal **income tax returns for the most recent 3 tax years**, or an explanation if fewer are submitted. Your **W-2s** for any of the most recent 3 tax years for which you filed a joint tax return but are using only your own income to qualify. Forms 1099 or evidence of other reported income *if* necessary to qualify.

For *SOME* sponsors:

☐ *If the immigrant you are sponsoring is bringing a spouse or children,* **photocopies of the immigrant's affidavit of support** for each spouse and/or child immigrating with the immigrant you are sponsoring.

☐ *If you are on active duty in the U.S. Armed Forces and are sponsoring a spouse or child using the 100 percent of poverty level exception,* **proof of your active military status.**

If you are using the income of persons in your household or dependents to qualify,

☐ A separate **Form I-864A** for each person whose income you will use. A sponsored immigrant/household member who is not immigrating with a spouse and/or child **does not need to complete Form I-864A.**

☐ Proof of their **residency and relationship** to you if they are not listed as dependents on your income tax return for the most recent tax year.

☐ Proof of their **current employment** or self-employment.

APPENDIX F: POVERTY GUIDELINES

☐ Copies of their individual Federal **income tax returns for the 3 most recent tax years,** or an explanation if fewer are submitted.

If you use your assets or the assets of the sponsored immigrant to qualify,

☐ **Documentation of assets** establishing location, ownership, date of acquisition, and value. Evidence of any liens or liabilities against these assets.

☐ A separate **Form I-864A** for each household member other than the sponsored immigrant/household member.

If you are a joint sponsor or the relative of an employment-based immigrant requiring an affidavit of support, **proof of your citizenship status.**

☐ For U.S. citizens or nationals, a copy of your birth certificate, passport, or certificate of naturalization or citizenship.

☐ For lawful permanent residents, a copy of both sides of your I-551, Permanent Resident Card.

APPENDIX F: POVERTY GUIDELINES

OMB No. 1115-0214

U.S. Department of Justice
Immigration and Naturalization Service

Affidavit of Support Under Section 213A of the Act

START HERE - Please Type or Print

Part 1. Information on Sponsor (You)

Last Name	First Name	Middle Name

Mailing Address *(Street Number and Name)*	Apt/Suite Number

City	State or Province

Country	ZIP/Postal Code	Telephone Number

Place of Residence if different from above *(Street Number and Name)*	Apt/Suite Number

City	State or Province

Country	ZIP/Postal Code	Telephone Number

Date of Birth *(Month, Day, Year)*	Place of Birth *(City, State, Country)*	Are you a U.S. Citizen? ☐ Yes ☐ No

Social Security Number	A-Number *(If any)*

FOR AGENCY USE ONLY

This Affidavit   Receipt

[ ] Meets

[ ] Does not
     meet

Requirements of
Section 213A

Officer or I.J.
Signature

Location

Date

Part 2. Basis for Filing Affidavit of Support

I am filing this affidavit of support because *(check one)*:

a. ☐ I filed/am filing the alien relative petition.

b. ☐ I filed/am filing an alien worker petition on behalf of the intending

immigrant, who is related to me as my _____ .
(relationship)

c. ☐ I have ownership interest of at least 5% _____
(name of entity which filed visa petition)

which filed an alien worker petition on behalf of the intending

immigrant, who is related to me as my _____ .
(relationship)

d. ☐ I am a joint sponsor willing to accept the legal obligations with any other sponsor(s).

Part 3. Information on the Immigrant(s) You Are Sponsoring

Last Name	First Name	Middle Name

Date of Birth *(Month, Day, Year)*	Sex ☐ Male ☐ Female	Social Security Number *(If any)*

Country of Citizenship	A-Number *(If any)*

Current Address *(Street Number and Name)*	Apt/Suite Number	City

State/Province	Country	ZIP/Postal Code	Telephone Number

List any spouse and/or children immigrating with the immigrant named above in this Part: *(Use additional sheet of paper if necessary.)*

Name	Relationship to Sponsored Immigrant			Date of Birth			A-Number *(If any)*	Social Security *(If any)*
	Spouse	Son	Daughter	Mo.	Day	Yr.		

Form I-864 (Rev. 11/05/01)Y

APPENDIX F: POVERTY GUIDELINES

Part 4.   Eligibility to Sponsor

To be a sponsor you must be a U.S. citizen or national or a lawful permanent resident. If you are not the petitioning relative, you must provide proof of status. To prove status, U.S. citizens or nationals must attach a copy of a document proving status, such as a U.S. passport, birth certificate, or certificate of naturalization, and lawful permanent residents must attach a copy of both sides of their Permanent Resident Card (Form I-551).

The determination of your eligibility to sponsor an immigrant will be based on an evaluation of your demonstrated ability to maintain an annual income at or above 125 percent of the Federal poverty line (100 percent if you are a petitioner sponsoring your spouse or child and you are on active duty in the U.S. Armed Forces). The assessment of your ability to maintain an adequate income will include your current employment, household size, and household income as shown on the Federal income tax returns for the 3 most recent tax years. Assets that are readily converted to cash and that can be made available for the support of sponsored immigrants if necessary, including any such assets of the immigrant(s) you are sponsoring, may also be considered.

The greatest weight in determining eligibility will be placed on current employment and household income. If a petitioner is unable to demonstrate ability to meet the stated income and asset requirements, a joint sponsor who *can* meet the income and asset requirements is needed. Failure to provide adequate evidence of income and/or assets or an affidavit of support completed by a joint sponsor will result in denial of the immigrant's application for an immigrant visa or adjustment to permanent resident status.

A. Sponsor's Employment

I am: 1. ☐ Employed by _____ *(Provide evidence of employment)*

Annual salary _____ or hourly wage $ _____ *(for _____ hours per week)*

2. ☐ Self employed _____ *(Name of business)*

Nature of employment or business _____

3. ☐ Unemployed or retired since _____

B. Sponsor's Household Size

Number

1. Number of persons (related to you by birth, marriage, or adoption) living in your residence, including yourself *(Do NOT include persons being sponsored in this affidavit.)* _____

2. Number of immigrants being sponsored in this affidavit *(Include all persons in Part 3.)* _____

3. Number of immigrants **NOT** living in your household whom you are obligated to support under a previously signed Form I-864. _____

4. Number of persons who are otherwise dependent on you, as claimed in your tax return for the most recent tax year. _____

5. Total household size. *(Add lines 1 through 4.)*   **Total** _____

List persons below who are included in lines 1 or 3 for whom you previously have submitted INS Form I-864, *if your support obligation has not terminated.*

(If additional space is needed, use additional paper)

Name	A-Number	Date Affidavit of Support Signed	Relationship

Form I-864 (Rev. 11/05/01)Y Page 2

C. Sponsor's Annual Household Income

Enter total unadjusted income from your Federal income tax return for the most recent tax year below. If you last filed a joint income tax return but are using only your *own* income to qualify, list total earnings from your W-2 Forms, or, *if* necessary to reach the required income for your household size, include income from other sources listed on your tax return. If your *individual* income does not meet the income requirement for your household size, you may also list total income for anyone related to you by birth, marriage, or adoption currently living with you in your residence if they have lived in your residence for the previous 6 months, or any person shown as a dependent on your Federal income tax return for the most recent tax year, even if not living in the household. For their income to be considered, household members or dependents must be willing to make their income available for support of the sponsored immigrant(s) and to complete and sign Form I-864A, Contract Between Sponsor and Household Member. A sponsored immigrant/household member only need complete Form I-864A if his or her income will be used to determine your ability to support a spouse and/or children immigrating with him or her.

You must attach evidence of current employment and copies of income tax returns as filed with the IRS for the most recent 3 tax years for yourself and all persons whose income is listed below. See "Required Evidence " in Instructions. Income from all 3 years will be considered in determining your ability to support the immigrant(s) you are sponsoring.

- ☐ I filed a single/separate tax return for the most recent tax year.
- ☐ I filed a joint return for the most recent tax year which includes only my own income.
- ☐ I filed a joint return for the most recent tax year which includes income for my spouse and myself.
    - ☐ I am submitting documentation of my individual income (Forms W-2 and 1099).
    - ☐ I am qualifying using my spouse's income; my spouse is submitting a Form I-864A.

Indicate most recent tax year	
	(tax year)
Sponsor's individual income	$ _____
or	
Sponsor and spouse's combined income *(If spouse's income is to be considered, spouse must submit Form I-864A.)*	$ _____
Income of other qualifying persons. *(List names; include spouse if applicable. Each person must complete Form I-864A.)*	
_____	$ _____
_____	$ _____
_____	$ _____
Total Household Income	$ _____

Explain on separate sheet of paper if you or any of the above listed individuals were not required to file Federal income tax returns for the most recent 3 years, or if other explanation of income, employment, or evidence is necessary.

D. Determination of Eligibility Based on Income

1. ☐ I am subject to the 125 percent of poverty line requirement for sponsors.
   ☐ I am subject to the 100 percent of poverty line requirement for sponsors on active duty in the U.S. Armed Forces sponsoring their spouse or child.
2. Sponsor's total household size, from Part 4.B., line 5 _____ .
3. Minimum income requirement from the Poverty Guidelines chart for the year of _____ is $ _____ for this household size.   *(year)*

If you are currently employed and your household income for your household size is equal to or greater than the applicable poverty line requirement (from line D.3.), you do not need to list assets (Parts 4.E. and 5) or have a joint sponsor (Part 6) unless you are requested to do so by a Consular or Immigration Officer. You may skip to Part 7, Use of the Affidavit of Support to Overcome Public Charge Ground of Admissibility. **Otherwise, you should continue with Part 4.E.**

APPENDIX F: POVERTY GUIDELINES

Part 4.   Eligibility to Sponsor   *(Continued)*

E. Sponsor's Assets and Liabilities

Your assets and those of your qualifying household members and dependents may be used to demonstrate ability to maintain an income at or above 125 percent (or 100 percent, if applicable) of the poverty line *if* they are available for the support of the sponsored immigrant(s) and can readily be converted into cash within 1 year. The household member, other than the immigrant(s) you are sponsoring, must complete and sign Form I-864A, Contract Between Sponsor and Household Member. List the cash value of each asset *after* any debts or liens are subtracted. Supporting evidence must be attached to establish location, ownership, date of acquisition, and value of each asset listed, including any liens and liabilities related to each asset listed. See "Evidence of Assets" in Instructions.

Type of Asset	Cash Value of Assets *(Subtract any debts)*
Savings deposits	$
Stocks, bonds, certificates of deposit	$
Life insurance cash value	$
Real estate	$
Other *(specify)*	$
Total Cash Value of Assets	$ _____

Part 5.   Immigrant's Assets and Offsetting Liabilities

The sponsored immigrant's assets may also be used in support of your ability to maintain income at or above 125 percent of the poverty line *if* the assets are or will be available in the United States for the support of the sponsored immigrant(s) and can readily be converted into cash within 1 year.

The sponsored immigrant should provide information on his or her assets in a format similar to part 4.E. above. Supporting evidence must be attached to establish location, ownership, and value of each asset listed, including any liens and liabilities for each asset listed. See "Evidence of Assets" in Instructions.

Part 6.   Joint Sponsors

If household income and assets do not meet the appropriate poverty line for your household size, a joint sponsor is required. There may be more than one joint sponsor, but each joint sponsor must individually meet the 125 percent of poverty line requirement based on his or her household income and/or assets, including any assets of the sponsored immigrant. By submitting a separate Affidavit of Support under Section 213A of the Act (Form I-864), a joint sponsor accepts joint responsibility with the petitioner for the sponsored immigrant(s) until they become U.S. citizens, can be credited with 40 quarters of work, leave the United States permanently, or die.

Part 7.   Use of the Affidavit of Support to Overcome Public Charge Ground of Inadmissibility

Section 212(a)(4)(C) of the Immigration and Nationality Act provides that an alien seeking permanent residence as an immediate relative (including an orphan), as a family-sponsored immigrant, or as an alien who will accompany or follow to join another alien is considered to be likely to become a public charge and is inadmissible to the United States unless a sponsor submits a legally enforceable affidavit of support on behalf of the alien. Section 212(a)(4)(D) imposes the same requirement on an employment-based immigrant, and those aliens who accompany or follow to join the employment- based immigrant, if the employment-based immigrant will be employed by a relative, or by a firm in which a relative owns a significant interest. Separate affidavits of support are required for family members at the time they immigrate if they are not included on this affidavit of support or do not apply for an immigrant visa or adjustment of status within 6 months of the date this affidavit of support is originally signed. The sponsor must provide the sponsored immigrant(s) whatever support is necessary to maintain them at an income that is at least 125 percent of the Federal poverty guidelines.

I submit this affidavit of support in consideration of the sponsored immigrant(s) not being found inadmissible to the United States under section 212(a)(4)(C) (or 212(a)(4)(D) for an employment-based immigrant) and to enable the sponsored immigrant(s) to overcome this ground of inadmissibility. I agree to provide the sponsored immigrant(s) whatever support is necessary to maintain the sponsored immigrant(s) at an income that is at least 125 percent of the Federal poverty guidelines. I understand that my obligation will continue until my death or the sponsored immigrant(s) have become U.S. citizens, can be credited with 40 quarters of work, depart the United States permanently, or die.

Form I-864 (Rev. 11/05/01)Y Page 4

APPENDIX F: POVERTY GUIDELINES

Notice of Change of Address.

Sponsors are required to provide written notice of any change of address within 30 days of the change in address until the sponsored immigrant(s) have become U.S. citizens, can be credited with 40 quarters of work, depart the United States permanently, or die. To comply with this requirement, the sponsor must complete INS Form I-865. Failure to give this notice may subject the sponsor to the civil penalty established under section 213A(d)(2) which ranges from $250 to $2,000, unless the failure to report occurred with the knowledge that the sponsored immigrant(s) had received means-tested public benefits, in which case the penalty ranges from $2,000 to $5,000.

> *If my address changes for any reason before my obligations under this affidavit of support terminate, I will complete and file INS Form I-865, Sponsor's Notice of Change of Address, within 30 days of the change of address. I understand that failure to give this notice may subject me to civil penalties.*

Means-tested Public Benefit Prohibitions and Exceptions.

Under section 403(a) of Public Law 104-193 (Welfare Reform Act), aliens lawfully admitted for permanent residence in the United States, with certain exceptions, are ineligible for most Federally-funded means-tested public benefits during their first 5 years in the United States. This provision does not apply to public benefits specified in section 403(c) of the Welfare Reform Act or to State public benefits, including emergency Medicaid; short-term, non-cash emergency relief; services provided under the National School Lunch and Child Nutrition Acts; immunizations and testing and treatment for communicable diseases; student assistance under the Higher Education Act and the Public Health Service Act; certain forms of foster-care or adoption assistance under the Social Security Act; Head Start programs; means-tested programs under the Elementary and Secondary Education Act; and Job Training Partnership Act programs.

Consideration of Sponsor's Income in Determining Eligibility for Benefits.

If a permanent resident alien is no longer statutorily barred from a Federally-funded means-tested public benefit program and applies for such a benefit, the income and resources of the sponsor and the sponsor's spouse will be considered (or deemed) to be the income and resources of the sponsored immigrant in determining the immigrant's eligibility for Federal means-tested public benefits. Any State or local government may also choose to consider (or deem) the income and resources of the sponsor and the sponsor's spouse to be the income and resources of the immigrant for the purposes of determining eligibility for their means-tested public benefits. The attribution of the income and resources of the sponsor and the sponsor's spouse to the immigrant will continue until the immigrant becomes a U.S. citizen or has worked or can be credited with 40 qualifying quarters of work, provided that the immigrant or the worker crediting the quarters to the immigrant has not received any Federal means-tested public benefit during any creditable quarter for any period after December 31, 1996.

> *I understand that, under section 213A of the Immigration and Nationality Act (the Act), as amended, this affidavit of support constitutes a contract between me and the U.S. Government. This contract is designed to protect the United States Government, and State and local government agencies or private entities that provide means-tested public benefits, from having to pay benefits to or on behalf of the sponsored immigrant(s), for as long as I am obligated to support them under this affidavit of support. I understand that the sponsored immigrants, or any Federal, State, local, or private entity that pays any means-tested benefit to or on behalf of the sponsored immigrant(s), are entitled to sue me if I fail to meet my obligations under this affidavit of support, as defined by section 213A and INS regulations.*

Civil Action to Enforce.

If the immigrant on whose behalf this affidavit of support is executed receives any Federal, State, or local means-tested public benefit before this obligation terminates, the Federal, State, or local agency or private entity may request reimbursement from the sponsor who signed this affidavit. If the sponsor fails to honor the request for reimbursement, the agency may sue the sponsor in any U.S. District Court or any State court with jurisdiction of civil actions for breach of contract. INS will provide names, addresses, and Social Security account numbers of sponsors to benefit-providing agencies for this purpose. Sponsors may also be liable for paying the costs of collection, including legal fees.

APPENDIX F: POVERTY GUIDELINES

I acknowledge that section 213A(a)(1)(B) of the Act grants the sponsored immigrant(s) and any Federal, State, local, or private agency that pays any means-tested public benefit to or on behalf of the sponsored immigrant(s) standing to sue me for failing to meet my obligations under this affidavit of support. I agree to submit to the personal jurisdiction of any court of the United States or of any State, territory, or possession of the United States if the court has subject matter jurisdiction of a civil lawsuit to enforce this affidavit of support. I agree that no lawsuit to enforce this affidavit of support shall be barred by any statute of limitations that might otherwise apply, so long as the plaintiff initiates the civil lawsuit no later than ten (10) years after the date on which a sponsored immigrant last received any means-tested public benefits.

Collection of Judgment.

I acknowledge that a plaintiff may seek specific performance of my support obligation. Furthermore, any money judgment against me based on this affidavit of support may be collected through the use of a judgment lien under 28 U.S.C 3201, a writ of execution under 28 U.S.C 3203, a judicial installment payment order under 28 U.S.C 3204, garnishment under 28 U.S.C 3205, or through the use of any corresponding remedy under State law. I may also be held liable for costs of collection, including attorney fees.

Concluding Provisions.

I, _____ , *certify under penalty of perjury under the laws of the United States that:*

    (a) *I know the contents of this affidavit of support signed by me;*

    (b) *All the statements in this affidavit of support are true and correct,*

    (c) *I make this affidavit of support for the consideration stated in Part 7, freely, and without any mental reservation or purpose of evasion;*

    (d) *Income tax returns submitted in support of this affidavit are true copies of the returns filed with the Internal Revenue Service; and*

    (e) *Any other evidence submitted is true and correct.*

_____   _____

      (Sponsor's Signature)   *(Date)*

Subscribed and sworn to (or affirmed) before me this

_____ day of _____ , _____

                (Month)   *(Year)*

at _____ .

My commission expires on _____ .

_____

(Signature of Notary Public or Officer Administering Oath)

_____

            (Title)

Part 8. If someone other than the sponsor prepared this affidavit of support, that person must complete the following:

I certify under penalty of perjury under the laws of the United States that I prepared this affidavit of support at the sponsor's request, and that this affidavit of support is based on all information of which I have knowledge.

Signature	Print Your Name	Date	Daytime Telephone Number

Firm Name and Address

Form I-864 (11/05/01)Y Page 6

APPENDIX F: POVERTY GUIDELINES

May 2004 Department of State Visa Bulletin

VISA BULLETIN

NUMBER 69
VOLUME VIII
WASHINGTON, D.C.

IMMIGRANT NUMBERS FOR MAY 2004

A. STATUTORY NUMBERS

1. This bulletin summarizes the availability of immigrant numbers during May. Consular officers are required to report to the Department of State documentarily qualified applicants for numerically limited visas; the Bureau of Citizenship and Immigration Services in the Department of Homeland Security reports applicants for adjustment of status. Allocations were made, to the extent possible under the numerical limitations, for the demand received by April 7th in the chronological order of the reported priority dates. If the demand could not be satisfied within the statutory or regulatory limits, the category or foreign state in which demand was excessive was deemed oversubscribed. The cut-off date for an Oversubscribed category is the priority date of the first applicant who could not be reached within the numerical limits. Only applicants who have a priority date earlier than the cut-off date may be allotted a number. Immediately that it becomes necessary during the monthly allocation process to retrogress a cut-off date, supplemental requests for numbers will be honored only if the priority date falls within the new cut-off date.

2. Section 201 of the Immigration and Nationality Act (INA) sets an annual minimum family-sponsored preference limit of 226,000. The worldwide level for annual employment-based preference immigrants is at least 140,000. Section 202 prescribes that the per-country limit for preference immigrants is set at 7% of the total annual family-sponsored and employment-based preference limits, i.e., 25,620. The dependent area limit is set at 2%, or 7,320.

3. Section 203 of the INA prescribes preference classes for allotment of immigrant visas as follows:

FAMILY-SPONSORED PREFERENCES

First: Unmarried Sons and Daughters of Citizens: 23,400 plus any numbers not required for fourth preference.

Second: Spouses and Children, and Unmarried Sons and Daughters of Permanent

Residents: 114,200, plus the number (if any) by which the worldwide family preference level exceeds 226,000, and any unused first preference numbers:

A. Spouses and Children: 77% of the overall second preference limitation, of which 75% are exempt from the per-country limit;

B. Unmarried Sons and Daughters (21 years of age or older): 23% of the overall second preference limitation.

Third: Married Sons and Daughters of Citizens: 23,400, plus any numbers not required by first and second preferences.

Fourth: Brothers and Sisters of Adult Citizens: 65,000, plus any numbers not required by first three preferences.

EMPLOYMENT-BASED PREFERENCES

First: Priority Workers: 28.6% of the worldwide employment-based preference level, plus any numbers not required for fourth and fifth preferences.

Second: Members of the Professions Holding Advanced Degrees or Persons of Exceptional Ability: 28.6% of the worldwide employment-based preference level, plus any numbers not required by first preference.

Third: Skilled Workers, Professionals, and Other Workers: 28.6% of the worldwide level, plus any numbers not required by first and second preferences, not more than 10,000 of which to "Other Workers."

Fourth: Certain Special Immigrants: 7.1% of the worldwide level.

Fifth: Employment Creation: 7.1% of the worldwide level, not less than 3,000 of which reserved for investors in a targeted rural or high-unemployment area, and 3,000 set aside for investors in regional centers by Sec. 610 of P.L. 102-395.

4. INA Section 203(e) provides that family-sponsored and employment-based preference visas be issued to eligible immigrants in the order in which a petition in behalf of each has been filed. Section 203(d) provides that spouses and children of preference immigrants are entitled to the same status, and the same order of consideration, if accompanying or following to join the principal. The visa prorating provisions of Section 202(e) apply to allocations for a foreign state or dependent area when visa demand exceeds the per-country limit. These provisions apply at present to the following oversubscribed chargeability areas: MEXICO, INDIA and PHILIPPINES.

5. On the chart below, the listing of a date for any class indicates that the class is oversubscribed (see paragraph 1); "C" means current, i.e., numbers are available for all qualified applicants; and "U" means unavailable, i.e., no numbers are available. (NOTE: Numbers are available only for applicants whose priority date is earlier than the cut-off date listed below.)

Priority Dates for Family Based Immigrant Visas

Family	ALL CHARGEABILITY AREAS EXCEPT THOSE LISTED	INDIA	MEXICO	PHILIPPINES
1st	22OCT00	22OCT00	15OCT94	15JUL90
2A*	15OCT99	15OCT99	01APR97	15OCT99
2B	15MAY95	15MAY95	01JAN92	15MAY95
3rd	15OCT97	15OCT97	01MAR95	01MAR90
4th	15JUN92	01APR91	15JUN92	15MAR82

*NOTE: For May, 2A numbers **EXEMPT from per-country limit** are available to applicants from all countries with priority dates earlier than 01APR97. 2A numbers **SUBJECT to per-country limit** are available to applicants chargeable to all countries EXCEPT MEXICO with priority dates beginning 01APR97 and earlier than 15OCT99. (All 2A numbers provided for MEXICO are exempt from the per-country limit; there are no 2A numbers for MEXICO subject to per-country limit.)

Priority Dates for Employment-Based Immigrant Visas

	ALL CHARGEABILITY AREAS EXCEPT THOSE LISTED	INDIA	MEXICO	PHILIPPINES
1st	C	C	C	C
2nd	C	U	C	C
3rd	C	U	C	C
Other Workers	C	U	C	C
4th	C	C	C	C
Certain Religious Workers	C	C	C	C
5th	C	C	C	C

The Department of State has available a recorded message with visa availability information which can be heard at (202) 663-1541. This recording will be updated in the middle of each month with information on cut-off dates for the following month.

B. DIVERSITY IMMIGRANT (DV) CATEGORY

Section 203(c) of the Immigration and Nationality Act provides a maximum of up to 55,000 immigrant visas each fiscal year to permit immigration opportunities for persons from countries other than the principal sources of current immigration to the United States. The Nicaraguan and Central American Relief Act (NACARA) passed by Congress in November 1997 stipulates that beginning with DV-99, and for as long as necessary, up to 5,000 of the 55,000 annually-allocated diversity visas will be made available for use under the NACARA program. **This reduction has resulted in the DV-2004 annual limit being reduced to 50,000.** DV visas are divided among six geographic regions. No one country can receive more than seven percent of the available diversity visas in any one year.

For **May,** immigrant numbers in the DV category are available to qualified DV-2004 applicants chargeable to all regions/eligible countries as follows. When an allocation cut-off number is shown, visas are available only for applicants with DV regional lottery rank numbers BELOW the specified allocation cut-off number:

All DV Chargeability Areas Except Those Listed Separately

Region
AFRICA: AF 26,200 Except: Ethiopia 24,100; Nigeria 16,500
ASIA: AS 11,500 Except: Bangladesh 7,850
EUROPE: EU 20,000
NORTH AMERICA (BAHAMAS): 15
OCEANIA: OC 825
SOUTH AMERICA, and the CARIBBEAN: 1,500

Entitlement to immigrant status in the DV category lasts only through the end of the fiscal (visa) year for which the applicant is selected in the lottery. The year of entitlement for all applicants registered for the DV-2004 program ends as of September 30, 2004. DV visas may not be issued to DV-2004 applicants after that date. Similarly, spouses and children accompanying or following to join DV-2004 principals are only entitled to derivative DV status until September 30, 2004. **DV visa availability through the very end of FY-2004 cannot be taken for granted. Numbers could be exhausted prior to September 30. Once all numbers provided by law for the DV-2004 program have been used, no further issuances will be possible.**

C. ADVANCE NOTIFICATION OF THE DIVERSITY (DV) IMMIGRANT CATEGORY RANK CUT-OFFS WHICH WILL APPLY IN JUNE

For **June**, immigrant numbers in the DV category are available to qualified DV-2004 applicants chargeable to all regions/eligible countries as follows. When an allocation cut-off number is shown, visas are available only for applicants with DV regional lottery rank numbers BELOW the specified allocation cut-off number:

All DV Chargeability Areas Except Those Listed Separately

Region

AFRICA: AF 28,300 Except: Nigeria 16,500, Ghana 11,500
ASIA: AS 12,800
EUROPE: EU 21,300 Except: Ukraine 8,000
NORTH AMERICA (BAHAMAS): 15
OCEANIA: OC 900
SOUTH AMERICA, and the CARIBBEAN: SA 1,600

D. OBTAINING THE MONTHLY VISA BULLETIN

The Department of State's Bureau of Consular Affairs offers the monthly Visa Bulletin on its Web site at

http://travel.state.gov

TO BE PLACED ON THE DEPARTMENT OF STATE'S E-MAIL SUBSCRIPTION LIST FOR THE VISA BULLETIN, PLEASE PROVIDE YOUR E-MAIL INFORMATION TO THE FOLLOWING E-MAIL ADDRESS:

listserv@calist.state.gov

and in the message body type:

Subscribe Visa-Bulletin First name/Last name

(example: Subscribe Visa-Bulletin Sally Doe)

To be removed from the Department of State's E-mail subscription list for the Visa Bulletin, send an e-mail message to the following e-mail address:

listserv@calist.state.gov

and in the message body type: Signoff Visa-Bulletin

The Department of State also has available a recorded message with visa cut-off dates which can be heard at (202) 663-1541. The recording is normally updated by the middle of each month with information on cut-off dates for the following month.

Readers may submit questions regarding Visa Bulletin related items by e-mail at the following address:

VISABULLETIN@STATE.GOV

(This address cannot be used to subscribe to the Visa Bulletin.)

Department of State Publication 9514

CA/VO: April 7, 2004

I-485 Application to Register Permanent Residence or Adjust Status

OMB No. 1115-0053

U.S. Department of Justice
Immigration and Naturalization Service

Form I-485, Application to Register Permanent Residence or Adjust Status

Purpose of This Form.
This form is used by a person who is in the United States to apply to the Immigration and Naturalization Service (INS) to adjust to permanent resident status or register for permanent residence. It may also be used by certain Cuban nationals to request a change in the date their permanent residence began.

Who May File.
Based on an immigrant petition. You may apply to adjust your status if:
- an immigrant visa number is immediately available to you based on an approved immigrant petition; or
- you are filing this application with a complete relative, special immigrant juvenile or special immigrant military petition, which if approved, would make an immigrant visa number immediately available to you.

Based on being the spouse or child (derivative) at the time another adjustment applicant (principal) files to adjust status or at the time a person is granted permanent resident status in an immigrant category that allows derivative status for spouses and children.
- **If the spouse or child is in the United States,** the individual derivatives may file their Form I-485 adjustment of status applications concurrently with the Form I-485 for the principal beneficiary, or file the Form I-485 at anytime after the principal is approved, if a visa number is available.
- **If the spouse or child is residing abroad,** the person adjusting status in the United States should file the **Form I-824, Application for Action on an Approved Application or Petition, concurrently** with the principal's adjustment of status application to allow the derivates to immigrate to the United States without delay, if the principal's adjustment of status application is approved. **No I-824 fee will be refunded if the principal's adjustment is not granted.**

Based on admission as the fiance(e) of a U. S. citizen and subsequent marriage to that citizen. You may apply to adjust status if you were admitted to the U. S. as the K-1 fiance(e) of a U. S. citizen and you married that citizen within 90 days of your entry. If you were admitted as the K-2 child of such a fiance(e), you may apply based on your parent's adjustment application.

Based on asylum status. You may apply to adjust status if you have been granted asylum in the U. S. after being physically present in the U. S. for one year after the grant of asylum, if you still qualify as an asylee or as the spouse or child of a refugee.

Based on Cuban citizenship or nationality. You may apply to adjust status if:
- you are a native or citizen of Cuba, were admitted or paroled into the U.S. after January 1, 1959, and thereafter have been physically present in the U.S. for at least one year; or
- you are the spouse or unmarried child of a Cuban described above, and regardless of your nationality, you were admitted or paroled after January 1, 1959, and thereafter have been physically present in the U.S. for at least one year.

Based on continuous residence since before January 1, 1972. You may apply for permanent residence if you have continuously resided in the U.S. since before January 1, 1972.

Applying to change the date your permanent residence began. If you were granted permanent residence in the U.S. prior to November 6, 1966, and are a native or citizen of Cuba, his or her spouse or unmarried minor child, you may ask to change the date your lawful permanent residence began to your date of arrival in the U.S. or May 2, 1964, whichever is later.

Other basis of eligibility. If you are not included in the above categories, but believe you may be eligible for adjustment or creation of record of permanent residence, contact your local INS office.

Persons Who Are Ineligible.
Unless you are applying for creation of record based on continuous residence since before January 1, 1972, or adjustment of status under a category in which special rules apply (such as asylum adjustment, Cuban adjustment, special immigrant juvenile adjustment or special immigrant military personnel adjustment), **you are not eligible for adjustment of status if any of the following apply to you:**
- you entered the U.S. in transit without a visa;
- you entered the U.S. as a nonimmigrant crewman;
- you were not admitted or paroled following inspection by an immigration officer;
- your authorized stay expired before you filed this application; you were employed in the U.S. prior to filing this application, without INS authorization; or you otherwise failed to maintain your nonimmigrant status, other than through no fault of your own or for technical reasons, unless you are applying because you are an immediate relative of a U.S. citizen (parent, spouse, widow, widower or unmarried child under 21 years old), a K-1 fiance(e) or K-2 fiance(e) dependent who married the U.S. petitioner within 90 days of admission or an "H" or "I" or special

immigrant (foreign medical graduates, international organization employees or their derivative family members);
- you are or were a J-1 or J-2 exchange visitor, are subject to the two-year foreign residence requirement and have not complied with or been granted a waiver of the requirement;
- you have an A, E or G nonimmigrant status, or have an occupation which would allow you to have this status, unless you complete Form I-508 (I-508F for French nationals) to wave diplomatic rights, privileges and immunities, and if you are an A or G nonimmigrant, unless you submit a complete Form I-566;
- you were admitted to Guam as a visitor under the Guam visa waiver program;
- you were admitted to the U.S. as a visitor under the Visa Waiver Pilot Program, unless you are applying because you are an immediate relative of a U.S. citizen (parent, spouse, widow, widower or unmarried child under 21 years old);
- you are already a conditional permanent resident;
- you were admitted as a K-1 fiance(e) but did not marry the U.S. citizen who filed the petition for you, or were admitted as the K-2 child of a fiance(e) and your parent did not marry the U.S. citizen who filed the petition.

General Filing Instructions.
Please answer all questions by typing or clearly printing in black ink. Indicate that an item is not applicable with **"N/A."** If the answer is **"none,"** write **"none."** If you need extra space to answer any item, attach a sheet of paper with your name and your alien registration number (A#), if any, and indicate the number of the item to which the answer refers. You must file your application with the required **Initial Evidence** described below, beginning on this page. Your application must be properly signed and filed with the correct fee. If you are under 14 years of age, your parent or guardian may sign your application.

Translations. Any foreign language document must be accompanied by a full English translation which the translator has certified as complete and correct, and by the translator's certification that he or she is competent to translate the foreign language into English.

Copies. If these instructions state that a copy of a document may be filed with this application, and you choose to send us the original, we may keep the original for our records.

Initial Evidence.
You must file your application with the following evidence:
- **Birth certificate.** Submit a copy of your foreign birth certificate or other record of your birth that meets the provisions of secondary evidence found in 8 CFR 103.2(b)(2).

- **Copy of passport page with nonimmigrant visa.** If you have obtained a nonimmigrant visa(s) from an American consulate abroad within the last year, submit a photocopy(ies) of the page(s) of your passport with the visa(s).

- **Photos.** Submit two (2) identical natural color photographs of yourself, taken within 30 days of the application. Photos must have a white background, be unmounted, printed on thin paper and be glossy and unretouched. They must show a three-quarter frontal profile showing the right side of your face, with your right ear visible and with your head bare. You may wear a headdress if required by a religious order of which you are a member. The photos must be no larger than 2 X 2 inches, with the distance from the top of the head to just below the chin about 1 and 1/4 inches. Lightly print your A# (or your name if you have no A#) on the back of each photo, using a pencil.

- **Fingerprints.** If you are between the ages of 14 and 75, you must be fingerprinted. After filing this application, INS will notify you in writing of the time and location where you must go to be fingerprinted. Failure to appear to be fingerprinted may result in denial of your application.

- **Police clearances.** If you are filing for adjustment of status as a member of a special class described in an I-485 supplement form, please read the instructions on the supplement form to see if you need to obtain and submit police clearances, in addition to the required fingerprints, with your application.

- **Medical examination (Section 232 of the Act).** When required, submit a medical examination report on the form you have obtained from INS.

Form I-485 (Rev. 02/07/00)N

A. Individuals applying for adjustment of status through the INS Service Center: 1) General: If you are filing your adjustment of status application with the INS Service Center, include your medical exam report with the application, unless you are a refugee or asylee. **2) Refugees:** If you are applying for adjustment of status one year after you were admitted as a refugee, you only need to submit a vaccination supplement with your adjustment of status application, not the entire medical report, **unless** there were medical grounds of inadmissibility that arose during the initial exam you had overseas.

B. Individuals applying for adjustment of status through the local INS office and asylees applying for adjustment of status through the Service Center: If you are filing your adjustment of status application with the local INS office, or if you are an asylee filing an adjustment of status application with the Service Center, one year after you were granted asylum, do not submit a medical report with your adjustment of status application. Wait for further instructions from INS about how and where to take the medical exam and submit the medical exam report.

Fiance(e)s: If you are a K-1 fiance(e) or K-2 dependent who had a medical exam within the past year as required for the nonimmigrant fiance (e) visa, you only need to submit a vaccination supplement, not the entire medical report. You may include the vaccination supplement with your adjustment of status application.

Individuals not required to have a medical exam: The medical report is not required if you are applying for creation of a record for admission as a lawful permanent resident under section 249 of the Act as someone who has continuously resided in the United States since January 1, 1972 (registry applicant).

- **Form G-325A, Biographic Information Sheet.** You must submit a completed G-325 if you are between 14 and 79 years of age.
- **Evidence of status.** Submit a copy of your Form I-94, Nonimmigrant Arrival/Departure Record, showing your admission to the U.S. and current status, or other evidence of your status.
- **Affidavit of Support/Employment Letter.**

  Affidavit of Support. Submit the Affidavit of Support (Form I-864) if your adjustment of status application is based on your entry as a fiance(e), or a relative visa petition (Form I-130) filed by your relative or on an employment based visa petition (Form I-140) based on a business that is five percent or more owned by your family.

  Employment Letter. If your adjustment of status application is based on an employment based visa petition (Form I-140), you must submit a letter on the letterhead of the petitioning employer which confirms that the job on which the visa petition is based is still available to you. The letter must also state the salary that will be paid.

(Note: The affidavit of support and/or employment letter are not required if you applying for creation of record based on continuous residence since before January 1, 1972, asylum adjustment, or a Cuban or a spouse or unmarried child of a Cuban who was admitted after January 1, 1959.)

- **Evidence of eligibility.**

  Based on an immigrant petition. Attach a copy of the approval notice for an immigrant petition which makes a visa number immediately available to you, or submit a complete relative, special immigrant juvenile or special immigrant military petition which, if approved, will make a visa number immediately available to you.

  Based on admission as the K-1 fiance(e) of a U.S. citizen and subsequent marriage to that citizen. Attach a copy of the fiance(e) petition approval notice, a copy of your marriage certificate and your Form I-94.

  Based on asylum status. Attach a copy of the letter or Form I-94 which shows the date you were granted asylum.

  Based on continuous residence in the U.S. since before January 1, 1972. Attach copies of evidence that shows continuous residence since before January 1, 1972.

  Based on Cuban citizenship or nationality. Attach evidence of your citizenship or nationality, such as a copy of your passport, birth certificate or travel document.

  Based on derivative status as the spouse or child of another adjustment applicant or person granted permanent residence based on issuance of an immigrant visa. File your application with the application of that other applicant, or with evidence that it is pending with the Service or has been approved, or evidence that your spouse or parent has been granted permanent residence based on an immigrant visa and:

  - If you are applying as the spouse of that person, also attach a copy of your marriage certificate and copies of documents showing the legal termination of all other marriages by you and your spouse;

  - If you are applying as the child of that person, also attach a copy of your birth certificate, and if the other person is not your natural mother, copies of evidence (such as a marriage certificate and documents showing the legal termination of all other marriages and an adoption decree) to demonstrate that you qualify as his or her child.

- **Other basis for eligibility.** Attach copies of documents proving that you are eligible for the classification.

Where to File.

File this application at the INS office having jurisdiction over your place of residence.

Fee. The fee for this application is **$220**, except that it is **$160** if you are less than 14 years old. There is no application fee if you are filing as a refugee under section 209(a) of the Act. If you are between the ages of 14 and 75, there is a $25 fingerprinting fee in addition to the application fee. For example, if your application fee is $220 and you are between the ages of 14 and 75, the total fee you must pay is $245. You may submit one check or money order for both the application and fingerprinting fees. Fees must be submitted in the exact amount. **DO NOT MAIL CASH.** Fees cannot be refunded. All checks and money orders must be drawn on a bank or other institution located in the United States and must be payable in United States currency. The check or money order should be made payable to the Immigration and Naturalization Service, except that:

- if you live in Guam and are filing this application in Guam, make your check or money order payable to the "Treasurer, Guam."

- if you live in the U.S. Virgin Islands and are filing this application in the U.S. Virgin Islands, make your check or money order payable to the "Commissioner of Finance of the Virgin Islands."

Checks are accepted subject to collection. An uncollected check in payment of an application fee will render the application and any document issued invalid. A charge of $30 will be imposed if a check in payment of a fee is not honored by the bank on which it is drawn.

Processing Information.

Acceptance. Any application that is not signed, or is not accompanied by the correct application fee, will be rejected with a notice that the application is deficient. You may correct the deficiency and resubmit the application. An application is not considered properly filed until accepted by the INS.

Initial Processing. Once an application has been accepted, it will be checked for completeness, including submission of the required initial evidence. If you do not completely fill out the form, or file it without required initial evidence, you will not establish a basis for eligibility, and we may deny your application.

Requests for More Information. We may request more information or evidence. We may also request that you submit the originals of any copy. We may return these originals when they are no longer required.

Interview. After you file your application you will be notified to appear at an INS office to answer questions about the application. You will be required to answer these questions under oath or affirmation. You must bring your Arrival-Departure Record (Form I-94) and any passport to the interview.

Decision. You will be notified in writing of the decision on your application.

Selective Service Registration. If you are a male at least 18 years old, but not yet 26 years old, and required according to the Military Selective Service Act to register with the Selective Service System, the INS will help you register. When your signed application is filed and accepted by the INS, we will transmit your name, current address, Social Security number, date of birth and the date you filed the application to the Selective Service to record your registration as of the filing date. If the INS does not accept your application, and if still so required, you are responsible to register with the Selective Service by other means, provided you are under 26 years of age. If you have already registered, the Selective Service will check its records to avoid any duplication. **(Note: men 18 through 25 years old, who are applying for student financial aid, government employment or job training benefits should register directly with the Selective Service or such benefits may be denied. Men can register at a local post office or on the Internet at http://www.sss.gov).**

Form I-485 (Rev. 02/07/00)N Page 2

APPENDIX H: I-485 APPLICATION

Travel Outside the U.S. for Adjustment of Status Applicants Under Sections 209 and 245 of the Act and Registry Applicants Under Section 249 of the Act. Your departure from the U.S. (including brief visits to Canada or Mexico) constitutes an abandonment of your adjustment of status application, unless you are granted permission to depart and you are inspected upon your return to the U.S. Such permission to travel is called "advance parole." To request advance parole, you must file Form I-131, with fee, with the INS office where you applied for adjustment of status.

- **Exceptions: 1) H and L nonimmigrants:** If you are an H or L nonimmigrant who continues to maintain his or her status, you may travel on a valid H or L visa without obtaining advance parole.
  2) Refugees and Asylees: If you are applying for adjustment of status one year after you were admitted as a refugee or one year after you were granted asylum, you may travel outside the United States on your valid refugee travel document, if you have one, without the need to obtain advance parole.

- **WARNING:** Travel outside of the U.S. may trigger the 3-and 10-year bars to admission under section 212(a)(9)(B)(i) of the Act for adjustment applicants, but not registry applicants. This ground of inadmissibility is triggered if you were unlawfully present in the U.S. (i.e., you remained in the United States beyond the period of stay authorized by the Attorney General) for more than 180 days before you applied for adjustment of status, and you travel outside of the U.S. while your adjustment of status application is pending. **(Note:** Only unlawful presence that accrued on or after April 1, 1997, counts towards the 3-and 10-year bars under section 212 (a)(9) (B)(i) of the Act.)

- If you become inadmissible under section 212(a)(9)(B)(i) of the Act while your adjustment of status application is pending, you will need a waiver of inadmissibility under section 212(a)(9)(B)(v) of the Act before your adjustment of status application can be approved. This waiver, however, is granted on a case-by-case basis and in the exercise of discretion. It requires a showing of extreme hardship to your U.S. citizen or lawful permanent resident spouse or parent, unless you are a refugee or asylee. For refugees and asylees, the waiver may be granted for humanitarian reasons, to assure family unity or if it is otherwise in the public interest.

Penalties. If you knowingly and willfully falsify or conceal a material fact or submit a false document with this request, we will deny the benefit you are filing for and may deny any other immigration benefit. In addition, you will face severe penalties provided by law and may be subject to criminal prosecution.

Privacy Act Notice. We ask for the information on this form and associated evidence to determine if you have established eligibility for the immigration benefit you are seeking. Our legal right to ask for this information is in 8 USC 1255 and 1259. We may provide this information to other government agencies, including the Selective Service System. Your failure to provide this information on this form and any requested evidence may delay a final decision or result in denial of your application.

Paperwork Reduction Act Notice. A person is not required to respond to a collection of information unless it displays a current valid OMB number. We try to create forms and instructions that are accurate, can be easily understood and which impose the least possible burden on you to provide us with information. Often this is difficult because some immigration laws are very complex. The estimated average time to complete and file this application is computed as follows: (1) 20 minutes to learn about the law and form; (2) 25 minutes to complete the form and (3) 270 minutes to assemble and file the application, including the required interview and travel time -- for a total estimated average of 5 hours and 15 minutes per application. If you have comments regarding the accuracy of this estimate or suggestions to make this form simpler, you should write to the Immigration and Naturalization Service, 425 I Street, N.W., Room 5307, Washington, D.C. 20536; OMB No. 1115-0053. **DO NOT MAIL YOUR COMPLETED APPLICATION TO THIS ADDRESS.**

OMB No. 1115-0053

U.S. Department of Justice
Immigration and Naturalization Service

**Form I-485, Application to Register
Permanent Resident or Adjust Status**

START HERE - Please Type or Print

Part 1. Information About You.

Family Name		Given Name		Middle Initial

Address - C/O

Street Number and Name		Apt. #

City

State		Zip Code

Date of Birth (month/day/year)		Country of Birth

Social Security #		A # (if any)

Date of Last Arrival (month/day/year)		I-94 #

Current INS Status		Expires on (month/day/year)

Part 2. Application Type. *(check one)*

I am applying for an adjustment to permanent resident status because:

a. ☐ an immigrant petition giving me an immediately available immigrant visa number has been approved. (Atttach a copy of the approval notice-- or a relative, special immigrant juvenile or special immigrant military visa petition filed with this application that will give you an immediately available visa number, if approved.)

b. ☐ my spouse or parent applied for adjustment of status or was granted lawful permanent residence in an immigrant visa category that allows derivative status for spouses and children.

c. ☐ I entered as a K-1 fiance(e) of a U.S. citizen whom I married within 90 days of entry, or I am the K-2 child of such a fiance(e). [Attach a copy of the fiance(e) petition approval notice and the marriage certificate.]

d. ☐ I was granted asylum or derivative asylum status as the spouse or child of a person granted asylum and am eligible for adjustment.

e. ☐ I am a native or citizen of Cuba admitted or paroled into the U.S. after January 1, 1959, and thereafter have been physically present in the U.S. for at least one year.

f. ☐ I am the husband, wife or minor unmarried child of a Cuban described in (e) and am residing with that person, and was admitted or paroled into the U.S. after January 1, 1959, and thereafter have been physically present in the U.S. for at least one year.

g. ☐ I have continuously resided in the U.S. since before January 1, 1972.

h. ☐ Other basis of eligibility. Explain. (If additional space is needed, use a separate piece of paper.)
_____
_____

I am already a permanent resident and am applying to have the date I was granted permanent residence adjusted to the date I originally arrived in the U.S. as a nonimmigrant or parolee, or as of May 2,1964, whichever date is later, and: *(Check one)*

i. ☐ I am a native or citizen of Cuba and meet the description in (e), above.

j. ☐ I am the husband, wife or minor unmarried child of a Cuban, and meet the description in (f), above.

Continued on back

FOR INS USE ONLY

Returned	Receipt
Resubmitted	
Reloc Sent	
Reloc Rec'd	
Applicant Interviewed	

Section of Law
☐ Sec. 209(b), INA
☐ Sec. 13, Act of 9/11/57
☐ Sec. 245, INA
☐ Sec. 249, INA
☐ Sec. 2 Act of 11/2/66
☐ Sec. 2 Act of 11/2/66
☐ Other _____

Country Chargeable

Eligibility Under Sec. 245
Approved Visa Petition
Dependent of Principal Alien
Special Immigrant
Other _____

Preference

Action Block

To be Completed by
Attorney or Representative, **if any**
☐ Fill in box if G-28 is attached to represent the applicant.
VOLAG # _____

ATTY State License # _____

Form I-485 (Rev. 02/07/00)N Page 1

Part 3. Processing Information.

A. City/Town/Village of Birth

Current Occupation

Your Mother's First Name

Your Father's First Name

Give your name exactly how it appears on your Arrival /Departure Record (Form I-94)

Place of Last Entry Into the U.S. (City/State)	In what status did you last enter? *(Visitor, student, exchange alien, crewman, temporary worker, without inspection, etc.)*
Were you inspected by a U.S. Immigration Officer? ☐ Yes ☐ No	
Nonimmigrant Visa Number	Consulate Where Visa Was Issued
Date Visa Was Issued (month/day/year)	Sex: ☐ Male ☐ Female	Marital Status ☐ Married ☐ Single ☐ Divorced ☐ Widowed

Have you ever before applied for permanent resident status in the U.S.? ☐ No ☐ Yes If you checked "Yes," give date and place of filing and final disposition.

B. List your present husband/wife and all your sons and daughters. (If you have none, write "none." If additional space is needed, use a separate piece of paper.)

Family Name	Given Name	Middle Initial	Date of Birth (month/day/year)
Country of Birth	Relationship	A #	Applying with You? ☐ Yes ☐ No
Family Name	Given Name	Middle Initial	Date of Birth (month/day/year)
Country of Birth	Relationship	A #	Applying with You? ☐ Yes ☐ No
Family Name	Given Name	Middle Initial	Date of Birth (month/day/year)
Country of Birth	Relationship	A #	Applying with You? ☐ Yes ☐ No
Family Name	Given Name	Middle Initial	Date of Birth (month/day/year)
Country of Birth	Relationship	A #	Applying with You? ☐ Yes ☐ No
Family Name	Given Name	Middle Initial	Date of Birth (month/day/year)
Country of Birth	Relationship	A #	Applying with You? ☐ Yes ☐ No

C. List your present and past membership in or affiliation with every political organization, association, fund, foundation, party, club, society or similar group in the United States or in other places since your 16th birthday. Include any foreign military service in this part. If none, write "none." Include the name(s) of the organization(s), location(s), dates of membership from and to, and the nature of the organization (s). If additional space is needed, use a separate piece of paper.

_____

_____

_____

_____

_____

_____

_____

APPENDIX H: I-485 APPLICATION

Part 3. Processing Information. *(Continued)*

Please answer the following questions. (If your answer is **"Yes"** to any one of these questions, explain on a separate piece of paper. Answering **"Yes"** does not necessarily mean that you are not entitled to adjust your status or register for permanent residence.)

1. Have you ever, in or outside the U. S.:

    a. knowingly committed any crime of moral turpitude or a drug-related offense for which you have not been arrested? ☐ Yes ☐ No

    b. been arrested, cited, charged, indicted, fined or imprisoned for breaking or violating any law or ordinance, excluding traffic violations? ☐ Yes ☐ No

    c. been the beneficiary of a pardon, amnesty, rehabilitation decree, other act of clemency or similar action? ☐ Yes ☐ No

    d. exercised diplomatic immunity to avoid prosecution for a criminal offense in the U. S.? ☐ Yes ☐ No

2. Have you received public assistance in the U.S. from any source, including the U.S. government or any state, county, city or municipality (other than emergency medical treatment), or are you likely to receive public assistance in the future? ☐ Yes ☐ No

3. Have you ever:

    a. within the past ten years been a prostitute or procured anyone for prostitution, or intend to engage in such activities in the future? ☐ Yes ☐ No

    b. engaged in any unlawful commercialized vice, including, but not limited to, illegal gambling? ☐ Yes ☐ No

    c. knowingly encouraged, induced, assisted, abetted or aided any alien to try to enter the U.S. illegally? ☐ Yes ☐ No

    d. illicitly trafficked in any controlled substance, or knowingly assisted, abetted or colluded in the illicit trafficking of any controlled substance? ☐ Yes ☐ No

4. Have you ever engaged in, conspired to engage in, or do you intend to engage in, or have you ever solicited membership or funds for, or have you through any means ever assisted or provided any type of material support to, any person or organization that has ever engaged or conspired to engage, in sabotage, kidnapping, political assassination, hijacking or any other form of terrorist activity? ☐ Yes ☐ No

5. Do you intend to engage in the U.S. in:

    a. espionage? ☐ Yes ☐ No

    b. any activity a purpose of which is opposition to, or the control or overthrow of, the government of the United States, by force, violence or other unlawful means? ☐ Yes ☐ No

    c. any activity to violate or evade any law prohibiting the export from the United States of goods, technology or sensitive information? ☐ Yes ☐ No

6. Have you ever been a member of, or in any way affiliated with, the Communist Party or any other totalitarian party? ☐ Yes ☐ No

7. Did you, during the period from March 23, 1933 to May 8, 1945, in association with either the Nazi Government of Germany or any organization or government associated or allied with the Nazi Government of Germany, ever order, incite, assist or otherwise participate in the persecution of any person because of race, religion, national origin or political opinion? ☐ Yes ☐ No

8. Have you ever engaged in genocide, or otherwise ordered, incited, assisted or otherwise participated in the killing of any person because of race, religion, nationality, ethnic origin or political opinion? ☐ Yes ☐ No

9. Have you ever been deported from the U.S., or removed from the U.S. at government expense, excluded within the past year, or are you now in exclusion or deportation proceedings? ☐ Yes ☐ No

10. Are you under a final order of civil penalty for violating section 274C of the Immigration and Nationality Act for use of fradulent documents or have you, by fraud or willful misrepresentation of a material fact, ever sought to procure, or procured, a visa, other documentation, entry into the U.S. or any immigration benefit? ☐ Yes ☐ No

11. Have you ever left the U.S. to avoid being drafted into the U.S. Armed Forces? ☐ Yes ☐ No

12. Have you ever been a J nonimmigrant exchange visitor who was subject to the two-year foreign residence requirement and not yet complied with that requirement or obtained a waiver? ☐ Yes ☐ No

13. Are you now withholding custody of a U.S. citizen child outside the U.S. from a person granted custody of the child? ☐ Yes ☐ No

14. Do you plan to practice polygamy in the U.S.? ☐ Yes ☐ No

Continued on back   Form I-485 (Rev. 02/07/00)N Page 3

APPENDIX H: I-485 APPLICATION

Part 4. **Signature.** *(Read the information on penalties in the instructions before completing this section. You must file this application while in the United States.)*

I certify, under penalty of perjury under the laws of the United States of America, that this application and the evidence submitted with it is all true and correct. I authorize the release of any information from my records which the INS needs to determine eligibility for the benefit I am seeking.

Selective Service Registration. The following applies to you if you are a man at least 18 years old, but not yet 26 years old, who is required to register with the Selective Service System: I understand that my filing this adjustment of status application with the Immigration and Naturalization Service authorizes the INS to provide certain registration information to the Selective Service System in accordance with the Military Selective Service Act. Upon INS acceptance of my application, I authorize INS to transmit to the Selective Service System my name, current address, Social Security number, date of birth and the date I filed the application for the purpose of recording my Selective Service registration as of the filing date. If, however, the INS does not accept my application, I further understand that, if so required, I am responsible for registering with the Selective Service by other means, provided I have not yet reached age 26.

Signature	*Print Your Name*	*Date*	*Daytime Phone Number*

Please Note: *If you do not completely fill out this form or fail to submit required documents listed in the instructions, you may not be found eligible for the requested benefit and this application may be denied.*

Part 5. **Signature of Person Preparing Form, If Other Than Above.** *(Sign Below)*

I declare that I prepared this application at the request of the above person and it is based on all information of which I have knowledge.

Signature	*Print Your Name*	*Date*	*Daytime Phone Number*

Firm Name and Address

APPENDIX H: I-485 APPLICATION

List of Countries
That Recognize Dual Citizenship
with the United States

This list is based on the best current information available. Some countries do not allow dual citizenship at all. Others have various restrictions regarding losing or acquiring dual citizenship and for that reason are not listed in the following. If you are concerned about losing your present citizenship when you naturalize as a U.S. citizen, speak to a representative of your government before filing for naturalization.

Dual Citizenship Generally Allowed After U.S. Naturalization

Albania	Cyprus	Jamaica	Romania
Antigua	Dominica	Latvia	St. Christopher
Barbados	Dominican	Lesotho	St. Kitts
Belize	Republic	Liechtenstein	St. Lucia
Benin	Ecuador	Macao	Slovenia
Bulgaria	El Salvador	Maldives	Sri Lanka
Burkina Faso	France	Mexico	Switzerland
Cambodia	Ghana	Morocco	Syria
Canada	Greece	Namibia	Togo
Cape Verde	Grenada	Nevis	Tunisia
Central African	Guatemala	New Zealand	Turkey
Republic	Hong Kong	Nigeria	Tuvalu
Colombia	Hungary	Panama	United Kingdom
Costa Rica	Iran	Peru	
Côte d'Ivoire	Ireland	Poland	
Croatia	Israel	Portugal	

Dual Citizenship Generally Not Allowed After U.S. Naturalization

Algeria	Burundi	Honduras	Libya
Andorra	Cameroon	India	Malawi
Azerbaijan	Chile	Indonesia	Malaysia
Bahrain	China	Iraq	Mali
Belarus	Congo	Japan	Monaco
Belgium	Cuba	Kazakhstan	Mongolia
Bhutan	Djibouti	Kiribati	Myanmar (Burma)
Bolivia	Equatorial Guinea	Kuwait	Nepal
Botswana	Gabon	Kyrgyzstan	New Guinea
Brunei	Guinea	Laos	Nicaragua

Niger	Príncipe Island	Sudan	United Arab
North Korea	Qatar	Swaziland	Emirates
Norway	Rwanda	Sweden	Uzbekistan
Oman	Saudi Arabia	Taiwan	Venezuela
Pakistan	Sierra Leone	Tonga	Vietnam
Palau	Singapore	Uganda	Yemen
Papua	South Korea	Ukraine	Zimbabwe

List of Aggravated Felonies

People convicted of aggravated felonies are permanently ineligible for naturalization and asylum. If you have a criminal record, see an immigration law expert before making any application to the USCIS. Here's a layperson's list of what may constitute an aggravated felony:

- Murder.
- Rape.
- Sexual abuse of a minor.
- Drug-trafficking crimes or any illicit trafficking in any controlled substances.
- Illicit trafficking in destructive devices.
- Many firearms offenses, though simple possession of an unlicensed firearm by a permanent resident is often not an aggravated felony.
- Any offense related to laundering of monetary instruments if the amount exceeds $10,000.
- Most offenses involving explosives or arson.
- Offenses relating to the receipt, manufacture, or possession of firearms without proper licenses or taxes.
- Most crimes of violence (not including a purely political offense) for which the term of imprisonment imposed (regardless of any suspension of such imprisonment) is at least one year.
- A theft offense (including receipt of stolen property) or burglary offense for which the term of imprisonment imposed (regardless of any suspension of such imprisonment) is at least one year.
- Ransom offenses, including using interstate communications to demand ransom or threaten kidnap; using mails to make threatening communications; making threatening communications from foreign countries; receiving, possessing, or disposing of ransom money or property.
- Child pornography offenses, including employing, using, or coercing minors to engage in pornography; selling or transferring custody of a child with knowledge that the child will be used for pornography; receiving or distributing child pornography.
- RICO (the Racketeer-Influenced and Corrupt Organizations Act) offenses for which a sentence of one year imprisonment or more may be imposed.
- Offenses relating to owning, controlling, managing, or supervising a prostitution business.
- Offenses relating to involuntary servitude.
- Offenses relating to spying and national security.
- Treason and concealing and failing to disclose treason.
- Fraud or deceit crimes in which the loss to the victim exceeds $10,000.
- Income tax evasion where the loss to the government exceeds $10,000.
- Alien smuggling for commercial gain (exception: only one offense where the person smuggled was your spouse, parent, or child).

- Document fraud under which the person's actions constitute trafficking in the documents and the sentence imposed (even if suspended) is at least one year (except where you committed the offense to assist your spouse, parent, or child).
- An offense for failing to appear for sentence where a defendant has been convicted of a crime with a possible sentence of 15 years or more.
- Offenses involving obstruction of justice, perjury, or subornation or helping another person commit perjury or bribery of a witness, for which a sentence of at least one year may be imposed.
- Offenses relating to commercial bribery, forgery, counterfeiting, or trafficking in vehicles, for which a sentence of at least one year may be imposed.
- Offenses committed by an alien ordered previously deported.
- Offenses relating to the failure to appear in court for a criminal offense for which a sentence of two or more years may be imposed.
- Any attempt or conspiracy to commit any of the above acts, committed within the United States.
- Any attempt or conspiracy to commit any of these acts violating a law in a foreign country where the term of imprisonment was completed within the previous 15 years.

The Oath of Allegiance

I hereby declare, on oath, that I absolutely, and entirely, renounce and abjure all allegiance and fidelity to any foreign prince, potentate, state or sovereignty of whom or which I have heretofore been a subject or citizen; that I will support and defend the Constitution, and laws, of the United States of America against all enemies, foreign and domestic; that I will bear true faith and allegiance to the same; that I will bear arms on behalf of the United States when required by the law; that I will perform noncombatant service in the armed forces of the United States when required by the law; that I will perform work of national importance, under civilian direction, when required by the law; and that I take this obligation freely, without any mental reservation, or purpose of evasion, so help me God.

N-400 Application
for Naturalization

U.S. Department of Justice
Immigration and Naturalization Service

OMB No. 1115-0009
Application for Naturalization

Print clearly or type your answers using CAPITAL letters. Failure to print clearly may delay your application. Use black or blue ink.

Part 1. Your Name *(The Person Applying for Naturalization)*

Write your INS "A"- number here:
A __ __ __ __ __ __ __ __ __

A. Your current legal name.

Family Name *(Last Name)*

FOR INS USE ONLY

Given Name *(First Name)*   Full Middle Name *(If applicable)*

Bar Code   Date Stamp

B. Your name **exactly** as it appears on your Permanent Resident Card.

Family Name *(Last Name)*

Remarks

Given Name *(First Name)*   Full Middle Name *(If applicable)*

C. If you have ever used other names, provide them below.

Family Name *(Last Name)*	Given Name *(First Name)*	Middle Name

D. Name change *(optional)*

Please read the Instructions before you decide whether to change your name.

1. Would you like to legally change your name? ☐ Yes ☐ No
2. If "Yes," print the new name you would like to use. Do not use initials or abbreviations when writing your new name.

Family Name *(Last Name)*

Action

Given Name *(First Name)*   Full Middle Name

Part 2. Information About Your Eligibility *(Check Only One)*

I am at least 18 years old AND

A. ☐ I have been a Lawful Permanent Resident of the United States for at least 5 years.

B. ☐ I have been a Lawful Permanent Resident of the United States for at least 3 years, AND I have been married to and living with the same U.S. citizen for the last 3 years, AND my spouse has been a U.S. citizen for the last 3 years.

C. ☐ I am applying on the basis of qualifying military service.

D. ☐ Other *(Please explain)* _____

Form N-400 (Rev. 07/23/02)N

Part 3. Information About You

Write your INS "A"- number here:

A __ __ __ __ __ __ __ __ __

A. Social Security Number

__ __ __ - __ __ - __ __ __ __

B. Date of Birth *(Month/Day/Year)*

__ __ / __ __ / __ __ __ __

C. Date You Became a Permanent Resident *(Month/Day/Year)*

__ __ / __ __ / __ __ __ __

D. Country of Birth

E. Country of Nationality

F. Are either of your parents U.S. citizens? *(if yes, see Instructions)* ☐ Yes ☐ No

G. What is your current marital status? ☐ Single, Never Married ☐ Married ☐ Divorced ☐ Widowed

☐ Marriage Annulled or Other *(Explain)* _____

H. Are you requesting a waiver of the English and/or U.S. History and Government requirements based on a disability or impairment and attaching a Form N-648 with your application? ☐ Yes ☐ No

I. Are you requesting an accommodation to the naturalization process because of a disability or impairment? *(See Instructions for some examples of accommodations.)* ☐ Yes ☐ No

If you answered "Yes", check the box below that applies:

☐ I am deaf or hearing impaired and need a sign language interpreter who uses the following language: _____

☐ I use a wheelchair.

☐ I am blind or sight impaired.

☐ I will need another type of accommodation. Please explain: _____

_____

_____

Part 4. Addresses and Telephone Numbers

A. Home Address - Street Number and Name *(Do NOT write a P.O. Box in this space)*

Apartment Number

City	County	State	ZIP Code	Country

B. Care of

Mailing Address - Street Number and Name *(If different from home address)*

Apartment Number

City	State	ZIP Code	Country

C. Daytime Phone Number *(If any)*

( )

Evening Phone Number *(If any)*

( )

E-mail Address *(If any)*

Form N-400 (Rev. 07/23/02)N Page 2

Part 5. Information for Criminal Records Search

Note: The categories below are those required by the FBI. See Instructions for more information.

A. Gender

☐ Male ☐ Female

B. Height

| Feet | Inches |

C. Weight

| Pounds |

D. Are you Hispanic or Latino? ☐ Yes ☐ No

E. Race *(Select one or more.)*

☐ White ☐ Asian ☐ Black or African American ☐ American Indian or Alaskan Native ☐ Native Hawaiian or Other Pacific Islander

F. Hair color

☐ Black ☐ Brown ☐ Blonde ☐ Gray ☐ White ☐ Red ☐ Sandy ☐ Bald (No Hair)

G. Eye color

☐ Brown ☐ Blue ☐ Green ☐ Hazel ☐ Gray ☐ Black ☐ Pink ☐ Maroon ☐ Other

Part 6. Information About Your Residence and Employment

A. Where have you lived during the last 5 years? Begin with where you live now and then list every place you lived for the last 5 years. If you need more space, use a separate sheet of paper.

Street Number and Name, Apartment Number, City, State, Zip Code and Country	Dates *(Month/Year)*	
	From	To
Current Home Address - Same as Part 4.A	__ __ / __ __ __ __	Present
	__ __ / __ __ __ __	__ __ / __ __ __ __
	__ __ / __ __ __ __	__ __ / __ __ __ __
	__ __ / __ __ __ __	__ __ / __ __ __ __
	__ __ / __ __ __ __	__ __ / __ __ __ __

B. Where have you worked (or, if you were a student, what schools did you attend) during the last 5 years? Include military service. Begin with your current or latest employer and then list every place you have worked or studied for the last 5 years. If you need more space, use a separate sheet of paper.

Employer or School Name	Employer or School Address *(Street, City and State)*	Dates *(Month/Year)*		Your Occupation
		From	To	
		__ __ / __ __ __ __	__ __ / __ __ __ __	
		__ __ / __ __ __ __	__ __ / __ __ __ __	
		__ __ / __ __ __ __	__ __ / __ __ __ __	
		__ __ / __ __ __ __	__ __ / __ __ __ __	
		__ __ / __ __ __ __	__ __ / __ __ __ __	

Form N-400 (Rev. 07/23/02)N Page 3

Part 7. Time Outside the United States
(Including Trips to Canada, Mexico, and the Caribbean Islands)

Write your INS "A"- number here:

A _ _ _ _ _ _ _ _ _

A. How many total days did you spend outside of the United States during the past 5 years? ☐ days

B. How many trips of 24 hours or more have you taken outside of the United States during the past 5 years? ☐ trips

C. List below all the trips of 24 hours or more that you have taken outside of the United States since becoming a Lawful Permanent Resident. Begin with your most recent trip. If you need more space, use a separate sheet of paper.

Date You Left the United States *(Month/Day/Year)*	Date You Returned to the United States *(Month/Day/Year)*	Did Trip Last 6 Months or More?	Countries to Which You Traveled	Total Days Out of the United States
_ _ / _ _ / _ _ _ _	_ _ / _ _ / _ _ _ _	☐ Yes ☐ No		
_ _ / _ _ / _ _ _ _	_ _ / _ _ / _ _ _ _	☐ Yes ☐ No		
_ _ / _ _ / _ _ _ _	_ _ / _ _ / _ _ _ _	☐ Yes ☐ No		
_ _ / _ _ / _ _ _ _	_ _ / _ _ / _ _ _ _	☐ Yes ☐ No		
_ _ / _ _ / _ _ _ _	_ _ / _ _ / _ _ _ _	☐ Yes ☐ No		
_ _ / _ _ / _ _ _ _	_ _ / _ _ / _ _ _ _	☐ Yes ☐ No		
_ _ / _ _ / _ _ _ _	_ _ / _ _ / _ _ _ _	☐ Yes ☐ No		
_ _ / _ _ / _ _ _ _	_ _ / _ _ / _ _ _ _	☐ Yes ☐ No		
_ _ / _ _ / _ _ _ _	_ _ / _ _ / _ _ _ _	☐ Yes ☐ No		
_ _ / _ _ / _ _ _ _	_ _ / _ _ / _ _ _ _	☐ Yes ☐ No		

Part 8. Information About Your Marital History

A. How many times have you been married (including annulled marriages)? ☐ If you have NEVER been married, go to Part 9.

B. If you are now married, give the following information about your spouse:

1. Spouse's Family Name *(Last Name)* | Given Name *(First Name)* | Full Middle Name *(If applicable)*

2. Date of Birth *(Month/Day/Year)* _ _ / _ _ / _ _ _ _ | 3. Date of Marriage *(Month/Day/Year)* _ _ / _ _ / _ _ _ _ | 4. Spouse's Social Security Number _ _ _ - _ _ - _ _ _ _

5. Home Address - Street Number and Name | Apartment Number

City | State | ZIP Code

C. Is your spouse a U.S. citizen? ☐ Yes ☐ No

D. If your spouse is a U.S. citizen, give the following information:

    1. When did your spouse become a U.S. citizen? ☐ At Birth ☐ Other

    If "Other," give the following information:

2. Date your spouse became a U.S. citizen

__ __/__ __/__ __ __ __

3. Place your spouse became a U.S. citizen *(Please see Instructions)*

City and State

E. If your spouse is NOT a U.S. citizen, give the following information :

1. Spouse's Country of Citizenship

2. Spouse's INS "A"- Number *(If applicable)*

A __ __ __ __ __ __ __ __ __

3. Spouse's Immigration Status

☐ Lawful Permanent Resident   ☐ Other _____

F. If you were married before, provide the following information about your prior spouse. If you have more than one previous marriage, use a separate sheet of paper to provide the information requested in questions 1-5 below.

1. Prior Spouse's Family Name *(Last Name)* | Given Name *(First Name)* | Full Middle Name *(If applicable)*

2. Prior Spouse's Immigration Status

☐ U.S. Citizen

☐ Lawful Permanent Resident

☐ Other _____

3. Date of Marriage *(Month/Day/Year)*

__ __/__ __/__ __ __ __

4. Date Marriage Ended *(Month/Day/Year)*

__ __/__ __/__ __ __ __

5. How Marriage Ended

☐ Divorce ☐ Spouse Died ☐ Other _____

G. How many times has your current spouse been married (including annulled marriages)? ☐

If your spouse has EVER been married before, give the following information about **your spouse's** prior marriage.
If your spouse has more than one previous marriage, use a separate sheet of paper to provide the information requested in questions 1 - 5 below.

1. Prior Spouse's Family Name *(Last Name)* | Given Name *(First Name)* | Full Middle Name *(If applicable)*

2. Prior Spouse's Immigration Status

☐ U.S. Citizen

☐ Lawful Permanent Resident

☐ Other _____

3. Date of Marriage *(Month/Day/Year)*

__ __/__ __/__ __ __ __

4. Date Marriage Ended *(Month/Day/Year)*

__ __/__ __/__ __ __ __

5. How Marriage Ended

☐ Divorce ☐ Spouse Died ☐ Other _____

Form N-400 (Rev. 07/23/02)N Page 5

APPENDIX L: N-400 APPLICATION FOR NATURALIZATION

| Part 9. Information About Your Children | Write your INS "A"- number here: A __ __ __ __ __ __ __ __ __ |

A. How many sons and daughters have you had? For more information on which sons and daughters you should include and how to complete this section, see the Instructions.

B. Provide the following information about all of your sons and daughters. If you need more space, use a separate sheet of paper.

Full Name of Son or Daughter	Date of Birth (Month/Day/Year)	INS "A"- number (if child has one)	Country of Birth	Current Address (Street, City, State & Country)
	__ __ / __ __ / __ __ __ __	A__ __ __ __ __ __ __ __		
	__ __ / __ __ / __ __ __ __	A__ __ __ __ __ __ __ __		
	__ __ / __ __ / __ __ __ __	A__ __ __ __ __ __ __ __		
	__ __ / __ __ / __ __ __ __	A__ __ __ __ __ __ __ __		
	__ __ / __ __ / __ __ __ __	A__ __ __ __ __ __ __ __		
	__ __ / __ __ / __ __ __ __	A__ __ __ __ __ __ __ __		
	__ __ / __ __ / __ __ __ __	A__ __ __ __ __ __ __ __		
	__ __ / __ __ / __ __ __ __	A__ __ __ __ __ __ __ __		

| Part 10. Additional Questions |

Please answer questions 1 through 14. If you answer "Yes" to any of these questions, include a written explanation with this form. Your written explanation should (1) explain why your answer was "Yes," and (2) provide any additional information that helps to explain your answer.

A. General Questions

1. Have you **EVER** claimed to be a U.S. citizen *(in writing or any other way)*? ☐ Yes ☐ No

2. Have you **EVER** registered to vote in any Federal, state, or local election in the United States? ☐ Yes ☐ No

3. Have you **EVER** voted in any Federal, state, or local election in the United States? ☐ Yes ☐ No

4. Since becoming a Lawful Permanent Resident, have you **EVER** failed to file a required Federal, state, or local tax return? ☐ Yes ☐ No

5. Do you owe any Federal, state, or local taxes that are overdue? ☐ Yes ☐ No

6. Do you have any title of nobility in any foreign country? ☐ Yes ☐ No

7. Have you ever been declared legally incompetent or been confined to a mental institution within the last 5 years? ☐ Yes ☐ No

Form N-400 (Rev. 07/23/02)N Page 6

APPENDIX L: N-400 APPLICATION FOR NATURALIZATION

Write your INS "A"- number here:

A __ __ __ __ __ __ __ __ __

B. Affiliations

8. a. Have you **EVER** been a member of or associated with any organization, association, fund, foundation, party, club, society, or similar group in the United States or in any other place?   ☐ Yes   ☐ No

   b. If you answered "Yes," list the name of each group below. If you need more space, attach the names of the other group(s) on a separate sheet of paper.

Name of Group	Name of Group
1.	6.
2.	7.
3.	8.
4.	9.
5.	10.

9. Have you **EVER** been a member of or in any way associated *(either directly or indirectly)* with:

   a. The Communist Party?   ☐ Yes   ☐ No

   b. Any other totalitarian party?   ☐ Yes   ☐ No

   c. A terrorist organization?   ☐ Yes   ☐ No

10. Have you **EVER** advocated *(either directly or indirectly)* the overthrow of any government by force or violence?   ☐ Yes   ☐ No

11. Have you **EVER** persecuted *(either directly or indirectly)* any person because of race, religion, national origin, membership in a particular social group, or political opinion?   ☐ Yes   ☐ No

12. Between March 23, 1933, and May 8, 1945, did you work for or associate in any way *(either directly or indirectly)* with:

   a. The Nazi government of Germany?   ☐ Yes   ☐ No

   b. Any government in any area (1) occupied by, (2) allied with, or (3) established with the help of the Nazi government of Germany?   ☐ Yes   ☐ No

   c. Any German, Nazi, or S.S. military unit, paramilitary unit, self-defense unit, vigilante unit, citizen unit, police unit, government agency or office, extermination camp, concentration camp, prisoner of war camp, prison, labor camp, or transit camp?   ☐ Yes   ☐ No

C. Continuous Residence

Since becoming a Lawful Permanent Resident of the United States:

13. Have you **EVER** called yourself a "nonresident" on a Federal, state, or local tax return?   ☐ Yes   ☐ No

14. Have you **EVER** failed to file a Federal, state, or local tax return because you considered yourself to be a "nonresident"?   ☐ Yes   ☐ No

Form N-400 (Rev. 07/23/02)N Page 7

Part 10. Additional Questions *(Continued)*	Write your INS "A"- number here: A __ __ __ __ __ __ __ __ __

D. Good Moral Character

For the purposes of this application, you must answer "Yes" to the following questions, if applicable, even if your records were sealed or otherwise cleared or if anyone, including a judge, law enforcement officer, or attorney, told you that you no longer have a record.

15. Have you **EVER** committed a crime or offense for which you were NOT arrested? ☐ Yes ☐ No

16. Have you **EVER** been arrested, cited, or detained by any law enforcement officer (including INS and military officers) for any reason? ☐ Yes ☐ No

17. Have you **EVER** been charged with committing any crime or offense? ☐ Yes ☐ No

18. Have you **EVER** been convicted of a crime or offense? ☐ Yes ☐ No

19. Have you **EVER** been placed in an alternative sentencing or a rehabilitative program (for example: diversion, deferred prosecution, withheld adjudication, deferred adjudication)? ☐ Yes ☐ No

20. Have you **EVER** received a suspended sentence, been placed on probation, or been paroled? ☐ Yes ☐ No

21. Have you **EVER** been in jail or prison? ☐ Yes ☐ No

If you answered "Yes" to any of questions 15 through 21, complete the following table. If you need more space, use a separate sheet of paper to give the same information.

Why were you arrested, cited, detained, or charged?	Date arrested, cited, detained, or charged *(Month/Day/Year)*	Where were you arrested, cited, detained or charged? *(City, State, Country)*	Outcome or disposition of the arrest, citation, detention or charge *(No charges filed, charges dismissed, jail, probation, etc.)*

Answer questions 22 through 33. If you answer "Yes" to any of these questions, attach (1) your written explanation why your answer was "Yes," and (2) any additional information or documentation that helps explain your answer.

22. Have you **EVER:**

    a. been a habitual drunkard? ☐ Yes ☐ No

    b. been a prostitute, or procured anyone for prostitution? ☐ Yes ☐ No

    c. sold or smuggled controlled substances, illegal drugs or narcotics? ☐ Yes ☐ No

    d. been married to more than one person at the same time? ☐ Yes ☐ No

    e. helped anyone enter or try to enter the United States illegally? ☐ Yes ☐ No

    f. gambled illegally or received income from illegal gambling? ☐ Yes ☐ No

    g. failed to support your dependents or to pay alimony? ☐ Yes ☐ No

23. Have you **EVER** given false or misleading information to any U.S. government official while applying for any immigration benefit or to prevent deportation, exclusion, or removal? ☐ Yes ☐ No

24. Have you **EVER** lied to any U.S. government official to gain entry or admission into the United States? ☐ Yes ☐ No

Form N-400 (Rev. 07/23/02)N Page 8

APPENDIX L: N-400 APPLICATION FOR NATURALIZATION

E. Removal, Exclusion, and Deportation Proceedings

25. Are removal, exclusion, rescission or deportation proceedings pending against you? ☐ Yes ☐ No

26. Have you **EVER** been removed, excluded, or deported from the United States? ☐ Yes ☐ No

27. Have you **EVER** been ordered to be removed, excluded, or deported from the United States? ☐ Yes ☐ No

28. Have you **EVER** applied for any kind of relief from removal, exclusion, or deportation? ☐ Yes ☐ No

F. Military Service

29. Have you **EVER** served in the U.S. Armed Forces? ☐ Yes ☐ No

30. Have you **EVER** left the United States to avoid being drafted into the U.S. Armed Forces? ☐ Yes ☐ No

31. Have you **EVER** applied for any kind of exemption from military service in the U.S. Armed Forces? ☐ Yes ☐ No

32. Have you **EVER** deserted from the U.S. Armed Forces? ☐ Yes ☐ No

G. Selective Service Registration

33. Are you a male who lived in the United States at any time between your 18th and 26th birthdays in any status except as a lawful nonimmigrant? ☐ Yes ☐ No

If you answered "NO", go on to question 34.

If you answered "YES", provide the information below.

If you answered "YES", but you did NOT register with the Selective Service System and are still under 26 years of age, you must register before you apply for naturalization, so that you can complete the information below:

Date Registered (Month/Day/Year) [   ]   Selective Service Number _ _ / _ _ _ _ _ _ / _

If you answered "YES", but you did NOT register with the Selective Service and you are now 26 years old or older, attach a statement explaining why you did not register.

H. Oath Requirements *(See Part 14 for the text of the oath)*

Answer questions 34 through 39. If you answer "No" to any of these questions, attach (1) your written explanation why the answer was "No" and (2) any additional information or documentation that helps to explain your answer.

34. Do you support the Constitution and form of government of the United States? ☐ Yes ☐ No

35. Do you understand the full Oath of Allegiance to the United States? ☐ Yes ☐ No

36. Are you willing to take the full Oath of Allegiance to the United States? ☐ Yes ☐ No

37. If the law requires it, are you willing to bear arms on behalf of the United States? ☐ Yes ☐ No

38. If the law requires it, are you willing to perform noncombatant services in the U.S. Armed Forces? ☐ Yes ☐ No

39. If the law requires it, are you willing to perform work of national importance under civilian direction? ☐ Yes ☐ No

Form N-400 (Rev. 07/23/02)N Page 9

Part 11. Your Signature

Write your INS "A"- number here:

A __ __ __ __ __ __ __ __ __

I certify, under penalty of perjury under the laws of the United States of America, that this application, and the evidence submitted with it, are all true and correct. I authorize the release of any information which INS needs to determine my eligibility for naturalization.

Your Signature

Date *(Month/Day/Year)*

__ __/__ __/__ __ __ __

Part 12. Signature of Person Who Prepared This Application for You *(if applicable)*

I declare under penalty of perjury that I prepared this application at the request of the above person. The answers provided are based on information of which I have personal knowledge and/or were provided to me by the above named person in response to the *exact questions* contained on this form.

Preparer's Printed Name

Preparer's Signature

Date *(Month/Day/Year)*

__ __/__ __/__ __ __ __

Preparer's Firm or Organization Name *(If applicable)*

Preparer's Daytime Phone Number

( )

Preparer's Address - Street Number and Name

City

State

ZIP Code

Do Not Complete Parts 13 and 14 Until an INS Officer Instructs You To Do So

Part 13. Signature at Interview

I swear (affirm) and certify under penalty of perjury under the laws of the United States of America that I know that the contents of this application for naturalization subscribed by me, including corrections numbered 1 through _____ and the evidence submitted by me numbered pages 1 through _____ , are true and correct to the best of my knowledge and belief.

Subscribed to and sworn to (affirmed) before me

Officer's Printed Name or Stamp

Date *(Month/Day/Year)*

Complete Signature of Applicant

Officer's Signature

Part 14. Oath of Allegiance

If your application is approved, you will be scheduled for a public oath ceremony at which time you will be required to take the following oath of allegiance immediately prior to becoming a naturalized citizen. By signing , you acknowledge your willingness and ability to take this oath:

I hereby declare, on oath, that I absolutely and entirely renounce and abjure all allegiance and fidelity to any foreign prince, potentate, state, or sovereignty, of whom or which which I have heretofore been a subject or citizen;

that I will support and defend the Constitution and laws of the United States of America against all enemies, foreign and domestic;

that I will bear true faith and allegiance to the same;

that I will bear arms on behalf of the United States when required by the law;

that I will perform noncombatant service in the Armed Forces of the United States when required by the law;

that I will perform work of national importance under civilian direction when required by the law; and

that I take this obligation freely, without any mental reservation or purpose of evasion; so help me God.

Printed Name of Applicant

Complete Signature of Applicant

Form N-400 (Rev. 07/23/02)N Page 10

National Listing of Voluntary Agencies (VOLAGs)

These not-for-profit agencies, known also as voluntary agencies, provide free or low-cost immigration law services. If you don't find your city listed, call a nearby organization. The quality of service provided by VOLAGs, just like those of attorneys, varies. If you're not happy with the services of a particular organization, shop around.

Alabama

Montgomery
International Assistance
   Project of Alabama, Inc.
P.O. Box 230238
4162 Carmichel Court
Montgomery, AL 36123-0238
Phone: 334-272-7092
Fax: 334-272-2247

Alaska

Anchorage
Catholic Social Services
   Center
3710 East 20th Avenue
Anchorage, AK 99508
Phone: 907-276-5590
Fax: 907-258-1091

Arizona

Florence
Florence Immigrant &
   Refugee Rights Project
P.O. Box 654
300 Main Street
Florence, AZ 85232
Phone: 520-868-0191
Fax: 520-868-0192

Phoenix
Catholic Social Service
   Phoenix
1825 West Northern Avenue
Phoenix, AZ 85201
Phone: 602-997-6105
Fax: 602-870-3891

San Luis
Proyecto San Pablo
23239 Archibald Street
San Luis, AZ 85349
Phone: 520-627-2042
Fax: 520-627-1614

Tucson
Catholic Social Services
155 West Helen Street
Tucson, AZ 85705
Phone: 520-623-0344
Fax: 520-770-8514

Tucson Ecumenical
   Council Assistance
   (TECLA)
631 South 6th Avenue
Tucson, AZ 85701
Phone: 520-623-5739
Fax: 520-623-7255

Yuma
Proyecto San Pablo
2215 South 8th Avenue
Yuma, AZ 85364
Phone: 520-783-5794
Fax: 520-783-2410

Arkansas

Little Rock
Catholic Immigration
   Services
2500 North Tyler Street
Little Rock, AR 72217-7565
Phone: 501-664-0340
Fax: 501-664-9075

California

Bakersfield
Catholic Charities
   Immigration and
   Refugee Services
415 East 19th Street
Bakersfield, CA 93305
Phone: 805-325-7751
Fax: 805-323-1106

Chico

Legal Services of Northern
California
P.O. Box 3728
Chico, CA 95928
Phone: 530-345-9491
Fax: 530-345-6913

Chula Vista

Proyecto San Pablo
1550 Broadway, Suite H
Chula Vista, CA 91911
Phone: 619-427-7213
Fax: 619-427-7752

Davis

Immigration Law Clinic
University of California
School of Law
Davis, CA 95616
Phone: 530-752-6942
Fax: 530-752-0822

El Centro

Proyecto San Pablo
428 South 5th Street
El Centro, CA 92243
Phone: 619-353-8013
Fax: 619-353-8013

El Monte

International Institute of
Los Angeles
10180 East Valley Boulevard
El Monte, CA 91737
Phone: 818-452-9421
Fax: 818-452-8520

Garden Grove

World Relief
7461 Garden Grove Boule-
vard, Suite B
Garden Grove, CA 92641
Phone: 714-890-0655
Fax: 714-890-0366

Los Angeles

Asian Pacific American
Legal Center
1010 South Flower Street,
Suite 302
Los Angeles, CA 90015
Phone: 213-748-2022
Fax: 213-748-0679

Asociacion de Salvadorenos
de Los Angeles
(ASOSAL)
660 South Bonnie Brae Street
Los Angeles, CA 90057
Phone: 213-483-1244
Fax: 213-483-9832

Barristers Aids Legal
Services Project,
Los Angeles County Bar
Association
P.O. Box 55020
Los Angeles, CA 90055
Phone: 213-896-6436
Fax: 213-896-6500

Central American Refugee
Center (CARECEN)
1636 West 8th Street, Suite
215
Los Angeles, CA 90017
Phone: 213-385-7800
Fax: 213-385-1094

International Institute of
Los Angeles
435 South Boyle Avenue
Los Angeles, CA 90033
Phone: 213-264-6217
Fax: 213-264-4623

International Rescue
Committee
3727 West 6th Street
Los Angeles, CA 90020
Phone: 213-386-6700
Fax: 213-386-7916

Jewish Family Service of
Los Angeles
6380 Wilshire Boulevard,
#1200
Los Angeles, CA 92057
Phone: 213-651-5573
Fax: 213-651-5649

Legal Aid Foundation of
Los Angeles
5228 East Whittier Boulevard
Los Angeles, CA 90022
Phone: 213-266-6550
Fax: 213-265-0566

One Stop
Immigration Center
3600 Whittier Boulevard
Los Angeles, CA 90023
Phone: 213-268-8472
Fax: 213-268-2231

One Stop
Immigration Center
20451 2 Cesar Chavez Avenue
Los Angeles, CA 90033
Phone: 213-268-2801

One Stop
Immigration Center
3440 Wilshire Boulevard,
Suite 400
Los Angeles, CA 90010
Phone: 213-383-1300 x 319
Fax: 213-427-2380

Public Counsel
601 South Ardmore Avenue
Los Angeles, CA 90005
Phone: 213-385-2977
Fax: 213 385-9089

El Rescate Legal Services
1340 South Bonnie Brae
Los Angeles, CA 90006
Phone: 213-387-3284

Lynwood

One Stop Immigration
Center
12435 Cookmore Avenue
Lynwood, CA 90262

Oakland

Immigration Project,
Catholic Charities
Diocese of Oakland
1232 33rd Avenue
Oakland, CA 94601
Phone: 510-261-1538
Fax: 510-532-3837

International Institute of
East Bay
297 Lee Street
Oakland, CA 94610
Phone: 510-451-2846
Fax: 510-465-3392

Oxnard

Immigrants Rights
Commission & National
Multi-Ethnic Families
Association (NAMEFA)
200 South "A" Street, Suite
202
Oxnard, CA 93030
Phone: 805-484-3787
Fax: 805-483-3009

Pacoima
San Fernando Valley
　　Neighborhood Legal
　　Services
13327 Van Nuys Boulevard
Pacoima, CA 91331
Phone: 818-896-5211
Fax: 818-896-6647

Palm Springs
Coachella Valley
　　Immigration Service &
　　Assistance, Inc.
　　(C-VISA)
934 Vella Road
Palm Springs, CA 92264
Phone: 619-327-1579
Fax: 619-325-2869

Redding
SEACM: A Ministry to
　　Refugees and
　　Immigrants
2315 Placer Street
Redding, CA 96001
Phone: 530-241-5802
Fax: 530-241-5897

Redwood City
International Institute of
　　San Mateo
2600 Middlefield Road
Redwood City, CA 94063
Phone: 415-780-7260
Fax: 415-364-4634

Reedley
One Stop
　　Immigration Center
1137 "G" Street
Reedley, CA 93654

San Bernardino
Libreria del Pueblo, Inc.
972 North Mount Vernon Ave
San Bernardino, CA 92324
Phone: 909-888-7678
Fax: 909-889-3895

San Diego
Access, Inc.
2602 Daniel Avenue
San Diego, CA 92111
Phone: 619-560-0871

Catholic Charities Diocese
　　of San Diego
4575 A Mission Gorge Place
San Diego, CA 92120
Phone: 619-287-9454
Fax: 619-287-6328

International Rescue
　　Committee
4535 30th Street, #110
San Diego, CA 92116
Phone: 619-641-7510
Fax: 619-641-7520

Legal Aid Society of
　　San Diego, Inc.
110 South Euclid Avenue
San Diego, CA 92114
Phone: 619-262-0896
Fax: 619-263-5697

San Fernando
Immigration Services of
　　Santa Rosa
132 North Maclay Avenue
San Fernando, CA 91340
Phone: 818-361-4341
Fax: 818-361-4316

San Francisco
　　Asian Law Caucus
468 Bush Street, 3rd Floor
San Francisco, CA 94408
Phone: 415-391-1655
Fax: 415-391-0366

Asylum Program,
　　Lawyers' Committee
　　for Civil Rights
301 Mission Street, Suite 400
San Francisco, CA 94105
Phone: 415-543-9444
Fax: 415-543-0296

Immigrants Assistance
　　Line of the Northern
　　California Coalition for
　　Immigrants' Rights
Phone: 415-543-6767
　　(Spanish, English)
Phone: 415-543-6769
　　(Chinese, Japanese)

Immigrant Legal Resource
　　Center (ILRC)
1663 Mission Street,
　　Suite 602
San Francisco, CA 94103
Phone: 415-255-9499
Fax: 415-255-9792

International Institute of
　　San Francisco
2209 Van Ness Avenue
San Francisco, CA 94109
Phone: 415-673-1720
Fax: 415-673-1763

International Rescue
　　Committee
1370 Mission Street,
　　4th Floor
San Francisco, CA 94103
Phone: 415-863-3777
Fax: 415-863-9264

Jewish Family &
　　Children's Services
423 Presidio Avenue
San Francisco, CA 94115
Phone: 415-474-0234
Fax: 415-474-4525

La Raza Centro Legal
474 Valencia Street, Suite 295
San Francisco, CA 94103
Phone: 415-575-3500
Fax: 415-255-7593

San Jose
Asian Law Alliance
184 Jackson Street
San Jose, CA 95112
Phone: 408-287-9710
Fax: 408-287-0864

Catholic Charities
　　Immigration Program
2625 Zanker Road, Suite 201
San Jose, CA 95137
Phone: 408-944-0691
Fax: 408-944-0347

Center for Employment
　　Training
701 Vine Street
San Jose, CA 95110
Phone: 408-287-7924
Fax: 408-294-5749

International Rescue
　　Committee
90 East Gish Road, Suite F
San Jose, CA 95112
Phone: 408-453-3536

Legal Aid Society of Santa
　　Clara County
480 North First Street
San Jose, CA 95112
Phone: 408-998-5200
Fax: 408-298-3782

Santa Ana
Catholic Charities of
　　Orange County
1506 Bookhollow Drive, #112
Santa Ana, CA 92705
Phone: 714-662-7500
Fax: 714-662-1861

Santa Barbara
Catholic Charities
    Immigration and
    Citizenship Department
609 East Haley Street
Santa Barbara, CA 93103
Phone: 805-966-3530
Fax: 805-966-6470

One Stop Immigration
    Center
110 North Milpas Street
Santa Barbara, CA 93103
Phone: 805-966-6470
Fax: 805-966-6470

Santa Rosa
Catholic Charities,
    Diocese of Santa Rosa,
    Immigration/
    Resettlement
555 Sebastopol Road
Santa Rosa, CA 95407
Phone: 707-578-6000
Fax: 707-575-4910

Stockton
Council for the Spanish
    Speaking
343 East Main Street, Suite
200
Stockton, CA 95201
Phone: 209-547-2855
Fax: 209-547-2870

Van Nuys
International Institute of
    Los Angeles
14701 Friar Street
Van Nuys, CA 91411
Phone: 818-988-1332
Fax: 818-988-1337

Visalia
OLA Raza, Inc.
115 West Main Street, Suite C
Visalia, CA 93291
Phone: 209-627-6291

Watsonville
Santa Cruz County
    Immigration Project
    (SCCIP)
406 Main Street, Suite 217
Watsonville, CA 95076
Phone: 408-724-5667

Colorado

Alamosa
San Luis Valley Christian
    Community Services
    Immigrant Assistance
    Program
309 San Juan Avenue
Alamosa, CO 81101
Phone: 719-589-5192
Fax: 719-589-4330

Denver
Catholic Immigration and
    Refugee Services
3417 West 38th Avenue
Denver, CO 80211
Phone: 303-458-0222
Fax: 303-458-0331

Colorado Rural Legal
    Services
655 Broadway, Suite 45D
Denver, CO 80203
Phone: 303-893-6468
Fax: 303-825-5532

Justice Information Center
1600 Downing Street,
    Suite 500
Denver, CO 80218
Phone: 303-832-1220
Fax: 303-832-1242

Connecticut

Bridgeport
Diocese of Bridgeport,
    Catholic Center
238 Jewett Avenue
Bridgeport, CT 06606-2845
Phone: 203-372-4301
Fax: 203-371-8698

International Institute of
    Connecticut, Inc.
670 Clinton Avenue
Bridgeport, CT 06605
Phone: 203-336-0141
Fax: 203-339-4400

Hartford
International Institute of
    Connecticut, Inc.
487 Main Street, Suite 15
Hartford, CT 06103
Phone: 860-520-4050
Fax: 860-520-4191

New Haven
Jerome N. Frank Legal
    Services Organization
P.O. Box 209090
New Haven, CT 06520-9090
Phone: 203-432-4800
Fax: 203-432-1426

Delaware

Wilmington
Service for Foreign Born
    820 North French
    Street,
    7th Floor
Wilmington, DE 19801
Phone: 302-577-3047
Fax: 302-577-3090

Wilmington Catholic
    Charities, Inc.
2601 West 4th Street
Wilmington, DE 19805
Phone: 302-654-6460
Fax: 302-655-9753

District of Columbia

Associated Catholic
    Charities
1221 Massachusetts Avenue,
    NW
Washington, DC 20005
Phone: 202-628-6861
Fax: 202-737-3421

Ayuda
1736 Columbia Road, NW
Washington, DC 20009
Phone: 202-387-4848
Fax: 202-387-0324

Catholic Immigration
    Services
1511 K Street, NW, Suite 703
Washington, DC 20005
Phone: 202-347-7401
Fax: 202-347-9191

Central American Resource
    Center (CARCEN)
3112 Mount Pleasant Street,
    NW
Washington, DC 20010
Phone: 202-328-9799
Fax: 202-328-0023

Lawyers' Committee for
Human Rights
100 Maryland Avenue, NE,
Suite 502
Washington, DC 20002
Phone: 202-547-5692
Fax: 202-543-5999

Lutheran Social Services
Refugee & Immigration
Services
4406 Georgia Avenue, NW
Washington, DC 20011
Phone: 202-723-3000
Fax: 202-723-3303

Spanish Catholic Center
3055 Mount Pleasant Street,
NW
Washington, DC 20009
Phone: 202-483-1520
Fax: 202-234-7349

Florida

Arcadia
Catholic Charities of
DeSoto County
1210 East Oak Street
Arcadia, FL 33821
Phone: 941-494-1068
Fax: 941-494-1671

Aventura
Rescue & Migration, Jewish
Family Service
18999 Biscayne Boulevard,
Suite 200
Aventura, FL 33180
Phone: 305-933-9820
Fax: 305-933-9843

Fort Myers
Catholic Hispanic Social
Services, Agency of
Catholic Charities
4235 Michigan Avenue Link
Fort Myers, FL 33916
Phone: 941-337-4193
Fax: 941-332-2799

Homestead
COFFO Immigration
Project
21 South Krome Avenue
Homestead, FL 33030
Phone: 305-247-4779
Fax: 305-242-0701

Lakeland
Florida Rural Legal
Services
P.O. Box 24688
963 East Memorial Boulevard
Lakeland, FL 33802-4688
Phone: 941-688-7376
Fax: 941-683-7861

Miami
Church World Service
701 SW 27th Avenue, Room
707
Miami, FL 33135
Phone: 305-541-8040
Fax: 305-642-2815

Florida Immigrant
Advocacy Center, Inc.
3000 Biscayne Boulevard,
Suite 400
Miami, FL 33137
Phone: 305-573-1106 x 104
Fax: 305-573-6273

Haitian American
Community
Association of Dade
County, Inc. (HACAD)
8037 NE 2nd Avenue
Miami, FL 33138
Phone: 305-751-3429
Fax: 305-751-0523

Immigration Latina
Community Services
8500 West Flagler Street,
Suite 203C
Miami, FL 33144
Phone: 305-220-7000
Fax: 305-223-3032

International Rescue
Committee
2750 Coral Way, Suite 200
Miami, FL 33145
Phone: 305-444-1417
Fax: 305-444-1517

Lutheran Ministries of
Florida, Inc.
4343 Flagler Street,
Suite 200
Miami, FL 33134
Phone: 305-567-2511
Fax: 305-567-2944

St. Thomas University
School of Law,
Immigration Clinic
16400 NW 32nd Avenue
Miami, FL 33054
Phone: 305-623-2309
Fax: 305-623-2390

Orlando
COFFO Immigration
Project
P.O. Box 540025
60 North Court Avenue, 2nd
Floor
Orlando, FL 32801
Phone: 407-481-8030
Fax: 407-481-9030

Pensacola
Catholic Social Services,
Refugee & Immigration
Services, Dioceses of
Pensacola/Tallahassee
222 East Government Street
Pensacola, FL 32501
Phone: 904-436-6420
Fax: 904-436-6419

South Miami
American Friends Service
Committee, Central
America Political
Asylum Project
1205 Sunset Drive
South Miami, FL 33143
Phone: 305-665-0022
Fax: 305-665-6422

St. Petersburg
Catholic Charities
6533 9th Avenue North, #1E
St. Petersburg, FL 33710
Phone: 813-893-1311
Fax: 813-893-1309

Tampa
Catholic Charities
2021 East Busch Boulevard
Tampa, FL 33612
Phone: 813-631-4370
Fax: 813-631-4395

Georgia

Atlanta
Latin American
Association
2665 Buford Highway
Atlanta, GA 30324
Phone: 404-638-1800
Fax: 404-638-1806

Clarkston

World Relief
964 North Indian Creek
    Drive, Suite A1
Clarkston, GA 30021
Phone: 404-294-4352
Fax: 404-294-6011

Tifton

Georgia Legal Services
    Program, Migrant Unit
P.O. Box 1669
150 South Ridge Avenue
Tifton, GA 31793
Phone: 912-386-3566
Fax: 912-386-3588

Hawaii

Honolulu

Catholic Charities
    Immigrant Services
712 North School Street
Honolulu, HI 96817
Phone: 808-528-5233
Fax: 808-531-1970

Immigrant Center
720 North King Street
Honolulu, HI 96817
Phone: 808-845-3918
Fax: 808-842-1962

Illinois

Chicago

ALAC-Catholic Charities
    Immigration & Refugee
    Resettlement Services
126 North Desplaines Street
Chicago, IL 60661
Phone: 312-427-7078
Fax: 312-427-3130

Chinese American Service
    League
310 West 24th Place
Chicago, IL 60616
Phone: 312-791-0418
Fax: 312-791-0509

Hebrew Immigrant Aid
    Society of Chicago
    (HIAS)
One South Franklin,
    Suite 411
Chicago, IL 60606
Phone: 312-357-4666
Fax: 312-855-3291

Lao American Community
    Services
4750 North Sheridan,
    Suite 355
Chicago, IL 60640
Phone: 312-271-0004
Fax: 312-271-1682

Legal Services Center for
    Immigrants, Legal
    Assistance Foundation
    of Chicago
1661 South Blue Island
    Avenue
Chicago, IL 60608
Phone: 312-226-0173
Fax: 312-421-4643

Lutheran Child &
    Family Services of
    Illinois (Hispanic Social
    Service Agency)
3859 West 26th Street
Chicago, IL 60623
Phone: 312-277-7330
Fax: 708-771-7184

Polish American
    Association
3834 North Cicero Avenue
Chicago, IL 60641
Phone: 312-282-8206
Fax: 312-282-1324

Travelers & Immigrants
    Aid, Midwest Immi
    grants Rights Center
208 South LaSalle
Chicago, IL 60604
Phone: 312-629-1960
Fax: 312-551-2214

United Network for
    Immigrants
1808 South Blue Island
    Avenue, Suite 2
Chicago, IL 60608
Phone: 312-563-0002
Fax: 312-563-9864

World Relief
3507 West Lawrence
Chicago, IL 60608
Phone: 312-583-9191
Fax: 312-583-9410

Elgin

Centro de Informacion y
    Progreso
62 South Grove Avenue
Elgin, IL 60120
Phone: 847-695-9050
Fax: 847-931-7991

Granite City

Immigrants Project
P.O. Box 753
1818 Cleveland Boulevard
Granite City, IL 62040
Phone: 618-452-7018

Rockford

Centro Hispano Sembrador
921 West State Street
Rockford, IL 61102
Phone: 815-964-8142
Fax: 815-969-2808

Wheaton

World Relief
1028 College Avenue, Suite A
Wheaton, IL 60187
Phone: 708-462-7566

Indiana

Gary

International Institute of
    Northwest Indiana
4333 Broadway
Gary, IN 46409
Phone: 219-980-4636
Fax: 219-980-3244

Goshen

La Casa of Goshen
202 North Cottage Avenue
Goshen, IN 46526
Phone: 219-533-4450
Fax: 219-533-4399

Indianapolis

The Hispanic Center
617 East North Street
Indianapolis, IN 46204
Phone: 317-631-9410
Fax: 317-631-9775

Iowa

Davenport

Diocesan Immigration
  Program, Diocese of
  Davenport
2706 North Gaines Street
Davenport, IA 52804-1998
Phone: 319-324-1911
Fax: 319-324-5811

Sioux City

La Casa Latina, Inc.
223 10th Street
Sioux City, IA 51103
Phone: 712-252-4259
Fax: 712-252-5655

Kansas

Dodge City

United Methodist Care
  Center
708 Avenue H
Dodge City, KS 67801
Phone: 316-225-0625

Garden City

Catholic Agency for
  Migration & Refugee
  Services
1510 Taylor Plaza East
Garden City, KS 67846
Phone: 316-276-7610
Fax: 316-276-9228

United Methodist Western
  Kansas Mexican-Ameri
  can Ministries
224 North Taylor, Box 766
Garden City, KS 67846
Phone: 316-275-1766
Fax: 316-275-4729

Kentucky

Louisville

Catholic Charities
  Migration & Refugee
  Services
2911 South Fourth Street
Louisville, KY 40208
Phone: 502-636-9263
Fax: 502-637-9780

Louisiana

New Orleans

Associated Catholic
  Charities of New
  Orleans, Immigration
  Legal Services
1000 Howard Avenue,
  Suite 600
New Orleans, LA 70113
Phone: 504-523-3755
Fax: 504-523-6962

Hispanic Apostolate,
  Archdiocese of
  New Orleans
P.O. Box 19104
3368 Esplanade Avenue
New Orleans, LA 70119
Phone: 504-486-1983
Fax: 504-486-8985

Loyola Law School Clinic
7214 St. Charles Avenue
New Orleans, LA 70118
Phone: 504-861-5590
Fax: 504-861-5440

Maryland

Baltimore

Catholic Charities,
  Immigration Legal
  Services
19 West Franklin Street
Baltimore, MD 21201
Phone: 410-659-4021
Fax: 410-659-4059

Columbia

Foreign-Born Information
  & Referral Network,
  Inc. (FIRN)
10630 Little Patuxent
  Parkway, Suite 209
Columbia, MD 21044
Phone: 410-992-1923
Fax: 410-730-0113

Silver Spring

Korean American
  Community Services
969 Thayer Avenue, Suite 3
Silver Spring, MD 20910
Phone: 301-589-6470
Fax: 301-589-4724

Takoma Park

Casa of Maryland
310 Tulip Street
Takoma Park, MD 20912
Phone: 301-270-0442
Fax: 301-270-8659

Massachusetts

Boston

Greater Boston Legal
  Services Asian
  Outreach Program
197 Friend Street
Boston, MA 02114
Phone: 617-371-1234
Fax: 617-371-1222

International Institute of
  Boston
287 Commonwealth Avenue
Boston, MA 02115
Phone: 617-536-1081
Fax: 617-536-1573

International Rescue
  Committee of Boston
162 Boylston Street, Suite 50
Boston, MA 02116
Phone: 617-482-1154
Fax: 617-482-7922

Cambridge

Centro Presente, Inc.
54 Essex Street
Cambridge, MA 02139
Phone: 617-487-9080
Fax: 617-497-7247

Community Legal Services
  and Counseling Center
One West Street
Cambridge, MA 02139
Phone: 617-661-1010

Dorchester

Haitian Multi Service
  Center, Refugee
  Program
12 Bicknell Street
Dorchester, MA 02121
Phone: 617-436-2848

Lowell

International Institute
  of Lowell
79 High Street
Lowell, MA 01852
Phone: 508-459-9031
Fax: 508-459-0154

Somerville

Catholic Charities Refugee
& Immigration Services
270 Washington Street
Somerville, MA 02143
Phone: 617-625-1920
Fax: 617-625-2246

Worcester

Catholic Charities of
Worcester, Refugee
Resettlement Program
15 Ripley Street
Worcester, MA 01610
Phone: 508-798-0191
Fax: 508-797-5659

National Council of
Jewish Women,
Immigration &
Naturalization Office
633 Salisbury Street
Worcester, MA 01609
Phone: 508-791-3438

Michigan

Detroit

Archdiocese of Detroit,
Office of Migration
305 Michigan Avenue,
5th Floor
Detroit, MI 48226
Phone: 313-237-4694
Fax: 313-237-5866

Freedom House
2630 West Lafayette
Detroit, MI 48216
Phone: 313-964-4320
Fax: 313-963-1077

International Institute of
Metropolitan Detroit
111 East Kirby
Detroit, MI 48202
Phone: 313-871-8600
Fax: 313-871-1651

Lansing

Refugee Services
1900 South Cedar, Room 302
Lansing, MI 48910-9145
Phone: 517-484-1010
Fax: 517-484-2610

Minnesota

Mankato

Southern Minnesota
Regional Legal
Services, Inc.
P.O. Box 3304
1302 South Riverfront Drive
Mankato, MN 56001
Phone: 507-387-5588
Fax: 507-387-2321

Minneapolis

Lutheran Social Service of
Minnesota, Refugee &
Immigration Services
Unit
2414 Park Avenue South
Minneapolis, MN 55404
Phone: 612-871-0221
Fax: 612-871-0354

Minnesota Advocates for
Human Rights, Refugee
& Asylum Project
400 Second Avenue South,
Suite 1050
Minneapolis, MN 55401
Phone: 612-341-3302
Fax: 612-341-2971

St. Paul

Catholic Charities MRS
215 Old 6th Street
St. Paul, MN 55102
Phone: 612-222-3001
Fax: 612-222-4581

Centro Legal, Inc.
2575 University Avenue West,
Suite 135
St. Paul, MN 55114-1024
Phone: 612-642-1890
Fax: 612-642-1875

International Institute of
Minnesota
1694 Como Avenue
St. Paul, MN 55108
Phone: 612-647-0191
Fax: 612-647-9268

Oficina Legal of Southern
Minnesota Regional
Legal Services
179 East Robie Street
St. Paul, MN 55107
Phone: 612-291-2579
Fax: 612-291-2549

Mississippi

Biloxi

Catholic Social &
Community Services,
Inc., Migration &
Refugee Center
870 Nativity Drive
Biloxi, MS 39533
Phone: 601-374-6507
Fax: 601-374-6560

Missouri

Kansas City

Don Bosco Center
531 Garfield
Kansas City, MO 64124
Phone: 816-691-2900

Legal Aid of Western
Missouri
920 Southwest Boulevard
Kansas City, MO 64108
Phone: 816-474-9868

St. Louis

Immigration Law Project
4232 Forest Park Avenue
St. Louis, MO 63108
Phone: 314-534-4200 x 1008
Fax: 314-534-7515

Montana

Billings

Montana Legal Services
2442 First Avenue North
Billings, MT 59101
Phone: 406-248-7113
Fax: 406-252-6055

Nebraska

Gering

NAF Multicultural
Human Development
Corporation
P.O. Box 552
3305 North 10th Street
Gering, NE 69341
Phone: 308-632-5831

Grand Island
NAF Multicultural Human
    Development Corpora
    tion, Regional Office
811 West 4th Street, Suite 3
Grand Island, NE 68801
Phone: 308-382-3956

Lincoln
NAF Multicultural Human
    Development
    Corporation,
    Regional Office
941 O Street, Suite 818
Lincoln, NE 68508
Phone: 402-434-2821

North Platte
NAF Multicultural Human
    Development Corpora
    tion, Regional Office
P.O. Box 2131
414 East 4th Street
North Platte, NE 69103
Phone: 308-534-2630

Omaha
Caridades Catolicas Centro
    Juan Diego
5211 31st Street
Omaha, NE 68107
Phone: 402-731-5413
Fax: 402-731-5865

South Sioux City
NAF Multicultural Human
    Development Corpora
    tion, Regional Office
2509 Dakota Avenue
South Sioux City, NE 68776
Phone: 402-494-6576

Nevada

Las Vegas
Catholic Charities of
    Southern Nevada
1501 Las Vegas Boulevard
North
Las Vegas, NV 89101
Phone: 702-383-8387
Fax: 702-385-7748

New Hampshire

Manchester
International Center
102 North Main Street
Manchester, NH 03102
Phone: 603-668-8602

New Hampshire Catholic
    Charities
215 Myrtle Street
Manchester, NH 03105
Phone: 603-669-3030
Fax: 603-626-1252

Nashua
St. Francis Xavier Parish
41 Chandler Street
Nashua, NH 03060
Phone: 603-881-8065
Fax: 603-594-9648

New Jersey

East Orange
Jewish Family Service of
    Metrowest
111 Prospect Street
East Orange, NJ 07017
Phone: 210-674-4210
Fax: 210-674-7137

Elizabeth
Human Rights Advocates
    International, Inc.
1341 North Avenue, Suite C-7
Elizabeth, NJ 07208-2622
Phone: 908-352-6032
Fax: 908-289-8540

Jersey City
International Institute of
    New Jersey
880 Bergen Avenue
Jersey City, NJ 07306
Phone: 201-653-3888 x 20
Fax: 201-963-0252

Newark
American Friends Service
    Committee, Immigrant
    Rights Program
972 Broad Street, 6th Floor
Newark, NJ 07102
Phone: 201-643-1924
Fax: 201-643-8924

Pennsduken
Diocese of Camden
    Immigration Services
6981 North Park Drive,
    Suite 104 W
Pennsduken, NJ 08110
Phone: 609-317-0202

Perth Amboy
Catholic Charities
    Immigration Program
    Service
295 Barclay Street
Perth Amboy, NJ 08861
Phone: 908-826-9160
Fax: 908-826-8342

Plainfield
El Centro Hispano-
    American
525 East Front Street
Plainfield, NJ 07060
Phone: 908-753-8730
Fax: 908-753-8463

Trenton
Lutheran Immigration
    Center, Lutheran Social
    Ministries of
    New Jersey
P.O. Box 30
189 South Broad Street
Trenton, NJ 08601
Phone: 609-393-4900
Fax: 609-393-1111

Union City
North Hudson Community
    Action Corporation
507 26th Street
Union City, NJ 07087-3798
Phone: 201-330-3804
Fax: 201-330-3803

St. Bridget's Church,
    Immigration Assistance
    Service
530 35th Street
Union City, NJ 07087
Phone: 201-865-8434

New Mexico

Albuquerque
Albuquerque Border
    City Project
115 2nd Street (Southwest
Basement)
Albuquerque, NM 87103-2121
Phone: 505-766-5404

Gallup
Casa Reina
217 East Wilson
Gallup, NM 87301
Phone: 505-722-5511

Santa Fe
Catholic Social Services of
Santa Fe, Inc.
1234-B San Felipe
Santa Fe, NM 87501
Phone: 505-982-0441
Fax: 505-984-1803

New York

Albany
Hispanic Outreach
Services
40 North Main Avenue
Albany, NY 12203
Phone: 518-453-6650
Fax: 518-453-6792

International Center of the
Capital Region
8 Russel Road
Albany, NY 12206-1307
Phone: 518-459-8812
Fax: 518-459-8980

Alton
Cornell Migrant Program
P.O. Box 181
8461 Ridge Road
Alton, NY 14413
Phone: 315-483-4092
Fax: 315-483-4040

Amityville
Migration Office of
Catholic Charities,
Diocese of Rockville
Centre
143 Schleigel Boulevard
Amityville, NY 11701
Phone: 516-789-5200
Fax: 516-789-5245

Astoria
Federation of Italian-
American Organizations
of Queens, Inc.
29-21 21st Avenue
Astoria, NY 11105
Phone: 718-204-2444
Fax: 718-204-9145

Immigration Advocacy
Services, Inc.
25-42 Steinway Street
Astoria, NY 11103
Phone: 718-956-8218
Fax: 718-274-1615

Binghamton
American Civic
Association
131 Front Street
Binghamton, NY 13905
Phone: 607-723-9419
Fax: 607-723-0023

Brooklyn
Catholic Migration Office,
Diocese of Brooklyn
1258 65th Street
Brooklyn, NY 11226
Phone: 718-826-2942
Fax: 718-826-2948

Central American Legal
Assistance
240 Hooper Street
Brooklyn, NY 11211
Phone: 718-486-6800

Liberty Immigration &
Citizenship Service, Inc.
P.O. Box 350-276
1424 Sheepshead Bay Road
Brooklyn, NY 11235
Phone: 718-743-5844
Fax: 718-743-6051

Southside Community
Mission
280 Mercy Avenue
Brooklyn, NY 11211
Phone: 718-387-3803
Fax: 718-387-6052

Buffalo
International Institute of
Buffalo, Inc.
864 Delaware Avenue
Buffalo, NY 14209
Phone: 716-883-1900
Fax: 716-883-9529

Corona
Concerned Citizens of
Queens
40-18 Junction Boulevard
Corona, NY 11368
Phone: 718-478-1600
Fax: 718-478-4318

Garden City
Nassau County Hispanic
Foundation, Inc.,
Immigration Law
Services
233 Seventh Street, 3rd Floor
Garden City, NY 11530
Phone: 516-742-0067
Fax: 516-742-2054

Hempstead
Central American Refugee
Center (CARECEN)
91 North Franklin Street,
Suite 211
Hempstead, NY 11550
Phone: 516-489-8330
Fax: 516-489-8308

Jackson Heights-Queens
Travelers Aid Immigration
Legal Services
74-09 37th Avenue, Room 412
Jackson Heights-Queens, NY
11372
Phone: 718-899-1233
Fax: 718-457-6071

New York City
Association of the Bar of
New York
Robert B. McKay
Community Outreach
Law Program
42 West 44th Street
New York, NY 10036
Phone: 212-382-6629
Fax: 212-354-7438

Catholic Charities,
Archdiocese of New
York, Office for
Immigrant Services
1011 First Avenue, 12th Floor
New York, NY 10022
Phone: 212-371-1000 x 2260
Fax: 212-826-6254

Gay Men's Health Crisis,
Inc., Immigrants with
HIV Project
129 West 20th Street
New York, NY 10011
Phone: 212-337-3504
Fax: 212-337-1160

Hebrew Immigrant
Aid Society (HIAS)
333 Seventh Avenue
New York, NY 10001
Phone: 212-967-4100
Fax: 212-967-4442

Interfaith Community
Services
308 West 46th Street,
3rd Floor
New York, NY 10036
Phone: 212-399-0899
Fax: 212-265-2238

Lawyers' Committee for
Human Rights,
Asylum Program
330 Seventh Avenue,
10th Floor
New York, NY 10001
Phone: 212-629-6170
Fax: 212-967-0916

New York Association
for New Americans, Inc.
(NYANA)
17 Battery Place
New York, NY 10004
Phone: 212-248-4100
Fax: 212-248-4138

Northern Manhattan
Coalition for Immigrant
Rights
Two Bennett Avenue
New York, NY 10033
Phone: 212-781-0355
Fax: 212-781-0943

Poughkeepsie
Prisoners' Legal Services
of New York Immigra
tion Law Project
205 South Avenue, Suite 200
Poughkeepsie, NY 12601
Phone: 914-473-3810
Fax: 914-473-2628

Rochester
Catholic Family Center
25 Franklin Street, 7th Floor
Rochester, NY 14604-1007
Phone: 716-262-7074
Fax: 716-232-6486

Legal Aid Society
65 West Broad Street,
Room 400
Rochester, NY 14614
Phone: 716-232-4090
Fax: 716-232-2352

White Plains
Westchester Hispanic
Coalition, Inc.
199 Main Street, 6th Floor
White Plains, NY 10601
Phone: 914-948-8466
Fax: 914-948-0311

North Carolina

Asheville
Catholic Social Services
35 Orange Street
Asheville, NC 28801
Phone: 704-258-2617
Fax: 704-253-7339

Greensboro
Lutheran Family Services
in the Carolinas
131 Manley Avenue
Greensboro, NC 27407
Phone: 910-855-0390
Fax: 910-855-6032

Raleigh
Lutheran Family Services
in the Carolinas
112 Cox Avenue
Raleigh, NC 27605
Phone: 919-832-2620
Fax: 919-832-0591

North Carolina Immigrants
Legal Assistance
Project
224 South Dawson Street
Raleigh, NC 27611
Phone: 888-251-2776
Fax: 919-856-2175

North Dakota

Fargo
Lutheran Social Services
1325 South 11th Street,
Box 389
Fargo, ND 58107
Phone: 701-235-7341
Fax: 701-235-7359

Migrant Legal Services
118 Broadway, Suite 305
Fargo, ND 58102
Phone: 701-232-8872
Fax: 701-232-8366

Ohio

Akron
International Institute
207 East Tallmadge Avenue
Akron, OH 44310-3298
Phone: 330-376-5106
Fax: 330-376-0133

Cincinnati
Catholic Social Services of
Southwestern Ohio
100 East 8th Street
Cincinnati, OH 45202
Phone: 513-241-7745
Fax: 513-241-4333

Travelers Aid International
of Greater Cincinnati
707 Race Street, Suite 300
Cincinnati, OH 45202
Phone: 513-721-7660
Fax: 513-287-7604

Cleveland
International Services
Center
1836 Euclid Avenue
Cleveland, OH 44115
Phone: 216-781-4560
Fax: 216-781-4565

Migration and Refugee
Services, Catholic
Diocese of Cleveland
1736 Superior Avenue, 2nd
Floor
Cleveland, OH 44114
Phone: 216-566-9500
Fax: 216-566-9161

Columbus
Community Refugee
& Immigration Services
3624 Bexvie Avenue
Columbus, OH 43227
Phone: 614-235-5747

Toledo
International Institute of
Greater Toledo
2040 Scottwood Avenue
Toledo, OH 43620
Phone: 419-241-9178
Fax: 419-241-9170

Oklahoma

Oklahoma City

Associated Catholic Charities, Immigration Assistance Program
1501 North Classen Boulevard, Suite 200
Oklahoma City, OK 73106
Phone: 405-523-3001
Fax: 405-523-3030

Hispanic American Mission
1836 NW 3rd
Oklahoma City, OK 73106
Phone: 405-272-0890

Legal Aid of Western Oklahoma
2901 Classen Boulevard, Suite 110
Oklahoma City, OK 73106
Phone: 405-557-0020
Fax: 405-557-0023

Tulsa

Migration and Refugee Services, Catholic Charities
751 North Denver
Tulsa, OK 74106
Phone: 918-582-0881

YWCA Intercultural Service Center
8145 East 17th Street
Tulsa, OK 74112
Phone: 918-663-0377
Fax: 918-628-1033

Oregon

Eugene

Lane County Law and Advocacy Center
376 East 11th Avenue
Eugene, OR 97401
Phone: 541-342-6056
Fax: 541-342-5091

Medford

Center for Nonprofit Legal Services, Inc.
P.O. Box 1586
225 West Main Street
Medford, OR 97501
Phone: 541-779-7292
Fax: 541-779-7308

Ontario

Oregon Legal Services Corporation
772 North Oregon Street
Ontario, OR 97914
Phone: 541-889-3121
Fax: 541-889-5562

Treasure Valley Immigration Counseling Service
772 North Oregon Street
Ontario, OR 97914
Phone: 541-889-3121
Fax: 541-889-5562

Pendleton

Oregon Legal Services Corporation
P.O. Box 1327
365 SE 3rd Street
Pendleton, OR 97801
Phone: 541-276-6685
Fax: 541-276-4549

Portland

Immigration Counseling Service
434 NW 6th Avenue, #202
Portland, OR 97209
Phone: 503-221-1689
Fax: 503-221-3063

Lutheran Family Service
605 SE 39th Avenue
Portland, OR 97214
Phone: 503-233-0042
Fax: 503-233-0667

One Stop Immigration Center
2936 NE Alberta Street
Portland, OR 97211
Phone: 503-288-2389

Sponsors Organized to Assist Refugees
5404 NE Alameda, Room 112
Portland, OR 97213
Phone: 503-284-3002
Fax: 503-284-6445

Woodburn

Centros de Servicios para Campesinos
300 Young Street
Woodburn, OR 97071
Phone: 503-982-0243
Fax: 503-982-1031

Pennsylvania

Allentown

Catholic Social Agency
928 Union Boulevard
Allentown, PA 18103
Phone: 610-435-1541
Fax: 610-435-4367

Erie

International Institute of Erie
517 East 26th Street
Erie, PA 16504
Phone: 814-452-3935
Fax: 814-452-3518

Harrisburg

Immigration & Refugee Services, Catholic Charities, Diocese of Harrisburg
900 North 17th Street
Harrisburg, PA 17103-1469
Phone: 717-232-0568
Fax: 717-234-7142

International Service Center
21 South River Street
Harrisburg, PA 17101
Phone: 717-236-9401
Fax: 717-236-3821

Philadelphia

Asian American Community Outreach Program of the Crime Prevention Association
2600 South Broad Street
Philadelphia, PA 19145
Phone: 215-467-1500
Fax: 215-467-1808

Catholic Social Services, Immigration Program
227 North 18th Street
Philadelphia, PA 19103
Phone: 215-854-7019
Fax: 215-854-7020

Hebrew Immigrant Aid Society (HIAS) & Council Migration Service of Philadelphia
226 South 16th Street, 18th Floor
Philadelphia, PA 19102
Phone: 215-735-1670
Fax: 215-735-8136

Nationalities Service
Center
1300 Spruce Street
Philadelphia, PA 19107
Phone: 215-893-8400
Fax: 215-735-9718

Reading
Apostolado Hispano de
Berks County
322 South 5th Street
Reading, PA 19602
Phone: 610-374-3351
Fax: 610-374-3351

Catholic Social Agency
138 North 9th Street
Reading, PA 19601
Phone: 610-374-4891
Fax: 610-374-4891

Rhode Island

Providence
Catholic Social Services
433 Elmwood Avenue
Providence, RI 02907
Phone: 401-467-7200
Fax: 401-467-6310

International Institute of
Rhode Island
645 Elmwood Avenue
Providence, RI 02907
Phone: 401-461-5940
Fax: 401-467-6530

South Dakota

Sioux Falls
Lutheran Social Services of
South Dakota, Refugee
& Immigration
Programs
620 West 18th Street
Sioux Falls, SD 57104
Phone: 605-357-0154
Fax: 605-357-0178

Tennessee

Nashville
Catholic Charities Refugee
Resettlement Program
10 South 6th Street
Nashville, TN 37206
Phone: 615-259-3567
Fax: 615-259-2851

Texas

Austin
Cristo Vive, C.S.S., Inc.
5800 Manor Road, Suite A
Austin, TX 78723
Phone: 512-929-9100
Fax: 512-926-1020

Immigration Counseling &
Outreach Services
(ICOS)
P.O. Box 13327
Austin, TX 78711-3327
Phone: 512-479-1009
Fax: 512-469-9537

Beaumont
Catholic Charities
1297 Calder
Beaumont, TX 77701
Phone: 409-832-7994
Fax: 409-833-9706

Brownsville
South Texas Immigration
Council
845 East 13th
Brownsville, TX 78520
Phone: 210-542-1991
Fax: 210-542-0490

Bryan
Chaplain Outreach
Services
717 South Main
Bryan, TX 77803
Phone: 409-775-8980
Fax: 409-823-7277

Corpus Christi
Catholic Social Services,
Immigration & Refugee
Program
1322 Comanche
Corpus Christi, TX 78401
Phone: 512-884-0651
Fax: 512-884-3956

Dallas
Catholic Charities,
Immigration Counseling
Services
3915 Lemmon Avenue
Dallas, TX 75219
Phone: 214-528-4870
Fax: 214-528-4874

Centro Social Hispano,
Cristo Rey Lutheran
Church
610 North Bishop
Dallas, TX 75208
Phone: 214-946-8661
Fax: 214-942-1278

Proyecto Adelante
3100 Crossman
Dallas, TX 75212
Phone: 214-741-2151
Fax: 214-741-2150

St. Matthew's Cathedral
5100 Ross Avenue
Dallas, TX 75206
Phone: 214-824-2942
Fax: 214-823-1048

Del Rio
Texas Rural Legal Aid, Inc.
P.O. Box 964
Del Rio, TX 78840
Phone: 210-775-1535
Fax: 210-774-0611

Edinburg
BARCA, Inc.
P.O. Box 715
Edinburg, TX 78540
Phone: 210-631-7447
Fax: 210-687-9266

Texas Rural Legal Aid, Inc.
316 South Closner
Edinburg, TX 78539
Phone: 210-383-5673
Fax: 210-383-4688

El Paso
Las Americas Refugee
Asylum Project
715 Myrtle Avenue
El Paso, TX 79901
Phone: 915-544-5126
Fax: 915-544-4041

Fort Worth
Catholic Charities,
Immigration Services
1216 West Magnolia
Fort Worth, TX 76104
Phone: 817-338-0774
Fax: 817-335-9749

Lutheran Social Services
of the South, Inc.
100 East 15th Street,
Suite 203
Fort Worth, TX 76102
Phone: 817-332-2820
Fax: 817-332-4606

Harlingen
Casa de Proyecto Libertad
113 North 1st
Harlingen, TX 78586
Phone: 210-425-9552
Fax: 210-425-8249

South Texas Immigration
Council
107 North 3rd Street
Harlingen, TX 78550
Phone: 210-425-6987
Fax: 210-425-7434

South Texas Pro Bono
Asylum Representation
Project (ProBar)
301 East Madison Avenue
Harlingen, TX 78550
Phone: 210-425-9231
Fax: 210-428-3731

Houston
Chaplain Outreach
Services, Inc.
6223 Richmond Avenue,
Suite 209
Houston, TX 77057
Phone: 713-974-4791

GANO/CARECEN
6006 Bellaire Boulevard,
Suite 100
Houston, TX 77053
Phone: 713-665-1284
Fax: 713-665-7967

Gulfton Area
Neighborhood
Organization
6006 Bellaire Boulevard,
Suite 100
Houston, TX 77081
Phone: 713-665-1284
Fax: 713-665-7967

Houston Community
Services
5115 Harrisburg
Houston, TX 77011
Phone: 713-926-8771

International Community
Service
3131 West Alabama Street,
Suite 100
Houston, TX 77098
Phone: 713-521-9083
Fax: 713-521-9086

International Immigration
Services
4402 Richmond Avenue,
Suite 109
Houston, TX 77027
Phone: 713-961-3118
Fax: 713-963-8271

Texas Center for
Immigration Legal
Assistance, Associated
Catholic Charities
3520 Montrose
Houston, TX 77006
Phone: 713-228-5200
Fax: 713-526-1546

YMCA International
Services
6315 Gulfton, Suite 100
Houston, TX 77081
Phone: 713-995-4005
Fax: 713-995-4776

Laredo
Asociacion Pro Servicios
Sociales, Inc.,
Centro Aztlan
406 Scott Street
Laredo, TX 78040
Phone: 210-724-6244
Fax: 210-724-5458

Catholic Social Services
of Laredo, Servicios
Para Inmigrantes
402 Corpus Christi Street
Laredo, TX 78040
Phone: 210-724-3604
Fax: 210-724-5051

Lubbock
Lubbock Catholic Family
Service, Inc.,
Legalization Project
102 Avenue J
Lubbock, TX 79401
Phone: 806-741-0409

McAllen
McAllen South Texas
Immigration Council
1201 Erie
McAllen, TX 78501
Phone: 210-682-5397
Fax: 210-682-8133

Utah

Salt Lake City
International Rescue
Committee (IRC)
530 East 500 South,
Suite 207
Salt Lake City, UT 84102
Phone: 801-328-1091
Fax: 801-328-1094

Salt Lake City Catholic
Community Services
of Utah, Immigration
Program
2300 West 1700 South
Salt Lake City, UT 84104
Phone: 801-977-9119
Fax: 801-977-9224

Virginia

Arlington
Community Refugee
Ecumenical Outreach
2315 South Grant Street
Arlington, VA 22202
Phone: 703-979-5180
Fax: 703-979-8138

Ethiopian Community
Development
Council, Inc.
1038 South Highland Street
Arlington, VA 22204
Phone: 703-685-0510
Fax: 703-685-0529

Norfolk
Refugee & Immigration
Services
1802 Ashland Avenue
Norfolk, VA 23509-1236
Phone: 804-623-9131
Fax: 804-623-9479

Richmond

Refugee & Immigration
Services, Catholic
Diocese of Richmond
16 North Laurel Street
Richmond, VA 23220-4801
Phone: 804-355-4559
Fax: 804-355-4697

Roanoke

Refugee & Immigration
Services, Catholic
Diocese of Richmond
1106 9th Street, SE
Roanoke, VA 24013
Phone: 540-342-7561
Fax: 540-344-7513

Washington

Granger

Immigration Project,
Northwest Communities
Education Center
P.O. Box 800
Granger, WA 98932
Phone: 509-854-2100
Fax: 509-854-2223

Seattle

Northwest Immigrant
Rights Project
909 8th Avenue
Seattle, WA 98104
Phone: 206-587-4009
Fax: 206-587-4025

Catholic Community
Services Refugee
Assistance Program
810 18th Avenue, Room 100
Seattle, WA 98122
Phone: 206-323-9450
Fax: 206-322-6711

Spokane

Refugee & Immigration
Multi-Service Center
South 130 Arthur
Spokane, WA 99202
Phone: 509-533-2075; 509-533-2076
Fax: 509-533-2179

Tacoma

Catholic Community
Services Refugee
Assistance Program
1323 South Yakima Street
Tacoma, WA 98405
Phone: 206-502-2600
Fax: 206-502-2751

West Virginia

Charleston

Catholic Community
Services, Migration &
Refugee Services
1033 Quarrier Street,
Suite 105
Charleston, WV 25301
Phone: 304-343-1036
Fax: 304-343-1040

Wisconsin

Green Bay

Department of Refugee
Migration & Hispanic
Services, Catholic
Diocese of Green Bay
P.O. Box 23825
Green Bay, WI 54305-3825
Phone: 414-437-7531 x 8247
Fax: 414-437-0694

Milwaukee

Centro Legal for Derechos
Humanos, Inc.
611 West National Avenue,
#209
Milwaukee, WI 53204
Phone: 414-384-7900
Fax: 414-384-6222

Council for the Spanish
Speaking, Inc., Social
Services
614 West National Avenue
Milwaukee, WI 53204
Phone: 414-384-3700
Fax: 414-384-7622

International Institute of
Wisconsin
1110 North Old World 3rd
Street, Suite 420
Milwaukee, WI 53203
Phone: 414-225-6220
Fax: 414-225-6235

Ractine

Catholic Social Services,
Hispanic Outreach
Program
800 Wisconsin Avenue
Racine, WI 53404
Phone: 414-635-9510
Fax: 414-635-9510

A List of NAFTA Professionals

Each occupation listed requires either a baccalaureate degree from a U.S. or Canadian college or university or a licenciatura degree from a Mexican college or university, unless otherwise specified. In certain occupations, a state license is an acceptable substitute for a baccalaureate or licenciatura degree (note where specified below). The degree need not be earned in a four-year program of study.

Other requirements apply to particular occupations. Disaster relief insurance claims adjusters require a baccalaureate or licenciatura degree or three years of experience in claims adjustment, and completion of training in disaster relief insurance adjustment. Management consultants require a baccalaureate or licenciatura degree or five years of experience in consulting or a related field. Librarians require a master's degree in library science. Where a specific educational requirement is imposed for a given occupation, it is applied strictly; it may not be met by the substitution of equivalent credentials, such as education and training.

Accountant
baccalaureate or licenciatura degree; or C.P.A., C.A., C.G.A., or C.M.A.

Architect
baccalaureate or licenciatura degree; or state/provincial license

Computer Systems Analyst
baccalaureate or licenciatura degree; or postsecondary diploma or certificate, and three years' experience

Disaster Relief Insurance Claims Adjuster
baccalaureate or licenciatura degree, and successful completion of training in disaster relief insurance adjustment; or three years' experience in claims adjustment and successful completion of training in disaster relief insurance adjustment

Economist
baccalaureate or licenciatura degree

Engineer
baccalaureate or licenciatura degree; or state/provincial license

Forester
baccalaureate or licenciatura degree; or state/provincial license

Graphic Designer
baccalaureate or licenciatura degree; or postsecondary diploma or certificate, and three years' experience

Hotel Manager
baccalaureate or licenciatura degree in hotel/restaurant management; or postsecondary diploma or certificate in hotel/restaurant management, and three years' experience

Industrial Designer
baccalaureate or licenciatura degree; or postsecondary diploma or certificate, and three years' experience

Interior Designer
baccalaureate or licenciatura degree; or postsecondary diploma or certificate, and three years' experience

Landscape Architect
baccalaureate or licenciatura degree

Land Surveyor

baccalaureate or licenciatura degree; or state/provincial/federal license

Lawyer (or Notary in province of Quebec)

LL.B., J.D., LL.L., B.C.L., or licenciatura degree (five years); or membership in a state/provincial bar

Librarian

M.L.S. or B.L.S. (for which another baccalaureate or licenciatura degree is a prerequisite)

Management Consultant

baccalaureate or licenciatura degree; or five years' experience in consulting or related field*

Mathematician (Statistician)

baccalaureate or licenciatura degree

Range Manager/Conservationist

baccalaureate or licenciatura degree

Research Assistant (in postsecondary educational institution)

baccalaureate or licenciatura degree

Scientific Technician/Technologist

must possess theoretical knowledge of any of the following disciplines: agricultural sciences, astronomy, biology, chemistry, engineering, forestry, geology, geophysics, meteorology, or physics; and must have the ability to solve practical problems in the discipline or apply principles of the discipline to basic or applied research

Silviculturist (Forestry Specialist)

baccalaureate or licenciatura degree

Social Worker

baccalaureate or licenciatura degree

Technical Publications Writer

baccalaureate or licenciatura degree; or postsecondary diploma or certificate, and three years' experience

Urban Planner (Geographer)

baccalaureate or licenciatura degree

Vocational Counselor

baccalaureate or licenciatura degree

MEDICAL/ALLIED PROFESSIONALS
Dentist

D.D.S., D.M.D., Doctor en Odontologia, or Doctor en Cirugia Dental; or state/provincial license

Dietitian

baccalaureate or licenciatura degree; or state/provincial license

Medical Laboratory Technologist (Canada)/Medical Technologist (Mexico and the United States)

baccalaureate or licenciatura degree; or postsecondary diploma or certificate, and three years' experience

Nutritionist

baccalaureate or licenciatura degree

Occupational Therapist

baccalaureate or licenciatura degree; or state/provincial license

Pharmacist

baccalaureate or licenciatura degree; or state/provincial license

Physician (teaching or research only)

M.D. or Doctor en Medicina; or state/provincial license

Physio/Physical Therapist

baccalaureate or licenciatura degree; or state/provincial license

Psychologist

state/provincial license or licenciatura degree

Recreational Therapist

baccalaureate or licenciatura degree

Registered Nurse

state/provincial license or licenciatura degree

Veterinarian

D.V.M., D.M.V., or Doctor en Veterinaria; or state/provincial license

SCIENTISTS
Agriculturist (Agronomist)

baccalaureate or licenciatura degree

Animal Breeder

baccalaureate or licenciatura degree

Animal Scientist

baccalaureate or licenciatura degree

Apiculturist

baccalaureate or licenciatura degree

Astronomer

baccalaureate or licenciatura degree

Biochemist

baccalaureate or licenciatura degree

Biologist

baccalaureate or licenciatura degree

Chemist

baccalaureate or licenciatura degree

Dairy Scientist

baccalaureate or licenciatura degree

Entomologist

baccalaureate or licenciatura degree

Epidemiologist

baccalaureate or licenciatura degree

Geneticist

baccalaureate or licenciatura degree

Geochemist

baccalaureate or licenciatura degree

Geologist

baccalaureate or licenciatura degree

Geophysicist (Oceanographer in the United States and Mexico)

baccalaureate or licenciatura degree

Horticulturist

baccalaureate or licenciatura degree

Meteorologist

baccalaureate or licenciatura degree

Oceanographer (see Geophysicist, Physicist)

Pharmacologist

baccalaureate or licenciatura degree

Physicist (Oceanographer in Canada)

baccalaureate or licenciatura degree

Plant Breeder

baccalaureate or licenciatura degree

Poultry Scientist

baccalaureate or licenciatura degree

Soil Scientist

baccalaureate or licenciatura degree

Zoologist

baccalaureate or licenciatura degree

TEACHERS

College

baccalaureate or licenciatura degree

Seminary

baccalaureate or licenciatura degree

University

baccalaureate or licenciatura degree

*Management consultants provide services that are directed toward improving the managerial, operating, and economic performance of public and private entities by analyzing and resolving strategic and operating problems and thereby improving the entity's goals, objectives, policies, strategies, administration, organization, and operation. Management consultants are usually independent contractors or employees of consulting firms under contracts to U.S. entities. They are only salaried employees of U.S. entities to which they are providing their services when they are not assuming existing positions or filling newly created positions. As salaried employees of such a U.S. entity, they may only fill supernumerary temporary positions. On the other hand, a Canadian citizen management consultant could temporarily fill a permanent position with a U.S. management consulting firm. Canadian citizens may qualify as management consultants by holding a baccalaureate degree, by having five years of experience in the field of management consulting, or by having five years of experience in a field of specialty relating to the consulting agreement.

Immigration Law and Policy Web Sites

The Web abounds with sites on immigration law and policy. Here are some of the best. This list is only a beginning. Good surfing!

Policy Research Sites

Information on the economics and politics of U.S. immigration policy.

Atlantic Monthly Immigration Resources
www.theatlantic.com/politics/immigrat/immigrat.htm
Interesting articles on policy, politics, current events surrounding immigration. Includes online discussion.

Center for Immigration Studies
www.cis.org/
A restrictionist research organization. (Wants to tightly restrict immigration.) Discusses immigration from this viewpoint: strategies, President Bush, labor, economics, overpopulation, etc. Find out what the other side thinks. I don't agree with their views, but they provide one of the best e-mail information services on current immigration news.

International Center for Migration, Ethnicity and Citizenship (ICMEC)
www.newschool.edu/icmec/
The center promotes scholarly research and public policy analysis bearing on international migration and refugees. The site is primarily for scholars and is a good research resource. It also includes an e-mail discussion list and event list, along with many relevant links.

Policy.Com Issue Analysis
www.speakout.com/activism/news/ (search words: "immigration" or "immigration policy")
This is an activist site with interesting articles on many topics, including immigration. It is also an online opinion research company. According to their promo, "By connecting people who want to be heard with their political and business leaders, we promote important dialogue, and create a more informed, better organized public. The insight we gain from those collective opinions allows us to provide our leaders with a better understanding of the will of the people."

RAND
www.rand.org/ (search word: "immigration")
The RAND corporation is a largely government-funded think tank, and the site is a bit dry. Still, I've always found them useful in providing data and analysis about immigration to the United States. "Our job is to help improve policy and decision making through research and analysis."

The Urban Institute
www.urban.org/
This site is full of information but is not user-friendly. Even a search was not very helpful. Go to "Research by Topic," look under "Social Welfare," and click on "Immigration." You will find high-

quality social science research that often influences governmental actions. "The Urban Institute investigates social and economic problems confronting the nation and analyzes efforts to solve these problems. The Institute seeks to increase Americans' awareness of important public choices and improve the formulation and implementation of government decisions."

University of California Migration Dialogue

migration.ucdavis.edu/
One of the best and most comprehensive online journals on immigration in the United States and migration around the world. The site provides two online journals, useful articles, an event list, and research. Articles are listed by region.

U.S. Commission on Immigration Reform

www.utexas.edu/lbj/uscir/
Created by the Immigration Act of 1990; dissolved in December 31, 1997. Includes research, reports to Congress, and congressional testimony. Of important historical significance. "The mandate of the commission was to review and evaluate the implementation and impact of U.S. immigration policy and to transmit to the Congress reports on its findings and recommendations." Scholarly site, with some emphasis on Mexico.

USCIS, Executive Office for Immigration Review, and Other Agencies Implementing and Enforcing Immigration Laws

U.S. Department of Justice Sites
Executive Office for Immigration Appeals

www.usdoj.gov/eoir/
This agency includes the Board of Immigration Appeals and immigration judges. Look here for information on how the board works, including questions and answers on motion and appeal practice.

Board of Immigration Appeals (BIA)

www.usdoj.gov/eoir/biainfo.htm
The BIA decides appeals from certain USCIS and immigration judge decisions. This site links you to recent BIA decisions. Includes free legal service providers, forms, and an immigration court directory.

U.S. Citizenship and Immigration Service (USCIS)

www.USCIS.usdoj.gov/
Very useful! Free forms to download and order. Information on eligibility for immigration benefits from the USCIS point of view. New regulations plus questions and answers on current USCIS practices and policies. Employer information, immigration-related news, and the USCIS Guide to Naturalization.

Office of Special Counsel for Unfair Immigration Related Employment Practices (Civil Rights Division)

www.usdoj.gov/crt/osc/
These people are responsible for investigating and countering immigration-related discrimination. Here you'll find a downloadable I-9 Employment Eligibility Verification form, brochures on immigration-related employment discrimination, and a list of organizations providing help to discrimination victims. Includes related news. Tambien en español.

U.S. Department of Labor (DOL)

www.dol.gov/ (search words: "labor certification" or "alien")
The DOL makes decisions on applications for permanent and temporary labor certifications. At their site, you'll find a national job bank, statistical data on U.S. employment, and regulations on labor certifications

DOL Law Library—Immigration Collection

www.oalj.dol.gov/libina.htm
This is the site of the U.S. Department of Labor and the Office of Administrative Law Judges. It has the purpose of "assisting judges in keeping abreast of developments in the law" and providing information to the public. The DOL is responsible for issuing labor certification applications in permanent and temporary visa cases. Includes the DOL's newsletter on immigration matters, case decisions, and immigration-related regulations and statutes.

U.S. Department of State (DOS)

www.state.gov/
Be patient—this site contains a lot of information, but you have to look for it. The Department of State grants nonimmigrant visas and, in some cases, immigrant visas. At the site you'll find information on nonimmigrant visa eligibility (search

word: "visa") and information on U.S. consulates and embassies abroad. You'll also find the nonimmigrant visa application (search word: "forms"). You can also look up information about other countries from the State Department point of view. Interesting.

Bureau of Democracy, Human Rights, and Labor (DRL)

www.state.gov/g/drl
Archive of information released prior to January 20, 2001:

www.state.gov/www/global/human_ rights/index.html
The DRL's responsibilities include promoting democracy and workers' rights worldwide, formulating U.S. human rights policies, and coordinating policy in human rights-related labor issues. Among the items you'll find here are the DRL's Annual Country Reports on Human Rights Practices. These reports are used by advocates, USCIS asylum officers, and immigration judges to help them analyze human rights conditions around the world.

Visa Bulletin

travel.state.gov/visa_bulletin.html
Check here to find out if your priority date under the preference system is current. The bulletin is usually posted on the 11th or 12th of the month with the cutoff numbers for the following month.

Federal Executive Branch: Departments and Agencies

Library of Congress

lcweb.loc.gov/global/executive/fed.html
Library of Congress resource page with extensive list of links.

Freedom of Information Act (Department of Justice)

www.usdoj.gov/foia/

Minority Business Development Agency

www.mbda.gov/
Practical articles to help minorities start and manage businesses. Includes news and links. Interesting and informative.

Office of Refugee Resettlement

www.acf.dhhs.gov/programs/orr/

Links to services and public and private support agencies.

Poverty Guidelines

aspe.os.dhhs.gov/poverty00poverty.htm
Guidelines and related information. These guidelines determine eligibility for many kinds of public aid.

FEDERAL LEGISLATIVE BRANCH

THOMAS Legislative Information on the Internet

thomas.loc.gov/home/legbranch/ legbranch.html
Service of the U.S. Congressional Library. See bills that are in Congress and may become law. Provides congressional and related links.

House of Representatives

www.house.gov/
Includes directories of members and committee offices.

Senate

www.senate.gov/
Hearing schedules, senator directory, and related information.

FEDERAL JUDICIAL BRANCH

U.S. Judicial Branch Resources: A Library of Congress Internet Resource

lcweb.loc.gov/global/judiciary.html
This page contains links to U.S. Judicial Branch resources as well as other Web sites specializing in legal information. Features law journals, law sites, court rules, and historic Supreme Court decisions. Good starting point for research.

Other Government Information Sites

Fedworld Information Network

www.fedworld.gov/
Hosted by the National Technical Information Service of the U.S. Department of Commerce. It does not have information on all government offices, but it does have extensive searchable databases including available information on tax forms, government job announcements, and U.S. customs.

U.S. Bureau of the Census

www.census.gov/population/www/ socdemo
Click on "immigration." This site directs you to important data on immigration and population growth. Particularly useful is their breakdown of immigration to the

United States by country of citizenship and nationality.

Legal Search Sites and Resources

AllLaw.com
www.alllaw.com/
"Comprehensive legal directory and search engine." Broad starting point for just about any kind of legal research.

American Law Sources On-line (ALSO)
www.lawsource.com/
"Provides a comprehensive, uniform, and useful compilation of links to freely accessible online sources of law for the United States, Canada, and Mexico." Divided into the areas of law, commentary, and practice. Introductions to legal systems, resources for research. Hay mucha información en español. Il a beaucoup d'information juridique en français.

National Archives and Records Administration (NARA)
www.nara.gov/
"NARA enables people to inspect for themselves the record of what government has done. It ensures continuing access to essential evidence that documents the rights of American citizens, the actions of federal officials, and the national experience." Offers research directions, archive contacts, and branch publications. Includes publicly available government records, such as genealogy, federal laws, and presidential documents.

FedLaw
www.legal.gsa.gov/
Comprehensive information related to federal law.

FindLaw Internet Legal Resources
www.findlaw.com/
"Searchable directory of all things law." Includes specialized community boards.

Government Printing Office Access
www.access.gpo.gov/su_docs/db2.html
"Specialized search pages for databases of U.S. government documents, including congressional records, bills, Supreme Court decisions, and Senate manual."

Law Reviews

Law Reviews On-line (Library of Congress)
www.loc.gov/law/guide/uslawr.html

Cornell University Legal Information Institute
www.law.cornell.edu/

Immigrant Rights, Immigration Law Advocacy, Human Rights, and Refugee Rights

American Civil Liberties Union Immigration Page
www.aclu.org/issues/immigrant/hmir.html
Very useful for those who need information on immigrants' rights. Covers news, relevant laws, court decisions, asylum, welfare, current legislation, and what you can do to help. Searchable archive. Algunos articulos en español.

American Immigration Lawyers Association (AILA)
aila.org/
AILA is the main organization of immigration lawyers. Their Web site provides limited information for nonmembers. For lawyers practicing immigration law, AILA is a great source of up-to-date information, and AILA's new Web site for members is a terrific addition to the many resources they provide.

Azteca Web Page—Immigration Section
www.azteca.net/aztec/immigrat/index.shtml
Essays, articles, and links on immigration and immigrant rights, with a focus on Mexicans, Chicanos, and/or Mexican Americans. Algunos articulos en español. The Azteca home page contains other interesting information on Mexico and Mexican Americans.

Forced Migration Projects of the Open Society Institute
www.soros.org/fmp2/index.html
Though this project closed in 1999, it was once the leading funder of immigrant rights initiatives. The site is still up and includes an archive of reports and articles, along with a discussion forum that is still somewhat active. Worth checking out even though the project has ended.

National Immigration Forum

www.immigrationforum.org/
The National Immigration Forum is the best-staffed and -funded pro-immigrant organization in the United States. Their site provides both broad policy analysis and up-to-date information on legislation and regulations. If you want to keep up with what's happening in Washington, DC, on immigration issues, this site is for you.

"The purpose of the National Immigration Forum is to embrace and uphold America's tradition as a nation of immigrants. The Forum advocates and builds public support for public policies that welcome immigrants and refugees and that are fair and supportive to newcomers in our country."

Lawyers' Committee for Human Rights

www.lchr.org/refugee/refugee.htm
The Lawyer's Committee is one of the leading defenders of the rights of asylees and refugees. In addition to policy advocacy, they help find lawyers to represent U.S. asylum applicants. The site contains relevant and inspiring articles.

Micasa-Sucasa

www.ilw.com/micasa/
A forum for advocacy against the restrictive immigration legislation signed by President Clinton in 1996 known as IIRAIRA. Stories, Internet discussion, and links.

NAFSA: Association of International Educators

www.nafsa.org/

Tons of excellent information on and for international students in the United States.

National Council of La Raza

www.nclr.org/
One of the largest organizations promoting Latino empowerment. Key advocates for immigrants' rights in Washington, DC. Lots of relevant information on topics like civil rights, foreign policy, education, and housing. News, events, and publications.

National Network for Immigrant and Refugee Rights (NNIRR)

www.nnirr.org/
The most unwavering defenders of the rights of immigrants. This site provides high-quality analyses of U.S. immigration law and policy. They are one of the few groups concerned with how immigrants are treated at the border and at work.

"The National Network for Immigrant and Refugee Rights (NNIRR) is composed of local coalitions and immigrant, community, religious, civil rights, and labor organizations and activists. It serves as a forum to share information and analyses, to educate communities and the general public, and to develop and coordinate plans of action on important immigrant and refugee issues. The organization works to promote a just immigration and refugee policy in the U.S. and to defend and expand the rights of all immigrants and refugees regardless of immigration status." Includes selected articles from their magazine, Network News.

Lawyers

The following sites were selected because they provide legal information, not just information about the attorneys or their firm.

Lots of lawyers have Web sites. My having listed these attorneys here is not a recommendation. Nor can I speak for the accuracy of the information they provide.

The leading company hosting sites of immigration lawyers is Immigration Lawyers on the Web, www.ilw.com/. Try them for lawyer sites not listed in the following text. Also includes relevant articles.

Everett P. Anderson, Esq.

www.ilw.com/anderson/

Robert F. Belluscio, Attorney at Law

www.ilw.com/belluscio
Informative. Algunos articulos en español.

Ramon Carrion, P.A.

www.ilw.com/carrion
Information on visas and permanent residency for businesspeople and entrepreneurs.

Capriotti & Associates International Law

www.ilw.com/capriotti

Community Legal Centers

www.enterusa.com/
Includes forms, articles, and links.

Copland and Brenner, Attorneys at Law

www.coplandandbrenner.com/
Informative newsletter.

Law Offices of Alan S. Gordon, P.A.

www.greencards.com/

Hammond and Associates

www.hammondlawfirm.com/

Particularly useful for human resource professionals wishing to hire non-U.S. nationals.

Immigration Lawnet

www.usgreencard.com/index.htm
Information, chats, discussion board, and forms.

Ingber & Aronson, P.A.

www.ingber-aronson.com/

Mark A. Ivener, A Law Corporation

www.ilw.com/ivener

**Allen C. Ladd
Immigration Law Office, P.C.**

www.ilw.com/ladd

Maggio & Kattar, P.C.

maggio-kattar.com/
Good Information for J-1 Exchange Visitors

Cyrus D. Mehta, Attorney at Law

www.ilw.com/mehta

Law Office of Sheela Murthy

www.murthy.com/

Jean Padberg & Associates, P.C.

jpadberg.com
Also in Russian.

Pederson & Freedman, L.L.P.

www.ilw.com/pederson

Serotte, Reich, Seipp & Kenmore

www.srs-usvisa.com/

Carl Shusterman

www.shusterman.com/
One of the best lawyer sites.

Siskind, Susser, Haas & Devine

www.visalaw.com/
Another of the best lawyer sites.

G. Wellington Smith, P.C.

www.ilw.com/smith

The American Immigration Law Center

www.ailc.com/

True, Walsh & Miller, LLP

www.twmlaw.com/

Law Offices of Bonnie Stern Wasser

www.ilw.com/wasser
Newsletter and Frequently Asked Questions

Allan Wernick, Esq.

www.allanwernick.com
Archive of my weekly columns from the New York Daily News and King Features Syndicate, links, and publications.

Margaret W. Wong & Associates Co., LPA

www.imwong.com/

Commercial Legal Sites

The following commercial legal sites will lead you to the wide world of Web legal information. Check them out for links to state laws and international laws and for lists of lawyers. More information about the law than you ever wanted to know.

LawInfo

www.lawinfo.com/

LawCrawler

www.lawcrawler.com/

FindLaw

www.findlaw.com/

WebLaw

www.weblaw1.com/

Legal Research Sites

CataLaw.com

CataLaw.com/

Hieros Gamos

www.hg.org/

Extensive legal research center. Deutsch, español, français, italiano.

Law Library of Congress

www.loc.gov/law/public/htdoc/index.html

Research Sites

Internet Legal Resource Guide

www.ilrg.com/
"Comprehensive guide to the most substantive legal resources on-line."

Law Crawler

www.lawcrawler.findlaw.com/
Legal Web and database search.

Law Research

www.lawresearch.com/
"Service providing legal resource links."

National Law Journal

www.nlj.com/index.shtml

"Weekly newspaper for the profession." Interesting articles for the professional or the layperson.

Meta-Index for U.S. Legal Research

heiwww.unige.ch/humanrts/lawform-new.html

Virtual Law Library

www.law.indiana.edu/v-lib/

Cornell Legal Information Institute

www.law.cornell.edu/

Excellent site for general legal information on recent and historic Supreme Court decisions; hypertext versions of the full U.S. Code, U.S. Constitution, Federal Rules of Evidence, and Federal Rules of Civil Procedure; and recent opinions of the New York Court of Appeals and commentary on them. It is host to the Cornell Law Review and offers information about Cornell Law School and the Cornell Law Library.

U.S. Citizenship and Immigration Service Laws and Regulations

www.USCIS.usdoj.gov/graphics/ lawsregs/index.htm

This site, hosted by the INS, provides a comprehensive database of documents pertaining to immigration and naturalization law.

Meta-Index for Legal Research

gsulaw.gsu.edu/metaindex/

An excellent guide to searchable legal materials on the Web. Here you can find Supreme Court, Federal Appeals Court, and Federal District Court decisions, federal statutes and codes, and links to many useful legal resources.

Web Sites Promising Employer Sponsors

The following Web sites say they are the place to go to find an employer prepared to sponsor workers for H-1B status and/or permanent residence. I cannot verify their accuracy, honesty, or integrity. As with any Web services, be cautious in using these sites.

VisaJobs

www.visajobs.com/

Y-Axis

www.y-axis.com/jobseekers.html

PJM Interconnection, L.L.C.

www.pjm.com/about/employment/ employ.html

h1visajobs.com

www.h1visajobs.com/

American Immigration Network

www.usavisanow.com/ immigrationusjobs.htm

J.E. Brown & Company

www.jebrown.com/

usjoboffer.com

www.usjoboffer.com/

h1bsponsors.com

www.h1bsponsors.com/

Washington Information Services

www.h1visajobfair.com/

Chapter 14 Sample 1: Fact Sheet on Labor Condition Applications for H-1B Nonimmigrants for Employers That Are not "H-1B Dependent or "Willful Violators"

Prepared by Phyllis Jewell, Jewell & Associates, San Francisco, California

February 6, 2001

Obtaining H-1B employment authorization for an employee is a two-step procedure: The first step is for the employer to file and receive approval of a Labor Condition Application ("LCA," or Form ETA-9035) from the Employment and Training Administration (ETA) of the U.S. Department of Labor (DOL) that is specific to the occupation and the place of employment. The second step is for the employer to file and receive approval of an H-1B petition (Form I-129) from the U.S. Citizenship and Immigration Service (USCIS). This fact sheet pertains to the LCA and is meant to assist employers (other than "H-1B dependent" employers and/or "willful violators," to which this fact sheet does not apply) in complying with the ongoing record-keeping requirements underlying each LCA. The LCA requirements are contained in the federal regulations at 20 CFR 655-700-855 and 29 CFR 507-700-855, effective January 19, 2001.

Contents of an LCA

The LCA is the employer's attestation that (1) the H-1B worker is being offered the higher of the local "prevailing wage" or the employer's "actual wage" paid to all other individuals with similar experience and qualifications for the specific employment in question; the H-1B worker will be paid the required wage even for time in nonproductive status due to the employer's decision or due to the H-1B employee's lack of a permit or license; and H-1B employees will be offered benefits and eligibility for benefits on the same basis, and in accordance with the same criteria, as offered to U.S. workers; (2) employment of the H-1B worker will not adversely affect the working conditions (e.g., hours, shifts, vacations, and fringe benefits) of workers "similarly employed," and that H-1B employees will be afforded working conditions on the same basis, and in accordance with the same criteria, as offered to U.S. workers; (3) that no strike, lockout, or work stoppage in the course of a labor dispute relating to the H-1B occupation is taking place, and that if such an action occurs after the LCA is submitted, the employer will notify the DOL within three days of the occurrence and will not use the LCA to support an H-1B petition involving the affected occupation and place of employment; and (4) a copy of the approved LCA (as well as the cover pages, if requested) will be given to the H-1B worker on or before the H-1B employment begins, and notice of the LCA has been or will be provided to other workers employed in the H-1B occupation at the work site where the H-1B worker will perform services. These attestations give rise to IMPORTANT EMPLOYER OBLIGATIONS as follows:

EMPLOYER OBLIGATIONS REGARDING WAGES. An employer must pay the H-1B worker the higher of either (1a) the "actual wage," which is defined as the wage that the employer pays all other individuals with similar experience and qualifications for the specific employment in question, or (2a) the "prevailing wage" for the occupation in the geographic area of intended employment. In addition, there is a "no benching" rule, meaning that the employer must pay the required wage rate even for time the H-1B worker spends in nonproductive status, if such nonproductive time is due to the employer's decision or due to the H-1B employee's lack of a permit or license.

The employer's obligation to pay the required wage generally begins on the date the H-1B nonimmigrant "enters into employment" (when he or she first makes himself or herself available for work or otherwise comes under the control of the employer). However, even if the H-1B nonimmigrant has not entered into employment, the employer must begin paying the required wage either 30 days after the H-1B worker is first admitted to the United States pursuant to the approved H-1B petition or, if the nonimmigrant is present in the United States on the date of petition approval, the employer must begin paying the required wage within 60 days of the date the nonimmigrant becomes eligible to work for the employer. Moreover, the employer's obligation to pay the required wage does not cease until there is a valid termination, which is defined as including notification to the USCIS of the termination.

EMPLOYER OBLIGATIONS REGARDING WORKING CONDITIONS. Employment of the H-1B worker must not adversely affect the working conditions (e.g., hours, shifts, vacations, and fringe benefits) of workers "similarly employed," and employers must afford H-1B employees working conditions on the same basis, and in accordance with the same criteria, as offered to U.S. workers.

EMPLOYER OBLIGATIONS REGARDING STRIKE OR LOCKOUT At the time the LCA is signed and filed, there must not be at the place of employment any strike, lockout, or work stoppage in the course of a labor dispute in the occupation in which the H-1B worker will be employed. In the event such a labor action occurs later, during the LCA's validity, the employer must notify the DOL within three days of the occurrence and must not place H-1B workers where such action is occurring.

EMPLOYER OBLIGATIONS REGARDING NOTICE. On or within 30 days before the day the LCA is filed, the employer must physically post a 10-day notice in two locations, or electronically post a 10-day notice, at each place of employment where the H-1B nonimmigrant will work. The "notice" may be a copy of the LCA form itself. (If the H-1B position is unionized, notice is accomplished by a letter to the bargaining representative rather than by posting.)

Finally, the employer must give the H-1B worker a copy of the approved LCA (as well as the LCA cover pages, if requested) no later than the first day of H-1B work covered by such LCA.

EMPLOYER OBLIGATIONS REGARDING MULTIPLE WORK SITES. The employer has LCA-related obligations for each "work site" (also called "place of employment") an H-1B employee is placed.

A place is not a "work site" if it is a place where only an "employee developmental activity" (e.g., management seminar, training course, etc.) takes place; or if it is a place where a "peripatetic" worker (one whose normal duties require frequent travel from location to location) spends no more than five days per visit; or if it is a place where a "nonperipatetic" worker (one who spends most work time at one location and travels occasionally to other locations) spends no more than 10 days per visit.

If an H-1B worker is placed at additional "work sites" not contemplated when the LCA was filed, the employer's additional obligations depend on whether the additional work site is within the same "area of intended employment" (which usually means an area comprising normal commuting distance) that is covered by the approved LCA. If the additional work site is within the same geographic area of intended employment, the employer must physically post a 10-day notice in two locations, or electronically post a 10-day notice, at such additional work site on or before the date the H-1B nonimmigrant begins work there.

On the other hand, if the additional work site is outside the "area of intended employment" covered by the approved LCA, the DOL regulations provide a "short-term placement" alternative to filing a new LCA. Specifically, if the placement will not exceed 30 workdays per year (or 60 workdays per year if the H-1B employee maintains an office or workstation at his or her permanent work site, spends a substantial amount of time at the permanent work site in a one-year period, and has his or her residence or place of abode in the area of the permanent work site and not in the area of the short-term work site), no new LCA is required. However, once an H-1B employee's placement has reached the 30- or 60-workday limit, the placement must terminate, or a new LCA must be filed.

EMPLOYER RECORD-KEEPING OBLIGATIONS.   No written material need be submitted to the DOL with the LCA form (Form ETA 9035). However, the employer must have and maintain certain documents, either at its principal place of business in the United States or at the place of H-1B employment.

Documents to Go in a "Public Access" File

Within one working day of filing the LCA, the employer must have a "public access" file available for public examination upon anyone's request. This file must contain:

- A copy of the completed LCA form (Form ETA 9035) bearing the original signature, as well as the cover pages (Form ETA 9035CP).

- A copy of the notice provided to workers at the work site, along with a record of the dates and locations of posting.

- Documentation of the local prevailing wage for the occupation: According to DOL regulations, the "prevailing wage" for the occupation must be determined by one of five sources of wage data: (1) a wage set by statute or regulation, including the McNamara-O'Hara Service Contract Act, or "SCA" (if an SCA wage exists for the occupation, the employer must use the SCA wage as the prevailing wage, unless the SCA wage is $27.63 per hour for an occupation in the computer industry, which the DOL regulations explain as an anomaly), (2) a wage covered by a union contract, or, if no SCA wage or union contract applies, (3) a written prevailing wage determination made by the State Employment Security Agency, or SESA (in California, it is the California Employment Development Department), (4) a published wage survey undertaken by an "independent authoritative source," or (5) wage information from another "legitimate source."

  Wage data from an "independent authoritative source" is acceptable only if the survey (a1) reflects the weighted average wage paid to workers similarly employed in the area of intended employment, (b2) is based on data collected within the 24-month period immediately preceding the date of publication of the survey, and (3c) represents the latest published prevailing wage finding by the independent authoritative source for the occupation in the area of intended employment.

  A prevailing wage provided by a "legitimate source" must meet the following three criteria: (1) it reflects the weighted average wage paid to workers employed in the area of intended employment, (2) it is based on the most recent and accurate information available, and (3) it is reasonable and consistent with recognized standards and principles to produce a prevailing wage.

- Documentation regarding the wage to be paid to the H-1B nonimmigrant: It is not clear in the DOL regulations whether an employer must maintain a separate public access document that states the wage to be paid to the H-1B nonimmigrant(s), or whether the wage stated on the LCA form itself (which must be maintained for public access) will suffice. Currently, it is our view that this documentation requirement is met by retaining the completed LCA for public access.

- Documentation regarding the employer's "actual wage": This may be a memo or other document(s), as long as it (1) fully and clearly explains the employer's own system for determining what it pays workers with similar experience and qualifications for the specific employment in question and (2) sets out any periodic wage adjustments provided for in the employer's system (such as increases for cost of living, increases for moving into a different grade level, a change in all salaries due to a change in the salary for entry-level employees, etc.). According to the DOL's preamble to the regulations, the explanation of the compensation system kept in the public access file must be sufficiently detailed for a third party to understand how the employer applied its pay system to arrive at the actual wage for its H-1B nonimmigrant(s); at a minimum, the documentation should identify the business-related factors that are considered and the manner in which they are implemented (e.g., stating the wage range for the specific employment in the employer's workforce and identifying the pay differentials for factors such as education and job duties).

- Documentation of employee benefits: The public access file must contain a summary of the benefits offered to U.S. workers in the same occupation as H-1B workers, including a statement of how employees are differentiated, if at all. Ordinarily, this requirement would be satisfied with a copy of the employer's employee handbook and summary plan descriptions. If the employer has workers receiving "home country" benefits, the employer may place a simple notation to that effect in the public access file.

- Documentation in the case of a change in corporate structure: When an employer corporation changes its corporate structure as the result of an acquisition, merger, spin-off, or other such action, the new employing entity is not required to file new LCAs or H-1B petitions with respect to the H-1B employees transferred to the new employing entity, provided that the new employing entity adds to the public access file(s) a sworn statement by a responsible official of the new employing entity that it accepts all obligations, liabilities, and undertakings under the LCAs filed by the predecessor employing entity, together with a list of each affected LCA and its date of certification, and a description of the actual wage system and federal Employer Identification Number (EIN) of the new employing entity. Curiously, DOL regulations state that unless such a statement is executed and made available for public access, the new employing entity shall not employ any of the predecessor employing entity's H-1B workers without filing new LCAs and new H-1B petitions for such workers. This regulatory provision, published by the DOL on December 20, 2000, directly contradicts the Visa Waiver Permanent Program Act (Public Law No.106-396), enacted on October 30, 2000, which states that an amended H-1B petition shall not be required where the petitioning employer is involved in a corporate restructuring, including but not limited to a merger, acquisition, or consolidation, where a new corporate entity succeeds to the interests and obligations of the original petitioning employer and where the terms and conditions of employment remain the same but for the identity of the petitioner.

The above "public access" documents must be retained for at least one year beyond the withdrawal or expiration of the LCA.

Payroll Records

The employer also must maintain (but not for public access) payroll records of all employees in the H-1B occupational classification (even U.S. workers) for three years from their creation. These payroll records must be made available to the DOL upon request. The payroll records must include (1) the employee's full name, address, and occupation, (2) employee's rate of pay, (3) hours worked each day and week except in the case of full-time, salaried employees, and (4) total additions to or deductions from pay each pay period covered by the payment, by employee.

Enforcement and Penalties

The DOL's Wage and Hour Division (WHD) of its Employment Services Administration (ESA) may initiate its own investigation or may investigate LCA compliance as the result of a complaint.

Penalties for noncompliance with LCA requirements may include the payment of back wages, a civil money penalty of $1,000 per violation, or such other administrative remedies as are deemed appropriate, if the employer is found to have done one or more of the following:

1. Filed an LCA that misrepresents a material fact.
2. Failed to pay wages (including benefits provided as compensation for services) as required.
3. Failed to provide working conditions as required.
4. Filed an LCA during a strike or lockout in the course of a labor dispute in the occupational classification at the place of employment.
5. Willfully or substantially failed to provide notice as required.
6. Willfully or substantially failed to specify accurately on the LCA the number of workers sought, the occupational classification in which the H-1B(s) will be employed, or the wage rate and conditions under which the H-1B(s) will be employed.
7. Required or accepted from an H-1B nonimmigrant payment or remittance of the $1,000 filing fee supplement incurred in filing an H-1B petition with the USCIS.
8. Required or attempted to require an H-1B nonimmigrant to pay a "penalty" (as distinguished from "liquidated damages") for ceasing employment prior to an agreed-upon date.
9. Discriminated against an employee for protected conduct (e.g., for reporting suspected H-1B/LCA violations or for participating in an investigation relating to such violations).
10. Failed to make available for public examination the required public access documents.
11. Failed to maintain other documentation as required.
12. Failed otherwise to comply in any other manner with the LCA requirements.

Administrative remedies that may be ordered if violations of the above requirements are found include, but are not limited to, payment of back wages or benefits, civil money penalties of up to $35,000 per violation, and "debarment" from approval of any of the employer's nonimmigrant or immigrant petitions for up to three years.

Aside from the penalties provided for in the LCA regulations, federal criminal statutes provide penalties of up to $10,000 and/or imprisonment of up to five years for knowing and willful submission of false statements to the federal government (18 USC 1001; see also 18 USC 1546)

Chapter 14 Sample 2:
Wage Paid to H-1B Employee

(To be prepared on employer's stationery.)

To: LCA Public Access File

From: [EMPLOYER or EMPLOYER'S REPRESENTATIVE]

Re: Actual wage used for the occupation of [JOB TITLE]

Date: [DATE of SIGNATURE]

The wage paid to the H-1B employee to whom this LCA pertains will be _____ for his/her employment in the position of [JOB TITLE].

_____

[EMPLOYER or EMPLOYER'S REPRESENTATIVE signature]

Chapter 14 Sample 3:
Employer's Letter Explaining
Basis for Actual Wage

(To be prepared on employer's stationery.)

To: LCA Public Access File

From: [EMPLOYER or EMPLOYER'S REPRESENTATIVE]

Re: Determination of actual wage used for the occupation of
           [JOB TITLE]

Date: [DATE of SIGNATURE]

The position of [JOB TITLE] has a range from _____ to _____. In determining the actual wage at our facility located in [CITY], [STATE], we consider the following factors:

(1) Experience, including whether the candidate has been previously employed in this position, the length of any such employment, the type of employment (e.g., whether supervisory in nature), and the depth and breadth of such experience;

(2) Educational background, including the level of education obtained, the existence of special academic achievements (such as superior class rank or other distinction), and the reputation of the educational facility/facilities attended;

(3) Job responsibility and function, including nature of duties and responsibilities to be performed and degree of supervision to be exercised;

(4) Possession of specialized knowledge, skills, or training; and

(5) Other indicators of performance and/or ability, including job references, performance evaluations, awards, achievements, and/or accomplishments.

Periodic wage adjustments to the actual wage in question are made to reflect employee annual increases, cost-of-living adjustments, moves to a greater responsibility level, and increases in entry-level pay that affect the overall salary structure.

_____

[EMPLOYER or EMPLOYER'S REPRESENTATIVE signature]

Chapter 14
Sample 4A and
Sample 4B

Sample 4A: Basis for Prevailing Wage Determination— SESA Wage or Published Survey

(To be prepared on employer's stationery.)

To: LCA Public Access File
From: [EMPLOYER or EMPLOYER'S REPRESENTATIVE]
Re: Basis for Prevailing Wage Determination for [JOB TITLE]
Date: [DATE of SIGNATURE]

The prevailing wage for the position of [JOB TITLE] was determined by using [SESA, OES, NAME of SURVEY]. A copy of the relevant portions of the survey are attached to this memo.

_____

[EMPLOYER or EMPLOYER'S REPRESENTATIVE signature]

Sample 4B: Basis for Prevailing Wage Determination— Employer Survey

(To be prepared on employer's stationery.)

To: LCA Public Access File
From: [EMPLOYER or EMPLOYER'S REPRESENTATIVE]
Re: Basis for Prevailing Wage Determination for [JOB TITLE]
Date: [DATE of SIGNATURE]

The prevailing wage for the position of [JOB TITLE] was determined by contacting eight employers and inquiring as to the wage paid to their employees in similar positions.

The employers contacted were [LIST EMPLOYERS SURVEYED, DATE CONTACTED, WAGE OBTAINED FROM EACH EMPLOYER].

The prevailing wage for the position of [JOB TITLE] was determined by adding together the wages found in the survey and dividing by the number of employees in the position. The result of that calculation was that the prevailing wage was determined to be [PREVAILING WAGE].

_____

[EMPLOYER or EMPLOYER'S REPRESENTATIVE signature]

Credential Evaluation Services

Center for Applied Research, Evaluation & Education, Inc.
P.O. Box 20348
Long Beach, CA 90801
Phone: 562-430-8215
E-mail: evalcaree@earthlink.net

Educational Credential Evaluators, Inc.
P.O. Box 92970
Milwaukee, WI 53202-0970
Phone: 562-289-3400
Fax: 562-289-3411
E-mail: eval@ece.org
Web: www.ece.org/

Educational International, Inc.
29 Denton Road
Wellesley, MA 02181
Phone: 781-235-7425
Fax: 781-235-6831
E-mail: edint@gis.net

Educational Records Evaluation Service, Inc.
777 Campus Commons Road, Suite 200
Sacramento, CA 95825-8309
Phone: 916-565-7475
Fax: 916-565-7476
E-mail: edu@eres.com
Web: www.eres.com/

Education Evaluators International, Inc.
P.O. Box 5397
Los Alamitos, CA 90720-5397
Phone: 562-431-2187
Fax: 562-493-5021

Evaluation Service, Inc.
P.O. Box 1455
Albany, NY 12201
Phone: 518-672-4522
Fax: 518-672-4877
E-mail: esi@capital.net

**Foreign Academic
Credential Service, Inc.**

P.O. Box 400
Glen Carbon, IL 62034
Phone: 618-288-1661

**Foreign Educational
Document Service**

P.O. Box 4091
Stockton, CA 95204
Phone: 209-948-6589

**Foundation for International
Services, Inc.**

19015 North Creek Parkway, #103
Bothell, WA 98011
Phone: 206-487-2245
Fax: 206-487-1989
E-mail: fis@mail.com

**International Consultants of
Delaware, Inc.**

109 Barksdale Professional Center
Newark, DE 19711
Phone: 302-737-8715
Fax: 302-737-8756
E-mail: icd@icdel.com

**International Education Research
Foundation, Inc.**

P.O. Box 66940
Los Angeles, CA 90066
Phone: 310-390-6276
Fax: 310-397-7686
E-mail: info@ierf.org
Web: www.ierf.org/

**Josef Silny & Associates, Inc.,
International Education
Consultants**

P.O. Box 248233
Coral Gables, FL 33124
Phone: 305-666-0233
Fax: 305-666-4133
E-mail: info@jsilny.com
Web: www.jsilny.com/

SpanTran Educational Services, Inc.

7211 Regency Square Boulevard, #205
Houston, TX 77036
Phone: 713-266-8805
Fax: 713-789-6022
Web: www.spantran-edu.com/

World Education Services, Inc.

P.O. Box 745
Old Chelsea Station
New York, NY 10113-0745
Phone: 800-937-3895
Fax: 212-966-6395
E-mail: info@wes.org
Web: www.wes.org/

I-129 Petition for a Nonimmigrant Worker

U.S. Department of Justice
Immigration and Naturalization Service

OMB No.1115-0168
Petition for a Nonimmigrant Worker

START HERE - Please Type or Print.

FOR INS USE ONLY

Part 1. Information about the employer filing this petition. If the employer is an individual, use the top name line. Organizations should use the second line.

Family Name	Given Name	Middle Initial

Company or Organization Name

Address - Attn:

Street Number and Name		Apt. #
City	State or Province	
Country	Zip/Postal Code	

IRS Tax #

Part 2. Information about this petition.
(See instructions to determine the fee.)

1. **Requested Nonimmigrant Classification**
    (Write classification symbol at right)

2. **Basis for Classification** *(Check one)*
    a. ☐ New employment
    b. ☐ Continuation of previously approved employment without change
    c. ☐ Change in previously approved employment
    d. ☐ New concurrent employment

3. **Prior Petition.** If you checked other than "New Employment" in item 2. (above) give the most recent prior petition number for the worker(s):

4. **Requested Action:** *(Check one)*
    a. ☐ Notify the office in Part 4 so the person(s) can obtain a visa or be admitted (NOTE: a petition is not required for an E-1, E-2 or R visa).
    b. ☐ Change the person(s) status and extend their stay since they are all now in the U.S. in another status (see instructions for limitations). This is available only where you check "New Employment" in item 2, above.
    c. ☐ Extend or amend the stay of ther person(s) since they now hold this status.

    Total number of workers in petition:
    (See instructions for where more than one worker can be included.)

Part 3. Information about the person(s) you are filing for.
Complete the blocks below. Use the continuation sheet to name each person included in this petition.

If an entertainment group, give their group name

Family Name	Given Name	Middle Initial
Date of Birth *(Month/Day/Year)*	Country of Birth	
Social Security #	A #	

If in the United States, complete the following:

Date of Arrival *(Month/Day/Year)*	I-94 #
Current Nonimmigrant Status	Expires *(Month/Day/Year)*

FOR INS USE ONLY

Returned	Receipt
Resubmitted	
Reloc Sent	
Reloc Rec'd	

Interviewed
☐ Petitioner
☐ Beneficiary

Class: _____
# of Workers: _____
Priority Number: _____
Validity Dates: From _____
To _____

☐ **Classification**
☐ Consulate/POE/PFI Notified
At: _____
☐ Extension Granted
☐ COS/Extension Granted

Partial Approval *(explain)*

Action Block

To Be Completed by Attorney or Representative, if any
☐ Fill in box if G-28 is attached to represent the applicant

VOLAG#

ATTY State License #

Continued on back.

Form I-129 (Rev. 12/10/01) Y

Part 4. Processing Information.

a. If the person named in Part 3 is outside the U.S. or a requested extension of stay or change of status cannot be granted, give the U.S. consulate or inspection facility you want notified if this petition is approved.

Type of Office *(Check one):* ☐ Consulate ☐ Pre-flight inspection ☐ Port of Entry

Office Address *(City)* U.S. State or Foreign Country

Person's Foreign Address

b. Does each person in this petition have a valid passport?
☐ Not required to have passport ☐ No - explain on separate paper ☐ Yes

c. Are you filing any other petitions with this one? ☐ No ☐ Yes - How many? _____

d. Are applications for replacement/initial I-94's being filed with this petition? ☐ No ☐ Yes - How many? _____

e. Are applications by dependents being filed with this petition? ☐ No ☐ Yes - How many? _____

f. Is any person in this petition in exclusion or deportation proceedings? ☐ No ☐ Yes - explain on separate paper

g. Have you ever filed an immigrant petition for any person in this petition? ☐ No ☐ Yes - explain on separate paper

h. If you indicated you were filing a new petition in Part 2, within the past 7 years has any person in this petition:

1) ever been given the classification you are now requesting? ☐ No ☐ Yes - explain on separate paper

2) ever been denied the classification you are now requesting? ☐ No ☐ Yes - explain on separate paper

i. If you are filing for an entertainment group, has any person in this petition not been with the group for at least 1 year? ☐ No ☐ Yes - explain on separate paper

Part 5. Basic information about the proposed employment and employer. *Attach the supplement relating to the classification you are requesting.*

Job Title Nontechnical Description of Job

Address where the person(s) will work if different from the address in Part 1.

Is this a full-time position?
☐ No - Hours per week ☐ Yes Wages per week or per year

Other Compensation *(Explain)* Value per week or per year Dates of intended employment From: To

Type of Petitioner - *Check* ☐ U.S. citizen or permanent resident ☐ Organization ☐ Other - explain on separate paper

Type of Business: Year established:

Current Number of Employees Gross Annual Income Net Annual Income

Part 6. Signature. *Read the information on penalties in the instructions before completing this section.*

I certify, under penalty of perjury under the laws of the United States of America, that this petition, and the evidence submitted with it, is all true and correct. If filing this on behalf of an organization, I certify that I am empowered to do so by that organization. If this petition is to extend a prior petition, I certify that the proposed employment is under the same terms and conditions as in the prior approved petition. I authorize the release of any information from my records, or from the petitioning organization's records, which the Immigration and Naturalization Service needs to determine eligibility for the benefit being sought.

Signature and Title Print Name Date

Please Note: If you do not completely fill out this form and the required supplement, or fail to submit required documents listed in the instructions, then the person(s) filed for may not be found eligible for the requested benefit, and this petition may be denied.

Part 7. Signature of person preparing form, if other than above.

I declare that I prepared this petition at the request of the above person and it is based on all information of which I have any knowledge.

Signature Print Name Date

Firm Name and Address

APPENDIX U: I-129 PETITION FOR A NONIMMIGRANT WORKER

OMB No. 1115-0168

E Classification
Supplement to Form I-129

U.S. Department of Justice
Immigration and Naturalization Service

Name of person or organization filing petition:	Name of person you are filing for:

Classification Sought *(Check one):*	Name of country signatory to treaty with U.S.
☐ E-1 Treaty trader ☐ E-2 Treaty investor	

Section 1.   **Information about the Employer Outside the U.S. (If any)**

Name	Address
Alien's Position - Title, duties and number of years employed	Principal Product, Merchandise or Service
Total Number of Employees	

Section 2.   **Additional information about the U.S. Employer**

The U.S. company is, to the company outside the U.S. *(Check one)*:
☐ Parent   ☐ Branch   ☐ Subsidiary   ☐ Affiliate   ☐ Joint Venture

Date and Place of Incorporation or establishment in the U.S.

Nationality of Ownership *(Individual or Corporate)*

Name	Nationality	Immigration Status	% Ownership

Assets	Net Worth	Total Annual Income

Staff in the U.S.	Executive Manager	Specialized Qualifications or Knowledge
Nationals of Treaty Country in E or L Status		
Total number of employees in the U.S.		

Total number of employees the alien would supervise; or describe the nature of the specialized skills essential to the U.S. company.

Section 3.   **Complete if filing for an E-1 Treaty Trader**

Total Annual Gross Trade/Business of the U.S. company	For Year Ending
$	

Percent of total gross trade which is between the U.S. and the country of which the treaty trader organization is a national.

Section 4.   **Complete if filing for an E-2 Treaty Investor**

Total Investment:	Cash	Equipment	Other
	$	$	$
	Inventory	Premises	Total
	$	$	$

Form I-129 Supplement E/L (Rev. 12/10/01)Y Page 3

APPENDIX U: I-129 PETITION FOR A NONIMMIGRANT WORKER

OMB No. 1115-0168

H Classification
Supplement to Form I-129

U.S. Department of Justice
Immigration and Naturalization Service

Name of person or organization filing petition:

Name of person or total number of workers or trainees you are filing for:

List the alien's and any dependent family members' prior periods of stay in H classification in the U.S. for the last six years. Be sure to list only those periods in which the alien and/or family members were actually in the U.S. in an H classification. If more space is needed, attach an additional sheet.

Classification sought *(Check one)*:

☐ H-1A   Registered professional nurse
☐ H-1B1   Specialty occupation
☐ H-1B2   Exceptional services relating to a cooperative research and development project administered by the U.S. Department of Defense
☐ H-1B3   Artist, entertainer or fashion model of national or international acclaim
☐ H-1B4   Artist or entertainer in unique or traditional art form

☐ H-1B5   Athlete
☐ H-1BS   Essential Support Personnel for H-1B entertainer or athlete
☐ H-2A   Agricultural worker
☐ H-2B   Nonagricultural worker
☐ H-3   Trainee
☐ H-3   Special education exchange visitor program

Section 1. Complete this section if filing for H-1A or H-1B classification.

Describe the proposed duties

Alien's present occupation and summary of prior work experience

Statement for H-1B specialty occupations only:

By filing this petition, I agree to the terms of the labor condition application for the duration of the alien's authorized period of stay for H-1B employment.

Petitioner's Signature   Date

Statement for H-1B specialty occupations and DOD projects:

As an authorized official of the employer, I certify that the employer will be liable for the reasonable costs of return transportation of the alien abroad if the alien is dismissed from employment by the employer before the end of the period of authorized stay.

Signature of authoried official of employer   Date

Statement for H-1B DOD projects only:

I certify that the alien will be working on a cooperative research and development project or a coproduction project under a reciprocal Government-to-governement agreement administered by the Department of Defense.

DOD project manager's signature   Date

Section 2. Complete this section if filing for H-2A or H-2B classification.

Employment is:
(Check one)
☐ Seasonal
☐ Peakload
☐ Intermittent
☐ One-time occurrence

Temporary need is:
(Check one)
☐ Unpredictable
☐ Periodic
☐ Recurrent annually

Explain your temporary need for the alien's services (attach a separate paper if additional space is needed).

Continued on back.   Form I-129 Supplement H (Rev. 12/10/01)Y Page 4

APPENDIX U: I-129 PETITION FOR A NONIMMIGRANT WORKER

Section 3. Complete this section if filing for H-2A classification.

The petitioner and each employer consent to allow government access to the site where the labor is being performed for the purpose of determining compliance with H-2A requirements. The petitioner further agrees to notify the Service in the manner and within the time frame specified if an H-2A worker absconds or if the authorized employment ends more than five days before the relating certification document expires, and pay liquidated damages of ten dollars for each instance where it cannot demonstrate compliance with this notification requirement. The petitioner also agrees to pay liquidated damages of two hundred dollars for each instance where it cannot be demonstrated that the H-2A worker either departed the United States or obtained authorized status during the period of admission or within five days of early termination, whichever comes first.

The petitioner must execute Part A. If the petitioner is the employer's agent, the employer must execute Part B. If there are joint employers, they must each execute Part C.

Part A. Petitioner:

By filing this petition, I agree to the conditions of H-2A employment, and agree to the notice requirements and limited liabilities defined in 8 CFR 214.2(h)(3)(vi).

Petitioner's signature _____ Date _____

Part B. Employer who is not petitioner:

I certify that I have authorized the party filing this petition to act as my agent in this regard. I assume full responsibility for all representations made by this agent on my behalf, and agree to the conditions of H-2A eligibility.

Employer's signature _____ Date _____

Part C. Joint Employers:

I agree to the conditions of H-2A eligibility.

Joint employer's signature(s) _____ Date _____

Joint employer's signature(s) _____ Date _____

Joint employer's signature(s) _____ Date _____

Joint employer's signature(s) _____ Date _____

Joint employer's signature(s) _____ Date _____

Section 4. Complete this section if filing for H-3 classification.

If you answer "yes" to any of the following questions, attach a full explanation.

		No	Yes
a.	Is the training you intend to provide, or similar training, available in the alien's country?	☐ No	☐ Yes
b.	Will the training benefit the alien in pursuing a career abroad?	☐ No	☐ Yes
c.	Does the training involve productive employment incidental to training?	☐ No	☐ Yes
d.	Does the alien already have skills related to the training?	☐ No	☐ Yes
e.	Is this training an effort to overcome a labor shortage?	☐ No	☐ Yes
f.	Do you intend to employ the alien abroad at the end of this training?	☐ No	☐ Yes

If you do not intend to employ this person abroad at the end of this training, explain why you wish to incur the cost of providing this training, and your expected return from this training.

OMB No.1115-0168

L Classification
Supplement to Form I-129

U.S. Department of Justice
Immigration and Naturalization Service

Name of person or organization filing petition:	Name of person you are filing for:

This petition is *(Check one)*:   ☐ An individual petition   ☐ A blanket petition

Section 1.   Complete this section if filing an individual.

Classification sought *(Check one)*:   ☐ L-1A manager or executive   ☐ L-1B specialized knowledge

List the alien's, and any dependent family member's prior periods of stay in an L classification in the U.S. for the last seven years. Be sure to list only those periods in which the alien and/or family members were actually in the U.S. in an L classification.

Name and address of employer abroad

Dates of alien's employment with this employer. Explain any interruptions in employment.

Description of the alien's duties for the past 3 years.

Description of alien's proposed duties in the U.S.

Summarize the alien's education and work experience.

The U.S. company is, to the company abroad: *(Check one)*
☐ Parent   ☐ Branch   ☐ Subsidiary   ☐ Affiliate   ☐ Joint Venture
Describe the stock ownership and managerial control of each company.

Do the companies currently have the same qualifying relationship as they did during the one-year period of the alien's employment with the company abroad?   ☐ Yes   ☐ No *(Attach explanation)*

Is the alien coming to the U.S. to open a new office?
☐ Yes *(Explain in detail on separate paper)*   ☐ No

Section 2.   Complete this section if filing a Blanket Petition.

List all U.S. and foreign parent, branches, subsidiaries and affiliates included in this petition. *(Attach a separate paper if additional space is needed.)*

Name and Address	Relationship

Explain in detail on separate paper.

APPENDIX U: I-129 PETITION FOR A NONIMMIGRANT WORKER

OMB No. 1115-0168

U.S. Department of Justice
Immigration and Naturalization Service

O and P Classification
Supplement to Form I-129

Name of person or organization filing petition: _____

Name of person or group or total number of workers you are filing for: _____

Classification sought *(Check one)*:

☐ O-1 Alien of extraordinary ability in sciences, art, education, or business.
☐ P-2 Artist or entertainer for reciprocal exchange program
☐ P-2S Essential Support Personnel for P-2.

Explain the nature of the event
_____
_____
_____
_____

Describe the duties to be performed
_____
_____
_____
_____
_____

If filing for O-2 or P support alien, dates of the alien's prior experience with the O-1 or P alien.
_____
_____
_____

Have you obtained the required written consulation(s)?   ☐ Yes - attached   ☐ No - Copy of request attached
If not, give the following information about the organization(s) to which you have sent a duplicate of this petition.

O-1 Extraordinary ability

Name of recognized peer group	Phone #
Address	Date sent

O-1 Extraordinary achievement in motion pictures or television

Name of labor organization	Phone #
Address	Date sent
Name of management organization	Phone #
Address	Date sent

O-2 or P alien

Name of labor organization	Phone #
Address	Date Sent

APPENDIX U: I-129 PETITION FOR A NONIMMIGRANT WORKER

OMB No.1115-0168

U.S. Department of Justice
Immigration and Naturalization Service

O & R Classifications
Supplement to Form I-129

Name of person or organization filing petition: | Name of person you are filing for:

Section 1.   Complete this section if you are filing for a Q international cultural exchange alien.

I hereby certify that the participant(s) in the international cultural exchange program:
- is at least 18 years of age,
- has the ability to communicate effectively about the cultural attributes of his or her country of nationality to the American public, and has not previously been in the United States as a Q nonimmigrant unless he/she has resided and been physically present outside the U.S.
- for the immediate prior year.

I also certify that the same wages and working conditions are accorded the participants as are provided similarly employed U.S. workers.

Petitioner's signature | Date

Section 2.   Complete this section if you are filing for an R religious worker.

List the alien's, and any dependent family members, prior periods of stay in R classification in the U.S. for the last six years. Be sure to list only those periods in which the alien and/or family members were actually in the U.S. in an R classification.

Describe the alien's proprosed duties in the U.S.

Describe the alien's qualifications for the vocation or occupation.

Description of the relationship between the U.S. religious organization and the organization abroad of which the alien was a member.

Form I-129 Supplement O/P/Q/R (Rev. 12/10/01)Y Page 8

APPENDIX U: I-129 PETITION FOR A NONIMMIGRANT WORKER

Supplement-1

Attach to Form I-129 when more than one person is included in the petition. *(List each person seperately. Do not include the person you named on the form).*

Family Name		Given Name	Middle Initial	Date of Birth *(Month/Day/Year)*
Country of Birth		Social Security No.		A#

IF IN THE U.S.	Date of Arrival *(Month/Day/Year)*		I-94#	
	Current Nonimmigrant Status:		Expires on *(Month/Day/Year)*	

Country where passport issued	Expiration Date *(Month/Day/Year)*	Date Started with group

Family Name		Given Name	Middle Initial	Date of Birth *(Month/Day/Year)*
Country of Birth		Social Security No.		A#

IF IN THE U.S.	Date of Arrival *(Month/Day/Year)*		I-94#	
	Current Nonimmigrant Status:		Expires on *(Month/Day/Year)*	

Country where passport issued	Expiration Date *(Month/DayYyear)*	Date Started with group

Family Name		Given Name	Middle Initial	Date of Birth *(Month/Day/Year)*
Country of Birth		Social Security No.		A#

IF IN THE U.S.	Date of Arrival *(Month/Day/Year)*		I-94#	
	Current Nonimmigrant Status:		Expires on *(Month/Day/Year)*	

Country where passport issued	Expiration Date *(Month/Day/Year)*	Date Started with group

Family Name		Given Name	Middle Initial	Date of Birth *(Month/Day/Year)*
Country of Birth		Social Security No.		A#

IF IN THE U.S.	Date of Arrival *(Month/Day/Year)*		I-94#	
	Current Nonimmigrant Status:		Expires on *(Month/Day/Year)*	

Country where passport issued	Expiration Date *(Month/Day/Year)*	Date Started with group

Family Name		Given Name	Middle Initial	Date of Birth *(Month/Day/Year)*
Country of Birth		Social Security No.		A#

IF IN THE U.S.	Date of Arrival *(Month/Day/Year)*		I-94#	
	Current Nonimmigrant Status:		Expires on *(Month/Day/Year)*	

Country where passport issued	Expiration Date *(Month/Day/Year)*	Date Started with group

Continued on back.   Form I-129 Supplement-1 (Rev. 12/10/01)Y Page 9

APPENDIX U: I-129 PETITION FOR A NONIMMIGRANT WORKER

Supplement-1

Attach to Form I-129 when more than one person is included in the petition. *(List each person separately. Do not include the person you named on the form).*

Family Name		Given Name	Middle Initial	Date of Birth *(Month/Day/Year)*
Country of Birth		Social Security No.		A#
IF IN THE U.S.	Date of Arrival *(Month/Day/Year)*		I-94#	
	Current Nonimmigrant Status:		Expires on *(Month/Day/Year)*	
Country where passport issued		Expiration Date *(Month/Day/Year)*	Date Started with group	

Family Name		Given Name	Middle Initial	Date of Birth *(Month/Day/Year)*
Country of Birth		Social Security No.		A#
IF IN THE U.S.	Date of Arrival *(Month/Day/Year)*		I-94#	
	Current Nonimmigrant Status:		Expires on *(Month/Day/Year)*	
Country where passport issued		Expiration Date *(Month/Day/Year)*	Date Started with group	

Family Name		Given Name	Middle Initial	Date of Birth *(Month/Day/Year)*
Country of Birth		Social Security No.		A#
IF IN THE U.S.	Date of Arrival *(month/day/year)*		I-94#	
	Current Nonimmigrant Status:		Expires on *(Month/Day/Year)*	
Country where passport issued		Expiration Date *(Month/Day/Year)*	Date Started with group	

Family Name		Given Name	Middle Initial	Date of Birth *(Month/Day/Year)*
Country of Birth		Social Security No.		A#
IF IN THE U.S.	Date of Arrival *(Month/Day/Year)*		I-94#	
	Current Nonimmigrant Status:		Expires on *(Month/Day/Year)*	
Country where passport issued		Expiration Date *(Month/Day/Year)*	Date Started with group	

Family Name		Given Name	Middle Initial	Date of Birth *(Month/Day/Year)*
Country of Birth		Social Security No.		A#
IF IN THE U.S.	Date of Arrival *(Month/Day/Year)*		I-94#	
	Current Nonimmigrant Status:		Expires on *(Month/Day/Year)*	
Country where passport issued		Expiration Date *(Month/Day/Year)*	Date Started with group	

Form I-129 Supplement-1 (Rev. 12/10/01)Y Page 10

Chapter 14 Sample 5: Employer's Letter in Support of H-1B Petition

(For the review and signature of employer. To be prepared on employer's stationery.)

[DATE of SIGNATURE]
United States Department of Justice
U.S. Citizenship and Immigration Service
[ADDRESS of USCIS REGIONAL SERVICE CENTER]

Re: I-129 Petition for H-1B Classification,
    Specialty Occupation: Software Engineer
    Petitioner: **SOFTWARE EXAMPLE, Inc.**
    Beneficiary: Sam Soft

Dear Sir/Madam:

This letter is in support of our H-1B petition filed on behalf of Sam Soft for the specialty occupation of software engineer. Mr. Soft is qualified for this position by virtue of his having attained a bachelor of science degree in **Information Systems from City College, CUNY.** A bachelor's degree in **Information Systems is a customary minimum degree requirement** for this position.

THE POSITION

The position of software engineer for **SOFTWARE EXAMPLE, Inc.** involves software testing and development, Unix administration, and database administration. A software engineer provides functional and empirical analysis related to the design, development, and implementation of software operating systems for our clients. This includes use of utility software, development software, and diagnostic software. The work requires knowledge of Visual Basic (5.), C, Sybase (Version 11.5), Team Teak, Unix, and Windows 95.

THE EMPLOYER/PETITIONER

Software Example, Inc. provides software consulting services. Our clients include Really Big Name Phone Co. and Famous Technologies. Our employees provide a broad range of software services including software development, systems engineering, quality assurance systems administration, and database design development and administration.

THE BENEFICIARY

Mr. Soft's transcript reveals appropriate preparation for a position at this level. He holds a **bachelor of science degree in Information Systems.** Among the subjects he studied that prepare him for the position are: Introduction to Business Data Processing (COBOL1), Introduction to Business Data Processing (COBOL2), Data Structure (Assembly Language), Introduction to Data Management, and Machine Organization (C Programming).

We urge your prompt and favorable review of our petition for Mr. Soft.

Very truly yours,

Edith Example
President
Software Example, Inc.

torture convention defense, 206
trafficking victims, 148
trainees, 144
transit, continuous, 141
transit without visa, 75
treaty investors, 141-142
treaty traders, 141-142
tuberculosis, 213
T visas. *See* trafficking victims.
TWOV. *See* transit without visa.

U

undocumented immigrants, xv
UNHCR. *See* United Nations High
  Commission on Refugees.
union contracts, 175
United Nations, 141, 142
United Nations High Commission on
Refugees, 213
U.S.A. Patriot Act provisions
    controlled departure, xviii
    detention under, xvii
    inadmissibility under, xviinew
    nonimmigrant visa procedures, xviii
    removal under, xvii
    tracking foreign students, xviii
U visas. *See* crimes.

V

Vietnam War, 124
Visa Bulletin, 68-70
visas. *See also* specific circumstances.

adjustment of status
    applying for, 80-84
    fees, 74-77
applying for
    cross-changeability, 71-72
    location, 72-73
    post-September 11 changes, xviii
    quota system, 67-68
    while living in the U.S.
        adjustment of status, 80-84
        consular processing, 80, 84-86
        qualification criteria, 82-84
    lottery. *See* lottery visas.
    waiver program, 153.
visitors
    business oriented, 150-152
    pleasure-oriented, 152-153
vocational schools, 146
voting, 117
V visas. *See* children; permanent
  residence; spouses.

W

wage. *See* actual wage; prevailing wage.
waivers. *See* exclusion grounds.
work cards. *See* employment.